Categorical Data Analysis for the Behavioral and Social Sciences

Categorical Data Analysis for the Behavioral and Social Sciences

Razia Azen
University of Wisconsin-Milwaukee

Cindy M. Walker
University of Wisconsin-Milwaukee

Routledge
Taylor & Francis Group
New York   London

Routledge
Taylor & Francis Group
270 Madison Avenue
New York, NY 10016

Routledge
Taylor & Francis Group
27 Church Road
Hove, East Sussex BN3 2FA

Printed in the United States of America on acid-free paper
10 9 8 7 6 5 4 3 2 1

International Standard Book Number: 978-1-84872-836-3 (Hardback)

Library of Congress Cataloging-in-Publication Data

Azen, Razia, 1969-
    Categorical data analysis for the behavioral and social sciences / Razia Azen, Cindy M. Walker.
      p. cm.
    Includes bibliographical references and index.
    ISBN 978-1-84872-836-3
    1. Social sciences--Statistical methods. I. Walker, Cindy M., 1965- II. Title.

HA29.A94 2011
519.5'35--dc22
                                                    2010014461

Visit the Taylor & Francis Web site at
http://www.taylorandfrancis.com

and the Psychology Press Web site at
http://www.psypress.com

Dedication

To our students: past, present, and future

Contents

Preface

While teaching categorical data analysis in an educational psychology department, we found that the textbooks currently available for categorical data analysis courses, although very good, are frequently too technical and require a more extensive understanding of mathematics than is typically the case for many students and researchers in the social sciences. Therefore, our approach in writing this book was to focus on the concepts and applications, rather than the technical details, of common categorical data analysis methods. We do present theory along with some technical details, as we believe these to be extremely important components of understanding statistical methods, but the main focus in this book is on conceptual understanding and application. In this way, not having extensive training should not prevent students and researchers from being able to understand and apply these statistical procedures.

The main goal of writing this book was to provide an accessible resource on categorical data analysis to students and researchers in the social and behavioral sciences. This book is intended to serve students and researchers in fields such as education, psychology, sociology, and business as well as many others that require the analysis of categorical variables. The book is primarily intended for a course in categorical data analysis or cross-classified data analysis, which is typically taught at the graduate level in the behavioral and social sciences, and will probably require one or two prerequisite statistics classes that cover conventional statistical methods (e.g., factorial analysis of variance, multiple regression). Some experience with statistical software is also expected, although we provide extensive examples and instructions for using both SAS (version 9.1.3) and IBM SPSS 18, which we refer to as SPSS in this book (SPSS was acquired by IBM in October 2009).

This book covers the most commonly used categorical data analysis techniques, and emphasis is placed on techniques that can be applied with variables measured in the nominal scale. Although the procedures presented can also be applied with ordinal variables, more advanced methods that are specific to ordinal variables are not covered extensively. The order of the chapters reflects the complexity of the material presented. We start with the building blocks of scales of measurement (Chapter 1), probability distributions (Chapter 2), and inferential methods for a single categorical variable (Chapter 3), and then move on to methods involving contingency tables with two (Chapter 4) and three (Chapter 5) categorical variables. The transition to modeling is made by introducing the overarching ideas of generalized linear models (Chapter 6) and then demonstrating these specifically as they apply to log-linear models (Chapter 7), logistic regression with continuous (Chapter 8) and categorical (Chapter 9) predictors, and concluding with logistic models for multicategory response variables (Chapter 10).

We intend the treatment to be both conceptual and practical, in that we present the concepts in general terms as well as demonstrate them with practical examples. In general, each chapter begins with a "Look Ahead" section that gives an overview of the material covered in the chapter, and concludes with a "Summary" section that summarizes the main topics covered. Each chapter typically contains a general conceptual development of the ideas and methods, illustrated with examples, along with a discussion of the relationships between and among the new procedure being introduced and existing schema (i.e., analytic procedures covered in prerequisite courses or previous chapters). The conceptual development is then followed by more extensive examples that use a data set to answer research questions with an explanation of how to obtain and interpret relevant output from statistical software packages. We demonstrate the examples using both SAS (version 9.1.3) and SPSS (version 18), and provide computing instructions as well as selected output from these packages in the chapters. We also include both conceptual and practical problems at the end of each chapter so that students can practice the concepts and methods covered in the chapter. The data sets used in the book can be accessed at http://www.researchmethodsarena.com/9781848728363.

Ultimately, our goal in writing this book was to create a resource that can be used extensively to train and assist students and researchers in appropriately conducting analyses that address the sorts of research questions they wish to answer. We want to thank those who reviewed the manuscript of our book at various stages, including Timothy D. Johnson from the University of Michigan, Sara Templin from the University of Alabama, Scott L. Thomas from Claremont Graduate University, Brandon Vaughn from the University of Texas at Austin, and three anonymous reviewers.

We were inspired by our students, and all of the satellite horseshoe crabs in the world, to write a book that would appeal to social scientists, and so the examples we use are primarily from the social sciences. We hope that we accomplished this goal and that you will find this book useful and informative.

chapter one

Introduction and overview

A LOOK AHEAD

There are a myriad of statistical procedures that can be used to address research questions in the social sciences. However, the required courses in most social science programs pay little to no attention to procedures that can be used with categorical data. There are good reasons for this, both pedagogical and conceptual. Statistical procedures for categorical data require a new set of "tools," or a new way of thinking because of the different distributional assumptions that must be made for these types of variables. Therefore, these procedures differ conceptually from those that we assume readers of this book are familiar with, such as multiple regression and analysis of variance (ANOVA). However, acquiring a conceptual understanding of the procedures that can be used to analyze categorical data opens a whole new world of possibilities to social science researchers. In this chapter we introduce the reader to these possibilities, explain categorical variables, and give a brief overview of the history of the methods for their analysis.

1.1 What is categorical data analysis?

Categorical data arises whenever a variable is measured on a scale that simply classifies respondents into a limited number of groups. For example, respondents' race, gender, marital status, and political affiliation are categorical variables that are often of interest to researchers in the social sciences. In addition to distinguishing a variable as either categorical (qualitative) or continuous (quantitative), variables can also be classified as either independent or dependent. The term *independent* refers to a variable that is experimentally manipulated (e.g., the treatment group each person is assigned to) but is also often applied to a variable that is used to predict another variable even if it cannot be externally manipulated (e.g., socioeconomic status). The term *dependent* refers to a variable that is of primary interest as an outcome or response variable; for example, the outcome of a treatment (based on treatment group) or the educational achievement level (predicted from socioeconomic status) can be considered dependent variables. Introductory statistics courses may give the impression that categorical variables can only be used as independent variables, because the analytic procedures typically learned in these courses are based on the assumption that the dependent variable follows a normal distribution in the population, which is obviously not the case for categorical variables. In addition, treating categorical variables exclusively as independent variables can ultimately restrict the types of research questions posed by social science researchers.

For example, suppose you wanted to determine whether charter schools differed in any substantial way from noncharter schools based on the demographics of the school (e.g., location: urban, suburban, or rural; type: public or private; predominant socioeconomic status of students: low, medium, or high; etc.). You would be unable to study this phenomenon without knowledge of categorical data analytic techniques because all variables involved are categorical. As another example, suppose that a researcher wanted to predict whether a student will graduate from high school based on information such as the student's attendance record (e.g., number of days in attendance), grade point average (GPA), income of parents, and so on. In this case a categorical analysis approach would be more appropriate because the research question requires that graduation status (yes or no) serve as the dependent variable. Indeed, a naïve researcher might decide to use the graduation status as an independent variable, but this approach would not directly address the research question and would ultimately limit the results obtained from the analysis. The purpose of this book is to describe and illustrate analytic procedures that are applicable when the variables of interest are categorical.

1.2   Scales of measurement

In general, measurement can be thought of as applying a specific rule to assign numbers to objects or persons for the sole purpose of differentiating between objects or persons on a particular attribute. For example, in the social sciences one might administer an aptitude test to a sample of college students to differentiate students in terms of their aptitude. In this case, the specific rule being applied is the administration of the same aptitude test to all students. Obviously if one were to use different aptitude tests for different respondents, then the scores could not be compared across students in a meaningful way. In the physical sciences, measurement can often be as precise as we want it to be. For example, we can measure the length of an object to the nearest centimeter, millimeter, or micromillimeter. However, this is typically not the case in the social sciences. The only way to ensure quality measurement in the social sciences is to use instruments with good psychometric properties, such as validity and reliability.

Measurement precision is typically defined by the presence or absence of the following four characteristics, which are ordered in terms of precision: (1) distinctiveness, (2) magnitude, (3) equal intervals, and (4) absolute zero. A measurement scale has the characteristic of distinctiveness if the numbers assigned to persons or objects differ on the property being measured. For example, if one were to assign a 0 to female respondents and a 1 to male respondents, then gender would be measured in a manner that had the characteristic of distinctiveness. A measurement scale has the characteristic of magnitude if the different numbers that are assigned to persons or objects can be ordered in a meaningful way. For example, if one were to assign a score of 1 to a respondent who was very liberal, 2 to a respondent who was somewhat liberal, 3 to a respondent who was somewhat conservative, and 4 to a respondent who was very conservative, then political affiliation would be measured in a manner that had the characteristic of magnitude. A measurement scale has the characteristic of equal intervals if *equivalent differences* between two numbers that are assigned to persons or objects have an equivalent meaning. For example, if one were to consider examinees' scores from a particular reading test as indicative of reading proficiency, then, assuming that an examinees' scores was created by summing the number of items answered correctly on the test, reading proficiency would be measured in a manner that had the characteristic of magnitude. Note that a score of 0 on the reading test does not necessarily represent an examinee who has no reading ability. It may simply imply that the test was too difficult, which would be the case if a second-grade student was given an eighth-grade reading test. This is an important distinction between measurement scales that have the property of equal intervals and those that have the property of having an absolute zero.

Table 1.1 Properties of the Four Levels of Measurement

Level of measurement	Characteristic				Examples
	Distinctiveness	Ordering	Equal intervals	Absolute zero	
Nominal	✓				Race, religious affiliation, sex, eye color, personality type
Ordinal	✓	✓			Proficiency classification, level of agreement to survey item, class rank
Interval	✓	✓	✓		Achievement, aptitude, temperature
Ratio	✓	✓	✓	✓	Time, age, length, height, weight, number of spelling errors

A measurement scale has the characteristic of having an absolute zero if assigning a score of 0 to persons or objects indicates an *absence* of the attribute being measured. For example, if a score of 0 represents no spelling errors on a spelling exam, then number of spelling errors would be measured in a manner that had the characteristic of having an absolute zero.

Table 1.1 indicates the four levels of measurement in terms of the four characteristics just described. Nominal measurement possesses only the characteristic of distinctiveness and can be thought of as the least precise form of measurement in the social sciences. Ordinal measurement possesses the characteristics of distinctiveness and ordering, and is a more precise form of measurement than nominal measurement. Interval measurement possesses the characteristics of distinctiveness, ordering, and equal intervals, and is a more precise form of measurement than ordinal measurement. Ratio measurement, which is rarely attained in the social sciences, possesses all four characteristics of distinctiveness, ordering, equal intervals, and having an absolute zero, and is the most precise form of measurement.

In categorical data analysis the dependent or response variable, which represents the characteristics or phenomena that we are trying to explain or predict in the population, is measured using either a nominal scale or an ordinal scale. Methods designed for ordinal variables make use of the natural ordering of the measurement categories, although the way in which we order the categories (i.e., from highest to lowest or from lowest to highest) is usually irrelevant. Methods designed for ordinal variables cannot be used for nominal variables. Methods designed for nominal variables will give the same results regardless of the order in which the categories are listed. These methods can be used for ordinal variables, although doing so will result in a loss of information (and usually loss of statistical power) since the information about the ordering is lost. In categorical data analysis techniques such as logistic regression, the independent variables, which are used to explain or predict variation in the dependent variable, can be measured using any of the four scales of measurement.

1.3   A brief history of categorical methods

The early development of categorical data analytical methods took place at the beginning of the 20th century and was spearheaded by the work of Karl Pearson and G. Udney Yule. As is typically the case when something new is introduced, the development of these procedures was not without controversy. While Pearson argued that categorical variables were simply proxies of continuous variables, Yule argued that categorical variables were inherently discrete (Agresti, 1996). This in turn led the two statisticians to approach the problem of how to summarize the relationship between two categorical variables in vastly different ways. Pearson maintained that the relationship between two categorical variables could be approximated by the underlying continuum and, given his prestige in the statistical community, he was rarely challenged by his peers. However, Yule challenged Pearson's approach to the problem and developed a measure to describe the relationship between two categorical variables that did not rely on trying to approximate the underlying continuum (Yule, 1912). Needless to say, Pearson did not take kindly to Yule's criticism and publicly denounced Yule's approach, going so far as to say that Yule would have to withdraw his ideas to maintain any credibility as a statistician (Pearson & Heron, 1913). One hundred years later, we realize that both statisticians were partially correct. While some categorical variables, especially those that are measured in an ordinal manner, can be thought of as proxies to variables that are truly continuous, others cannot.

Pearson's work was also critiqued by R. A. Fisher, who maintained that one of Pearson's formulas was incorrect (Fisher, 1922) and, even though statisticians eventually realized that Fisher was correct, it was difficult for Fisher to get his work published due to Pearson's reputation in the field (Agresti, 1996). Moreover, while Pearson's criticisms of Fisher's work were published (Pearson, 1922), Fisher was unable to get his rebuttals to these criticisms published, which ultimately led him to resign from the Royal Statistical Society (Cowles, 2001). Although Fisher's scholarly reputation among statisticians today is primarily due to other theoretical work, particularly in the area of ANOVA, he did make several contributions to the field of categorical data analysis, not the least of which is his approach to small sample techniques for analyzing categorical data.

1.4   Organization of this book

Given the fact that most of the groundwork for categorical data analysis was developed in the early part of the 20th century, it goes without saying that the procedures presented in this book are relatively new. Indeed, it was not until the middle of the 20th century that strong theoretical advances were made in the field and it is clear that there is still more work to be done. However, in this book we chose to present a few of the more widely used analytic procedures for categorical data in great detail, as opposed to inundating the reader with all of the various models that can be used for categorical data and their associated nuances. The primary goal of this book is to help social scientists develop a conceptual understanding of the categorical data analytic techniques presented. Therefore, while extensive training in mathematics will certainly be of benefit to the reader, a lack of it should not prevent students and researchers from being able to understand and apply these statistical procedures. This is accomplished by utilizing examples that are reflective of realistic applications of data analytic techniques in the social sciences and by emphasizing specific research questions that can be addressed by each analytic procedure.

This book begins by introducing the reader to the different types of distributions that are used most often with categorical data. This is followed by a discussion of the estimation procedures and goodness-of-fit tests that are used with all of the subsequent categorical data analytical procedures. Procedures designed to analyze the relationship between two categorical variables are then presented, followed by a discussion of procedures designed to analyze the relationships among three categorical variables. This is followed by a discussion of the generalized linear model. Finally, specific applications of the generalized linear model are presented in chapters on log-linear models, binomial logistic regression models, and multinomial logistic regression models.

1.5 Summary

In this chapter we introduced the reader to the types of research questions that can be addressed with statistical procedures designed to be used for categorical data. We gave a brief history on the development of these procedures, discussed scales of measurement, and provided the readers with the organizational structure of this book. In the next chapter we turn to the different distributions that are assumed to underlie categorical data.

Problems

1.1 Indicate the scale of measurement used for each of the following variables:
   a. Sense of belongingness, as measured by a 20-item scale
   b. Satisfaction with life, as measured by a one-item scale
   c. Level of education, as measured by a demographic question with five categories

1.2 Indicate the scale of measurement used for each of the following variables:
   a. Self-efficacy, as measured by a 10-item scale
   b. Race, as measured by a demographic question with six categories
   c. Income, as measured by yearly gross income

1.3 For each of the following research scenarios, identify the dependent and independent variables as well as the scale of measurement used for each variable. Explain your answers.
   a. A researcher would like to determine if boys are more likely than girls to be proficient in mathematics.
   b. A researcher would like to determine if people in a committed relationship are more likely to be satisfied with life than those who are not in a committed relationship.
   c. A researcher is interested in whether females tend to have lower self-esteem, in terms of body image, than males.
   d. A researcher is interested in the relationship between religious affiliation and level of education.

1.4 For each of the following research scenarios, identify the dependent and independent variables as well as the scale of measurement used for each variable. Explain your answers.
   a. A researcher would like to determine if people living in the United States are more likely to be obese than people living in France.
   b. A researcher would like to determine if the cholesterol levels of men who suffered a heart attack are higher than the cholesterol levels of women who suffered a heart attack.
   c. A researcher is interested in whether gender is related to political party affiliation.
   d. A researcher is interested in the relationship between amount of sleep and grade point average for high school students.

1.5 Determine whether procedures for analyzing categorical data are needed to address each of the following research questions. Provide a rationale for each of your answers by identifying the dependent and independent variables as well as their scales of measurement.

    a. A researcher would like to determine whether a respondent is likely to vote for the Republican or Democratic candidate in the U.S. presidential election based on the respondent's annual income.

    b. A researcher would like to determine whether respondents who vote for the Republican candidate in the U.S. presidential election have a different annual income than those who vote for the Democratic candidate.

    c. A researcher would like to determine whether males who have suffered a heart attack have higher fat content in their diets than males who have not suffered a heart attack in the past 6 months.

    d. A researcher would like to predict whether a man is likely to suffer a heart attack in the next 6 months based on the fat content in his diet.

1.6 Determine whether procedures for analyzing categorical data are needed to address each of the following research questions. Provide a rationale for each of your answers by identifying the dependent and independent variables as well as their scales of measurement.

    a. A researcher would like to determine whether a student is likely to complete high school based on the student's grade point average.

    b. A researcher would like to determine whether students who complete high school have a different grade point average than students who do not complete high school.

    c. A researcher would like to determine whether the families of students who attend college have a higher annual income than the families of students who do not attend college.

    d. A researcher would like to determine whether a student is likely to attend college based on his or her family's annual income.

1.7 Determine whether procedures for analyzing categorical data are needed to address each of the following research questions. Indicate what analytic procedure (e.g., ANOVA, regression) you would use for those cases that do *not* require categorical methods, and provide a rationale for each of your answers.

    a. A researcher would like to determine if scores on the verbal section of the SAT help to predict whether students are proficient in reading on a state-mandated test administered in 12th grade.

    b. A researcher is interested in the relationship between income and gender.

    c. A researcher is interested in whether level of education helps to predict income.

    d. A researcher is interested in the relationship between political party affiliation and gender.

1.8 Provide a substantive research question of interest that would need to be addressed using procedures for categorical data analysis. In your answer be sure to identify the scale of measurement for the dependent and independent variables, as well as how these variables would be measured.

chapter two

Probability distributions

A LOOK AHEAD

The ultimate goal of most any inferential statistics endeavor is to determine how likely it is to have obtained a particular **sample** given certain assumptions about the **population** the sample was drawn from. For example, suppose that in a random sample of students obtained from a large school district 40% of the students are classified as minority students. Based on this result, what can we infer about the proportion of students who are minority students in the school district as a whole? This type of inference is accomplished by determining the **probability** of randomly selecting a particular sample from a specific population, and this probability is obtained from a sampling distribution. In this chapter we introduce the most common probability and sampling distributions that are appropriate for categorical variables.

The properties of a sampling distribution typically depend on the properties of the underlying distribution of the random variable of interest, a distribution that also provides the probability of randomly selecting a particular observation, or value of the variable, from a specific population. The most familiar example of this concept involves the sampling distribution of the mean, from which the probability of obtaining particular samples (with particular sample mean values) can be determined. The properties of this sampling distribution depend on the properties of the probability distribution of the random variable in the population (e.g., its mean and variance). In the case of continuous variables, for sufficient sample sizes the sampling distribution of the mean and the probabilities obtained from it are based on the normal distribution. In general, probability distributions form the basis for inferential procedures and in this chapter we discuss these distributions as they apply to categorical variables.

2.1   Probability distributions for categorical variables

Suppose, for example, that the population of interest is a fifth-grade class at a middle school consisting of 50 students: 10 females and 40 males. In this case, if a teacher randomly selected one student from the class, the teacher would be more likely to choose a male student than a female student. In fact, because the exact number of male and female students in the population is known, the exact probability of randomly selecting a male or female student can be determined. Specifically, the probability of any particular outcome is defined as the number of ways a particular outcome can occur out of the total number of possible outcomes; therefore, the probability of randomly selecting a male student in this example is 40/50 = 0.8, and the probability of randomly selecting a female student is 10/50 = 0.2.

However, contrary to the example with the population of fifth-grade students, it is atypical to know the exact specifications (i.e., distribution) of the population. The goal of inferential statistical procedures is to make inferences about the population from observed sample data, not the other way around. This is accomplished by considering a value that is obtained as the result of some experiment or data collection activity to be only one possible outcome out of a myriad of different outcomes that may have occurred; that is, this value is a variable because it can vary across different studies or experiments. For example, if 10 students were randomly selected from the fifth grade discussed earlier, the proportion of males in that sample of 10 students could be used to infer the proportion of males in the larger group or population (of all 50 students). If another random sample of 10 students was obtained, the proportion of males may not be equal to the proportion in the first sample; in that sense, the proportion of males is a variable. **Random variable** is a term that is used to describe the possible outcomes that a particular variable may take on. It does not describe the actual outcome itself and cannot be assigned a value, but rather is used to convey the fact that the outcome that was obtained was the result of some underlying random process. A **probability distribution** is a table or mathematical function that links the actual outcome obtained from the result of an experiment or data collection activity (e.g., a random sample) to the probability of its occurrence.

Most methods that deal with continuous dependent variables make the assumption that the values that are obtained are random observations that come from a normal distribution. In other words, when the dependent variable is continuous it is assumed that the underlying random process in the population from which the variable was obtained was a normal distribution. However, there are many other probability distributions, and when the dependent variable is categorical, it can no longer be assumed that it was obtained from a population that is normally distributed. The purpose of this chapter is to describe probability distributions that are assumed to underlie the population from which categorical data are obtained.

2.2   *Frequency distribution tables for discrete variables*

A discrete variable is a variable that can only take on a finite number of values. Categorical data almost always consist of discrete variables. One way to summarize data of this type is to construct a frequency distribution table, which depicts the number of responses in each category of the measurement scale, as well as the probability of occurrence of a particular response category and the percentage of responses in each category. In fact, a frequency distribution table is a specific example of a probability distribution. For example, suppose a random sample of individuals in the United States were asked to identify their political affiliation using a 7-point response scale that ranged from extremely liberal to extremely conservative, with higher values reflecting a more liberal political affiliation. Table 2.1 is a frequency distribution table summarizing the (hypothetical) responses.

Note that the **probabilities** depicted in the table are also the **proportions**, computed by simply dividing the **frequency** of responses in a particular category by the total number of respondents (e.g., the proportion of those who are extremely liberal is $30/1443 \approx .021$), and the **percentages** depicted in the table can be obtained by multiplying these values by 100 (e.g., the percentage of those who are extremely liberal is $(100)(.021) = 2.1\%$). More formally, if the frequency is denoted by f and the total number of respondents is denoted by N, then the probability or proportion is $\frac{f}{N}$ and the percentage is $100\left(\frac{f}{N}\right)\%$. Note also that the frequency can be obtained from the proportion (or probability) by $f = N(\text{proportion})$.

A frequency distribution table such as the one depicted in Table 2.1 summarizes the data obtained so that a researcher can easily determine, for example, that respondents were most

Table 2.1 Frequency Distribution Table Depicting Political Affiliation of Respondents

Political affiliation (X)	Frequency (f)	Percentage	Probability
Extremely liberal (7)	30	2.1	0.021
Liberal (6)	163	11.3	0.113
Slightly liberal (5)	193	13.4	0.134
Moderate (4)	527	36.5	0.365
Slightly conservative (3)	248	17.2	0.172
Conservative (2)	241	16.7	0.167
Extremely conservative (1)	41	2.8	0.028
Total	1443	100.0	1.000

likely to consider their political affiliation to be moderate and least likely to consider themselves to be extremely liberal. However, how might these data be summarized more succinctly?

Descriptive statistics, such as the mean and standard deviation, can be used to summarize discrete variables just as they can for continuous variables. However, the manner in which these descriptive statistics are computed differs with categorical data. In addition, because it is no longer appropriate to assume that a normal distribution is the underlying random mechanism that produces the categorical responses in a population, distributions appropriate to categorical data must be used for inferential statistics with these data (just as the normal distribution is commonly the appropriate distribution used for inferential statistics with continuous data). The two most common probability distributions assumed to underlie responses in the population when data are categorical are the binomial distribution and the Poisson distribution, although there are also other distributions that are appropriate for categorical data. The remainder of this chapter is devoted to introducing and describing common probability distributions appropriate for categorical data.

2.3 The hypergeometric distribution

The hypergeometric distribution can be used with discrete variables when trying to determine the number of "successes" in a sequence of n draws from a finite population where sampling is conducted without replacement. It should be noted that "success" is simply a label for the occurrence of a particular event of interest. For example, suppose the admissions committee at a medical college has 15 qualified applicants, 3 of which are minority applicants, and can only admit 2 new students. In this case, a success is defined as the admission of a minority applicant, and the hypergeometric distribution can be used to determine the probability of admitting at least one minority student if the admissions committee were to randomly select two new students from the 15 qualified applicants. In general, if Y denotes the total number of minority students selected for admission (i.e., the number of successes), m denotes the number of minority applicants, N denotes the total number of qualified applicants, and n denotes the total number of applicants to be admitted, then the probability that $Y = k$ (where k is a specific number) can be expressed by

$$P(Y = k) = \frac{\binom{m}{k}\binom{N-m}{n-k}}{\binom{N}{n}}, \tag{2.1}$$

where the notation $\begin{pmatrix} m \\ k \end{pmatrix}$ is read as *"m choose k"* and refers to the number of ways that k individuals (or objects) can be selected from a total of m individuals (or objects). This is computed as

$$\begin{pmatrix} m \\ k \end{pmatrix} = \frac{m!}{k!(m-k)!} = \frac{m(m-1)(m-2)\cdots(1)}{[k(k-1)(k-2)\cdots(1)][(m-k)(m-k-1)(m-k-2)\cdots(1)]}.$$

Note that 1! and 0! (1 factorial and 0 factorial, respectively) are both defined to be equal to 1. This general formulation can be conceptualized using the theory of combinatorics. The number of ways to select or choose n applicants from the total number of applicants, N, is $\begin{pmatrix} N \\ n \end{pmatrix}$. Similarly, the number of ways to choose k minority applicants from the total number of minority applicants, m, is $\begin{pmatrix} m \\ k \end{pmatrix}$ and for each possible manner of choosing k minority applicants from the total number of minority applicants, m, there are $\begin{pmatrix} N-m \\ n-k \end{pmatrix}$ possible ways to select the remaining number of nonminority applicants to fulfill the requirement of admitting n applicants. Therefore, the number of ways to form a sample consisting of exactly k minority applicants is

$$\begin{pmatrix} m \\ k \end{pmatrix}\begin{pmatrix} N-m \\ n-k \end{pmatrix}$$

and, since each of the samples is equally likely, the probability of selecting exactly k minority applicants is

$$\frac{\begin{pmatrix} m \\ k \end{pmatrix}\begin{pmatrix} N-m \\ n-k \end{pmatrix}}{\begin{pmatrix} N \\ n \end{pmatrix}}.$$

Using the numerical example provided earlier, $m = 3$ minority applicants, $k = 1$ minority admission, $N = 15$ qualified applicants, and $n = 2$ total admissions, so the probability of admitting exactly one minority student if applicants are selected at random can be computed as follows:

$$P(Y=1) = \frac{\begin{pmatrix} 3 \\ 1 \end{pmatrix}\begin{pmatrix} 15-3 \\ 2-1 \end{pmatrix}}{\begin{pmatrix} 15 \\ 2 \end{pmatrix}} = \frac{\begin{pmatrix} 3 \\ 1 \end{pmatrix}\begin{pmatrix} 12 \\ 1 \end{pmatrix}}{\begin{pmatrix} 15 \\ 2 \end{pmatrix}} = \frac{\left(\frac{3!}{1!(2!)}\right)\left(\frac{12!}{1!(11!)}\right)}{\left(\frac{15!}{2!13!}\right)} = \frac{3(12)}{\frac{15(14)}{2}} = \frac{36}{105} = 0.34.$$

Similarly, the probability of admitting exactly two minority students if applicants are selected at random can be computed as follows:

$$P(Y=2) = \frac{\binom{3}{2}\binom{15-3}{2-2}}{\binom{15}{2}} = \frac{\binom{3}{2}\binom{12}{0}}{\binom{15}{2}} = \frac{\left(\frac{3!}{2!(1!)}\right)\left(\frac{12!}{0!(12!)}\right)}{\left(\frac{15!}{2!13!}\right)} = \frac{3(1)}{\frac{15(14)}{2}} = \frac{3}{105} = 0.03.$$

Therefore, the probability of admitting at least one minority student is

$$P(Y=1) + P(Y=2) = 0.34 + 0.03 = 0.37.$$

We could also use this procedure to compute the probability of admitting no minority students, but it is easier to make use of the laws of probability to determine this: Since only two applicants are to be admitted, either none of those admitted can be minority students, one could be a minority student, or both could be minority students. Therefore, these three probabilities must sum to one and, because the probability of one or two minority student admissions was shown to be 0.37, the probability that no minority students are admitted can be obtained by $1.0 - 0.37 = 0.63$.

In this case, if applicants are randomly selected from the qualified applicant pool, it is more likely (with 63% probability) that none of the applicants selected by the admissions committee will be minority students, so the committee may want to select applicants in a nonrandom manner.

Most any distribution can be described by its mean and variance. In the case of the hypergeometric distribution the mean (μ) and variance (σ^2) can be computed using the following formulas:

$$\mu = \frac{nm}{N}$$

and

$$\sigma^2 = \frac{n(m/N)(1-m/N)(N-n)}{N-1}.$$

Therefore, for our example, the mean of the distribution is

$$\mu = \frac{3(2)}{15} = \frac{6}{15} = 0.4$$

and the variance is

$$\sigma^2 = \frac{n(m/N)(1-m/N)(N-n)}{N-1} = \frac{3(2/15)(1-2/15)(15-3)}{15-1} = \frac{3(.13)(.87)(12)}{14} = 0.297,$$

which implies that the standard deviation is $\sigma = \sqrt{0.297} = 0.525$.

What do these values represent? The mean can be interpreted as the expected number of minority applicants chosen, if they are randomly selected from the applicant pool. Since this value is less than one, the expected number of minority applicants selected is less than one, which mirrors the information that was obtained when the probabilities were calculated directly. The standard deviation can be interpreted in the usual manner; basically, it can be thought of as the average difference between the observed number of minority applicants selected in any given sample and the expected number of minority applicants selected (which in this case is 0.4) assuming the hypergeometric distribution underlies the selection process. The hypergeometric distribution is the appropriate distribution to use for research problems of this kind.

2.4   The Bernoulli distribution

The Bernoulli distribution is perhaps the simplest probability distribution for discrete variables and can be thought of as the building block for more complicated probability distributions used with categorical data. A discrete variable that comes from a Bernoulli distribution can only take on one of two values, such as pass/fail or proficient/not proficient. This distribution can be used to determine the probability of success (i.e., the outcome of interest) if only one draw is made from a finite population. Therefore, this distribution is actually a special case of the hypergeometric distribution with $n = 1$. Using the example presented earlier, if $n = 1$ then only one applicant is to be selected for admission and, because this candidate can either be a minority applicant or not, to compute the probability of a success, the number of successes, k, is also equal to one. In this case, Equation 2.1 can be simplified as follows:

$$P(Y = k = 1) = \frac{\binom{m}{k}\binom{N-m}{n-k}}{\binom{N}{n}} = \frac{\binom{m}{1}\binom{N-m}{0}}{\binom{N}{1}} = \frac{\left(\frac{m!}{(m-1)!(1!)}\right)\left(\frac{(N-m)!}{(N-m)!}\right)}{\left(\frac{N!}{(N-1)!(1!)}\right)} = \frac{m}{N}. \qquad (2.2)$$

Therefore, the probability of selecting a minority applicant from the pool, which can be thought of as the probability of a single success, is simply the number of minority candidates divided by the total number of candidates. In other words, it simply represents the proportion of minority candidates in the pool. This probability is typically denoted by π in the population (or p in the sample), and is equal to $\pi = 3/15 = 0.2$ in this example. Using the laws of probability, the probability of not selecting a minority candidate from the pool can be obtained by $1 - \pi$, which in our example is $1 - 0.2 = 0.8$. The mean, or expected value, for this distribution is simply $\mu = \pi$ and the variance for this distribution can be calculated using the formula $\sigma^2 = \pi(1 - \pi)$, which is $0.2(0.8) = 0.16$ for the example presented.

2.5   The binomial distribution

Categorical variables that follow the binomial distribution can only take on one of two possible outcomes, as is the case with variables that follow the Bernoulli distribution. However, whereas the Bernoulli distribution only deals with one trial, outcome, or event, the binomial distribution deals with multiple trials (denoted by *n*). Therefore, the binomial distribution can be thought of as an extension of the Bernoulli distribution and can also be considered to be akin to the hypergeometric distribution. Like the hypergeometric distribution, the binomial distribution can be used with discrete variables when trying to determine the number of successes in a sequence of *n* trials that are drawn from a finite population. However, whereas sampling is conducted without replacement when the hypergeometric distribution underlies responses, the events or trials are independent when they follow a binomial distribution. With the hypergeometric distribution there is a dependency among the events considered because sampling is done without replacement. Therefore, the probability of success becomes smaller in subsequent trials and this change can be dramatic if the population is small. However, with the binomial distribution the probability of success does not change in subsequent trials because the probability of success for each trial is independent of previous or subsequent trials; in other words, sampling is conducted *with* replacement. For example, to draw 2 applicants from a total of 15, sampling without replacement proceeds such that once the first applicant has been selected for admission there are only 14 remaining applicants from which to select the second admission. Therefore, the probability of success for the second selection differs from the probability of success for the first selection, and is in fact higher than the probability of success for the first selection. On the other hand, sampling with replacement proceeds such that each selection is considered to be drawn from the pool of all 15 individuals. In other words, the first selection is not removed from the total sample before the second selection is made, and each selection has the same probability of being selected thereby making each selection independent of all other selections. In this case, it is possible that the same applicant will be selected on both draws, which is conceptually nonsensical. However, this is very unlikely with large samples, which is why the binomial distribution is often used with large samples even though conceptually the hypergeometric distribution may be more appropriate. In fact, the binomial distribution is an excellent approximation to the hypergeometric distribution if the size of the population is relatively large compared to the number of cases that are to be sampled from the population (Sheskin, 2007). In addition, the binomial distribution is more appropriate when selections are truly independent of each other. For example, suppose the probability that a female applicant will be admitted to an engineering program (a success) is 0.8 across all such programs. In this case, to determine the probability that 3 out of 15 (or, more generally, *k* out of *n*) engineering programs would admit a female applicant, the number of trials would be *n* = 15 and the trials would be considered independent given that each program's admission decision is not influenced by any other program's decision.

In general, for a series of *n* independent trials, each resulting in only one of two particular outcomes, where π is the probability of success and $1 - \pi$ is the probability of "failure," the probability that $Y = k$ can be expressed by:

$$P(Y = k) = \binom{n}{k} \pi^k (1 - \pi)^{(n-k)}.$$

(2.3)

For example, suppose that the probability of being proficient in mathematics (a success) is 0.7 and three students are chosen at random from a particular school. The binomial distribution can be used, for example, to determine the probability that of three randomly selected students ($n = 3$) all three students are proficient in mathematics ($k = 3$):

$$P(Y = 3) = \binom{3}{3} 0.7^3 (0.3)^{(3-3)} = 0.7^3 = 0.343.$$

In addition, all possible outcomes can be exhausted to determine the most likely number of students that will be found to be proficient. Specifically:

- The probability that none of the three students is proficient
  $$= P(Y = 0) = \binom{3}{0} 0.7^0 (0.3)^{(3-0)} = 0.3^3 = 0.027.$$

- The probability that one of the three students is proficient
  $$= P(Y = 1) = \binom{3}{1} 0.7^1 (0.3)^{(3-1)} = 3(0.7)^1 (0.3)^2 = 0.189.$$

- The probability that two of the three students are proficient
  $$= P(Y = 2) = \binom{3}{2} 0.7^2 (0.3)^{(3-2)} = 3(0.7)^2 (0.3)^1 = 0.441.$$

Therefore, it is most likely that the number of mathematically proficient students selected will be two. Note that, since the preceding computations exhausted all possible outcomes, their probabilities should and do sum to one.

The mean and variance of the binomial distribution are expressed by $\mu = n\pi$ and $\sigma^2 = n\pi(1 - \pi)$, respectively. Therefore, for our example, the mean of the distribution is $\mu = 3(0.7) = 2.1$, so the expected number of students found to be proficient in mathematics is 2.1, which is comparable to the information that was obtained when the probabilities were calculated directly. Moreover, the variance of the distribution is $\sigma^2 = 3(.7)(.3) = 0.63$, which implies that the standard deviation is $\sigma^2 = \sqrt{0.63} = 0.794$.

2.6   The multinomial distribution

The multinomial distribution is a multivariate extension of the binomial distribution when there are I possible outcomes, as opposed to only two. The binomial distribution can be used to represent the number of successes in n independent Bernoulli trials when the probability of success is the same for each trial. However, in a multinomial distribution each trial results in one of I outcomes, where I is some fixed finite number and the probability of each possible outcome can be expressed by $\pi_1, \pi_2, ..., \pi_I$ such that the sum of all probabilities is $\sum_{i=1}^{I} \pi_i = 1$. Therefore, while the binomial distribution depicts the probability of obtaining a specific outcome pattern across two categories in n trials, the multinomial distribution depicts the probability of obtaining a specific outcome pattern across I categories in n trials. In this sense, the binomial distribution is a special case of the multinomial distribution with $I = 2$. In the illustrative example provided for the binomial distribution, students were classified as either proficient or not proficient, and the probability of observing a particular number of proficient students was of interest so the binomial distribution was appropriate. However, if students were instead categorized into one of four proficiency classifications, such as minimal, basic, proficient, and advanced, and the probability of observing a particular number of students in each of the four proficiency classifications was of interest, then the multinomial distribution would be appropriate.

In general, for n trials with I possible outcomes, where π_i = the probability of the ith outcome, the probability that $Y_1 = k_1$, $Y_2 = k_2$, ..., and $Y_I = k_I$ can be expressed by

$$P(Y_1 = k_1, Y_2 = k_2, \ldots, \text{and } Y_I = k_I) = \frac{n!}{k_1! k_2! \cdots k_I!} \pi_1^{k_1} \pi_2^{k_2} \cdots \pi_I^{k_I}. \qquad (2.4)$$

Note that the sum of probabilities is

$$\sum_{i=1}^{I} \pi_i = 1$$

and the sum of outcome frequencies is

$$\sum_{i=1}^{I} k_i = n.$$

For example, suppose that the probability of being a minimal reader is 0.12, the probability of being a basic reader is 0.23, the probability of being a proficient reader is 0.47, and the probability of being an advanced reader is 0.18. If five students are chosen at random from a particular classroom, the multinomial distribution can be used to determine the probability that one student selected at random is a minimal reader, one student is a basic reader, two students are proficient readers, and one student is an advanced reader:

$$P(Y_1 = 1, Y_2 = 1, \ Y_3 = 2, \text{ and } Y_4 = 1) = \frac{5!}{(1!)(1!)(2!)(1!)}(0.12)^1(0.23)^1(0.47)^2(0.18)^1$$

$$= \frac{5(4)(3)(2)(1)}{2}(0.12)(0.23)(0.47)(0.47)(0.18) = 0.066.$$

There are 120 different permutations in which the proficiency classification of students can be randomly selected (e.g., the probability that all five students were advanced, the probability that one student is advanced and the other four students are proficient, and so on), thus we do not enumerate all possible outcomes here. However, the multinomial distribution could be used to determine the probability of any of the 120 different permutations in a similar manner.

There are I means and variances for the multinomial distribution, each dealing with a particular outcome, i. Specifically, for the ith outcome the mean can be expressed by $\mu_i = n\pi_i$ and the variance can be expressed by $\sigma_i^2 = n\pi_i(1 - \pi_i)$. Table 2.2 depicts these descriptive statistics for each of the four proficiency classifications in the previous example.

Table 2.2 Descriptive Statistics for Proficiency Classifications
Following a Multinomial Distribution

Proficiency classification (i)	π_i	μ_i	σ_i^2	σ_i
Minimal	0.12	$5(0.12) = 0.60$	$5(0.12)(0.88) = 0.53$	0.73
Basic	0.23	$5(0.23) = 1.15$	$5(0.23)(0.77) = 0.89$	0.94
Proficient	0.47	$5(0.47) = 2.35$	$5(0.47)(0.53) = 1.25$	1.12
Advanced	0.18	$5(0.18) = 0.90$	$5(0.18)(0.82) = 0.74$	0.86

2.7 The Poisson distribution

The Poisson distribution is similar to the binomial distribution in that both distributions are used to model count data that varies randomly over time. In fact, as the number of trials gets larger (i.e., $n \to \infty$), the binomial distribution and the Poisson distribution tend to converge when the probability of success remains fixed. The major difference between the binomial and the Poisson distributions is that for the binomial distribution the number of observations (trials) is fixed, whereas for the Poisson distribution the number of observations is not fixed but rather the period of time in which the observations occur must be fixed. In other words, when categorical data arise from the binomial distribution all eligible cases are studied, whereas when data arise from the Poisson distribution only those cases with a particular outcome in a fixed time interval are studied. For example, suppose that a researcher was interested in studying the number of accidents at a particular highway interchange in a 24-hour period. To study this phenomenon using the binomial distribution the researcher would have to know the total number of cars (i.e., n) that had traveled through the particular interchange in a 24-hour period as well as the number of cars that had been involved in an accident at the particular interchange in this 24-hour period (which, when divided by n, provides π or p). This is because the binomial distribution assumes that there are two possible outcomes to the phenomenon: success or failure. On the other hand, to study this phenomenon using the Poisson distribution the researcher would only need to know the mean number of cars that had been involved in an accident at the particular interchange in a 24-hour period, which is obviously much easier to obtain. For this reason, the Poisson distribution is often used when the probability of success is very small.

In general, if λ equals the number of successes expected to occur in a fixed interval of time, then the probability of observing k successes in that time interval can be expressed by

$$P(Y = k) = \frac{e^{-\lambda}\lambda^k}{k!}. \tag{2.5}$$

For example, suppose that over the last 50 years the average number of suicide attempts that occurred at a particular correction facility each year is approximately 2.5. The Poisson distribution can be used to determine the probability that five suicide attempts will occur at this particular correction facility in the next year. Specifically,

$$P(Y = 5) = \frac{e^{-\lambda}\lambda^5}{5!} = \frac{e^{-2.5}2.5^5}{5!} = \frac{(0.082)(2.5)^5}{5(4)(3)(2)(1)} = 0.067.$$

In addition, all possible outcomes can be exhausted to determine the most likely number of suicides that will occur at this particular correction facility in the next year. Specifically,

$$P(1 \text{ suicide attempt will occur}) = \frac{e^{-2.5}2.5^1}{1!} = \frac{(0.082)(2.5)}{1} = 0.205,$$

$$P(2 \text{ suicide attempts will occur}) = \frac{e^{-2.5}2.5^2}{2!} = \frac{(0.082)(2.5)^2}{2(1)} = 0.256,$$

$$P(3 \text{ suicide attempts will occur}) = \frac{e^{-2.5}2.5^3}{3!} = \frac{(0.082)(2.5)^3}{3(2)(1)} = 0.214,$$

$$P(4 \text{ suicide attempts will occur}) = \frac{e^{-2.5}2.5^4}{4!} = \frac{(0.082)(2.5)^4}{4(3)(2)(1)} = 0.138,$$

$$P(5 \text{ suicide attempts will occur}) = \frac{e^{-2.5}2.5^5}{5!} = \frac{(0.082)(2.5)^5}{5(4)(3)(2)(1)} = 0.067,$$

$$P(6 \text{ suicide attempts will occur}) = \frac{e^{-2.5}2.5^6}{6!} = \frac{(0.082)(2.5)^6}{6(5)(4)(3)(2)(1)} = 0.028,$$

$$P(7 \text{ suicide attempts will occur}) = \frac{e^{-2.5}2.5^7}{7!} = \frac{(0.082)(2.5)^7}{7(6)(5)(4)(3)(2)(1)} = 0.010,$$

$$P(8 \text{ suicide attempts will occur}) = \frac{e^{-2.5}2.5^8}{8!} = \frac{(0.082)(2.5)^8}{8(7)(6)(5)(4)(3)(2)(1)} = 0.003, \text{ and}$$

$$P(9 \text{ suicide attempts will occur}) = \frac{e^{-2.5}2.5^9}{9!} = \frac{(0.082)(2.5)^8}{9(8)(7)(6)(5)(4)(3)(2)(1)} < 0.001.$$

Figure 2.1 depicts this distribution graphically and Figure 2.2 depicts a comparable distribution if the average number of suicide attempts in a year had only been equal to one. Comparing the two figures, note that the expected (i.e., average) number of suicides in any given year at this particular correctional facility, assuming that the number of suicides follows the Poisson distribution, is greater in Figure 2.1 than in Figure 2.2, as would be expected. Moreover, the likelihood of having a high number of suicides (e.g., four or more) is much lower in Figure 2.2 than in Figure 2.1, as would be expected.

Figure 2.3 illustrates a comparable distribution where the average number of suicide attempts in a year is equal to five. Notice that Figure 2.3 is somewhat reminiscent of a normal distribution. In fact, as λ gets larger the Poisson distribution tends to more closely resemble the normal distribution and, for sufficiently large λ, the normal distribution is an excellent approximation to the Poisson distribution (Cheng, 1949).

The mean and variance of the Poisson distribution are both expressed by $\mu = \sigma^2 = \lambda$. This implies that as the average number of times an event is expected to occur gets larger, so does the expected variability of that event occurring, which also makes sense intuitively. However, with real count data the variance often exceeds the mean, a phenomenon known as **overdispersion**.

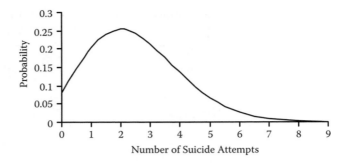

Figure 2.1 Illustration of Poisson distribution when $\lambda = 2.5$.

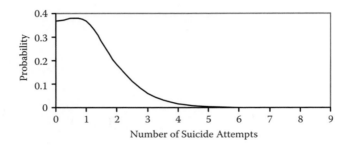

Figure 2.2 Illustration of Poisson distribution when $\lambda = 1.0$.

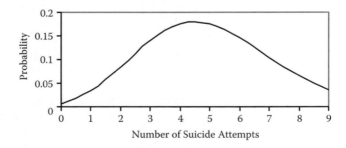

Figure 2.3 Illustration of Poisson distribution when $\lambda = 5.0$.

Table 2.3 Summary of Common Probability Distributions for Categorical Variables

Distribution	Process modeled	Parameters
Hypergeometric	Probability of k successes in n dependent trials	m (total number of successes available) n (total number of selections) N (total number available)
Bernoulli	Probability of a success in one trial	$\pi = m/N$ (probability of success)
Binomial	Probability of k successes in n independent trials	n (total number of trials) π (probability of success)
Multinomial	Probability of k_i successes in each of I categories in n independent trials	n (total number of trials) $\pi_1, \pi_2, \dots \pi_I$ (probability of success in each of I categories)
Poisson	Probability of k successes in a fixed time interval	λ (number of successes expected to occur in a fixed interval)

2.8   Summary

In this chapter we discussed various probability distributions that are often used to model discrete random variables. The distribution that is most appropriate for a given situation depends on the random process that is modeled and the parameters that are needed or available in that situation. A summary of the distributions we discussed is provided in Table 2.3.

In the next chapter we make use of some of these distributions for inferential procedures; specifically, we will discuss how to estimate and test hypotheses about a population proportion based on the information obtained from a random sample.

Problems

2.1   A divorce lawyer must choose 5 out of 25 people to sit on the jury that is to help decide how much alimony should be paid to his client, the ex-husband of a wealthy business woman. As luck would have it, 12 of the possible candidates are very bitter about having to pay alimony to their ex-spouses. If the lawyer were to choose jury members at random, what is the probability that none of the five jury members he chooses are bitter about having to pay alimony?

2.2   At Learn More School, 15 of the 20 students in second grade are proficient in reading.
   a.   If the principal of the school were to randomly select two second-grade students to represent the school in a poetry reading contest, what is the probability that both of the students chosen will be proficient in reading?
   b.   What is the probability that only one of the two students selected will be proficient in reading?
   c.   If two students are selected, what is the expected number of students that are proficient in reading?

2.3 Suppose there are 48 Republican senators and 52 Democrat senators in the United States Senate and the president of the United States must appoint a special committee of 6 senators to study the issues related to poverty in the United States. If the special committee is appointed by randomly selecting senators, what is the probability that half of the committee consists of Republican senators and half of the committee consists of Democrat senators?

2.4 The CEO of a toy company would like to hire a vice president of sales and marketing. Only two of the five qualified applicants are female and the CEO would really like to hire a female VP if at all possible to increase the diversity of his administrative cabinet. If he randomly chooses an applicant from the pool, what is the probability that the applicant chosen will be a female?

2.5 Suppose that the principal of Learn More School from Problem 2.2 is only able to choose one second-grade student to represent the school in a poetry contest. If he randomly selects a student, what is the probability that the student will be proficient in reading?

2.6 Researchers at the Food Institute have determined that 67% of women tend to crave sweets over other alternatives. If 10 women are randomly sampled from across the country, what is the probability that only 3 of the women sampled will report craving sweets over other alternatives?

2.7 For a multiple choice test item with four response options, the probability of obtaining the correct answer by simply guessing is 0.25. If a student simply guessed on all 20 items in a multiple choice test:
a. What is the probability that she would obtain the correct answers to 15 of the 20 items?
b. What is the expected number of items the student would answer correctly?

2.8 The probability that an entering college freshman will obtain his or her degree in 4 years is 0.4. What is the probability that at least 1 out of 5 admitted freshmen will graduate in 4 years?

2.9 An owner of a boutique store knows that 45% of the customers who enter her store will make purchases that total less than $200, 15% of the customers will make purchases that total more than $200, and 40% of the customers will simply be browsing. If five customers enter her store on a particular afternoon, what is the probability that exactly two customers will make a purchase that totals less than $200 and exactly one customer will make a purchase that totals more than $200?

2.10 On average, 10 people enter a particular bookstore every 5 minutes.
a. What is the probability that only four people enter the bookstore in a 5-minute interval?
b. What is the probability that eight people enter the bookstore in a 5-minute interval?

2.11 Telephone calls are received by a college switchboard at the rate of four calls every 3 minutes. What is the probability of obtaining five calls in a 3-minute interval?

2.12 Provide a substantive illustration of a situation that would require the use of each of the five probability distributions described in this chapter.

chapter three

Proportions, estimation, and goodness-of-fit

A LOOK AHEAD

Categorical variables are typically measured on nominal or ordinal scales, as discussed in Chapter 1. Therefore, categorical data are typically examined in terms of the proportion of cases observed in each category, and common probability distributions appropriate for proportions were discussed in Chapter 2. In this chapter, we examine proportions in more detail and discuss how to estimate proportions in the population using sample data, as well as inferential procedures for generalizing this information from the sample to the population. For example, suppose that we would like to know whether the proportion of students in the United States who are proficient in mathematics meet the expectations of the federal government. In this case, the population consists of all students in the United States and we would need to *estimate* the exact proportion of students in the United States who are proficient in mathematics because it is unfeasible to observe all of the students in the United States. This estimate can be obtained by selecting a random sample of students from the United States and computing the proportion of students in the sample who are proficient in mathematics. Next, we may wish to *infer* how well the sample proportion represents the population proportion and test whether this proportion is significantly larger or smaller than the expectations set by the federal government. In this chapter we will discuss these topics as they relate to a binary (or dichotomous) variable and then extend this discussion to a variable that consists of more than two categories.

3.1   Maximum likelihood estimation: a single proportion

In estimating a population parameter (e.g., a population proportion), we use information from the sample to compute a statistic (e.g., a sample proportion) that optimally represents the parameter in some way. The term **maximum likelihood estimate** refers to the value of the parameter that is most probable, given the sample data, according to the appropriate underlying probability distribution.

To demonstrate this estimation procedure with a computationally simple example, suppose that we select a random sample of 10 students from the population of all students in the United States and record whether each student is proficient (a "success," in the terminology of Chapter 2) or not proficient in mathematics. Since the proficiency outcome for each student is a Bernoulli trial, and there are $n = 10$ such trials, the appropriate underlying distribution for this process is the binomial. Recall (from Chapter 2) that the binomial probability of k successes in n independent "trials" is computed as

$$P(Y = k) = \binom{n}{k} \pi^k (1 - \pi)^{(n-k)}. \tag{3.1}$$

Using Equation 3.1, suppose that in our example 4 of the 10 students were proficient in mathematics. The probability would thus be computed by substituting $n = 10$ and $k = 4$ into Equation 3.1, so

$$P(Y = 4) = \binom{10}{4} \pi^4 (1 - \pi)^{(10-4)}.$$

By evaluating this probability for different values of π, the maximum likelihood estimate is the value of π at which the probability (likelihood) is highest (maximized). For example, if $\pi = 0.3$, the probability of 4 (out of the 10) students being proficient is

$$P(Y = 4) = \binom{10}{4} (0.3)^4 (1 - 0.3)^{(10-4)}$$

$$= \frac{(10 \times 9 \times 8 \times 7 \times 6 \times 5 \times 4 \times 3 \times 2 \times 1)}{(4 \times 3 \times 2 \times 1)(6 \times 5 \times 4 \times 3 \times 2 \times 1)} (0.3)^4 (0.7)^6 = 210(0.0081)(0.1176) = 0.20.$$

Similarly, if $\pi = 0.4$, the probability is

$$P(Y = 4) = \binom{10}{4} (0.4)^4 (1 - 0.4)^{(10-4)} = 210(0.4)^4 (0.6)^6 = 0.25.$$

The probabilities for the full range of possible π values are shown in Figure 3.1, which demonstrates that the value of π that maximizes the probability (or likelihood) in our example is 0.40. This means that the value of 0.40 is an ideal estimate of π in the sense that it is most probable, or likely, given the observed data. In fact, the **maximum likelihood estimate of a proportion** is equal to the sample proportion, computed as $p = k/n = 4/10 = 0.40$.

In general, the maximum likelihood estimation method is an approach to obtaining sample estimates that is useful in a variety of contexts as well as in cases where a simple computation does not necessarily provide an ideal estimate. We will use the concept of maximum likelihood estimation throughout this book.

So far we have discussed the concept of maximum likelihood estimation and showed that we can use the sample proportion, $p = k/n$, to obtain the maximum likelihood estimate (MLE) of the population proportion, π. This is akin to what is done with more familiar parameters, such as the population mean. In this case, the MLE of the population mean is the sample mean, when it is assumed that responses follow an underlying normal distribution. The inferential step, in the case of the population mean, involves testing whether the

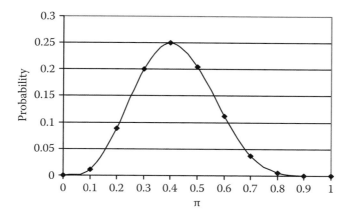

Figure 3.1 Binomial probabilities for various values of π with $k = 4$ successes and $n = 10$ trials.

sample mean differs from what it is hypothesized to be in the population and constructing a confidence interval for the value of the population mean based on its sample estimate. Similarly, in our example we can infer whether the proportion of students found to be proficient in mathematics in the sample differs from the proportion of students hypothesized to be proficient in mathematics in the population. We can also construct a confidence interval for the proportion of students proficient in mathematics in the population based on the estimate obtained from the sample. We now turn to a discussion of inferential procedures for a proportion.

3.2   Hypothesis testing for a single proportion

In testing a null hypothesis for a single population mean, where the variable of interest is continuous, a test statistic is constructed and evaluated against the probabilities of the normal distribution. In the case of testing a null hypothesis for a single population proportion, however, the variable of interest is discrete and several hypothesis-testing methods are available. We will discuss methods that use the probabilities from the binomial distribution as well as methods that use a continuous distribution to approximate the binomial distribution. Computer programs and output for the examples presented are provided at the end of the chapter.

3.2.1   Hypothesis testing using the binomial distribution

Recall from Chapter 2 that the probability of any dichotomous outcome (i.e., number of successes, k) can be computed using the binomial probability distribution. For example, suppose that federal guidelines state that 80% of students should demonstrate proficiency in mathematics, and in a randomly selected sample of 10 students only 70% of students were found to be proficient in mathematics. In such a case, we may wish to test whether the proportion of students who are proficient in mathematics in the population is significantly different than the federal guideline of 80%. In other words, we would like to know whether our obtained sample proportion of 0.7 is significantly lower than 0.8, so we would test the null hypothesis H_0: $\pi = 0.8$ against the (one-sided, in this case) alternative H_1: $\pi < 0.8$.

Table 3.1 Probabilities of the Binomial
Distribution With $n = 10$ and $\pi = 0.8$

k	Probability $= P(Y = k)$	Cumulative probability $= P(Y \leq k)$
0	0.0000	0.0000
1	0.0000	0.0000
2	0.0001	0.0001
3	0.0008	0.0009
4	0.0055	0.0064
5	0.0264	0.0328
6	0.0881	0.1209
7	0.2013	0.3222
8	0.3020	0.6242
9	0.2684	0.8926
10	0.1074	1.0000

In this example, using our sample of $n = 10$ students, the probability for each outcome ($k = 0, 1, \ldots, 10$) can be computed under the null hypothesis (where $\pi = 0.8$) using

$$P(Y = k) = \binom{10}{k} 0.8^k (1 - 0.8)^{(10-k)}.$$

The resulting probabilities (which make up the null distribution) are shown in Table 3.1 and Figure 3.2. Using the conventional significance level of $\alpha = 0.05$, any result that is in the lowest 5% of the null distribution would lead to rejection of H_0. From the cumulative probabilities in Table 3.1, which indicate the sum of the probabilities up to and including a given value of k, we can see that the lowest 5% of the distribution consists of the k values 0 through 5. For values of k above 5, the cumulative probability is greater than 5%. Since our sample result of $p = 0.7$ translates to $k = 7$ when $n = 10$, we can see that this result is not in the lowest 5% of the distribution and does not provide sufficient evidence for rejecting H_0.

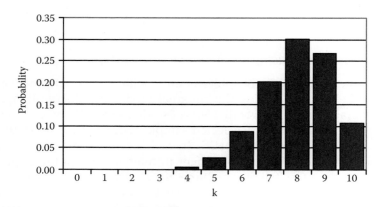

Figure 3.2 Probabilities of the binomial distribution with $n = 10$ and $\pi = 0.8$.

In other words, our result is not all that unusual under the null distribution so we cannot reject the hypothesis that $\pi = 0.8$. The sample result of $p = 0.7$ is not inconsistent with the notion that 80% of the students in the *population* (represented by the sample) are indeed proficient in mathematics. On the other hand, if we had obtained a sample proportion of $p = 0.5$ (i.e., $k = 5$), our result would have been in the lowest 5% of the distribution and therefore we would have rejected the null hypothesis that $\pi = 0.8$. In this case we would have concluded that, based on our sample proportion, it would be unlikely that 80% of the students in the population are proficient in mathematics.

In addition, *p*-values can be computed for these tests using the null distribution probabilities by observing that, if the null hypothesis was true, the lower-tailed probability of obtaining a result *at least as extreme* as the sample result of $p = 0.7$ (or $k = 7$) is

$$P(Y = 0) + P(Y = 1) + P(Y = 2) + \ldots + P(Y = 7) = 0.322,$$

which is also the cumulative probability (see Table 3.1) corresponding to $k = 7$.

To conduct a two-tailed test, in which the alternative hypothesis is $H_1: \pi \neq 0.8$, the one-tailed *p*-value is typically doubled. In our example, the two-tailed *p*-value would thus be $2(0.322) = 0.644$. If, in our sample, only 50% of the students were found to be proficient in mathematics then the lower-tailed probability of obtaining a result *at least as extreme* as the sample result of $p = 0.5$ (or $k = 5$) would be

$$P(Y = 0) + P(Y = 1) + P(Y = 2) + \ldots + P(Y = 5) = 0.032,$$

which is also the cumulative probability (see Table 3.1) corresponding to $k = 5$.

There are two main drawbacks to using this method for hypothesis testing. First, if the number of observations (or trials) is large, the procedure requires computing and summing a large number of probabilities. In such a case, approximate methods work just as well and these are discussed in the following sections. Second, the *p*-values obtained from this method are typically a bit too high and the test is thus conservative, meaning that when the significance level is set at 0.05 and the null hypothesis is true, it is not rejected 5% of the time, as would be expected, but rather less than 5% of the time (Agresti, 2007). Methods that adjust the *p*-value so that it is more accurate are beyond the scope of this book, but are discussed in Agresti (2007) as well as Agresti and Coull (1998).

3.2.2   *Hypothesis testing using the normal approximation*

When the sample size (i.e., value of n) is relatively large, the binomial distribution can be approximated by the normal distribution so test statistics can be constructed and evaluated using the familiar standard normal distribution. Specifically, the normal approximation can be used when both $n\pi \geq 5$ and $n(1 - \pi) \geq 5$. In our example, $n\pi = 10(0.8) = 8 > 5$ but $n(1 - \pi) = 10(0.2) = 2 < 5$ so the normal approximation may not be accurate. However, we will proceed with our example to illustrate this method.

The normal approximation test statistic is very similar to the test statistic used in comparing a sample mean against a hypothesized population mean when the dependent variable is continuous. Specifically, a *z*-statistic is constructed using the standard formula

$$z = \frac{\text{Estimate} - \text{Parameter}}{\text{Standard error}}.$$

In testing a mean, the estimate is the sample mean, the parameter is the population mean specified under the null hypothesis, and the standard error is the standard deviation of the appropriate sampling distribution. In our case, recall from Chapter 2 (Section 2.5) that the variance for the distribution of frequencies that follow the binomial distribution is $\sigma^2 = n\pi(1 - \pi)$.

Because a proportion is a frequency divided by the sample size, n, using the properties of linear transformations the variance of the distribution of proportions is equal to the variance of the distribution of frequencies divided by n^2, or $\sigma^2/n^2 = n\pi(1 - \pi)/n^2 = \pi(1 - \pi)/n$, which is estimated in the sample by $p(1 - p)/n$. The standard error can thus be estimated from sample information using $\sqrt{p(1-p)/n}$, and the test statistic for testing the null hypothesis $H_0: \pi = \pi_0$ is

$$z = \frac{p - \pi_0}{\sqrt{p(1-p)/n}}.$$

This test statistic follows a standard normal distribution when the sample size is large. For our example,

$$z = \frac{p - \pi_0}{\sqrt{p(1-p)/n}} = \frac{0.7 - 0.8}{\sqrt{(0.7)(0.3)/10}} = \frac{-0.1}{0.145} = -0.69.$$

To reject a two-tailed test at the 0.05 significance level using the standard normal distribution, the test statistic must be greater than 1.96 or smaller than –1.96, so this test statistic does not lead to rejection of H_0. Therefore, the null hypothesis is not rejected and we conclude that the sample estimate of 0.7 is consistent with the notion that 80% of the students in the population are proficient in math. This procedure is called the **Wald test**, and it may be less reliable than some other methods discussed in this section, especially for small samples. One of the problems with this test is that it relies on the estimate of the population proportion (p) to compute the standard error, and this could lead to unreliable values for the standard error, especially when the estimate is based on a small sample. A variation on this test that uses the null hypothesis proportion π_0 (instead of p) to compute the standard error is called the **score test**. Using the score test, the test statistic becomes

$$z = \frac{p - \pi_0}{\sqrt{\pi_0(1-\pi_0)/n}}$$

and it too follows a standard normal distribution when the sample size is large. For our example,

$$z = \frac{p - \pi_0}{\sqrt{0.8(1-0.8)/n}} = \frac{0.7 - 0.8}{\sqrt{(0.8)(0.2)/10}} = \frac{-0.1}{0.126} = -0.79.$$

In this case our conclusions do not change: We do not reject the null hypothesis based on this result.

In general, and thus applicable to both the Wald and score tests, squaring the value of z produces a test statistic that follows the χ^2 (chi-squared) distribution with one degree of freedom, which is equivalent to the z-test (but can only be used when the hypothesis test is two-tailed). Another general hypothesis testing method that is based on the χ^2 distribution, the likelihood ratio method, will be used in different contexts throughout the book and is introduced next.

3.2.3   Hypothesis testing using the likelihood ratio method

The likelihood ratio method compares the likelihood (probability) of the observed data obtained using the proportion specified under the null hypothesis to the likelihood of the observed data obtained using the observed sample estimate. The likelihood obtained under the null hypothesis is denoted by L_0 and the likelihood obtained using the sample estimate is denoted by L_1. The ratio L_0/L_1 represents the **likelihood ratio**. If L_1 (the likelihood obtained from the observed data) is much larger than L_0 (the likelihood under H_0), the likelihood ratio will be much smaller than one and will indicate that the data provide evidence against the null hypothesis. The likelihood ratio test statistic is obtained by taking the natural logarithm (ln) of the likelihood ratio and multiplying it by –2. Specifically, the test statistic is

$$G^2 = -2\ln\left(\frac{L_0}{L_1}\right) = -2\,[\ln(L_0) - \ln(L_1)].$$
(3.2)

The **natural logarithm function** is illustrated in Figure 3.3, where the horizontal axis represents values of a random variable, X, and the vertical axis represents the value of its natural logarithm, $\ln(X)$. Note that when the natural log function is applied to a variable, X, it will be negative when the value of X is less than one, positive when the value of X is greater than one, and zero when the value of X is equal to one. Therefore, at the extreme, when the two likelihoods (L_0 and L_1) are equivalent, the likelihood ratio will be one and

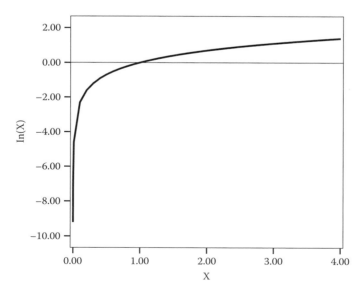

Figure 3.3 Illustration of the natural logarithm function for values of the variable X.

the G^2 test statistic will be zero. As the likelihood computed from the data (L_1) becomes larger relative to the likelihood under the null hypothesis (L_0), the likelihood ratio will become smaller than one, its (natural) log will become more negative, and the test statistic will become more positive. Thus, a larger (more positive) G^2 test statistic indicates stronger evidence against H_0, as is typically the case with test statistics. In fact, under H_0 and with reasonably large samples, the G^2 test statistic follows a χ^2 distribution with degrees of freedom (df) equal to the number of parameters restricted under H_0 (i.e., $df = 1$ in the case of a single proportion). Because the χ^2 distribution consists of squared (i.e., positive) values, it can only be used to test two-tailed hypotheses. In other words, the p-value obtained from this test is based on a two-tailed alternative.

For our example, with $n = 10$ and $k = 7$, L_0 is the likelihood of the observed data, $P(Y = 7)$, computed using the binomial probability distribution with the parameter (π) specified under the null hypothesis (H_0: $\pi = 0.8$):

$$L_0 = P(Y = 7) = \binom{10}{7} 0.8^7 (1 - 0.8)^{(10-7)} = 0.201.$$

Similarly, the likelihood, L_1, of the observed data given the data-based estimate for the parameter (π), $p = 0.7$, is

$$L_1 = P(Y = 7) = \binom{10}{7} 0.7^7 (1 - 0.7)^{(10-7)} = 0.267,$$

so the test statistic is

$$G^2 = -2\ln\left(\frac{L_0}{L_1}\right) = -2\ln(0.201/0.267) = -2\ln(0.753) = 0.567.$$

The critical value of a χ^2 distribution with one degree of freedom at the 0.05 significance level is 3.84 (see Appendix), so the null hypothesis is not rejected using this two-tailed test.

3.2.4 Summary of test results

We discussed several approaches to null hypothesis testing for a single proportion: the binomial (exact) test, the Wald test, the score test, and the likelihood ratio test. A summary of the results using these various approaches for our example is presented in Table 3.2, and

Table 3.2 Summary of Various Approaches for Testing H_0: $\pi = 0.8$
With $n = 10$ and $k = 7$

Testing approach	Test statistic	One-tailed *p*-value	Two-tailed *p*-value
Exact test	Not applicable	0.322	0.644
Wald test	−0.69	0.245	0.490
Score test	−0.79	0.215	0.429
Likelihood ratio test	0.57	Not applicable	0.451

the computing section at the end of this chapter shows how to obtain the results for the exact and score tests using computer software.

3.3   Confidence intervals for a single proportion

While hypothesis testing gives an indication as to whether the observed proportion is consistent with a population proportion of interest (specified under H_0), a confidence interval for the population proportion provides information on the possible value of the "true" proportion in the population of interest. In general, the formula for a confidence interval is

$$\text{Statistic} \pm (\text{Critical value})(\text{Standard error})$$

where the statistic is the sample estimate of the parameter, the critical value depends on the level of confidence desired and is obtained from the sampling distribution of the statistic, and the standard error is the standard deviation of the sampling distribution of the statistic. For example, in constructing a confidence interval for the population mean, one would typically use the sample mean as the statistic, a value from the t-distribution (with $n - 1$ degrees of freedom at the desired confidence level) as the critical value, and $s/\sqrt{n}$ for the standard error (where s is the sample standard deviation).

Generalizing this to a confidence interval for a proportion, the sample proportion, p, is used as the statistic and the critical value is obtained from the standard normal distribution (e.g., $z = 1.96$ for a 95% confidence interval). To compute the standard error, we refer back to the Wald statistic, which uses $\sqrt{p(1-p)/n}$ as the standard error of a proportion. Therefore, the confidence interval for a proportion is computed using

$$p \pm z_{\alpha/2}\sqrt{p(1-p)/n},$$

where $z_{\alpha/2}$ is the critical value from the standard normal distribution for a $(1 - \alpha)$% confidence level. For example, to construct a 95% confidence interval using our sample (where $n = 10$ and $k = 7$), we have $p = 0.7$, $\alpha = 0.05$ so $z_{\alpha/2} = 1.96$, and $\sqrt{p(1-p)/n} = 0.145$. Therefore, the 95% confidence interval for our example is

$$0.7 \pm 1.96(0.145) = 0.7 \pm 0.284 = [0.416, 0.984].$$

Based on this result, we can be 95% confident that the proportion of students in the population (from which the sample was obtained) who are proficient in mathematics is somewhere between (approximately) 42% and 98%. This is a very large range due to the fact that we have a very small sample (and, thus, a relatively large standard error). As we mentioned previously in our discussion of the Wald test, it is somewhat unreliable to compute the standard error based on the sample proportion, especially when the sample size is small. However, here we do not have the option of replacing p with π_0 (as we did for the score test) because a confidence interval does not require the specification of a null hypothesis. Although there are other available methods for computing confidence intervals for a proportion, they are beyond the scope of this book. We refer the interested reader to Agresti (2007), who suggests using the hypothesis testing formula to essentially "work backward" and solve for a confidence interval. Other alternatives include the Agresti–Coull confidence interval, which is an approximation of the method that uses the hypothesis testing formula (Agresti & Coull, 1998), and the *F* distribution method (Collett, 1991; Leemis & Trivedi, 1996) that provides exact confidence limits for the binomial proportion. The latter (confidence interval computed by the *F* distribution method) is also provided by SAS (as shown at the end of this chapter).

3.4   Goodness-of-fit: comparing distributions for a single discrete variable

In the previous sections we discussed a variable (proficiency in mathematics) that took on only two values (yes or no) because it was measured in a dichotomous manner. While the methods discussed so far are appropriate for such dichotomous variables, when a categorical variable consists of more than two categories it may be necessary to evaluate several proportions. For example, the Wisconsin Department of Public Instruction (2006b) uses four categories to measure mathematics proficiency: advanced, proficient, basic, and minimal. To determine if there has been a change in the proficiency classification of Wisconsin students after a year of implementing an intensive program designed to increase student proficiency in mathematics across the four categories, a test can be performed that compares the **expected** and **observed** frequency distributions. This test is called the chi-squared (χ^2) **goodness-of-fit test**, because it tests whether the observed data "fit" with expectations. The null hypothesis of this test states that the expected and observed frequency distributions are the same, so a rejection of this null hypothesis indicates that the observed frequencies exhibit significant departures from the expected frequencies.

For example, suppose that the values in the second column of Table 3.3 (Expected Proportions) represent the proportion of Wisconsin 10th-grade students in each of the four proficiency classifications in 2005. If there has been no change in the proficiency distribution, these would constitute the proportions expected in 2006 as well. Suppose further that the last column of Table 3.3 represents (approximately) the observed mathematics proficiency classifications (frequencies) for 71,709 10th-grade Wisconsin students in 2006 (Wisconsin Department of Public Instruction, 2006a). Using these data, we may wish to determine whether there has been a change in the proficiency level distribution from 2005 to 2006.

The **Pearson chi-squared** test statistic for comparing two frequency distributions is

$$X^2 = \sum_{\text{all categories}} \frac{(\text{observed frequency} - \text{expected frequency})^2}{\text{expected frequency}} = \sum_{i=1}^{c} \frac{(O_i - E_i)^2}{E_i},$$

Table 3.3 Distribution of Wisconsin Tenth-Grade Students According to Four Proficiency Classification Levels ($n = 71{,}709$)

Proficiency Level	Expected Proportion	Expected Frequency	Observed Frequency
Advanced	15%	10,756.35	18,644
Proficient	40%	28,683.60	32,269
Basic	30%	21,512.70	10,039
Minimal	15%	10,756.35	10,757

where O_i represents the observed frequency in the ith category and E_i represents the expected frequency in the ith category. This X^2 test statistic follows a χ^2 distribution with $c - 1$ degrees of freedom, where c is the total number of categories. The reason for this is that, for a given total sample size, only $c - 1$ category frequencies can vary "freely" because the c frequencies must add up to the total sample size, n. Therefore, once $c - 1$ frequencies are known, the last category frequency can be determined by subtracting those frequencies from the total sample size. The expected frequencies are specified by the null hypothesis; that is, they are the frequencies one expects to observe if the null hypothesis is true. In our example, the null hypothesis would state that there is no change in frequencies between 2005 and 2006, so the two distributions should be the same. Therefore, if the null hypothesis is true, the 2006 expected frequencies would follow the 2005 distribution. Because the test statistic uses frequencies rather than proportions, we must convert the 2005 proportions in the second column of Table 3.3 to frequencies based on 71,709 students. These values are shown in the third column of Table 3.3, under Expected Frequency (for example, 15% of 71,709 is 10,756.35). Thus, we can test whether the frequency distributions are the same or different by comparing the last two columns of Table 3.3 using a goodness-of-fit test. The test statistic comparing these two frequency distributions is

$$X^2 = \frac{(18644 - 10756.35)^2}{10756.35} + \frac{(32269 - 28683.6)^2}{28683.6} + \frac{(10039 - 21512.7)^2}{21512.7} + \frac{(10757 - 10756.35)^2}{10756.35}$$

$$= 5784.027 + 448.1688 + 6119.445 + 0 = 12351.64.$$

The critical value of the χ^2 distribution with $c - 1 = 4 - 1 = 3$ degrees of freedom at the 0.05 significance level is 7.82 (see the Appendix), so the test statistic of $X^2 = 12351.64$ exceeds this critical value and the null hypothesis is rejected (in fact, the p-value is less than 0.0001). That is, the mathematics proficiency distribution of Wisconsin 10th-grade students in 2006 is significantly different than (or does not fit with) the 2005 distribution. More specifically, it appears that the numbers of students who were in the advanced or proficient categories in 2006 are higher than those expected under the 2005 distribution while the number of students who were at the basic level in 2006 is lower than expected under the 2005 distribution. Note that the number of students who are at the minimal proficiency level is almost identical under the 2005 and 2006 distributions.

This test is very sensitive to sample size. If there are any categories, also referred to as cells, with very few expected frequencies (generally less than 5), the test may be very inaccurate because it relies on a large-sample approximation to the χ^2 distribution. However, if the sample size is very large, the null hypothesis may be rejected even if it is true (i.e., a Type II error will occur) because the frequencies will be very large and any deviations between the observed and expected distributions will be magnified. The sample size in our example is most likely too large for this test.

As was the case with a single proportion, the Pearson chi-squared test (which is a score test) also has an alternative that is based on the likelihood ratio method (see Section 3.2.3). The **likelihood ratio test statistic** is

$$G^2 = 2\sum(\text{observed frequency})\ln\left(\frac{\text{observed frequency}}{\text{expected frequency}}\right) = 2\sum_{i=1}^{c}O_i\ln\left(\frac{O_i}{E_i}\right)$$

and it also follows a χ^2 distribution with $c - 1$ degrees of freedom. For our example,

$$G^2 = 2\sum_{i=1}^{c} O_i \ln\left(\frac{O_i}{E_i}\right)$$

$$= 2\left[18644 \times \ln\left(\frac{18644}{10756.35}\right) + 32269 \times \ln\left(\frac{32269}{28683.60}\right) + 10039 \times \ln\left(\frac{10039}{21512.70}\right)\right.$$

$$\left. + 10757 \times \ln\left(\frac{10757}{10756.35}\right)\right]$$

$$= 2(10254.72 + 3800.69 - 7651.38 + 0.65) = 12809.36.$$

This result is similar to the Pearson (score) test, as will typically be the case with large samples.

Note that both test statistics (X^2 and G^2) will be zero if the expected and observed frequencies are equal to each other in each category, and will become more positive (i.e., larger) as the expected and observed frequencies become less similar. The individual components (i.e., one value for each category) that are summed to obtain each test statistic can be examined to determine which categories tend to contribute most to the test statistic, or in which categories deviations between the observed and expected frequencies are most prominent. For example, in our computations we can see that in the last (minimal proficiency) category the deviations, or differences between observed and expected frequencies, were very small (0 and 0.65 for the X^2 and G^2 test statistics, respectively). This indicates that in this category the frequencies did not change much from 2005 to 2006. Moreover, there are more students classified as advanced and proficient in 2006, and less students classified as basic, than would be expected if the frequency distribution observed in 2006 followed the same distribution as 2005. Therefore, one might conclude that the efforts the school engaged in were effective, although this is merely speculative since no experiment was conducted. We will revisit the topic of these deviations, or residuals, when we discuss two-way contingency tables in the next chapter.

3.5 Computer output: single proportion example

3.5.1 SAS

The SAS program for obtaining most of the results discussed in Sections 3.2 and 3.3 is provided in Figure 3.4 and the results are provided in the output shown in Figure 3.5. In the program (Figure 3.4):

- Two variables are entered: the proficiency level (prof) and the frequency (count).
  - Note that if raw data for 10 individuals (i.e., 10 rows of data) were analyzed, where the variable called "prof" consisted of 7 yes responses and 3 no responses, the counts would be computed by the program and would not be needed as input.
  - Note also that the prof variable is followed by $ in the input line to indicate that it is a string (rather than a numeric) variable.
- The frequency procedure (proc freq) is used to obtain the results.
  - The first line of the frequency procedure uses the option order=data to indicate that the yes responses should be examined first (as they are entered first in the data). The SAS default is to order the categories in alphabetical order, so in this case the no responses would have been analyzed if this option was omitted.

```
data ch3example1;
 input prof $ count;
 datalines;
 yes 7
 no 3
 ;
proc freq order=data;
 weight count;
 tables prof /binomial (p=0.8) alpha=.05;
 exact binomial;
run;
```

Figure 3.4 SAS program for inference about a single proportion.

```
                    The FREQ Procedure

                              Cumulative    Cumulative
 prof   Frequency    Percent    Frequency      Percent
 -------------------------------------------------------
 yes         7        70.00           7         70.00
 no          3        30.00          10        100.00


                 Chi-Square Test
                for Equal Proportions
                ----------------------
                Chi-Square     1.6000
                DF                  1
                Pr > ChiSq     0.2059


          Binomial Proportion for prof = yes
          ------------------------------------
          Proportion (P)               0.7000
          ASE                          0.1449
          95% Lower Conf Limit         0.4160
          95% Upper Conf Limit         0.9840

          Exact Conf Limits
          95% Lower Conf Limit         0.3475
          95% Upper Conf Limit         0.9333

            Test of H0: Proportion = 0.8

          ASE under H0                 0.1265
          Z                           -0.7906
          One-sided Pr <  Z            0.2146
          Two-sided Pr > |Z|           0.4292

          Exact Test
          One-sided Pr <=  P           0.3222
          Two-sided = 2 * One-sided    0.6444

                Sample Size = 10
```

Figure 3.5 SAS output for inference about a single proportion.

- The second line specifies that the count variable is to be used as a "weight" for the number of observations in each category, essentially indicating that the count variable is to be treated as a frequency. Note that if raw data were used, the weight command would be omitted.
- The third line requests a frequency table for the proficiency variable, and the options (that follow the slash) are:
    - The binomial option requests output for analyses that treat the proportion as a binomial variable.
    - The ($p = 0.8$) option specifies the null proportion against which to test the observed proportion. The default null hypothesis used by SAS is H_0: $\pi = 0.5$, so this option can be omitted if the null proportion is 0.5.
    - The alpha= .05 option is used to set the (1-alpha) confidence level for the confidence interval computations; once again, the default is .05 (or a 95% confidence interval) but the option is included here for completeness.
    - Finally, the fourth line requests that the output for the exact test, using binomial distribution probabilities, be provided.
- The run command executes the program.

You may wish to refer back to and compare the results summarized in Table 3.2 and discussed in Section 3.3 as you examine the output in Figure 3.5. The output (Figure 3.5) provides

- the frequency table;
- the Chi-Square Test for Equal Proportions, which is *not* the likelihood ratio test but rather the squared version of the score test; and
- the Binomial Proportion for prof = yes section, which includes the hypothesis tests and confidence intervals for the proportion of students who are proficient, as discussed in this chapter. Specifically, the following are provided in this part of the output:
    - The proportion of yes responses (i.e., the sample estimate of 0.7).
    - The ASE (which stands for the asymptotic standard error) of the proportion, 0.1449, computed using the sample proportion (i.e., as in the Wald test).
    - The 95% confidence interval with limits 0.416 and 0.984, which is computed using the ASE.
    - The exact 95% confidence interval limits (0.3475, 0.9333), which are based on the *F* distribution method referred to in Section 3.3.
    - The results of the test of the null hypothesis H_0: $\pi = 0.8$:
        - The "ASE under H_0" of 0.1265 refers to the asymptotic standard error computed by replacing the sample proportion (p) with the null hypothesis value (π_0), which is the standard error used by the score test.
        - The "Z test-statistic" provided by in this part of the output (−0.79) is based on the score test, as are the p-values that follow it (0.2146 and 0.4292 for one- and two-tailed tests, respectively).
- Finally, results of the exact test (using the binomial distribution probabilities) are provided in the form of one- and two-tailed p-values (0.3222 and 0.6444, respectively).

3.5.2   SPSS

The data are entered in SPSS in the same manner used for data entry in SAS. That is, two variables are entered: the proficiency level (Proficiency) and the frequency (Count). In this

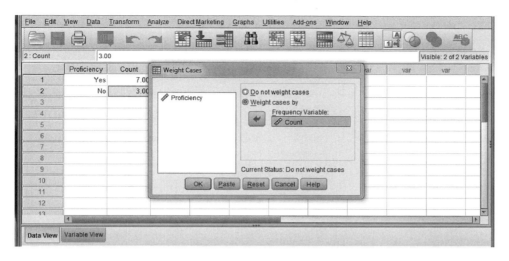

Figure 3.6 SPSS data window showing how to specify count as a weight variable.

example, summary information was entered with Proficiency coded as 1 = Yes and 0 = No. These variables were then coded, using the label function under the Variable tab, so that the labels (i.e., yes and no) appear in the data window, as opposed to the numeric values. If raw data for 10 individuals were entered, the counts would be computed by the program and would not be needed as input. If counts are to be used as weights (when summary information rather than raw data are analyzed), this must be specified in SPSS by

- Clicking on the Data menu and selecting Weight Cases....
- In the dialogue box that opens, click on Weight cases by, then click on the Count variable and move it to the Frequency Variable box.
- Click OK.

This is shown in Figure 3.6.

   To obtain the exact (binomial) test:

- Choose Nonparametric Tests in the Analyze menu and click on One Sample.... This will bring up a window with three file tabs on the top.
- Select the third file tab, Settings, then the option that is titled Customized Tests, and then select the first button, Compare observed binary probability to hypothesized (Binomial test). This is illustrated in Figure 3.7.
- Click on Options and move the count variable into the Test Variable List box on the left, then specify the null hypothesis proportion (i.e., 0.8) in the Test Proportion box.
- Select the value that defines success, then click OK. This is shown in Figure 3.8.
- Click Run to obtain the output.

   To obtain the score test:

- Choose Nonparametric Tests in the Analyze menu and click on One Sample.... This will bring up the same window that was obtained when performing the binomial test, with three file tabs on the top.

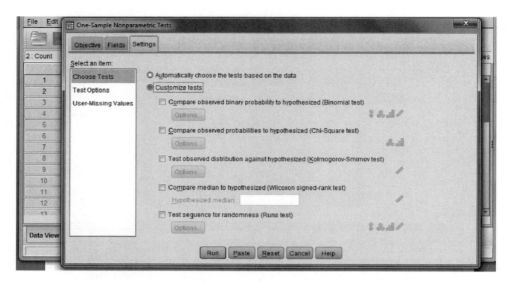

Figure 3.7 SPSS data window for selecting the binomial or score test.

- Once again select the third file tab, Settings, select the option that is titled Customized Tests, and then select the second button, Compare observed probability to hypothesized (Chi-Square test). Refer to Figure 3.7 for this screenshot.
- The expected proportions (i.e., 2 and 8) need to be specified by clicking on Options under the second button. The analysis window is shown in Figure 3.9.
- Click OK and then Run.

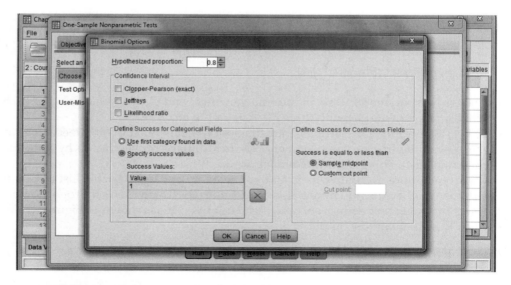

Figure 3.8 SPSS data window for specifying options to use when conducting a binomial test.

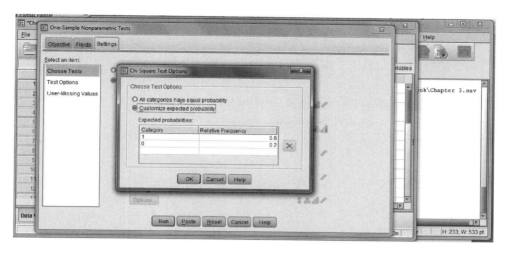

Figure 3.9 SPSS data window specifying expected proportions for the score test.

The output that automatically appears in the output window when conducting the binomial exact test is shown in Figure 3.10.

- The Hypothesis Test Summary table in Figure 3.10 provides the one-tailed p-value for the exact test, which is 0.322.

The output obtained from conducting the score tests is graphically depicted in Figure 3.11.

- The Hypothesis Test Summary table at the top of Figure 3.11 appears automatically and provides the two-tailed p-value for the score test, which is 0.429.
- Clicking on this box in the output window will open the model output view and provide the output shown on the bottom of Figure 3.11.
- In the model output view (Figure 3.11) additional statistics are provided, such as the squared test statistic of the score test, 0.625; its degrees of freedom, 1; and the two-tailed p-value of 0.429. In addition, the squared and the observed and hypothesized distributions are graphically depicted.

Hypothesis Test Summary

	Null Hypothesis	Test	Sig.	Decision.
1	The categories defined by proficiency = (Yes) and (No) occur with probabilities 0.8 and 0.2.	One-sample Binomial Test	0.322[1]	Retain the null hypothesis.

Asymptotic significances are displayed. The significance level is 0.05.

[1]Exact significance is displayed for this test.

Figure 3.10 SPSS output obtained from testing a single proportion using the binomial test.

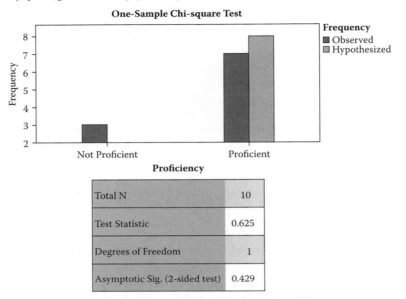

Hypothesis Test Summary

	Null Hypothesis	Test	Sig.	Decision.
1	The categories of proficiency occur with the specified probabilities.	One-sample Chi-Square Test	0.429	Retain the null hypothesis.

Asymptotic significances are displayed. The significance level is 0.05.

One-Sample Chi-square Test

Total N	10
Test Statistic	0.625
Degrees of Freedom	1
Asymptotic Sig. (2-sided test)	0.429

1. There are 1 cells (50%) with expected values less than 5. The minimum expected value is 2.

Figure 3.11 SPSS output obtained from conducting the score test for a single proportion.

3.6   Computer output: goodness-of-fit example

3.6.1   SAS

The SAS program for obtaining most of the results discussed in Section 3.4 is provided in Figure 3.12 and the output is provided in Figure 3.13. In the program (Figure 3.12):

- Two variables are specified: proficiency level (prof) and frequency (count). As was the case with a single proportion, the count variable is not necessary when raw data are analyzed.
- The proc freq and weight statements (lines one and two of the procedure) are the same as they were in the previous example.
- The tables statement (third line of proc freq) requests the frequency table for the proficiency categories and includes the option testp=, which is followed by the proportions of the expected frequency distribution.
  - Note that SAS will automatically compute the expected frequencies based on these expected proportions and the total number of observations (which the program obtains by summing the observed frequencies from the data).

```
data ch3example2;
 input prof $ count;
 datalines;
  advanced 18644
  proficient 32269
  basic 10039
  minimal 10757
 ;
proc freq order=data;
 weight count;
 tables prof / testp=(0.15 0.40 0.30 0.15);
run;
```

Figure 3.12 SAS program for the Pearson chi-squared goodness-of-fit test.

- Due to the use of the order=data option in the proc freq statement, the proportions entered after testp= must be ordered according to the order of the categories as they appear in the data set.

The output, shown in Figure 3.13, provides:

- The frequency table, including the observed frequencies and proportions as well as the expected proportions (as specified in the program).
- The Chi-Square Test output, consisting of the Pearson test statistic (Chi-Square = 12351.64) as well as the degrees of freedom ($df = 3$) and p-value ($< .0001$) of the test.

Other options (and more extensive output) are available when several variables (i.e., two-way tables) are analyzed, as is the case in the next chapter.

3.6.2   SPSS

The data are entered in SPSS in the same manner used for data entry in SAS. That is, two variables are entered: the proficiency level (prof) and the frequency (count). If raw data were used, the counts would be computed by the program and would not be needed as input.

```
                        The FREQ Procedure

                                   Test     Cumulative    Cumulative
  prof        Frequency   Percent  Percent  Frequency     Percent
  --------------------------------------------------------------------
  advanced      18644     26.00    15.00      18644         26.00
  proficie      32269     45.00    40.00      50913         71.00
  basic         10039     14.00    30.00      60952         85.00
  minimal       10757     15.00    15.00      71709        100.00

                        Chi-Square Test
                     for Specified Proportions
                     -------------------------
                     Chi-Square     12351.6415
                     DF                      3
                     Pr > ChiSq        <.0001

                     Sample Size = 71709
```

Figure 3.13 SAS output for the Pearson chi-squared goodness-of-fit test.

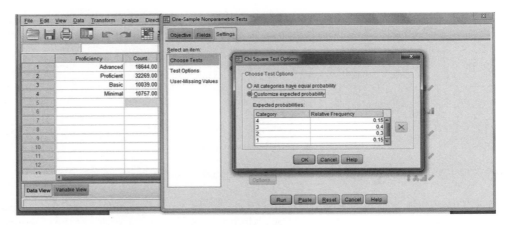

Figure 3.14 Specifying expected values for goodness-of-fit test in SPSS.

Note that the proficiency categories were entered as nominal data such that Advanced = 4, Proficient = 3, Basic = 2, and Minimal = 1. These variables were then coded, using the label function under the Variable tab, so that the labels (i.e., advanced, proficient, basic, and minimal) appear in the data window, as opposed to the numeric values.

Again, since frequencies rather than raw data are used, this must be specified in SPSS (see Figure 3.6) by

- Clicking on the Data menu and selecting Weight Cases....
- In the dialogue box that opens, click on Weight cases by, then click on the count variable and move it to the Frequency variable box, then click OK.

To obtain the chi-squared goodness-of-fit test:

- Choose Nonparametric Tests in the Analyze menu and click on One Sample....
- This will bring up the same window that was obtained when performing the binomial and score tests, with three file tabs on the top. Again select the third file tab, Settings, select the option that is titled Customized Tests, and then select the second button, Compare observed probability to hypothesized (Chi-Square test). Refer to Figure 3.7 for this screenshot.
- The expected proportions (i.e., 0.15, 0.40, 0.30, and 0.15) need to be specified by clicking on the Options button. The analysis window is shown in Figure 3.14.

Hypothesis Test Summary

	Null Hypothesis	Test	Sig.	Decision.
1	The categories of proficiency occur with the specified probabilities.	One-Sample Chi-Square Test	0.000	Reject the null hypothesis.

Asymptotic significances are displayed. The significance level is 0.05.

Figure 3.15 SPSS output for the Pearson chi-squared goodness-of-fit test.

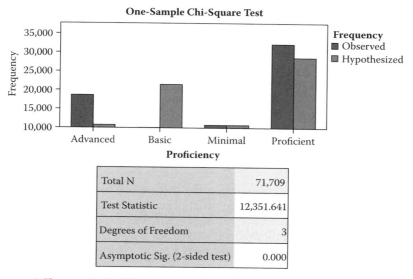

1. There are 0 cells (0%) with expected values less than 5. The minimum expected value is 10,756.350.

Figure 3.16 SPSS model output for the Pearson chi-squared goodness-of-fit test obtained by clicking on the output shown in Figure 3.15.

The output that is automatically displayed in the output window is shown in Figure 3.15. Double clicking this box in the output window will provide the model view output illustrated in Figure 3.16, which includes

- a graphic display (bar graph) of the observed and expected frequencies; and
- the Pearson chi-squared test statistic of 12351.64, with 3 degrees of freedom and a p-value of .000 (which implies $p < 0.0001$).

3.7   Summary

In this chapter we discussed estimation and inferential procedures for a single categorical variable. Specifically, we discussed how to estimate a proportion of interest, or the probability of a given category of the variable, and how to test hypotheses as well as construct confidence intervals for a single proportion. We introduced the concept of maximum likelihood estimation as well as tests such as the Wald, score, and likelihood ratio tests, all of which will be used throughout the book.

In addition, we also discussed how to use the goodness-of-fit test to compare the observed distribution of a single categorical variable to the distribution that would be expected or hypothesized. This again is a general approach to testing hypotheses in categorical data analysis that will be utilized in subsequent chapters.

Whereas this chapter introduced some general approaches and concepts as applied to a single categorical variable, the next chapter demonstrates these ideas in the context of investigating the relationship between two categorical variables.

Problems

3.1   In a certain school the proportion of students who are proficient in mathematics is 40%. A new teaching approach is introduced in the school, and after a year it is found that in a random sample of 20 students 13 are proficient.

a.   What is the maximum likelihood estimate of the proficiency rate with the new teaching approach?

b.   Did the new teaching approach significantly improve proficiency? State the null and alternative hypotheses and report the p-value of the exact test (binomial distribution).

3.2   Suppose that in the general population the proportion of obese men who have heart disease is 10%. In a random sample of 50 obese men who were placed on a low-fat diet, two men were found to have heart disease after 6 months.

a.   What is the maximum likelihood estimate of heart disease rate in the population of obese men who are on a low-fat diet?

b.   Is there evidence that heart disease rate is significantly lower in the population of obese men placed on a low-fat diet? State the null and alternative hypotheses and report the p-value of the exact test (binomial distribution).

3.3   Repeat Problem 3.1 using the score test.

3.4   Repeat Problem 3.2 using the score test.

3.5   Use the results of Problems 3.1 and 3.3 to explain why the exact test (based on the binomial distribution) is considered to be more conservative than the score test (based on the normal approximation).

3.6   Use the results of Problems 3.2 and 3.4 to explain why the exact test (based on the binomial distribution) is considered to be more conservative than the score test (based on the normal approximation).

3.7   Repeat Problem 3.1 using the likelihood ratio test. State the null and alternative hypotheses (note that this method requires a two-tailed test). Report the p-value and state the conclusions.

3.8   In a recent poll, 120 registered voters from a random sample of 200 indicated that they plan to vote for Candidate X. Based on these results, a researcher would like to determine whether it is fair to say that Candidate X will receive the majority of votes.

a.   What are the null and alternative hypotheses?

b.   Use the score test to compute the p-value of the hypothesis test.

c.   Use the Wald test to compute the p-value of the hypothesis test.

d.   State the conclusions.

3.9   Use the information in Problem 3.8 to construct and interpret:

a.   The results of a 95% confidence interval for the proportion of votes for Candidate X.

b.   The results of a 99% confidence interval for the proportion of votes for Candidate X.

c.   Based on the results of the confidence intervals, is it fair to say that Candidate X will likely receive the majority of votes?

3.10 After introducing a new teaching curriculum, a principal would like to determine whether the grade distribution in her school is significantly different than it has been in previous years. Suppose that Table 3.4 represents the distribution over previous years. Further, suppose that in a random sample of 100 students, 25 got an A, 30 got a B, 30 got a C, 14 got a D, and 1 got an F.

   a. Use the Pearson chi-squared test to determine whether there is sufficient evidence to conclude that this grade distribution is significantly different than it had been in previous years.

   b. Using the results from part (a), which grade contributes the least and greatest amounts to the overall chi-squared test statistic? How can this be interpreted?

Table 3.4 Grades Distribution from Previous Years for Problem 3.10

Grade	A	B	C	D	F
Percentage	20%	40%	20%	15%	5%

3.11 In a study on whether voters place different levels of importance on various issues, a random sample of 200 registered voters were asked to rate which of four issues they consider most important. The results obtained are shown in Table 3.5.

   a. State the null and alternative hypotheses.

   b. Do the data indicate that voters place the same or different levels of importance on each of these issues? Use the Pearson chi-squared test to answer this question.

Table 3.5 Frequency Distribution on Issues of Importance to Voters for Problem 3.11

Issue	Economy	Health	Security	Environment
Frequency	80	40	65	15

3.12 Repeat Problem 3.10 using the likelihood ratio test statistic.

3.13 Repeat Problem 3.11 using the likelihood ratio test statistic.

3.14 With dichotomous variables, tests can be conducted using either single proportion methods or the goodness-of-fit methods (with $c = 2$). Repeat Problem 3.1 using the Pearson chi-squared goodness-of-fit test.

chapter four

Association between two categorical variables

A LOOK AHEAD

In this chapter we turn to research questions concerning the association between two categorical variables. Typically, with categorical data, rather than simply estimating a single population proportion, we are interested in determining whether there is an association, a relationship, or a dependency between two or more categorical variables. With continuous variables, an association between two variables is typically described and tested using the correlation coefficient, which measures the covariance between two variables using their joint distribution. Here we extend these ideas to the case of categorical variables. Some examples of research questions that can be answered with the material in this chapter include:

- Is there an association between gender and political affiliation?
- Is there an association between type of treatment and improvement in depression symptoms?
- Is there an association between educational proficiency and socioeconomic status?

In this chapter we will discuss how these associations are measured and how inferential procedures can be used to evaluate the statistical significance of the observed association.

4.1   Contingency tables for two categorical variables

To measure the association between two categorical variables, we use a **contingency table** that summarizes the (joint) frequencies observed in each category of the variables. For example, as we wrote this, the race between Hillary Clinton and Barack Obama for the 2008 democratic presidential candidacy was still undecided and very much in the news. Suppose that we would like to know whether there is an association between voter gender and candidate choice in the Wisconsin democratic primary. An exit poll of 1,442 Wisconsin voters, 42% males and 58% females, showed that 67% of the males and 50% of the females voted for Obama (CNN Election Center, 2008). Table 4.1 presents the 2-by-2 (2 × 2) contingency table showing the frequencies for the variables of gender (male or female) and candidate (Clinton or Obama).

Table 4.1 Observed Frequencies for a Wisconsin Democratic Primary Exit Poll

		Candidate		
		Clinton	Obama	Total
Gender	Male	200	406	606
	Female	418	418	836
	Total	618	824	1442

We use Table 4.1 to introduce some notation and terminology for contingency tables. First, the total number of categories for the row variable is denoted by I, with each category indexed by i, while for the column variable the total number of categories is denoted by J and each category is indexed by j. In our example, gender has $I = 2$ categories ($i = 1$ for males; $i = 2$ for females) and candidate has $J = 2$ categories ($j = 1$ for Clinton; $j = 2$ for Obama). In general, the size of the contingency table is denoted as $I \times J$ (i.e., 2×2 in our example).

The frequency in each cell of the table, called a **joint frequency**, is denoted by n_{ij}. For example, n_{12} in Table 4.1 represents the number of voters who are male ($i = 1$) and voted for Obama ($j = 2$), so $n_{12} = 406$. Taken together, the cell frequencies represent the joint distribution of the two categorical variables. It is important to note that each individual observation can only be counted once so it must appear in (or be classified into) one and only one cell of the table. Each frequency appearing in the margins of the table is called a **marginal frequency** and represents the row or column total for one category of one variable. A marginal frequency for a row is denoted by n_{i+} and a marginal frequency for a column is denoted by n_{+j}. For example, the row total for females in Table 4.1, representing the total number of females in the sample, is $n_{2+} = 836$. The marginal frequencies for the rows (or columns) represent the marginal distribution of the row (or column) variable. Finally, the overall total number of observations is denoted by n_{++}, so in this example $n_{++} = 1442$.

Each of the cell frequencies can be converted to a joint proportion (or probability) by dividing the cell frequency by the total number of observations. In the population, these are denoted by $\pi_{ij} = n_{ij}/n_{++}$, whereas in the sample the cell proportions are denoted by p_{ij}. Similarly, each of the marginal frequencies (n_{i+} or n_{+j}) can be converted to a marginal proportion or probability when divided by the total number of observations. For example, from Table 4.1 the joint proportion of voters who are female and voted for Clinton is $p_{21} = n_{21}/n_{++} = 418/1442 = 0.29$, and the marginal proportion of voters who voted for Clinton is $p_{+1} = n_{+1}/n_{++} = 618/1442 = 0.43$.

4.2   Independence

Just as we typically use the correlation coefficient to evaluate the association between two continuous variables, we use a value called the **odds ratio** to evaluate the association between two categorical variables. Before we define and discuss the odds ratio, however, we expand a bit on the idea of **independence** between two variables, which is a key concept in categorical data analysis. When two categorical variables are independent of each other, they are not associated. Intuitively, for example, if gender and candidate choice are independent variables then one is not associated with the other. More specifically, if these variables are independent then we would be able to predict candidate choice just as well regardless of whether we had knowledge of the voter's gender. Thus, if knowing whether the voter is male or female does not help in predicting the candidate chosen by that voter then there is no relationship between gender and candidate choice and these two variables are independent. Further, if knowing the value (category) of one variable has no effect on predicting the value (category) of the other then the column probability distribution should be the same in each row and the row probability distribution should be the same in each column. In our example this would mean that the overall candidate (column) probability distribution of 43% (618/1442) for Clinton and 57% (824/1442) for Obama should also be the candidate choice distribution obtained for either males or females. So using our data in Table 4.1, if independence holds then 43% of the 606 males would vote for Clinton and 57% of the 606 males would vote for Obama. Similarly, 43% of the 836 females would vote for Clinton and 57% of the 836 females would vote for Obama. Formally this can be stated as $\pi_{ij}/\pi_{i+} = \pi_{+j}$ for each column ($j = 1, 2, ..., J$), or $\pi_{ij}/\pi_{+j} = \pi_{i+}$ for each row ($i = 1, 2, ..., I$). Rearranging either of these formulas, this relationship can also be formally stated as $\pi_{ij} = \pi_{i+}\pi_{+j}$.

In statistical terms, if, in the population, two variables are independent, then their joint probability (π_{ij}) can be computed directly as the product of the corresponding marginal probabilities ($\pi_{i+}\pi_{+j}$). As usual, these population parameters can be estimated using sample data. For instance, using our example in Table 4.1, if gender and voting preference are independent then the probability of a woman voting for Clinton can be obtained from multiplying the probability of a voter being female by the probability of a voter choosing Clinton:

$$p_{21} = (p_{2+})(p_{+1})$$

$$= \text{(Proportion of females)(Proportion voting for Clinton)}$$

$$= (836/1442)(618/1442) = (0.58)(0.43) = 0.25.$$

So if independence holds, we would expect that 25% of all 1,442 voters would be females who voted for Clinton, and so forth for all other cells in the contingency table. This relationship between the joint and marginal probabilities will not hold if there is an association between the two variables. These computations are further discussed and demonstrated in Section 4.4.

4.3   Odds ratio

The odds ratio is a special measure that can be computed for any 2×2 contingency table (or a 2×2 subset of a larger contingency table). To define the odds ratio, we start with a definition of the odds. The **odds** of an event occurring (sometimes also labeled a "success," as in Chapter 2) are the probability that the event occurs relative to the probability that the event does not occur. For example, if the odds that a student in the United States will graduate from high school are 2.5, then the probability that the student will graduate is 2.5 times greater than the probability that the student will not graduate. If the probability that the event occurs in the population is π, then the odds that the event occurs are

$$\text{Odds} = \frac{\pi}{1-\pi}.$$ (4.1)

Rearranging Equation 4.1 to solve for the probability, we obtain

$$Odds = \frac{\pi}{1-\pi}$$

$$Odds(1 - \pi) = \pi$$

$$Odds - Odds(\pi) = \pi$$

$$Odds = \pi + Odds(\pi)$$

$$Odds = \pi (1 + Odds)$$

$$\frac{Odds}{1 + Odds} = \pi$$

In other words, while the odds are expressed in terms of the probability in Equation 4.1, the probability can be expressed in terms of the odds by the equation

$$\pi = \frac{Odds}{1 + Odds}. \qquad (4.2)$$

So, for example, the probability that a student will graduate from high school given the odds of 2.5 would be

$$\pi = \frac{2.5}{1 + 2.5} = \frac{2.5}{3.5} = 0.71.$$

As usual, these population parameters can be estimated using sample data. From Table 4.1 we can say that the probability that a voter voted for Clinton in the Wisconsin primary was

$$P(\text{voted for Clinton}) = \frac{618}{1442} = 0.43,$$

so the odds of voting for Clinton were

$$Odds = \frac{0.43}{1 - 0.43} = \frac{0.43}{0.57} = 0.75.$$

Therefore, the probability of voting for Clinton is 0.75 times the probability of not voting for Clinton, and because the odds are less than 1 the probability of voting for Clinton was lower than the probability of not voting for her (i.e., voting for Obama). Another way to say this is that the probability of a vote for Clinton was 75% of the probability of a vote for Obama. Additionally, because there are only two outcomes (candidates), the odds of voting for Obama can be computed as the reciprocal of the odds of voting for Clinton, or $1/0.75 = 1.33$. To show this, note that because the probability of voting for Clinton is 0.43 (and there are only two candidates), the probability of voting for Obama must be $(1 - 0.43) = 0.57$, thus the odds of voting for Obama are $0.57/(1 - 0.57) = 0.57/0.43 = 1.33$, which is indeed the reciprocal of the odds of voting for Clinton. So, while the probability of a Clinton vote was 0.75 times the probability of an Obama vote, the probability of an Obama vote was 1.33 times the probability of a Clinton vote. In general, when the odds equal 1 the probability of the event occurring is 50% so it is just as likely to occur as not; when the odds are greater than 1 the event is more likely to occur than not, and when the odds are less than 1 the event is less likely to occur than not.

The **odds ratio** is simply defined as the ratio of two odds. Although the definition seems simple enough, interpreting the odds ratio can be tricky (and easily confused with the interpretation of the odds). For example, suppose that we want to compare the odds of voting for Clinton across the genders: males (group 1) and females (group 2). This is achieved through the odds ratio:

$$\text{Odds ratio} = \theta = \frac{\text{odds for group 1}}{\text{odds for group 2}}.$$

It is important to note that the interpretation of the odds ratio requires two components: (1) the category or event of interest (i.e., "success") in the computation of the odds, and (2) the groups defined as "group 1" and "group 2" in the computation of the odds ratio. In our example, we need to define whether the odds of voting for Clinton or for Obama are being examined (as the event or category of interest) as well as whether males or females are considered as the first comparison group. If we consider the odds of voting for Clinton and use males as "group 1", then within the male group the probability of voting for Clinton is

$$P(\text{voting for Clinton if male}) = \frac{n_{11}}{n_{1+}} = \frac{200}{606} = 0.33,$$

and the odds of voting for Clinton for males are

$$\text{Odds (males)} = \frac{0.33}{1-0.33} = \frac{0.33}{0.67} = 0.49.$$

Similarly, for females the probability of voting for Clinton is

$$P(\text{voting for Clinton if female}) = \frac{n_{21}}{n_{2+}} = \frac{418}{836} = 0.50$$

and the odds of voting for Clinton for females are

$$\text{Odds (females)} = \frac{0.50}{1-0.50} = \frac{0.50}{0.50} = 1.00.$$

The odds ratio, then, is

$$\text{Odds ratio} = \frac{\text{Odds (males)}}{\text{Odds (females)}} = \frac{0.49}{1.00} = 0.49.$$

This means that the odds of a male voting for Clinton are 0.49 times (about half) the odds of a female voting for Clinton, or that for males the odds of a Clinton vote are 49% of the odds for females. If we switch the group labels, the odds would be

$$\text{Odds ratio} = \frac{\text{Odds (females)}}{\text{Odds (males)}} = \frac{1.00}{0.49} = 2.0$$

and we can say that the odds of a female voting for Clinton are about 2 times (or 200% of) the odds of a male voting for Clinton. Therefore, to interpret the odds ratio correctly it is important to specify which group is in the numerator and which is in the denominator of the odds ratio. This decision is somewhat arbitrary and can be made by the researcher according to his or her preference and ease of interpretability.

In general, for a 2×2 contingency table, the odds ratio in the population is

$$\theta = \frac{\pi_{11}/\pi_{12}}{\pi_{21}/\pi_{22}} = \frac{\pi_{11}\pi_{22}}{\pi_{12}\pi_{21}}. \tag{4.3}$$

As indicated previously, p is used to denote the sample estimate of π and, therefore, the odds ratio is estimated from sample data by

$$\hat{\theta} = \frac{p_{11}/p_{12}}{p_{21}/p_{22}} = \frac{p_{11}p_{22}}{p_{12}p_{21}} = \frac{(n_{11}/n_{++})(n_{22}/n_{++})}{(n_{12}/n_{++})(n_{21}/n_{++})} = \left(\frac{n_{11}n_{22}}{n_{++}^2}\right)\left(\frac{n_{++}^2}{n_{12}n_{21}}\right) = \frac{n_{11}n_{22}}{n_{12}n_{21}}.$$

Note than when the odds ratio is 1, the odds for the first group (e.g., first row of the table) is equal to the odds for the second group (e.g., the second row of the table). This implies that the probability distribution is the same for both rows, and thus is indicative of statistical independence between the two variables. When the odds ratio is greater than 1, the odds (note: not the probability!) are higher in the first group than in the second, and when the odds ratio is smaller than 1 the odds are lower in the first group than in the second. Therefore, an odds ratio of 1 indicates a lack of association between the two variables, whereas greater deviations from the value of 1 indicate a greater degree of association.

Finally, when any of the cell frequencies (n_{ij} values) are zero or close to zero (i.e., very small) the odds ratio will be either zero (if there is a zero in the numerator) or undefined (if there is a zero in the denominator). Therefore, in cases such as this, one-half (0.5) should be added to each of the cell frequencies prior to computing the odds ratio (Agresti, 1996). For example, suppose that we observe the following frequencies in a 2×2 contingency table: $n_{11}=15$, $n_{12} = 25$, $n_{21} = 0$, and $n_{22} = 10$. The odds ratio in this case would be computed as follows:

$$\hat{\theta} = \frac{(n_{11}+0.5)(n_{22}+0.5)}{(n_{12}+0.5)(n_{21}+0.5)} = \frac{(15.5)(10.5)}{(25.5)(0.5)} = \frac{162.75}{12.75} = 12.8.$$

In general, for $I \times J$ contingency tables that are larger than 2×2, the odds ratio can be computed for any 2×2 subset of cells from the larger table. In this case, the odds in any given row of the table are compared to the corresponding odds in any other row of the table. For example, suppose that we have a 5×5 table and we would like to compare the odds, defined as the probability in column 2 relative to column 5, for Group (row) 1 and Group (row) 3. In this case the odds ratio would be

$$\hat{\theta} = \frac{\text{odds for group 1}}{\text{odds for group 3}} = \frac{P_{12}/P_{15}}{P_{32}/P_{35}} = \frac{n_{12}/n_{15}}{n_{32}/n_{35}} = \frac{n_{12}n_{35}}{n_{15}n_{32}}.$$

In general, the odds ratio can be used to compare the ratio of frequencies (or probabilities) from any pair of columns in a given row, which represents the odds between two column categories in that row, to the ratio of frequencies from the same two columns in another row.

4.3.1 Relative risk and odds ratios

The relative risk is a measure that might be confused with the odds ratio because it also compares two groups, but it compares the probability of success (rather than the odds of success) between the two groups:

$$\text{Relative risk} = \frac{\text{Probability for Group 1}}{\text{Probability for Group 2}}.$$

For example, using Table 4.1 once again, if we want to compare males (Group 1) and females (Group 2) on the probability of voting for Clinton, the probability for males is

$$P(\text{voting for Clinton if male}) = \frac{n_{11}}{n_{1+}} = \frac{200}{606} = 0.33,$$

the probability for females is

$$P(\text{voting for Clinton if female}) = \frac{n_{21}}{n_{2+}} = \frac{418}{836} = 0.50,$$

and the relative risk would be $0.33/0.50 = 0.66$. Therefore, the probability that a male voted for Clinton is 66% of the probability that a female voted for Clinton. Similarly, if we compare males and females on the probability of voting for Obama, the relative risk would be $0.67/0.50 = 1.34$. The ratio of these two relative risk measures provides us with the odds ratio ($0.66/1.34 = 0.49$), but each one in itself is a ratio of probabilities rather than a ratio of odds. In general, the relative risk can be defined as the probability of the jth event occurring in group i relative to the probability of the jth event occurring in group i', or

$$\frac{p_{ij}}{p_{i'j}} = \frac{n_{ij}/n_{i+}}{n_{i'j}/n_{i'+}}.$$

Alternatively, the relative risk of the ith event occurring in group j relative to group j' is

$$\frac{p_{ij}}{p_{ij'}} = \frac{n_{ij}/n_{+j}}{n_{ij'}/n_{+j'}}.$$

4.3.2   Inference for odds ratios

When two variables are independent in the population, the odds ratio is exactly one. However, as with all parameters, when the odds ratio is estimated based on a random sample drawn from the population, it will likely not be exactly one even if the variables are independent in the population. Therefore, to infer or provide an estimate of the odds ratio parameter (population value) from its value in the sample, we can estimate the parameter by constructing a confidence interval. In addition to providing an estimate of the value of the odds ratio in the population, a confidence interval for the odds ratio can be used to test whether independence is plausible in the population. For example, if a 95% confidence interval for the odds ratio includes the value of 1, then the null hypothesis of independence would not be rejected at the 0.05 significance level. Similarly, if the 95% confidence interval for the odds ratio does not include the value of 1, then the null hypothesis of independence can be rejected at the 0.05 significance level.

Because the odds ratio must be positive, as it is based on either frequencies or proportions, its distribution is not symmetric around the value of 1 (i.e., theoretically the distribution varies from a minimum of zero to a maximum of infinity). Therefore, the odds ratio is typically transformed by taking its natural logarithm, denoted by ln, to obtain what is referred to as the "log odds ratio":

$$\text{log odds ratio} = \ln(\text{odds ratio}) = \ln(\theta).$$

Recall (see Figure 3.3) that the natural logarithm of a variable X is zero when X is one, negative when X is lower than one and positive when X is greater than one. Therefore, under independence ($\theta = 1$) the log odds ratio will be zero, when the odds ratio is less than one its log will be negative, and when the odds ratio is greater than one its log will be positive:

$$\text{If } \theta = 1, \ln(\theta) = \ln(1) = 0;$$

$$\text{If } \theta < 1, \ln(\theta) < 0;$$

$$\text{If } \theta > 1, \ln(\theta) > 0.$$

Because the log function varies from negative infinity to positive infinity, and the log of one is zero, this transformation allows us to use a distribution that approximates the standard normal distribution (i.e., symmetric around the value of zero) to infer whether there is enough evidence to suggest that the odds ratio reflects a statistically significant association (i.e., lack of independence). In addition, the inverse of the natural logarithm function is the **exponential function**. Specifically, exponentiating a value that has been transformed using the natural log function has the effect of "canceling out" the log transformation and returning the variable to its original value, such that $\exp[\ln(x)] = e^{\ln(x)} = x$, where the exponential value is a constant ($e \approx 2.718$).

Given that the distribution of the log odds ratio, $\ln(\theta)$, can be approximated using the normal distribution, to construct a confidence interval for the value of the odds ratio in the population, θ, we first transform it to the log odds ratio, $\ln(\theta)$, then use the normal distribution to construct the confidence interval for $\ln(\theta)$, and finally transform the limits of the confidence interval back (using the exponential function) to obtain the confidence interval for θ. Readers familiar with constructing confidence intervals for the Pearson correlation will recognize that the log odds ratio transformation is conceptually very similar to Fisher's r-to-z transformation. The general formula for the confidence interval around the log odds ratio is $\ln(\theta) \pm z^* \, \mathrm{SE}_{\ln(\theta)}$, where z^* is a value from the standard normal table corresponding to the desired confidence level and $\mathrm{SE}_{\ln(\theta)}$ is the standard error of the log odds ratio, computed as

$$\mathrm{SE}_{\ln(\theta)} = \sqrt{\frac{1}{n_{11}} + \frac{1}{n_{12}} + \frac{1}{n_{21}} + \frac{1}{n_{22}}}.$$

As was mentioned earlier, if any of the cell frequencies are zero or very small, a value of 0.5 is added to each n_{ij} before computing the odds ratio and the standard error.

Using the aforementioned formulas, the upper limit of the confidence interval is $\ln(\theta) + z^* \, \mathrm{SE}_{\ln(\theta)}$ and the lower limit is $\ln(\theta) - z^* \, \mathrm{SE}_{\ln(\theta)}$. Once computed, these two values (limits) are exponentiated to obtain the confidence interval for the odds ratio, θ. To illustrate this process with an example, we will compute a 95% confidence interval for the odds ratio relating gender and candidate choice using the data from the 2008 Wisconsin Democratic Primary discussed earlier (see Table 4.1). Recall that the odds ratio of $1.0/0.49 = 2.0$ was interpreted to mean that the odds of a female voting for Clinton rather than Obama are 2 times (or 200% of) the odds of a male voting for Clinton rather than Obama. The standard error of the log odds ratio is

$$\mathrm{SE}_{\ln(\theta)} = \sqrt{\frac{1}{200} + \frac{1}{406} + \frac{1}{418} + \frac{1}{418}} = 0.111$$

and the 95% confidence interval for the log odds ratio is

$$\ln(2) \pm 1.96(0.111) = 0.693 \pm 0.217 = [0.476, \, 0.910].$$

Finally, the 95% confidence interval for the odds ratio itself is

$$[e^{0.476}, \, e^{0.910}] = [1.6, \, 2.5].$$

Therefore, with 95% confidence, the odds ratio in the population (e.g., all Wisconsin voters) is between 1.6 and 2.5. Since the value of one is not included in the interval (i.e., both limits are higher than one), gender and candidate choice are most likely associated in the population such that the odds of a female voting for Clinton are higher than the odds of a male voting for Clinton. Finally, note that if we had switched the order of the candidates, the odds ratio would be 0.49, indicating that the odds of a male voting for Clinton rather than Obama are about half (or 49% of) the odds of a female voting for Clinton rather than Obama. In this case, the 95% confidence interval for the log odds is

$$\ln(0.49) \pm 1.96(0.111) = -0.713 \pm 0.217 = [-0.930, -0.496]$$

and the 95% confidence interval for the odds ratio itself is

$$[e^{-0.930}, \, e^{-0.496}] = [0.39, \, 0.61].$$

So, with 95% confidence, we can say that in the population the odds of a male voting for Clinton rather than Obama are between 39% and 61% of the odds of a female voting for

Clinton rather than Obama. While the confidence interval for the odds ratio can be used to infer whether two variables are independent in the population, the odds ratio is somewhat limited in that it measures the association only for the special case of 2×2 tables. In the next section we discuss how to test whether two variables are independent in the general case, for any $I \times J$ table.

4.4 Testing the association between two categorical variables

There are two general approaches to examining and testing the association between two variables in a contingency table and both approaches involve comparing observed and expected frequencies using the test statistics introduced in Chapter 3. While the two approaches are computationally identical, they are conceptually different, so the choice of approach typically depends on the research question and the way in which the data were obtained. In the first approach, none of the marginal frequencies are fixed. Rather the marginal totals are the end result of obtaining a random sample of individuals that are simply classified into their corresponding cells. Therefore, the cell probabilities, as well as the marginal probabilities, are all random as opposed to fixed. The voter preference example used earlier in this chapter is an example of a design for which this first approach is appropriate because in an exit poll it is unlikely that any marginal means were fixed. Rather, 1,442 respondents were polled and the cell frequencies were used to determine the marginal frequencies. Therefore, in this case, the research question of interest is: Is there an association between gender and choice of candidate, or to put it another way, Are the two variables, gender and choice of candidate, independent?

In the second approach the marginal totals for the independent variable are experimentally fixed. For example, suppose one is interested in studying the efficacy of a new drug developed to help alleviate depression. To conduct this study, a researcher could obtain a sample of patients in treatment for depression and randomly assign patients to one of three groups: a control group, a group treated with the new drug for depression, and a group treated with an existing drug used to treat depression. The outcome variable could be measured as whether the patient reports a decrease (or shows an improvement) in depressive symptoms. In this situation, the marginal totals for the independent variable (groups) are experimentally fixed, and one can examine whether, within each treatment group, the distribution of the proportions for the outcome categories (improved/not improved) is the same. In this case the research question of interest is: Is the proportion of patients that report a decrease in depressive symptoms the same for each of the three treatment groups?

To summarize, there are two general approaches to testing association in contingency tables. In the first approach one assumes that only the overall sample size is experimentally fixed and the null hypothesis that is tested is that the two variables are statistically independent. In this approach the joint distribution of the cell frequencies is examined to determine whether it is consistent with a pattern of independence, or lack of association, between the two variables. In this case, it does not make sense to treat one variable as independent and the other as dependent, because both are obtained observationally and neither is subject to experimental manipulation or control. In the second approach the set of marginal frequencies for the independent variable is experimentally fixed and the null hypothesis tested is that the probability distribution of the outcome (or dependent) variable is the same across all categories of the manipulated (or independent) variable. Note that while the research questions that arise from the two approaches are similar, there is a subtle difference in the way in which they are posed and conceptualized.

Recall from Chapter 3 that expected frequencies are computed based on the null hypothesis. We now turn to the computations of expected frequencies using these two approaches. We should emphasize that although the two approaches pose the null hypothesis in slightly different ways, computationally they are equivalent because the expected frequencies are mathematically identical regardless of the approach, as was shown in Section 4.2. Nonetheless, we discuss the computations separately for each approach as a reminder that they pose different research questions and assume that different components of the data are fixed.

4.4.1   Expected frequencies under independence

Under the first approach to testing the association between two categorical variables, the null hypothesis states that the two variables are **statistically independent**. This means (recall from Section 4.2) that the frequency or probability in a particular cell of the contingency table can be determined using its row and column categories and their associated (marginal) probabilities. In other words, under statistical independence, the marginal probabilities (or frequencies) can be used to determine the joint probabilities (or frequencies). More specifically, under statistical independence the cell (joint) probability is equal to the product of its row and column (marginal) probabilities: $\pi_{ij} = \pi_{i+}\pi_{+j}$.

Using sample notation, the expected joint probability p_{ij} can be computed as

$$p_{ij} = p_{i+}p_{+j} = \left(\frac{n_{i+}}{n_{++}}\right)\left(\frac{n_{+j}}{n_{++}}\right).$$

Converting this expected probability to the corresponding **expected frequency**, we multiply the probability by the total number of observations:

$$n_{ij} = n_{++}\, p_{ij} = n_{++}\left(\frac{n_{i+}}{n_{++}}\right)\left(\frac{n_{+j}}{n_{++}}\right) = \frac{n_{i+}n_{+j}}{n_{++}}. \tag{4.4}$$

Using our voter preference and gender example (Table 4.1), under the null hypothesis of independence the expected probability of a male who voted for Clinton can be computed as follows:

$$P(\text{voter is male and votes for Clinton}) = p_{11}$$

$$= P(\text{voter is male}) \times P(\text{vote for Clinton})$$

$$= p_{1+}p_{+1} = \left(\frac{n_{1+}}{n_{++}}\right)\left(\frac{n_{+1}}{n_{++}}\right)$$

$$= (606/1442)(618/1442)$$

$$= (0.42)(0.43) = 0.18.$$

To convert this probability to a frequency, we multiply it by the total number of observations (in our case, 1,442) to obtain $n_{11} = n_{++}p_{11} = (1442)(0.18) = 259.71$. Alternatively, this

Table 4.2 Expected Frequencies for the Wisconsin
Democratic Primary Exit Poll Data Shown in Table 4.1

		Candidate		
		Clinton	Obama	Total
Gender	Male	259.71	346.29	606
	Female	358.29	477.71	836
	Total	618	824	1442

expected frequency and all others can be obtained directly using the expected frequencies formula shown in Equation 4.4:

$$\text{Males voting for Clinton} = n_{11} = (n_{1+}n_{+1})/n_{++} = (606)(618)/1442 = 259.71;$$

$$\text{Males voting for Obama} = n_{12} = (n_{1+}n_{+2})/n_{++} = (606)(824)/1442 = 346.29;$$

$$\text{Females voting for Clinton} = n_{21} = (n_{2+}n_{+1})/n_{++} = (836)(618)/1442 = 358.29; \text{ and}$$

$$\text{Females voting for Obama} = n_{22} = (n_{2+}n_{+2})/n_{++} = (836)(824)/1442 = 477.71.$$

These expected frequencies are summarized in Table 4.2. Note that the expected marginal frequencies in Table 4.2 are identical to the observed marginal frequencies in Table 4.1, and this should always be the case (so you can check your computations accordingly).

4.4.2   Expected frequencies under equal proportion distributions

Under the second approach to testing the association between two categorical variables, which compares frequency or probability distributions, the null hypothesis states that the probability distribution of the dependent variable (e.g., decrease in depressive symptoms) is the same in each category of the independent variable (e.g., each of the three treatment groups). In other words, the null hypothesis for this example states that the distribution of the depressive symptoms outcome should be the same across the three different treatment groups. If that is the case, then the overall distribution of decreased depressive symptoms, or the marginal distribution of symptoms, would be the same for each treatment group. Therefore, the expected distribution of decreased depressive symptoms within each treatment group is computed based on the marginal distribution of the depressive symptoms outcome. Hypothetical data for our example is presented in Table 4.3. Using the observed

Table 4.3 Observed Frequencies for a Hypothetical Example

		Decreased depressive symptoms		
		Yes	No	Total
Treatment Group	New Drug	16	9	25
	Existing Drug	12	13	25
	Control Group	5	20	25
	Total	33	42	75

Table 4.4 Expected Frequencies for a Hypothetical Example

| | | Decreased depressive symptoms | | |
		Yes	No	Total
Treatment Group	New Drug	11	14	25
	Existing Drug	11	14	25
	Control Group	11	14	25
	Total	33	42	75

frequencies, the marginal probability distribution of the depressive symptoms outcome is as follows:

$$P(\text{decrease in depressive symptoms} = \text{Yes}) = p_{+1} = 33/75 = 0.44;$$

$$P(\text{decrease in depressive symptoms} = \text{No}) = p_{+2} = 42/75 = 0.56.$$

Under independence, this probability distribution should hold for each of the treatment groups. For example, since there are 25 individuals who received the new drug, under independence 44% of them are expected to show a decrease in depressive symptoms and 56% of them are not expected to show a decrease in depressive symptoms. Therefore, the frequency distribution for that group (or in that row of the table) is expected to be:

Expected frequency of a decrease in depressive symptoms = (0.44)(25) = 11;

Expected frequency of no decrease in depressive symptoms = (0.56)(25) = 14.

Moreover, assuming the null hypothesis is true, the marginal probabilities of 0.44 and 0.56 for whether or not patients reported less depressive symptoms, respectively, holds for all three of the treatment groups and, since all groups happen to have 25 individuals, the same frequency distribution is expected for all three treatment groups. These expected frequencies are summarized in Table 4.4 and reflect the fact that under the null hypothesis the overall probabilities of 0.44 and 0.56 across the outcome categories are expected to hold within each of the groups. Note once again that the expected marginal frequencies in Table 4.4 are identical to the observed marginal frequencies in Table 4.3.

4.4.3   Test statistics

To compute the test statistic for either approach, the observed and expected frequencies are compared using the goodness-of-fit test statistics discussed in Chapter 3 (Section 3.4). Specifically, for two variables the test the Pearson chi-squared test statistic is

$$X^2 = \sum_{i=1}^{I} \sum_{j=1}^{J} \frac{(O_{ij} - E_{ij})^2}{E_{ij}}$$

and the likelihood ratio test statistic is

$$G^2 = 2 \sum_{i=1}^{I} \sum_{j=1}^{J} O_{ij} \ln \left(\frac{O_{ij}}{E_{ij}} \right),$$

where O_{ij} *and* E_{ij} refer to the observed and expected joint frequencies, respectively, in a two-way contingency table.

The Pearson chi-squared test statistic for a contingency table consists of a summation over all cells and results in a test statistic with $(I - 1)(J - 1)$ degrees of freedom. The degrees of freedom can be determined using the same reasoning provided in Chapter 3; that is, given the marginal frequencies, only $(I - 1)(J - 1)$ cell frequencies are "free" to vary, while the remaining cell frequencies are determined based on the marginal frequencies. Try it for yourself: Given the marginal frequencies in Table 4.3 (or Table 4.4), how many cell frequencies could you "freely" choose? Therefore, for the drug treatment example, the degrees of freedom are $(3 - 1)(2 - 1) = 2$, and the test statistic is

$$X^2 = \sum_{i=1}^{I} \sum_{j=1}^{J} \frac{(O_{ij} - E_{ij})^2}{E_{ij}}$$

$$= \frac{(O_{11} - E_{11})^2}{E_{11}} + \frac{(O_{12} - E_{12})^2}{E_{12}} + \frac{(O_{21} - E_{21})^2}{E_{21}} + \frac{(O_{22} - E_{22})^2}{E_{22}} + \frac{(O_{31} - E_{31})^2}{E_{31}} + \frac{(O_{32} - E_{32})^2}{E_{32}}$$

$$= \frac{(16-11)^2}{11} + \frac{(9-14)^2}{14} + \frac{(12-11)^2}{11} + \frac{(13-14)^2}{14} + \frac{(5-11)^2}{11} + \frac{(20-14)^2}{14} = 10.065.$$

Note that here O_{ij} *and* E_{ij} represent the observed and expected frequencies, respectively, for the cell in the ith row and jth column. Comparing the obtained value of 10.065 to a chi-squared distribution with 2 degrees of freedom, we see that the test statistic exceeds the critical value of 5.99 at the 5% significance level (see the Appendix) and so the null hypothesis can be rejected. In this case we would conclude (under the second approach) that the probability of a decrease in depressive symptoms is not the same for all three treatment groups.

The likelihood ratio test statistic introduced in Chapter 3 would also follow a chi-squared distribution with $(I - 1)(J - 1) = 2$ degrees of freedom and, summed over all cells in the table, results in

$$G^2 = 2 \sum_{i=1}^{I} \sum_{j=1}^{J} O_{ij} \ln\left(\frac{O_{ij}}{E_{ij}}\right)$$

$$= 2\left[O_{11} \ln\left(\frac{O_{11}}{E_{11}}\right) + O_{12} \ln\left(\frac{O_{12}}{E_{12}}\right) + O_{21} \ln\left(\frac{O_{21}}{E_{21}}\right) + O_{22} \ln\left(\frac{O_{22}}{E_{22}}\right) + O_{31} \ln\left(\frac{O_{31}}{E_{31}}\right) + O_{32} \ln\left(\frac{O_{32}}{E_{32}}\right)\right]$$

$$= 2\left[16\ln\left(\frac{16}{11}\right) + 9\ln\left(\frac{9}{14}\right) + 12\ln\left(\frac{12}{11}\right) + 13\ln\left(\frac{13}{14}\right) + 5\ln\left(\frac{5}{11}\right) + 20\ln\left(\frac{20}{14}\right)\right]$$

$$= 2\left[16(0.375) + 9(-0.442) + 12(0.087) + 13(-0.074) + 5(-0.788) + 20(0.357)\right]$$

$$= 10.581.$$

Again comparing the obtained test statistic of 10.581 to a chi-squared distribution with 2 degrees of freedom, we see that the test statistic exceeds the critical value of 5.99 at the 5% significance level and so the null hypothesis can be rejected. The conclusions here are the same as those obtained with the X^2 statistic earlier; that is, the probability of a decrease in depressive symptoms is not the same for all three treatment groups.

There is, of course, a correspondence between testing for independence using the odds ratio (as discussed in Section 4.3) and the test statistics discussed in this section. To show this correspondence using the first example in this chapter (Table 4.1), recall (from Section 4.3) that when two variables are statistically independent or unassociated we expect the odds ratio to be one. Indeed, if we use the expected frequencies (computed under the assumption of independence and shown in Table 4.2) to compute the odds ratio for this example, we obtain

$$\theta = \frac{n_{11}n_{22}}{n_{12}n_{21}} = \frac{(259.71)(477.71)}{(346.29)(358.29)} = 1.0.$$

If we repeat the same calculation for the observed frequencies, we obtain $\theta = 0.49$, as was shown in Section 4.3. Therefore, because we expect the odds ratio to be one under the null hypothesis, a rejection of the null hypothesis would indicate that the observed odds ratio is significantly different than one, and in Subsection 4.3.2 we indeed show that the value of one is not in the 95% confidence interval for the odds ratio. Alternatively, using the Pearson chi-squared test for this example, the test statistic is

$$X^2 = \sum_{i=1}^{I}\sum_{j=1}^{J} \frac{(O_{ij} - E_{ij})^2}{E_{ij}}$$
$$= \frac{(200 - 259.71)^2}{259.71} + \frac{(406 - 346.29)^2}{346.29} + \frac{(418 - 358.29)^2}{358.29} + \frac{(418 - 477.71)^2}{477.71} = 41.44.$$

Therefore, because at the 5% significance level with $(2 - 1)(2 - 1) = 1$ degree of freedom, the critical value of the chi-squared distribution is 3.84, the null hypothesis is rejected, and we conclude that the choice of candidate is not independent of gender, or that choice of candidate and gender are associated with each other. In order to further understand the nature of the association between these two variables, we compare the expected frequencies computed under the null hypothesis (see Table 4.2) to the observed frequencies from the actual sample (see Table 4.1). The larger the differences between these values, the less support we have for the null hypothesis of independence. For example, we can see that under the null hypothesis of independence we would have expected that fewer females would vote for Clinton (358.3) than actually did (418). Therefore, one way to explain the nature of the association between gender and candidate choice is to say that Clinton gets a higher proportion of the female vote than would be expected if these variables were unrelated (or, alternatively, one can say that Obama gets a higher proportion of the male vote than would be expected under independence, and so forth). As discussed in Chapter 3, the residuals (or observed and expected frequency discrepancies) can be examined more closely to determine how certain cells contribute to the overall lack of independence.

4.4.4   *Residuals*

Residuals are typically defined as the discrepancies or differences between the observed and expected frequency in each of the cells, where the residual in the ith row and jth column is denoted as $r_{ij} = O_{ij} - E_{ij}$.

It is often useful to divide this difference by its standard error to obtain standardized residuals. The standardized residual for the ith row and j^{th} column is

$$\text{Standardized } r_{ij} = \frac{O_{ij} - E_{ij}}{\sqrt{E_{ij}(1-p_{i+})(1-p_{+j})}},$$

where p_{i+} refers to the marginal probability (n_{i+}/n_{++}) of an observation in row i and p_{+j} refers to the marginal probability (n_{+j}/n_{++}) of an observation in row j. The distribution of these standardized residuals is approximately standard normal, so standardized residuals that are larger than 2 or smaller than -2 are usually considered large as these values indicate that the observed frequency is more than 2 standard deviations away from the corresponding expected frequency. For example, using the information from Table 4.1 and Table 4.2, the observed number of males who voted for Clinton was 200, while the corresponding expected frequency was 259.71. Therefore, the residual is $r_{11} = 200 - 259.71 = -59.71$, and the standardized residual is

$$\text{Standardized } r_{11} = \frac{O_{11} - E_{11}}{\sqrt{E_{11}(1-p_{1+})(1-p_{+1})}} = \frac{200 - 259.71}{\sqrt{259.71(1 - 606/1442)(1 - 618/1442)}}$$

$$= \frac{-59.71}{9.28} = -6.44.$$

If the null hypothesis was true we would expect the residual to be zero, so a standardized residual of -6.4 indicates that the observed value is more than 6 standard deviations below the expected value, representing a very large discrepancy.

In addition, we can compute the contribution of each discrepancy to the overall chi-squared statistic by calculating, for each cell, the value of $(O_{ij}-E_{ij})^2/E_{ij}$. For example, the contribution of the males who voted for Clinton cell to the overall chi-squared statistic is $(O_{11} - E_{11})^2/E_{11} = (200-259.71)^2/259.71 = 13.73$, which constitutes more than a quarter of the overall chi-squared value (of 41.44). The standardized residuals and contributions to the chi-squared statistic are shown in Table 4.5 for all cells. Note that, while all standardized residuals are equally large and demonstrate substantial deviations from expectation (under independence), the highest discrepancy in terms of contribution to chi-squared is in the males voting for Clinton cell and the lowest is in the females voting for Obama cell.

Table 4.5 Residuals, Standardized Residuals (in Bold), and Contributions to the Overall Chi-Squared Statistic (in Parentheses) for the Wisconsin Democratic Primary Exit Poll Data Shown in Table 4.1

		Candidate		
		Clinton	Obama	Total
Gender	Male	−59.71	59.71	606
		−6.44	**6.44**	
		(13.73)	(10.30)	
	Female	59.71	−59.71	836
		6.44	**−6.44**	
		(9.95)	(7.46)	
	Total	618	824	1442

4.4.5 Fisher's exact test

As we discussed in Chapter 3, tests based on the chi-squared distributions are large sample approximations and are typically not valid for small samples. With small samples, the underlying probability distribution for a two-way table, the hypergeometric distribution (see Chapter 2), can be used to perform an exact test. The exact test uses the distribution of all contingency tables possible under the assumption of independence (i.e., when the null hypothesis is true). The table actually observed is then located on this distribution and its *p*-value is found using the fact that two-way table frequencies follow a hypergeometric distribution; thus, if the placement of the observed table is extreme on this distribution, then the null hypothesis can be rejected. The computational details of this test are omitted here (the interested reader can consult other books, such as Agresti, 2007), but we show how to obtain the exact test results using computer software at the end of this chapter.

4.4.6 Ordinal data

When both of the categorical variables are measured on an ordinal scale, there is an alternative test for independence that incorporates information on the order of the categories. This test requires that a rank or score is given to each category, which is then used to compute what is essentially the ordinal correlation between the variables. For example, suppose that one of the variables is socioeconomic status (SES; measured as high, middle, or low) and the other variable is proficiency on a standardized test (measured as advanced, proficient, basic, or minimal). In this case, although we cannot assume that the categories of each variable are equally spaced, they are clearly ordinal variables. Therefore, it is possible to assign numbers to the categories of each variable to indicate the ordering of the categories from high to low. If the row and column variables are independent, we expect that the ordinal correlation between them would be zero in the population. Therefore, the null hypothesis that this correlation is zero (in the population) can be tested. This test is typically more powerful than the test discussed so far, which treats both variables as nominal. This test can also be used when one of the two variables is nominal, provided that this variable consists of only two categories. For computational details on testing independence among ordinal variables, we refer the interested reader to Clogg and Shihadeh (1994) or Agresti (2007) among other sources.

4.5 Applications: inter-rater agreement

When the rows and columns of a contingency table represent the same set of categories, the association (or independence) between the variables is a measure of agreement. For instance, in studies that employ the collection of data from raters or observers who use the same rating categories, the agreement between the raters can be measured as the degree of association between their classifications. Agreement among independent observers in the way they classified individuals strengthens the reliability of the observational classification process and the conclusions that can be drawn from it. This is referred to as inter-rater agreement or *inter-rater reliability*. Because both raters are using the same categories, the resulting contingency table will be square (i.e., the number of rows is the same as the number of columns), and values along the diagonal cells of the table will represent agreement between the raters.

For example, Table 4.6 presents a hypothetical example in which two raters were asked to rate the same 80 students by classifying each of the students into one of four categories that

Table 4.6 Hypothetical Example of Student Rating Frequencies and Probabilities (in Italics) From Two Raters

		Rater 2				
		A	B	C	D	Total
	A	25	7	5	3	40
		0.3125	*0.0875*	*0.0625*	*0.0375*	*0.5*
Rater 1	B	4	10	4	0	18
		0.05	*0.125*	*0.05*	*0.00*	*0.225*
	C	3	2	7	0	12
		0.0375	*0.025*	*0.0875*	*0.00*	*0.15*
	D	3	1	2	4	10
		0.0375	*0.0125*	*0.025*	*0.05*	*0.125*
	Total	35	20	18	7	80
		0.4375	*0.25*	*0.225*	*0.0875*	*1.00*

represent the student's level of engagement in the class: (A) engaged in the class, (B) somewhat distracted, (C) appears to be bored, or (D) is disruptive. This results in a 4 × 4 contingency table, with the rows representing classifications made by Rater 1 and the columns representing classifications made by Rater 2. Using the hypothetical data shown in Table 4.6, 25 of the students were classified into Category A by both raters, whereas 7 of the students were classified into Category A by Rater 1 and into Category B by Rater 2. When both raters classify a student into the same category, the student is counted in what is referred to as a diagonal cell of the table. Similarly, when the two raters classify the same student into different categories, the student is counted in an off-diagonal cell. As can be seen from Table 4.6, the classifications made by the two raters in this example do not agree with each other perfectly because, if they did, values of zero would be observed in all of the off-diagonal cells of the table.

To measure the degree of agreement or reliability of the classifications, **Cohen's kappa** (κ) coefficient is computed as a measure of the degree of agreement beyond what would be expected under independence (e.g., Cohen, 1960; Fleiss, 1973). The degree of agreement under independence is that which is expected to be obtained simply by chance, or in the absence of any systematic relationship between the classifications made by the two raters. The formula for computing κ (in the population) is

$$\kappa = \frac{\sum_{i=1}^{I} \pi_{ii} - \sum_{i=1}^{I} \pi_{i+} \pi_{+i}}{1 - \sum_{i=1}^{I} \pi_{i+} \pi_{+i}}.$$

The numerator of κ measures the difference between the observed probability of agreement (sum of the probabilities in the table's diagonal cells) and the expected probability of agreement computed under independence (see Section 4.4.1). The denominator measures the maximum possible difference, which is the difference between perfect agreement (value of 1) and the expected probability of agreement under independence. Note that under independence the numerator would be zero (because $\pi_{ii} = \pi_{i+}\pi_{+i}$ for all i) and so $\kappa = 0$, and under perfect agreement the numerator and denominator would be equal to each other so $\kappa = 1$. Therefore, κ must be greater than zero to demonstrate that the raters' classifications are in agreement and are associated (rather than independent), and the closer κ is to 1, the higher the level of agreement or association between ratings.

Cohen's kappa is estimated from sample data by replacing the population probabilities with the sample probabilities. Using the data in Table 4.6, the observed probability of agreement is

$$\sum_{i=1}^{I} p_{ii} = 0.3125 + 0.125 + 0.0875 + 0.05 = 0.575,$$

and the probability of agreement under independence is

$$\sum_{i=1}^{I} p_{i+}p_{+i} = (0.5)(0.4375) + (0.225)(0.25) + (0.15)(0.225) + (0.125)(0.0875) = 0.320,$$

so the estimate of kappa is

$$\frac{\sum_{i=1}^{I} p_{ii} - \sum_{i=1}^{I} p_{i+}p_{+i}}{1 - \sum_{i=1}^{I} p_{i+}p_{+i}} = \frac{0.575 - 0.320}{1 - 0.320} = 0.375.$$

The large-sample approximation for the standard error of kappa (Fleiss, Cohen, & Everitt, 1969) can also be computed and used to construct confidence intervals for κ. In this case, the 95% confidence interval for κ (obtained using computer software, as shown in Section 4.7) is [0.22, 0.53], so the level of agreement between the raters seems to be significantly better than chance, or significantly greater than zero, because zero is not included in the interval. More specifically, in the population, the level of agreement is estimated to be somewhere between 0.22 and 0.53 with 95% confidence. Finally, a weighted kappa measure exists when the categories can be ordered (i.e., for ordinal variables) such that more weight is given to disagreements across categories that are farther apart (e.g., Cohen, 1968; Fleiss, Cohen, & Everitt, 1969). Because kappa relies heavily on the marginal distributions, some researchers have also proposed various alternatives or adjustments to the reporting of kappa; see, for example, Byrt, Bishop, and Carlin, (1993) and Zwick (1988).

4.6   Computer output: test of independence

To obtain computer output for tests of association and most of the results discussed in Sections 4.3 and 4.4, syntax and output for SAS, as well as menu instructions and output for SPSS, are discussed in this section.

4.6.1   SAS

The SAS program to analyze the data of Table 4.1 is provided in Figure 4.1 and the results are provided in the output shown in Figure 4.2. The data set (given the name dem08) consists of three columns: the row and column variables of the table (gender and candidate) as well as the cell frequency (count). Note that if raw data were used there would be 1,442 rows in the data set, each consisting of an individual's gender and candidate choice, and the counts would be computed by the program. The frequency procedure (proc freq) is used to obtain the results.

- The first line of the frequency procedure invokes the procedures and uses the option order=data to indicate that the row and column categories should be arranged in the order with which they first appear in the data set as entered (the SAS default is to arrange the categories in alphabetical order).

```
data dem08;
  input gender $ candidate $ count;
  datalines;
  Male Clinton 200
  Male Obama 406
  Female Clinton 418
  Female Obama 418
  ;
proc freq order=data;
  weight count;
  tables gender*candidate /expected deviation cellchi2 chisq relrisk;
run;
```

Figure 4.1 SAS program for tests of independence using the data from Table 4.1.

- The second line specifies that the count variable is to be used as a "weight" for the number of observations in each category, essentially indicating that the count variable is to be treated as a frequency. Note that if raw (rather than summary) data were used, the weight command would be omitted.
- The third line requests the contingency table with the rows represented by the first variable listed and the columns represented by the second variable (to the left of the asterisk [*]). The remaining options, listed after the slash, request the following values:
  - Expected frequencies under independence ("expected")
  - Deviation or discrepancy between the observed and expected frequencies ("deviation")
  - Contribution of each cell deviation to the overall chi-squared statistic ("cellchi2")
  - Chi-squared test for independence ("chisq")
  - Odds ratio ("relrisk")

The output, shown in Figure 4.2, begins with the contingency table; an ordered list of the values appearing in each cell is shown in the upper left corner of the table:

- The first value appearing in each cell is the observed frequency.
- The second value is the expected frequency (under independence).
- The third value is the deviation between observed and expected frequencies.
- The fourth value is the contribution of this deviation to the overall chi-squared test statistic.
- The fifth, sixth, and seventh values appear by default (but can be suppressed by using appropriate options), and represent the cell proportion relative to the total number of observations, the proportion relative to the total observations in the row, and the proportion relative to the total observations in the column, respectively.

The next part of the output in Figure 4.2 consists of the statistics for the test of independence (including the chi-squared, likelihood ratio, and Fisher's exact tests). According to the output:

- The Pearson chi-squared test statistic is 41.44 and, with 1 degree of freedom, has a *p*-value less than 0.0001 so the null hypothesis of independence is rejected.
- The likelihood ratio test yields similar results (test statistic of 41.92, 1 degree of freedom, and a *p*-value less than 0.0001).

```
                        The FREQ Procedure

                    Table of gender by candidate

                gender          candidate

                Frequency      |
                Expected       |
                Deviation      |
                Cell Chi-Square|
                Percent        |
                Row Pct        |
                Col Pct        |Clinton | Obama  | Total
                ---------------|--------|--------|-------
                Male           |    200 |    406 |   606
                               | 259.71 | 346.29 |
                               | -59.71 | 59.714 |
                               |  13.73 | 10.297 |
                               |  13.87 |  28.16 |  42.02
                               |  33.00 |  67.00 |
                               |  32.36 |  49.27 |
                ---------------|--------|--------|-------
                Female         |    418 |    418 |   836
                               | 358.29 | 477.71 |
                               | 59.714 | -59.71 |
                               | 9.9524 | 7.4643 |
                               |  28.99 |  28.99 |  57.98
                               |  50.00 |  50.00 |
                               |  67.64 |  50.73 |
                ---------------|--------|--------|-------
                Total               618      824     1442
                                  42.86    57.14   100.00

            Statistics for Table of gender by candidate

       Statistic                    DF      Value      Prob
       --------------------------------------------------------
       Chi-Square                    1     41.4436    <.0001
       Likelihood Ratio Chi-Square   1     41.9121    <.0001
       Continuity Adj. Chi-Square    1     40.7525    <.0001
       Mantel-Haenszel Chi-Square    1     41.4149    <.0001
       Phi Coefficient                     -0.1695
       Contingency Coefficient              0.1671
       Cramer's V                          -0.1695

                        Fisher's Exact Test
                   --------------------------------
                   Cell (1,1) Frequency (F)      200
                   Left-sided Pr <= F       6.885E-11
                   Right-sided Pr >= F         1.0000

                   Table Probability (P)    3.547E-11
                   Two-sided Pr <= P        1.261E-10

            Estimates of the Relative Risk (Row1/Row2)

     Type of Study              Value      95% Confidence Limits
     ------------------------------------------------------------
     Case-Control (Odds Ratio)   0.4926      0.3966      0.6119
     Cohort (Col1 Risk)          0.6601      0.5784      0.7533
     Cohort (Col2 Risk)          1.3399      1.2272      1.4630

                      Sample Size = 1442
```

Figure 4.2 SAS output for tests of independence.

- Although it is not needed here (due to a large sample size), Fisher's exact test shows that under the hypothesis of independence the probability (obtained from the hyper-geometric distribution) of observing this specific table is 3.5×10^{-11}, or very close to zero, and the two-tailed p-value associated with this table is also very close to zero (1.3×10^{-10}).
- Finally, the Relative Risk part of the output provides the odds ratio of 0.49 and its 95% confidence interval (0.397, 0.612). The row labeled Cohort (Col1 Risk) refers to comparing the row probabilities in column 1 to each other and the row labeled Cohort (Col2 Risk) refers to comparing the row probabilities in column 2 to each other.
  - For example, the column 1 relative risk (of 0.66) is computed as the proportion of males who voted for Clinton (200/606 = 0.33) divided by the proportion of females who voted for Clinton (418/836 = 0.5).
  - Therefore, the "risk" of voting for Clinton is relatively lower (66%) for males than for females. Similarly, the "risk" of voting for Obama is relatively higher (134%) for males than for females, and the odds ratio is the ratio of these two values (0.66/1.34 = 0.49).

4.6.2 SPSS

The data of Table 4.1 are entered in SPSS as three variables: gender, candidate (pres_choice), and the frequency (count). If raw data for all 1,442 individuals (that included gender and candidate choice for each) were used, the counts would be computed by the program and would not be needed as input. As stated previously, if counts are to be used as weights (when summary information rather than raw data are analyzed), this must be specified in SPSS by clicking on the Data menu and selecting Weight Cases.... In the dialogue box that opens, click on the count variable and move it to the "Weight cases by" box on the left, then click OK. This is illustrated in Figure 4.3.

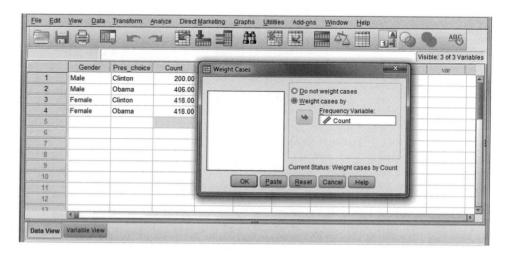

Figure 4.3 SPSS data window illustrating how to enter data from Table 4.1.

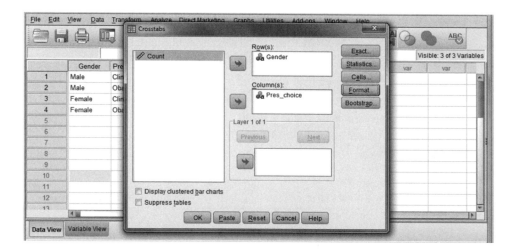

Figure 4.4 SPSS analysis window illustrating how to conduct the test of independence.

To conduct the tests of independence using SPSS menus:

- Choose Descriptive Statistics in the Analyze menu and click on Crosstabs.
- Move the row variable (gender) into the Row(s) box and the column variable (pres_choice) into the Column(s) box. This is illustrated in Figure 4.4.
- Click on the Statistics… button and select the desired statistics: for this output Chi-square and Risk were selected. Click Continue.
- Click on the Cells… button and select the desired options: for this output Observed and Expected were selected under Counts, and Unstandardized as well as Adjusted standardized were selected under Residuals. Click Continue and then OK to obtain the output.

The output, shown in Figure 4.5, contains:

- The contingency table, including the observed frequencies and expected frequencies (under independence) as well as the differences between the two (called residuals on the output) and the standardized residuals (called **adjusted residuals**).
  - By default, SPSS arranges the category values in ascending alphabetical order. This default can be changed so that the output is arranged in descending alphabetical order by clicking on the Format button (see Figure 4.4) and selecting the descending option.
- The contingency table is followed by the tests of independence, including the Pearson chi-squared and likelihood ratio tests as well as the p-values for Fisher's exact test.
- The Risk Estimate table shows the odds ratio and its 95% confidence interval as well as the cohort relative risks (proportion of females to males) computed by column (candidate).
  - Note, for example, that the proportion of females voting for Clinton is about 150% the proportion of males voting for Clinton, the proportion of females voting for Obama is about 75% of the proportion of males voting for Obama, and the odds ratio is the ratio of these two values (1.5/0.75 = 2.0).

Gender* Pres_choice Crosstabulation

| | | | Pres_choice | | Total |
			Clinton	Obama	
Gender	Female	Count	418.000	418.000	836.000
		Expected Count	358.3	477.7	836.0
		Residual	59.7	−59.7	
		Adjusted Residual	6.4	−6.4	
	Male	Count	200.000	406.000	606.000
		Expected Count	259.7	346.3	606.0
		Residual	−59.7	59.7	
		Adjusted Residual	−6.4	6.4	
Total		Count	618.000	824.000	1442.000
		Expected Count	618.0	824.0	1442.0

Chi-Square Tests

	Value	df	Asymp.Sig. (2-sided)	Exact Sig. (2-sided)	Exact Sig. (1-sided)
Pearson Chi-Square	41.444[a]	1	.000		
Continuity Correction[b]	40.752	1	.000		
Likelihood Ratio	41.912	1	.000		
Fisher's Exact Test				.000	.000
N of Valid Cases	1442				

a. 0 cells (.0%) have expected count less than 5. The minimum expected count is 259.71.
b. Computed only for a 2×2 table

Risk Estimate

| | Value | 95% Confidence interval | |
		Lower	Upper
Odds Ratio for Gender (Female/Male)	2.030	1.634	2.522
For cohort Pres_Choice = Clinton	1.515	1.327	1.79
For cohort Pres_Choice = Obama	.746	.684	.815
N of Valid Cases	1442		

Figure 4.5 SPSS output for tests of independence.

4.7   Computer output: inter-rater agreement

Data are entered as was described in Section 4.6 for both programs, so these instructions are omitted here. Three variables must be entered: the category value for Rater 1, the category value for Rater 2, and the count in the resulting cell. The commands to generate coefficient kappa and its confidence interval are discussed next.

4.7.1   SAS

The SAS commands are shown in Figure 4.6. The tables command generates the contingency table and requests several options:

- The norow, nocol, and nopercent options suppress printing the row, column, and overall cell proportions, respectively.
- The expected option requests expected cell frequencies (under independence) and the agree option requests that Cohen's kappa and its 95% confidence interval be computed.

The output is shown in Figure 4.7 and can be compared to the results discussed in Section 4.5. In the output, the contingency table is followed by a Kappa Statistics table that includes

- Cohen's kappa of 0.375,
- its asymptotic standard error (0.079), and
- its 95% confidence interval (0.22, 0.53), which does not include zero.

Therefore, agreement between these two raters is significantly better than chance and, in the population, the level of agreement is estimated to be somewhere between 0.22 and 0.53 with 95% confidence.

4.7.2   SPSS

To conduct a test of inter-rater agreement using SPSS menus:

- Enter the data as depicted in Figure 4.8 and be sure to select the weight cases option under the Data menu (as discussed previously).
- Choose Descriptive Statistics in the Analyze menu and click on Crosstabs.
- Move the row variable (rater_1) into the Row(s) box and the column variable (rater_2) into the Column(s) box.
- Click on Statistics and select the desired statistics: for this output only Kappa was selected. Click Continue. A screenshot of this is provided in Figure 4.9.
- Now click on Cells and select the desired options: for this output, only Observed and Expected were selected. Click Continue and then OK to obtain the output.

The output, shown in Figure 4.10, contains

- the contingency table, including the observed and expected frequencies (under independence);

```
proc freq;
 weight freq;
 tables rater1*rater2 /norow nocol nopercent expected agree;
run;
```

Figure 4.6 SAS program for evaluating inter-rater agreement.

```
                    The FREQ Procedure

                 Table of rater1 by rater2

      rater1      rater2

      Frequency,
      Expected |a       |b       |c       |d       | Total
      ---------|--------|--------|--------|--------|
      a        |    25 |     7 |     5 |     3 |   40
               |  17.5 |    10 |     9 |   3.5 |
      ---------|--------|--------|--------|--------|
      b        |     4 |    10 |     4 |     0 |   18
               | 7.875 |   4.5 |  4.05 | 1.575 |
      ---------|--------|--------|--------|--------|
      c        |     3 |     2 |     7 |     0 |   12
               |  5.25 |     3 |   2.7 |  1.05 |
      ---------|--------|--------|--------|--------|
      d        |     3 |     1 |     2 |     4 |   10
               | 4.375 |   2.5 |  2.25 | 0.875 |
      ---------|--------|--------|--------|--------|
      Total         35      20      18       7     80

            Statistics for Table of rater1 by rater2

                    Test of Symmetry
                 -----------------------
                 Statistic (S)    4.9848
                 DF                    6
                 Pr > S           0.5458

                    Kappa Statistics

    Statistic        Value      ASE     95% Confidence Limits
    --------------------------------------------------------------
    Simple Kappa     0.3753    0.0791    0.2203        0.5302
    Weighted Kappa   0.3785    0.0916    0.1991        0.5580

                  Sample Size = 80
```

Figure 4.7 SAS output for evaluating inter-rater agreement.

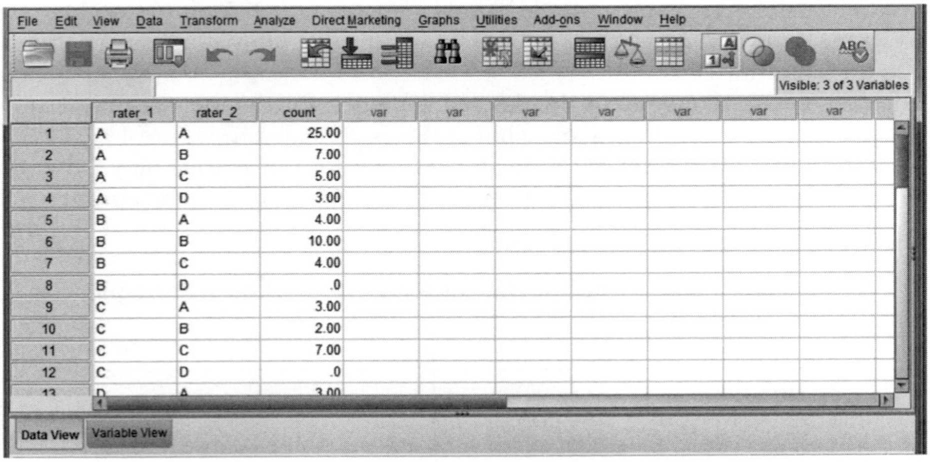

Figure 4.8 SPSS data window illustrating how to enter the data in Table 4.6.

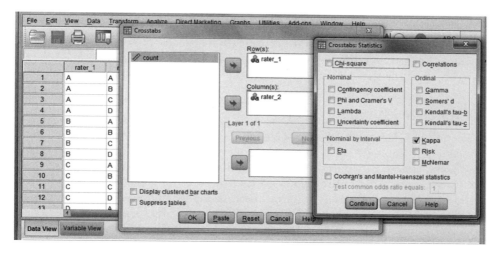

Figure 4.9 SPSS analysis window illustrating how to obtain statistics for inter-rater agreement.

rater_1 * rater_2 Crosstabulation

			rater_2				
			A	B	C	D	Total
rater_1	A	Count	25	7	5	3	40
		Expected Count	17.5	10.0	9.0	3.5	40.0
	B	Count	4	10	4	0	18
		Expected Count	7.9	4.5	4.1	1.6	18.0
	C	Count	3	2	7	0	12
		Expected Coun	5.3	3.0	2.7	1.1	12.0
	D	Count	3	1	2	4	10
		Expected Count	4.4	2.5	2.3	.9	10.0
Total		Count	35	20	18	7	80
		Expected Count	35.0	20.0	18.0	7.0	80.0

Symmetric Measures

	Value	Asymp. Std. Error[a]	Approx. T[b]	Approx. Sig.
Measure of Agreement Kappa	.375	.079	5.457	.000
N of Valid Cases	80			

a. Not assuming the null hypothesis.
b. Using the asymptotic standard error assuming the null hypothesis.

Figure 4.10 SPSS output for evaluating inter-rater agreement.

- the value of kappa (0.375);
- its asymptotic standard error (0.079); and
- the results of testing the null hypothesis (that agreement is zero). Since the *p*-value (called "Approx. Sig." on the output) is very small, the null hypothesis is rejected and we can conclude that agreement is significantly better than chance.

4.8   Complete example

In this section we demonstrate a complete analysis of a two-way contingency table. The data, presented in Table 4.7, were obtained from the 2006 General Social Survey (http://gss.norc.org/), and specifically pertain to the educational attainment of respondents and their attitude toward removing antireligious books from the library. For our purposes, educational attainment was defined as whether the respondent has at least a bachelor's degree. The attitude was measured using two categories, a yes or no response to the question: If some people in your community suggested a book against churches and religion should be taken out of your public library, would you favor removing this book or not? The data are shown in Table 4.7. The odds of favoring removal of the books for those without a bachelor's degree are $439/1015 = 0.433$, and the odds of favoring removal of the books for those with a bachelor's degree (or higher) are $81/437 = 0.185$. The odds ratio comparing the odds of favoring removal of the books for those without a bachelor's degree to those who have at least a bachelor's is, therefore, $0.433/0.185 = 2.3$. This indicates that the odds of endorsing the removal of antireligious books by respondents who did not attain at least a bachelor's degree are about 2.3 times the odds for those who did.

The SAS program and output for these data are shown in Figures 4.11 and 4.12, respectively, and the SPSS output is shown in Figure 4.13.

The odds ratio reported on the SAS output (Figure 4.12) is 2.333 with a 95% confidence interval of [1.795, 3.033]. This indicates that in the population we can estimate the odds ratio to be between about 1.8 and 3.0 with 95% confidence. These results also indicate that this odds ratio is significantly greater than 1 and so educational attainment level is most likely associated with attitude toward removal of antireligious books from the public library. The reciprocal of this odds ratio, $1/2.3 = 0.429$, is reported by SPSS (Figure 4.13) and indicates that the odds of opposing the removal of antireligious books by respondents who did not attain at least a bachelor's degree are about 0.4 times the odds for those who did.

The goodness-of-fit tests further indicate that there is a significant association between educational attainment and attitude toward removing books as we have defined them

Table 4.7 Data on Educational Attainment and Attitude Toward Removing Antireligious Books From the Public Library

Attitude	Bachelor's (or Higher)		Total
	No	Yes	
Remove	439	81	520
Do not remove	1015	437	1452
Total	1454	518	1972

Source: 2006 General Social Survey.

```
data gss06;
  input bachelors $ remove $ count;
  datalines;
n            y            439
n            n            1015
y            y            81
y            n            437
;
proc freq data=gss06 order=data;
  weight count;
  tables remove*bachelors /nocol norow nopercent expected deviation cellchi2
chisq relrisk;
run;
```

Figure 4.11 SAS syntax for the educational attainment and attitude toward removing antireligious books from the public library example.

(Pearson $X^2 = 41.7$, likelihood ratio $G^2 = 44.9$, $df = 1$, $p < .0001$). Therefore, the overall conclusion is that these variables are significantly associated such that the odds of supporting the removal of antireligious books are higher for those respondents with lower educational attainment (less than a bachelor's degree).

The adjusted residuals are provided in the SPSS output (in the contingency table of Figure 4.13). These are all quite large (with an absolute value of 6.5) and indicate large deviations from expectation in each cell. In other words, all observed cell frequencies deviate substantially from what we would expect under independence. The contributions to Pearson's X^2 are included in the SAS output (in the contingency table of Figure 4.12, under Cell Chi-square). From these, we can see that the smallest contribution (of 2.9) to X^2 came from the cell for those who do not support removal of antireligious books and do not have at least a bachelor's degree, while the largest contribution (22.6) to X^2 came from the cell for those who support removal of anti-religious books and have at least a bachelor's degree. In fact, the largest contribution in this case constitutes over half of the total test statistic (of 41.7), so it appears to be quite substantial. Combined with the residual for this cell, which is negative, we can say that those who attained a higher level of education tend to support the removal of anti-religious books at a very low rate relative to what would be expected under independence, and this discrepancy is largely responsible for the overall association observed between the variables of educational attainment and attitude toward the removal of antireligious books.

4.9   Summary

In this chapter we introduced the concept and notation of contingency tables, and used these to examine the relationship or association between two categorical variables. To that end, we also introduced the concept of independence between variables, and defined the odds as well as the odds ratio, which are fundamental in categorical data analysis.

To investigate the association between categorical variables, we discussed inferential procedures designed to estimate the odds ratio and test whether it is significantly different than what would be expected under independence, or lack of association. Whereas the odds ratio is very useful when each variable has two categories, for variables with more than two categories we also discussed investigating the association using goodness-of-fit statistics that compare the observed joint distribution of two variables to that expected

```
                        The FREQ Procedure

                   Table of remove by bachelors

           remove              bachelors

           Frequency     |
           Expected      |
           Deviation     |
           Cell Chi-Square|n       |y       |   Total
           ---------------|--------|--------|
           y              |   439  |    81  |   520
                          | 383.41 | 136.59 |
                          | 55.592 | -55.59 |
                          | 8.0606 | 22.626 |
           ---------------|--------|--------|
           n              |  1015  |   437  |   1452
                          | 1070.6 | 381.41 |
                          | -55.59 | 55.592 |
                          | 2.8867 | 8.1029 |
           ---------------|--------|--------|
           Total             1454     518      1972


                Statistics for Table of remove by bachelors

     Statistic                     DF      Value      Prob
     ------------------------------------------------------------
     Chi-Square                     1      41.6760    <.0001
     Likelihood Ratio Chi-Square    1      44.9019    <.0001
     Continuity Adj. Chi-Square     1      40.9297    <.0001
     Mantel-Haenszel Chi-Square     1      41.6548    <.0001
     Phi Coefficient                       0.1454
     Contingency Coefficient               0.1439
     Cramer's V                            0.1454

                        Fisher's Exact Test
                   ----------------------------------
                   Cell (1,1) Frequency (F)      439
                   Left-sided Pr <= F         1.0000
                   Right-sided Pr >= F      1.654E-11

                   Table Probability (P)    9.575E-12
                   Two-sided Pr <= P        2.762E-11


                Statistics for Table of remove by bachelors
                Estimates of the Relative Risk (Row1/Row2)

     Type of Study               Value    95% Confidence Limits
     ------------------------------------------------------------
     Case-Control (Odds Ratio)   2.3334    1.7952       3.0330
     Cohort (Col1 Risk)          1.2077    1.1488       1.2697
     Cohort (Col2 Risk)          0.5176    0.4175       0.6416

                        Sample Size = 1972
```

Figure 4.12 SAS output for the educational attainment and attitude toward removing antireligious books from the public library example.

under independence. In addition, we discussed an application of these concepts as they relate to estimating and evaluating inter-rater reliability.

Many of the concepts introduced in this chapter, for the analysis of two categorical variables and their association, will be used and extended in the next chapter for the analysis of three categorical variables.

Remove * Bachelors Crosstabulation

			Bachelors		Total
			n	y	
Remove	y	Count	439	81	520
		Expected Count	383.4	136.6	520.0
		Residual	55.6	−55.6	
		Adjusted Residual	6.5	−6.5	
	n	Count	1015	437	1452
		Expected Count	1070.6	381.4	1452.0
		Residual	-55.6	55.6	
		Adjusted Residual	-6.5	6.5	
Total		Count	1454	518	1972
		Expected count	1454.0	518.0	1972.0

Chi-Square Tests

	Value	df	Asymp. Sig. (2-sided)	Exact. Sig. (2-sided)	Exact. Sig. (1-sided)
Pearson Chi-Square	41.676[b]	1	.000		
Continuity Correction[a]	40.930	1	.000		
Likelihood Ratio	44.902	1	.000		
Fisher's Exact Test				.000	.000
N of Valid Cases	1972				

a. Computed only for a 2×2 table

b. 0. cells (.0%) have expected count less than 5. The minimum expected count is 136.59.

Risk Estimate

	Value	95% Confidence Interval	
		Lower	Upper
Odds Ratio for Remove (n /y)	.429	.330	.557
For cohort Bachelors = n	.828	.788	.870
For cohort Bachelors = y	1.932	1.558	2.395
N of Valid Cases	1972		

Figure 4.13 SPSS output for the educational attainment and attitude toward removing antireligious books from the public library example.

Problems

4.1 Suppose that fourth-grade students from a national random sample were classified as either proficient or not proficient in mathematics as well as whether each was a native English speaker (NES). Possible results (loosely based on data from the National Center for Education Statistics) are shown in Table 4.8.
   a. Compute the odds of proficiency based on these data and interpret this value.
   b. Compute the odds ratio for this table and interpret this value.

Table 4.8 Contingency Table of
Mathematics Proficiency by Native
English Speaker Status for Problem 4.1

		Proficient	
		No	Yes
NES	No	35	5
	Yes	93	67

4.2 Find the 95% confidence interval for the odds ratio in Problem 4.1 and interpret the result.

4.3 Is there an association between proficiency and NES status based on the data in Problem 4.1? State the null hypothesis and interpret the results of the hypothesis test.

4.4 Repeat Problems 4.1, 4.2, and 4.3 using computer software.

4.5 Think of two categorical variables that theoretically should be independent and explain why you believe they should be independent.

4.6 Use computer software and the data in Table 4.9 to test whether there is an association between Vitamin C and the incidence of colds.
   a. Report the results of the Pearson chi-squared statistic and its *p*-value.
   b. Report the results of the likelihood ratio test statistic and its *p*-value.
   c. Report the conclusions.

Table 4.9 Contingency Table of Colds Incidence by
Vitamin C Use for Problem 4.6

		Regularly take vitamin C		
		Yes	No	Total
Colds/year	Few	32	16	48
	Some	13	27	40
	Many	5	7	12
	Total	50	50	100

4.7 Obtain the residuals and contributions to chi-squared for each of the cells in Problem 4.6.
a. Which cells show the largest and smallest deviations from the results expected under independence?
b. Would any of these deviations be considered large? Explain.

4.8 In a random sample of 996 Americans, individuals were classified according to their marital status and whether they considered life dull, routine, or exciting. The results (based on a subset of the 1993 General Social Survey) are shown in Table 4.10.
a. Is there an association between marital status and attitude about life? Report the test statistic and explain your answer.
b. Are any of the deviations particularly large or small? If so, which cells tend to deviate most from independence?
c. Select two categories for each variable and compute the odds ratio for the resulting subtable. Interpret this value.

Table 4.10 Contingency Table of Marital Status by Attitude Toward Life for Problem 4.8

		Attitude about life			
		Dull	Routine	Exciting	Total
	Married	21	241	251	513
Marital Status	Widowed	17	54	40	111
	Divorced	10	74	65	149
	Separated	6	11	8	25
	Never married	11	79	108	198
	Total	65	459	472	996

4.9 A study was conducted to determine the level of agreement between the ratings of prospective job candidates made by two personnel officers. The officers rated each of 20 job candidates as unacceptable (A); acceptable (B); or recommended (C). The results are shown in Table 4.11.
a. Compute (by hand) the value of Cohen's kappa for these data and interpret this value.
b. Obtain (by computer) the 95% confidence interval for Cohen's kappa and interpret the results.

Table 4.11 Contingency Table of Ratings by Two Personnel Officers for Problem 4.9

		Officer 1		
		A	B	C
	A	2	1	0
Officer 2	B	1	5	4
	C	1	3	3

4.10 If the two officers in Problem 4.10 agreed perfectly, what might the observed contingency table have been? Provide an example of such a table and compute the value of Cohen's kappa that would be obtained for this table.

4.11 Find a contingency table from a recent news story or study to use for this problem. Cite the source of the data and use it to:
   a. Provide a research question that can be answered with the data.
   b. Run the analysis (by computer) to obtain the appropriate results.
   c. Using the results from part (b), provide the substantive conclusion as it relates to the research question in part (a).

chapter five

Association between three categorical variables

A LOOK AHEAD

Research questions often involve more than two variables because researchers are usually interested in the interrelationship among several variables. For example, a researcher may hypothesize that the presence or severity of attention deficit disorder (ADD) is dependent on gender, age, and family history. In this case one would likely be interested in whether the presence or severity of ADD can be explained or predicted by gender, age, or family history, or the interaction of any of these variables. In other words, the relationship among and between these variables is of interest. In other situations, a researcher may want to take into consideration independent variables that may be influencing the relationship among the variables of interest. These variables are referred to as **covariates**. For example, a researcher may be primarily interested in the relationship between political affiliation and income, but hypothesize that this relationship depends on religious affiliation. In this case religious affiliation would be considered a covariate. In either situation, and with either continuous or categorical variables, to examine the interrelationships among several variables or control for the effects of covariates we typically focus on examining the relationship between two variables of interest while holding the other variable(s) or covariate(s) constant. However, the way in which we accomplish this differs depending on whether the variables are categorical or continuous in nature. In this chapter, we will focus on categorical variables and, specifically, cases that involve three categorical variables. Examples of research questions that can be addressed by the methods presented in this chapter include

- Is there an association between gender, political affiliation, and age?
- How does age affect the relationship between smoking status and a person's ability to breathe normally?
- Is there an association between education, religious attitudes, and income?
- Is there an association between marital status and happiness after controlling for gender?

In these examples we assume that all of the variables were measured as categorical, and in this chapter we extend the ideas presented in the previous chapter so that we can deal with research questions that pertain to the association between three categorical variables.

5.1   Contingency tables for three categorical variables

5.1.1   Partial tables and conditional associations

Three-way contingency tables depict the relationship between three categorical variables by considering two-way contingency tables, known as **partial tables**, at fixed levels of the third variable. While the notation and terminology introduced in the previous chapter for two-way contingency tables generalizes to three-way contingency tables, it must be extended to take into consideration the third variable. Specifically, the total number of categories for the row variable, X, is still denoted by I, with each category indexed by i; the total number of categories for the column variable, Y, is still denoted by J, with each category indexed by j; but now we have a third variable, Z, for which the total number of categories is denoted by K, with each category indexed by k. Figure 5.1 illustrates a three-way table, which can be partitioned or "sliced up" in three different ways to create partial tables. Specifically, one could either create K partial tables, one for each level of variable Z; J partial tables, one for each level of variable Y; or I partial tables, one for each level of X. The slices for each level of Z are depicted in the figure and the frequency in any cell of the table (i.e., the number of observations falling into the ith category of X, j^{th} category of Y, and k^{th} category of Z) is denoted by n_{ijk}.

A substantive example of a three-way contingency table depicting the relationship between political affiliation, age, and gender is illustrated in Table 5.1. In our example, political affiliation has $I = 3$ categories ($i = 1$ for liberal; $i = 2$ for moderate; and $i = 3$ for conservative), age group has $J = 4$ categories ($j = 1$ for those 18–29 years of age; j = 2 for those 30–39 years of age; $j = 3$ for those 40–49 years of age; and $j = 4$ for those 50-plus years of age), and gender has $K = 2$ categories ($k = 1$ for males; $k = 2$ for females). In general, the size of three-way contingency tables is denoted as $I \times J \times K$ (i.e., $3 \times 4 \times 2$ in our example) and the frequency in each cell of the table is denoted by n_{ijk}. For example, n_{342} in Table 5.1 represents the number of respondents who are conservative ($i = 3$), 50-plus years of age ($j = 4$), and female ($k = 2$), so $n_{342} = 133$. Taken together, the cell frequencies represent the joint distribution of the three categorical variables.

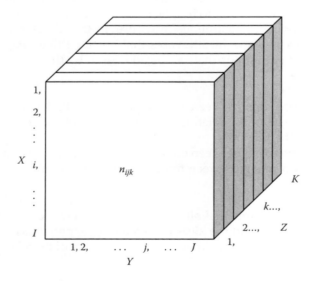

Figure 5.1 Three-dimensional representation of a three-way contingency table.

Table 5.1 Three-Way Contingency Table of Political Affiliation
by Age Group by Gender

Gender	Political affiliation	Age category				
		18–29	30–39	40–49	50+	Total
Male	Liberal	27	44	37	49	157
	Moderate	49	54	48	64	215
	Conservative	44	58	49	101	252
Female	Liberal	59	56	51	63	229
	Moderate	54	76	64	118	312
	Conservative	44	55	46	133	278

In this example, we can create a partial table by "conditioning" on gender, politi-cal affiliation, or age category. A partial table is, therefore, a two-way contingency table (involving two of the categorical variables) at one specific level of the third variable, such as the two-way contingency table involving the variables of age category and political affiliation for males only, which is illustrated in Table 5.2. The associations in partial tables are called **conditional associations** because they reflect the relationship between two of the variables conditional at a fixed level of the third. Conditional associations are also sometimes referred to as **partial associations** because they reflect the associations in par-tial tables. Because they are two-way contingency tables, the statistical procedures that were described in Chapter 4 can be used on each of the partial tables to determine whether a conditional association exists. For example, to determine whether a conditional asso-ciation exists between political affiliation and age group in Table 5.1 we could calculate two separate χ^2 statistics: one for males and one for females. Recall (from Chapter 4) that these statistics compare the observed frequencies with those that would be expected if the variables were statistically independent; in other words, the null hypothesis tested is that political affiliation and age are independent within each gender (separately). Computing these statistics for the data presented in Table 5.1, we find that there is a conditional asso-ciation between political affiliation and age group for females ($\chi^2 = 24.946$, $df = 6$, $p < 0.001$) but not for males ($\chi^2 = 8.193$, $df = 6$, $p = 0.224$).

The standardized residuals associated with each of the cells in Table 5.1 are depicted in Table 5.3 and can be used to assist in the interpretation of the results (as discussed in Chapter 4). The standardized residuals for the male partial table are relatively small, but some of those in the female partial table (namely, r_{112}, r_{142}, and r_{342}) are relatively large. Specifically, for female respondents, there are more liberals between the ages of 18 to 29, less liberals that are 50 years or older, and more conservatives that are 50 years or older than would be expected if political affiliation and age group were independent.

Table 5.2 Partial Table of Political Affiliation by Age Group for Males

Political affiliation	Age category				
	18–29	30–39	40–49	50+	Total
Liberal	27	44	37	49	157
Moderate	49	54	48	64	215
Conservative	44	58	49	101	252

Table 5.3 Standardized Residuals for Three-Way Contingency Table of Political Affiliation by Age Group by Gender

Gender	Political affiliation	Age category 18–29	30–39	40–49	50+
Male	Liberal	−0.6	0.8	0.6	−0.7
	Moderate	1.2	0.0	0.3	−1.1
	Conservative	−0.6	−0.6	−0.7	1.6
Female	Liberal	2.3	0.5	0.9	−2.6
	Moderate	−0.8	0.6	0.3	−0.1
	Conservative	−1.3	−1.1	−1.2	2.6

Odds ratios can also be used to describe the conditional associations in three-way tables. For $2 \times 2 \times K$ tables, the odds ratios can be calculated for each of the K partial tables because each partial table is a 2×2 contingency table. However, multiple odds ratios must be used to describe the conditional associations in higher-way tables such as Table 5.1. This is accomplished by partitioning the higher-way table into multiple 2×2 tables. For example, the partial table for males, depicted in Table 5.2, could be partitioned into four 2×2 tables as depicted in Figure 5.2. Then the odds ratios obtained for each of the 2×2 subtables could be used to describe the associations in the larger table. It should be noted that, because the order of the rows and columns is somewhat arbitrary, any two rows and two columns could be used to form a 2×2 subtable of a higher-way table. In other words, there are numerous different ways to partition a higher-way table into 2×2 tables to understand the associations present in the table. In fact, the best partitions are those that enable a researcher to better understand the data from a substantive perspective. An example of this is presented later in this chapter.

5.1.2   Marginal tables and marginal associations

Combining the frequencies from the partial tables formed for any two variables (e.g., X and Y) by adding the frequencies across all levels of the third variable (e.g., Z) results in a two-way table known as the **marginal table**. For instance, using the example in Table 5.1, a 3×4 marginal table (representing political affiliation and age category) can be formed by adding the frequencies across males and females, as depicted in Table 5.4. The associations in marginal tables are called **marginal associations**. For those familiar with analysis

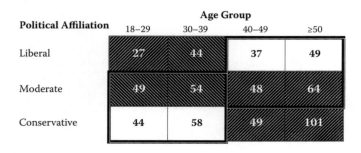

Figure 5.2 One possible way to partition Table 5.2 into four 2×2 tables.

Table 5.4 Marginal Table of Political Affiliation by Age Group

| | Age category | | | | |
Political affiliation	18–29	30–39	40–49	50+	Total
Liberal	86	100	88	112	386
Moderate	103	130	112	182	527
Conservative	88	113	95	234	530
Total	277	343	295	528	1443

of variance (ANOVA), conditional associations are analogous to three-way interactions in ANOVA (where the interaction between any two factors depends on the level of the third factor) and marginal associations are analogous to two-way interactions in a three-way ANOVA (where the interaction between any two factors is averaged across all levels of the third factor). In other words, conditional associations examine two-way associations separately at each level of the third variable, while marginal associations examine two-way associations overall, essentially ignoring the level of the third variable. Therefore, conditional associations can be very different than the associations obtained from marginal tables.

To further illustrate these concepts, Table 5.5 depicts the results of a study adapted from Agresti (1990), that examined the association between smoking status and the ability to breathe normally for two age groups. A marginal table that depicts the overall association between smoking status and the ability to breathe normally regardless of age is shown in Table 5.6. The estimated odds ratio for the marginal association between breathing test and smoking status (computed using the frequencies in Table 5.6) is

$$\hat{\theta} = \frac{741 \times 131}{927 \times 38} = 2.756,$$

which is a statistically significant marginal association ($\chi^2 = 30.242$, $df = 1$, $p < 0.001$). However, in computing this association we have ignored the effect of age, which surely might be hypothesized to have an impact on the ability to breathe. In fact, using the partial tables shown in Table 5.5, for the participants in the study who were less than 50 years of age the estimated odds ratio between breathing test and smoking status is $\hat{\theta} = 1.418$, which

Table 5.5 Partial Tables for Smoking Status and Breathing Test Results by Age

		Breathing test result		
	Smoking status	Normal	Not normal	Total
Age < 50	Never	577	34	611
	Yes/Past	682	57	739
	Total	1259	91	1350
Age > 50	Never	164	4	168
	Yes/Past	245	74	319
	Total	409	78	487

Table 5.6 Marginal Table for Smoking Status and Breathing Test Results

Smoking status	Breathing test result		Total
	Normal	Not normal	
Never	741	38	779
Yes	927	131	1058
Total	1668	169	1837

is not a statistically significant conditional association ($\chi^2 = 2.456$, $df = 1$, $p = 0.112$). On the other hand, for participants in the study who were 50 years of age or older the estimated odds ratio is $\hat{\theta} = 12.38$, which is a statistically significant conditional association ($\chi^2 = 35.45$, $df = 1$, $p < 0.001$). Therefore, age is an important covariate in studying the relationship between smoking status and the ability to breathe.

The results from the example just discussed suggest that, although smoking status is related to the ability to breathe even if age is ignored, the strength of the association is affected by age. This is because there was not a statistically significant association between smoking status and the ability to breathe for participants in the study who were less than 50 years of age, but there was a statistically significant association between smoking status and the ability to breathe for those 50 years of age or older. Whereas the odds of having an abnormal breathing test were only 2.7 times greater if one were a smoker when age is ignored, the odds of having an abnormal breathing test were more than 12 times greater if one is a smoker over the age of 50. Therefore, in some sense the marginal association misrepresents the full story provided by the data because it ignores age, which turns out to be an important factor in fully understanding the association between smoking status and the ability to breathe normally. Interpreting the marginal association in the presence of differing conditional associations is analogous to reporting and interpreting a two-way interaction when a three-way interaction is present in ANOVA.

5.2 Marginal and conditional independence

In the discussion that follows, we discuss the relationship between two variables, X and Y, either conditional on or combined across levels of the third variable, Z. Although the labels given to the variables (i.e., which variable is called X, Y, or Z) are rather arbitrary, it is somewhat conventional to denote the primary variables of interest as X and Y while denoting the covariate as Z. Therefore, this is the approach we take in the general discussion that follows.

5.2.1 Marginal independence

Marginal independence implies that the there is no association in the marginal table, whereas marginal dependence implies that there is an association in the marginal table. For a 2×2 marginal table representing the relationship between the two variables, X and Y, marginal independence implies that (in the population) the **marginal odds ratio**, θ_{XY}, is equal to one, whereas marginal dependence implies that (in the population) θ_{XY} is not equal to one. For instance, in our second example (Table 5.6) there was marginal dependence (in the sample) between smoking status and the ability to breathe normally because the estimated marginal odds ratio was, $\hat{\theta}_{XY} = 2.756$.

In general, for an $I \times J$ marginal table, marginal independence implies that all of the odds ratios that can be formed using *any* two levels of the variables, X and Y, is equal to one. On the other hand, marginal dependence implies that *at least one* of the odds ratios formed by using two levels of the variables X and Y is not equal to one.

5.2.2   *Conditional independence*

Conditional independence implies that there is no association between the variables X and Y in any of the K partial tables that are conditional on each level of the third variable, Z. For a 2×2 partial table, this implies that, in the population, the odds ratios in all of the K partial tables are equal to one, or $\theta_{XY|Z_k} = 1$ for *all* $k = 1, 2, \ldots, K$. We use the conditional odds ratio notation $\theta_{XY|Z_k}$ to represent the association between any two levels of X with any two levels of Y conditional on the kth level of Z. Note that in conditional probability notation the variables to the left of the vertical line represent the association of interest and the variables to the right of the vertical line represent the variables on which the association is conditioned. In general, for any $I \times J$ partial table, conditional independence implies that the odds ratio that can be formed by using any two levels of X and Y is equal to one for all K partial tables (i.e., conditional on the levels of Z). Conditional dependence implies that there is an association in at least one of the partial tables. For 2×2 partial tables, conditional dependence implies that, in the population, the odds ratio in *at least one* of the partial tables is not equal to one, or $\theta_{XY|Z_k} \neq 1$ for *at least one* $k = 1, 2, \ldots, K$. In general, for any $I \times J$ partial table, conditional dependence implies that *at least one* of the odds ratios that can be formed by using any two levels of two variables, X and Y, is not equal to one for at least one of the Z partial tables. In both of our examples, conditional dependence was evident because a significant partial association between two of the variables was found in (at least) one of the partial tables. In our first example (Table 5.1) there was a significant partial association between political affiliation and age for females ($\chi^2 = 24.496$, $df = 6$, $p < 0.001$), though not for males ($\chi^2 = 8.193$, $df = 6$, $p = 0.224$). This implies that at least one of the odds ratios that can be computed from the political affiliation and age group partial table for females is not equal to one. In fact, given the residual analysis described previously (Table 5.3) and examining the cells that most deviated from independence, it is likely that the odds ratio formed by considering the 2×2 table for liberal and conservative females in the age groups 18–29 and 50 or older will reflect a statistically significant association. This is because these cells have the largest residuals and thus deviate most from what would be expected under independence. The frequency counts for these four cells are shown in Table 5.7 and the estimated odds ratio for this table is $\hat{\theta} = 2.83$, indicating that the odds of being affiliated as liberal rather than conservative are approximately 3 times greater for females between the ages of 18 and 29 than for females who are at least 50 years old. In our

Table 5.7 Subset of Partial Table from Table 5.1 Depicting Political Affiliation and Age for Females

		Age group	
		18–29	50+
Political Affiliation	Liberal	59	63
	Conservative	44	133

Table 5.8 Possible Outcomes for Three-Way Tables, With Shaded Rows Representing Simpson's Paradox

Marginal table	Conditional table	Result
Independence	Independence	Marginal independence/ conditional independence
Independence	Dependence	Marginal independence/ conditional dependence
Dependence	Independence	Marginal dependence/ conditional independence
Dependence	Dependence	Marginal dependence/ conditional dependence

second example (Table 5.5), we found a significant conditional association between smoking status and the ability to breathe normally for study participants older than 50 years of age but not for those who were 50 years of age or younger. Therefore, the null hypothesis of conditional independence would be rejected in both of these examples.

Interestingly, marginal independence *does not* imply conditional independence and conditional independence *does not* imply marginal independence. In fact, it is possible for the marginal association to be in the opposite direction from the conditional association, which is known as **Simpson's paradox**. In examining the association between three (or more) variables, the possible outcomes can be summarized by the four scenarios shown in Table 5.8. These different scenarios highlight the importance of considering confounding variables when studying the relationships between categorical variables. A thorough investigation of both the partial and marginal associations is necessary to ensure that all of the existing relationships are uncovered. Again, this is analogous to investigating both three-way and two-way interactions in an ANOVA with three factors; an analysis of both is needed to ensure that the results are interpreted thoroughly and accurately.

5.2.3 *Homogeneous association*

When the conditional associations between X and Y are equal across all K partial tables (representing levels of Z), we have **homogeneous association** between X and Y. This is analogous to the absence of a three-way interaction in a three-way ANOVA, and implies that the two-way interaction between any two variables (or factors) is the same across all levels of the third variable (or factor). Neither of the examples presented thus far demonstrated the presence of homogeneous association because the partial associations between X and Y were not the same across all K partial tables. In other words, in both of the examples presented thus far there was a "three-way interaction" between the variables considered. In our first example, there was a three-way interaction between gender, age, and political affiliation because there was an association between political affiliation and age for females, but not for males. In other words, the association between political affiliation and age depended on one's gender. Likewise, in our second example there was a three-way interaction between ability to breathe normally, smoking, and age because there was an association between smoking and the ability to breathe normally for respondents older than 50 years of age but not for those 50 years of age or younger. In general, however, it is not necessary for some conditional associations to be significant and others to be insignificant to reject the null hypothesis of homogeneous association.

A rejection of this null hypothesis only implies that the partial associations are not equivalent. It could be the case, for example, that one of the partial associations is simply stronger than another (yet both are statistically significant).

Formally, a homogeneous association implies that the following equalities hold:

$$\theta_{XY|Z_1} = \theta_{XY|Z_2} = \ldots = \theta_{XY|Z_K}, \tag{5.1}$$

$$\theta_{XZ|Y_1} = \theta_{XZ|Y_2} = \ldots = \theta_{XZ|Y_J}, \text{ and} \tag{5.2}$$

$$\theta_{YZ|X_1} = \theta_{YZ|X_2} = \ldots = \theta_{YZ|X_I}. \tag{5.3}$$

It should be noted that if any one of these is true then the other two equalities will also be true. For example, suppose that homogeneous association was found between reading proficiency (yes or no), type of instruction (whole language or phonics), and school locale (urban or rural). This would imply that there was no three-way interaction between these three variables. Therefore, the odds of being proficient in reading if taught using a whole language approach, as opposed to a phonics approach, would be statistically equivalent for students in urban and rural schools. Moreover, the odds of being proficient in reading if one went to an urban school, as opposed to a rural school, would be statistically equivalent regardless of the method of instruction. Finally, the odds of being taught from a whole language approach if one went to an urban school, as opposed to a rural school, would be comparable for students who were proficient in reading and those who were not.

Conditional independence is a special case of homogeneous association because it implies that the odds ratios in each of the K partial tables are both equal to each other (homogeneous association) and also equal to one. Formally, this can be expressed by

$$\theta_{XY|Z_1} = \theta_{XY|Z_2} = \ldots = \theta_{XY|Z_K} = 1. \tag{5.4}$$

Note that although *conditional independence implies homogeneous association*, the converse is not necessarily true; that is, *homogeneous association does not necessarily imply conditional independence*. In the section that follows we discuss how to statistically test for these types of associations.

5.3   *Inferential statistics for three-way tables*

Although a three-way ANOVA includes a continuous dependent variable, whereas exploring the relationships among three categorical variables does not, the two analyses are analogous in that a researcher begins by investigating whether a three-way interaction exists between the factors (or categorical variables). If a three-way interaction is found, then it is unwise to interpret any lower two-way interactions or main effects that may exist because they cannot be interpreted unambiguously. However, if there is no evidence for the presence of a three-way interaction then a researcher would want to test whether any two-way interactions exist.

With categorical data, testing for homogeneous association is analogous to testing for a three-way interaction. If the data do not show a pattern of homogeneous association, then one can conclude that a three-way interaction exists between the three categorical variables. If the data follow a pattern that is consistent with homogeneous association, then one can conclude that a three-way interaction does not exist and the conditional odds ratios for the K partial tables are statistically equal. In other words, the conditional association between any two of the variables is the same regardless of the level of the third variable. In the first example discussed in this chapter (Table 5.1), this would mean that the association between age and political affiliation (whatever it may be) is the same for both males and females. Therefore, a **common odds ratio** can be computed to summarize the two-way associations that exist in the partial tables, which may or may not be reflective of a two-way association, or interaction. To evaluate whether the common two-way association is significant, one would conduct a test of conditional independence, although one need not necessarily conduct a test of homogeneous association prior to conducting a test of conditional independence. The presence of a homogeneous association allows us to estimate the K conditional odds ratios with one common odds ratio, but the absence of homogeneous association indicates that we should keep the K conditional odds ratios separate because the associations in the K partial tables are not all the same. The presence of conditional independence, on the other hand, tells us that not only can the K conditional odds ratios be estimated with one common odds ratio, but that this common odds ratio is equal to one (in the population); in other words, the conditional association that is common to all K partial tables is not significant. It should be noted that a researcher who is interested in the relationships among three categorical variables should not collapse the partial tables and study the two-way associations in the marginal table without first investigating the conditional associations, because this could lead to incomplete and, possibly, misleading interpretations (as demonstrated in the example exploring the relationship between smoking status, breathing, and age). Marginal associations, which essentially involve only two categorical variables, can be investigated using the procedures discussed in Chapter 4. The inferential procedures described in this section are specific to three categorical variables and as such involve conditional (not marginal) associations.

There are two inferential test statistics that can be used with three-way tables. The **Breslow–Day test** statistic can be used to test for a three-way interaction or association. The null hypothesis of this test is that the data satisfy homogeneous association, so if the results of this test are statistically significant then one can conclude that there is a three-way interaction among the three variables. If the results of this test are not statistically significant then one can conclude that there is not a three-way interaction, or that there is a homogeneous association and the conditional association between any two of the variables is the same at each level of the third. In other words, if the null hypothesis is *not* rejected then we can assume that homogeneous associations exist in the data. However, this test can only be used for $2 \times 2 \times K$ tables.

The **Cochran–Mantel–Haenszel (CMH) test** statistic can be used to test for conditional independence in three-way tables of any size and can be thought of as a test to determine if a two-way interaction exists. The null hypothesis of the CMH test is that all conditional odds ratios are equal to 1, so if this null hypothesis is rejected we can conclude that at least one conditional odds ratio is not equal to 1 and some partial or conditional association exists in the data. These testing procedures are summarized in Figure 5.3, which shows that one typically begins by testing for homogeneous association across the K partial tables. If there is insufficient evidence to reject the presence of homogeneous association (i.e., homogeneous association appears plausible) then one may proceed with estimating the conditional odds ratio using one common value, the **Mantel–Haenszel estimate**, and testing whether this (common) conditional association is significant. However, if there is sufficient evidence to reject the presence of homogenous association (i.e., homogeneous association appears to be implausible), the partial tables must be examined and interpreted separately.

Similarly, in the presence of homogeneous association, if there is sufficient evidence to reject the presence of conditional independence, the common conditional association should be examined and interpreted as this would indicate that the variables are conditionally associated. However, if there is insufficient evidence to reject the presence of

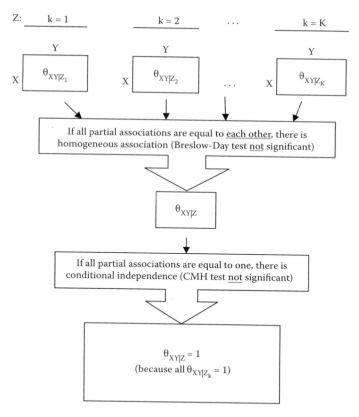

Figure 5.3 Summary of testing procedures for three-way contingency tables.

conditional independence (and, by implication, homogeneous association), one may conclude that the three variables are not associated with each other; that is, X and Y are independent at every level of Z. The remainder of this chapter is devoted to describing these tests. It should also be noted that a statistical modeling approach, known as log-linear modeling, can be used to test the same hypotheses tested by these inferential procedures. Moreover, the log-linear modeling approach can be used with three-way tables of any size and can also be used for higher-way tables. This approach will be covered in Chapter 7.

5.3.1 *Breslow–Day test statistic for homogeneous association*

The Breslow–Day statistic tests the null hypothesis of homogeneous association, expressed mathematically in Equations 5.1 to 5.3, which states that the odds ratios are the same in each of the K partial tables. As previously stated, this test can only be used with $2 \times 2 \times K$ tables. Moreover, it should only be used when each partial table has fairly large sample sizes, or when approximately 80% or more of the expected cell counts are at least five. It is computed by taking the sum of the squared difference between the observed and expected cell counts divided by the expected cell counts, and thus it is an approximate χ^2 statistic with degrees of freedom equal to $K - 1$. The expected cell counts are based on the assumption, made under the null hypothesis of homogeneous association, that a common odds ratio can be used to describe the conditional associations. Computing the expected

Table 5.9 Three-Way Contingency Table Classifying
Characteristics of Firearm Injuries

Location of injury	Type of injury	Fatal injury?		
		Yes	No	Total
Victim's Home	Suicide	45	20	65
	Accident	15	29	44
	Total	60	49	109
Friend/Relative's Home	Suicide	13	12	25
	Accident	14	27	41
	Total	27	39	66
Other	Suicide	18	11	29
	Accident	11	29	40
	Total	29	40	69

values is quite complex when assuming a common odds ratio, and therefore will not be further explicated here.

To illustrate the use of this test, consider the data about firearm injuries, adapted from a study by Grossman, Reay, and Baker (1999), presented in Table 5.9. Each injury was classified as to the location of the injury, the type of injury that was incurred, and whether the injury was fatal. One way to state the null hypothesis of homogeneous association in this example is that the association between type of injury and fatal outcome is the same regardless of location. Using SAS, the Breslow–Day test statistic obtained for these data was not statistically significant ($\chi^2 = 1.43$, $df = 2$, $p = 0.49$). Therefore, we are not able to reject the null hypothesis of homogeneous association and we conclude that the conditional associations between fatal outcome and injury type do not differ significantly by location. In other words, there is insufficient evidence to refute the presence of homogeneous association in the data and we conclude that the conditional association between fatal outcome and injury type is (statistically) the same for all locations.

5.3.2 Mantel–Haenszel estimate of a common odds ratio

Given that (based on the Breslow–Day test results) we presume the presence of homogeneous association in the data pertaining to the firearm injuries (Table 5.9), we may compute a common odds ratio to describe the conditional association between fatal outcome and injury type in the partial tables. In other words, since all $\theta_{XY|Z_k}$ are equal to each other, we may combine them into one common value, denoted by $\theta_{XY|Z}$, that represents the one conditional association between outcome (fatal or not) and injury type (suicide or accident) that is common to all locations. Prior to computing a common odds ratio, it makes sense to calculate the odds ratios for each of the partial tables because a common odds ratio can be thought of as a weighted average of the odds ratios in each of the partial tables. For our firearm injury example, when the injury happened at the victim's home the odds of a firearm injury being fatal, if it was a result of suicide, were 4.35 times greater than if the injury was accidental:

$$\theta_{XY|Z_1} = \frac{45 \times 29}{15 \times 20} = 4.35.$$

When the injury happened at a friend or relative's home, the odds of a firearm injury being fatal, if it was a result of suicide, were 2.09 times greater than if the injury was accidental:

$$\theta_{XY|Z_2} = \frac{13 \times 27}{14 \times 12} = 2.09.$$

Finally, when the injury happened at someplace other than home or a friend or relative's home, the odds of a firearm injury being fatal if it was a result of suicide were 4.31 times greater than if the injury was accidental:

$$\theta_{XY|Z_3} = \frac{18 \times 29}{11 \times 11} = 4.31.$$

Since the results of the Breslow–Day test for homogeneous association indicated that these three odds ratios are not statistically significantly different from each other, they can thus be summarized by one value that is common to all three locations.

For a $2 \times 2 \times K$ table, a common odds ratio, known as the Mantel–Haenszel estimate, can be calculated using the following formula:

$$\hat{\theta}_{XY|Z} = \hat{\theta}_{MH} = \frac{\sum_k (n_{11k} n_{22k} / n_{++k})}{\sum_k (n_{12k} n_{21k} / n_{++k})}.$$

For example, the Mantel–Haenszel estimate of a common odds ratio for our firearm injury example is computed as follows:

$$\hat{\theta}_{MH} = \frac{\sum_k (n_{11k} n_{22k} / n_{++k})}{\sum_k (n_{12k} n_{21k} / n_{++k})} = \frac{45(29)/109 + 13(27)/66 + 18(29)/69}{20(15)/109 + 12(14)/66 + 11(11)/69} = 3.53.$$

Therefore, we can conclude that, on average, the odds of a firearm injury being fatal if it was a result of suicide were 3.53 times greater than if the injury was accidental for all three locations.

It is important to understand that the common odds ratio, $\theta_{XY|Z}$, is different from the marginal odds ratio, θ_{XY}, both conceptually and mathematically. The common (but still conditional) odds ratio, $\theta_{XY|Z}$, is a measure of the association between X and Y after controlling for Z, whereas the marginal odds ratio, θ_{XY}, is a measure of the association between X and Y that completely ignores the presence of the Z variable. In our example, θ_{XY} would indicate the overall association between fatal outcome and injury type that is computed from the marginal table for these two variables and does not involve the location variable at all. On the other hand, $\theta_{XY|Z}$ indicates the association that exists between fatal outcome and injury type once location is accounted or controlled for, and is computed by averaging the individual conditional associations. In other words, the partial tables are needed for the computation of $\theta_{XY|Z}$ but are not needed for the computation of θ_{XY} (which is computed directly from the marginal table). The appropriate measure to use depends on the research question; namely, whether one wishes to ignore the effects of Z or control for them. Neither of these measures is appropriate, however, in the absence of homogeneous association.

5.3.3   Cochran–Mantel–Haenszel test for conditional independence

The Cochran–Mantel–Haenszel (CMH) statistic tests the null hypothesis that the odds ratios in each of the partial tables are equal to one, which was mathematically presented in Equation 5.4 for a $2 \times 2 \times K$ table. It is assumed that the cell counts are independently sampled from either a Poisson, multinomial, or binomial distribution. Although there is a generalization of the CMH statistic that can be used for three-way tables of any size, the computations involved are very complex. Moreover, as previously stated, using a log-linear model fitting approach also allows a researcher to test the null hypothesis of conditional independence, making the generalization of the CMH statistic somewhat unnecessary. Therefore, to simplify our discussion, we only provide an illustration of how to calculate the CMH test statistic for the special case of $2 \times 2 \times K$ tables. Assuming that the null hypothesis is true, for a $2 \times 2 \times K$ table the mean and variance of the cell in the first row and first column of the kth partial table are

$$\mu_{11k} = E(n_{11k}) = \frac{n_{1+k}n_{+1k}}{n_{++k}}, \tag{5.5}$$

$$VAR(n_{11k}) = \frac{n_{1+k}n_{2+k}n_{+1k}n_{+2k}}{n_{++k}^2(n_{++k}-1)}. \tag{5.6}$$

Therefore, if the null hypothesis is true then the count in this cell of table k (n_{11k}) is expected to be equal to the mean of this cell of table k (μ_{11k}), and the difference between them is expected to be zero: $n_{11k} - \mu_{11k} = 0$. If the null hypothesis is not true, and the population partial odds ratio in table k ($\theta_{XY|Z_k}$) is greater than one, the difference between the observed count and expected mean of this cell of table k is expected to be greater than zero: $n_{11k} - \mu_{11k} > 0$. Similarly, if the null hypothesis is not true, and the population partial odds ratio in table k ($\theta_{XY|Z_k}$) is less than one, the difference between the observed count and the expected mean of this cell of table k is expected to be less than zero: $n_{11k} - \mu_{11k} < 0$. The CMH test statistic basically sums the differences $n_{11k} - \mu_{11k}$ across all K partial tables using the following formula:

$$CMH = \frac{[\Sigma_k(n_{11k} - \mu_{11k})]^2}{\Sigma_k VAR(n_{11k})}. \tag{5.7}$$

If the CMH statistic is large, it is indicative of large discrepancies between the observed frequencies and the frequencies expected under the null hypothesis, so a large CMH statistic provides evidence against the null hypothesis (of conditional independence). This statistic has a large-sample χ^2 distribution with one degree of freedom. Note that it is inappropriate to use this statistic when the directions of the associations vary dramatically across the k partial tables. This is due to the fact that when the associations are positive in some partial tables and negative in others the differences between the actual cell counts and the expected cell counts across the partial tables will cancel each other out in the numerator of the test statistic (Equation 5.7). Therefore, this statistic should only be used when the directions of large associations are similar across the partial tables, and this can be evaluated by computing and examining the direction of the partial associations before conducting this test.

To illustrate how the CMH statistic is computed, consider again the data about firearm injuries presented in Table 5.7. Each injury was classified as to the location of the injury, the type of injury incurred, and whether the injury was fatal. A test of conditional independence could be used to answer any of the following research questions:

1. Is there an association between where a firearm injury occurred and whether the injury was fatal, after controlling for the type of injury that was incurred?
2. Is there an association between where a firearm injury occurred and the type of injury that incurred after controlling for whether the injury was fatal?
3. Is there an association between the type of firearm injury incurred and whether the injury was fatal, after controlling for where the injury occurred?

To calculate the CMH test statistic we first need to calculate the expected cell counts for fatal injuries from a suicide at the three different locations (i.e., μ_{111}, μ_{112}, and μ_{113}). This can be accomplished using Equation 5.5, as follows:

$$\mu_{111} = E(n_{111}) = \frac{n_{1+1}n_{+11}}{n_{++1}} = \frac{65(60)}{109} = 35.78,$$

$$\mu_{112} = E(n_{112}) = \frac{n_{1+2}n_{+12}}{n_{++2}} = \frac{25(27)}{66} = 10.23,$$

$$\mu_{113} = E(n_{113}) = \frac{n_{1+3}n_{+13}}{n_{++3}} = \frac{29(29)}{69} = 12.19,$$

We then need to calculate the difference between the observed cell counts and the expected cell counts for fatal injuries from a suicide at the three different locations. This can be accomplished by subtraction, as follows:

$$n_{111} - \mu_{111} = 45 - 35.78 = 9.22,$$

$$n_{112} - \mu_{112} = 13 - 10.23 = 2.77, \text{ and}$$

$$n_{113} - \mu_{113} = 18 - 12.19 = 5.81.$$

Note that for each of the three partial tables, the difference between the observed and expected cell counts is positive, which indicates that the directions of the (three) partial associations are all the same and we are utilizing the CMH statistic appropriately. Note that this was also confirmed in the previous section, where the partial odds ratios were computed and were all found to be greater than one. Next, we need to calculate the variances for each of the cells pertaining to fatal injuries from a suicide at the three different locations. This can be accomplished using Equation 5.6, as follows:

$$VAR(n_{111}) = \frac{n_{1+1}n_{2+1}n_{+11}n_{+21}}{n_{++1}^2(n_{++1}-1)} = \frac{65(44)(60)(49)}{109^2(109-1)} = 6.55,$$

$$VAR(n_{112}) = \frac{n_{1+2}n_{2+2}n_{+12}n_{+22}}{n_{++2}^2(n_{++2}-1)} = \frac{25(41)(27)(39)}{66^2(66-1)} = 3.81, \text{ and}$$

$$VAR(n_{113}) = \frac{n_{1+3}n_{2+3}n_{+13}n_{+23}}{n_{++3}^2(n_{++3}-1)} = \frac{29(40)(29)(40)}{69^2(69-1)} = 4.16.$$

Finally, the CMH test statistic can be computed using Equation 5.7:

$$CMH = \frac{[\Sigma_k(n_{11k} - \mu_{11k})]^2}{\Sigma_k VAR(n_{11k})} = \frac{[9.22 + 2.77 + 5.81]^2}{6.55 + 3.81 + 4.16} = 21.82.$$

With 1 *df*, the *p*-value of this test statistic is $p < 0.0001$. Therefore, we can conclude that there is a conditional association in at least one of the three partial tables and that, after controlling for the location of the injury, there is a relationship between whether a firearm injury is fatal and the type of injury.

5.4 Computer output: test of association

To obtain computer output for tests of association and most of the results discussed in Section 5.1, syntax and output for SAS, as well as menu instructions and output for SPSS, are discussed in this section.

5.4.1 SAS

The SAS program to analyze the data of Table 5.1 is provided in Figure 5.4. Note that the primary difference between this program and the one provided in Chapter 4 (to analyze the associations in a two-way table) is that we now have an additional column in our data set representing the additional variable. In addition, the "tables" command of proc freq includes three variables:

- The first variable listed is considered the conditional (Z) variable.
- The second variable listed is the row (X) variable.
- The third variable listed is the column (Y) variable.

Thus, the output shown in Figure 5.5 depicts the partial tables controlling for gender. Note that two χ^2 statistics are provided in the output: one testing for independence in the partial

```
data political;
  input gender $ affiliat $ age $ count;
  cards;
  male liberal 18-29 27
  male liberal 30-39 44
  male liberal 40-49 37
  male liberal 50+ 49
  male moderate 18-29 49
  male moderate 30-39 54
  male moderate 40-49 48
  male moderate 50+ 64
  male conservative 18-29 44
  male conservative 30-39 58
  male conservative 40-49 49
  male conservative 50+ 101
  female liberal 18-29 59
  female liberal 30-39 56
  female liberal 40-49 51
  female liberal 50+ 63
  female moderate 18-29 54
  female moderate 30-39 76
  female moderate 40-49 64
  female moderate 50+ 118
  female conservative 18-29 44
  female conservative 30-39 55
  female conservative 40-49 46
  female conservative 50+ 133
  ;

proc freq order = data;
  weight count;
  tables gender*affiliat*age/nopercent nocol norow chisq;
run;
```

Figure 5.4 SAS program for tests of conditional association for three-way tables using the data from Table 5.1.

```
                          The FREQ Procedure

                      Table 1 of political by age
                      Controlling for gender=male

           political      age

           Frequency|18-29   |30-39   |40-49   |50+     |  Total
           ---------|--------|--------|--------|--------|
           liberal  |    27  |    44  |    37  |    49  |    157
           ---------|--------|--------|--------|--------|
           moderate |    49  |    54  |    48  |    64  |    215
           ---------|--------|--------|--------|--------|
           conserva |    44  |    58  |    49  |   101  |    252
           ---------|--------|--------|--------|--------|
           Total         120      156      134      214      624


                Statistics for Table 1 of political by age
                      Controlling for gender=male

           Statistic                     DF       Value      Prob
           ------------------------------------------------------------
           Chi-Square                     6      8.1935     0.2243
           Likelihood Ratio Chi-Square    6      8.0800     0.2323
           Mantel-Haenszel Chi-Square     1      1.9922     0.1581
           Phi Coefficient                       0.1146
           Contingency Coefficient               0.1138
           Cramer's V                            0.0810

                         Sample Size = 624


                      Table 2 of political by age
                      Controlling for gender=female

           political      age

           Frequency|18-29   |30-39   |40-49  |50+     |  Total
           ---------|--------|--------|-------|--------|
           liberal  |    59  |    56  |   51  |    63  |    229
           ---------|--------|--------|-------|--------|
           moderate |    54  |    76  |   64  |   118  |    312
           ---------|--------|--------|-------|--------|
           conserva |    44  |    55  |   46  |   133  |    278
           ---------|--------|--------|-------|--------|
           Total         157      187     161      314      819


                Statistics for Table 2 of political by age
                      Controlling for gender=female

           Statistic                     DF       Value      Prob
           ------------------------------------------------------------
           Chi-Square                     6     24.9458     0.0003
           Likelihood Ratio Chi-Square    6     24.9325     0.0004
           Mantel-Haenszel Chi-Square     1     18.8021     <.0001
           Phi Coefficient                       0.1745
           Contingency Coefficient               0.1719
           Cramer's V                            0.1234

                         Sample Size = 819
```

Figure 5.5 SAS output for tests of conditional association for three-way tables using the data from Table 5.1.

table for males and one testing for independence in the partial table for females. Also note that it is not possible to obtain the standardized residuals, depicted in Table 5.3, using SAS PROC FREQ. These were obtained using SPSS.

5.4.2 *SPSS*

The data of Table 5.1 are entered in SPSS as four variables: gender, political affiliation, age group, and frequency (cell count) as depicted in Figure 5.6. It should be noted that numeric values were used for each of the categories of each variable to simplify data entry. These values were then given labels (in SPSS Variable View) to simplify interpretation of the output. If raw data for all 1,443 individuals were available, then the counts would be computed by the program and would not be needed as input. To conduct the tests of association using SPSS menus (after weighting the cases by count):

- Select Crosstabs from the Descriptive Statistics option under the Analyze menu.
- The variable that is to be used to create the partial tables (in this example, gender) needs to be moved into the Layer 1 of 1 box, as depicted in Figure 5.7.
- Select the Chi-square test under the Statistics button and the Standardized residuals under the Cells button.

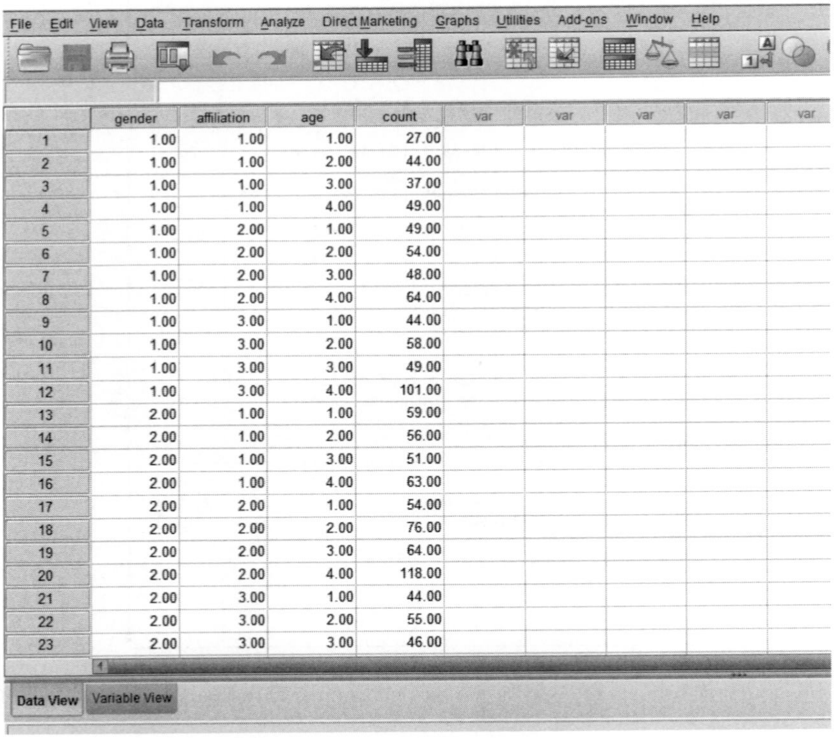

	gender	affiliation	age	count	var	var	var	var	var
1	1.00	1.00	1.00	27.00					
2	1.00	1.00	2.00	44.00					
3	1.00	1.00	3.00	37.00					
4	1.00	1.00	4.00	49.00					
5	1.00	2.00	1.00	49.00					
6	1.00	2.00	2.00	54.00					
7	1.00	2.00	3.00	48.00					
8	1.00	2.00	4.00	64.00					
9	1.00	3.00	1.00	44.00					
10	1.00	3.00	2.00	58.00					
11	1.00	3.00	3.00	49.00					
12	1.00	3.00	4.00	101.00					
13	2.00	1.00	1.00	59.00					
14	2.00	1.00	2.00	56.00					
15	2.00	1.00	3.00	51.00					
16	2.00	1.00	4.00	63.00					
17	2.00	2.00	1.00	54.00					
18	2.00	2.00	2.00	76.00					
19	2.00	2.00	3.00	64.00					
20	2.00	2.00	4.00	118.00					
21	2.00	3.00	1.00	44.00					
22	2.00	3.00	2.00	55.00					
23	2.00	3.00	3.00	46.00					

Figure 5.6 SPSS screenshot illustrating how to enter the data from Table 5.1.

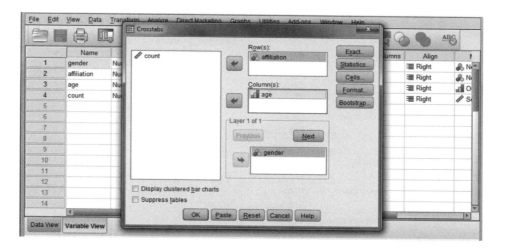

Figure 5.7 SPSS analysis window illustrating how to select variables when analyzing three-way contingency tables.

The output, depicted in Figure 5.8, contains

- the contingency table, including the observed frequencies and the standardized residuals; and
- the tests of independence, including the chi-squared and likelihood ratio tests for each of the partial tables.

5.5 Computer output: inferential tests for three-way tables

In this section we show how to obtain results from our second example, on the association between location, injury type, and whether it was fatal (see Table 5.9). Data are entered as was described in Section 5.4 for both programs, so these instructions are omitted here. In this section we discuss the commands to conduct the CMH test for conditional independence, to conduct the Breslow–Day test for homogeneous association, and to obtain the Mantel–Haenszel estimate of a common odds ratio.

5.5.1 SAS

The SAS program for obtaining the CMH test statistic, the Breslow–Day test statistic, and the Mantel–Haenszel estimate of a common odds ratio is presented in Figure 5.9.

- Note that the difference between this program and the program depicted in Figure 5.4 is the use of the command "cmh," rather than the "chisq" command, in the tables statement under proc freq.
- This command will invoke SAS to produce both of the inferential statistics described in Section 5.3. However, the Breslow–Day test statistic, as well as an estimate of a

gender					age				Total
					18–29	30–39	40–49	4.00	
male	affiliation	liberal	Count		27	44	37	49	157
			Std. Residual		−.6	.8	.6	−.7	
		moderate	Count		49	54	48	64	215
			Std. Residual		1.2	.0	.3	−1.1	
		conservative	Count		44	58	49	101	252
			Std. Residual		−.6	−.6	−.7	1.6	
	Total		Count		120	156	134	214	624
female	affiliation	liberal	Count		59	56	51	63	229
			Std. Residual		2.3	.5	.9	−2.6	
		moderate	Count		54	76	64	118	312
			Std. Residual		−.8	.6	.3	−.1	
		conservative	Count		44	55	46	133	278
			Std. Residual		−1.3	−1.1	−1.2	2.6	
	Total		Count		157	187	161	314	819

affiliation * age * gender Crosstabulation

Chi-Square Tests

gender		Value	df	Asymp. Sig. (2-sided)
male	Pearson Chi-Square	8.193[a]	6	.224
	Likelihood Ratio	8.080	6	.232
	Linear-by-Linear Association	1.992	1	.158
	N of Valid Cases	624		
female	Pearson Chi-Square	24.946[b]	6	.000
	Likelihood Ratio	24.932	6	.000
	Linear-by-Linear Association	18.802	1	.000
	N of Valid Cases	819		

a. 0 cells (.0%) have expected count less than 5. The minimum expected count is 30.19.

b. 0.cells (.0%) have expected count less than 5. The minimum expected count is 43.90.

Figure 5.8 SPSS output for tests of association for three-way tables using the data from Table 5.1.

common odds ratio, will only be present in the output if the three-way table that is being analyzed is a $2 \times 2 \times K$ table.

- The CMH test statistic will be provided in the output regardless of the size of the table, since there is a generalization of this test statistic for higher-way tables.
- The "relrisk" command was used to obtain the odds ratios for each of the partial tables.

```
data injury;
input location $ type $ fatal count;
datalines
  home suicide yes 45
  home accident yes 15
  friend/rel suicide yes 13
  friend/rel accident yes 14
  other suicide yes 18
  other accident yes 11
  home suicide no 20
  home accident no 29
  friend/rel suicide no 12
  friend/rel accident no 27
  other suicide no 11
  other accident no 29
;
proc freq order=data;
  weight count;
  tables location*type*fatal/ nopercent nocol norow cmh relrisk;
  run;
```

Figure 5.9 SAS program to conduct inferential tests for three-way tables using the data from Table 5.9.

Figure 5.10 illustrates the output that was obtained from running the SAS program in Figure 5.9. This output provides

- each of the partial tables, followed by the odds ratio for that partial table;
- the results of the CMH tests, including the test statistic (of 21.8), the degrees of free-dom (of 1), and the p-value (Prob < .0001);
- the estimate of the common odds ratio (of 3.53); and
- the results of the Breslow–Day test, including the test statistic (of 1.4), the degrees of freedom (of 2), and the p-value (Prob = 0.4891).

Again, note that the latter two statistics would not be provided if the three-way table ana-lyzed was not a $2 \times 2 \times K$-sized table.

5.5.2   SPSS

To obtain the CMH test statistic, the Breslow–Day test statistic, and the Mantel–Haenszel estimate of a common odds ratio using SPSS menus, simply open the Crosstabs Statistics window (from the Descriptive Statistics option under the Analyze menu), and select the Risk option and the Cochran's and Mantel–Haenszel statistics option, both located under the Statistics button as illustrated in Figure 5.11.

Figure 5.12 illustrates the output that was obtained from running this analysis in SPSS. Similar to the SAS output, this output includes

- each of the partial tables, followed by the odds ratio for each partial table;
- the results from statistical tests conducted to test for homogeneous association, including the Breslow–Day test statistic; and
- the results of tests conducted to test for conditional independence, including the esti-mate of the common odds ratio.

```
                      Table 1 of type by fatal
                     Controlling for location=home

              type       fatal

                 Frequency|yes     |no      |  Total
                 ---------|--------|--------|
                 suicide  |    45  |    20  |    65
                 ---------|--------|--------|
                 accident |    15  |    29  |    44
                 ---------|--------|--------|
                 Total         60       49      109


                 Statistics for Table 1 of type by fatal
                      Controlling for location=home

              Estimates of the Relative Risk (Row1/Row2)

     Type of Study                   Value      95% Confidence Limits
     ---------------------------------------------------------------
     Case-Control (Odds Ratio)      4.3500       1.9234      9.8381
     Cohort (Col1 Risk)             2.0308       1.3057      3.1584
     Cohort (Col2 Risk)             0.4668       0.3061      0.7120

                        Sample Size = 109


                      Table 2 of type by fatal
                     Controlling for location=friend/r

              type       fatal

                 Frequency|yes     |no      |  Total
                 ---------|--------|--------|
                 suicide  |    13  |    12  |    25
                 ---------|--------|--------|
                 accident |    14  |    27  |    41
                 ---------|--------|--------|
                 Total         27       39      66


                 Statistics for Table 2 of type by fatal
                     Controlling for location=friend/r

              Estimates of the Relative Risk (Row1/Row2)

     Type of Study                   Value      95% Confidence Limits
     ---------------------------------------------------------------
     Case-Control (Odds Ratio)      2.0893       0.7564      5.7709
     Cohort (Col1 Risk)             1.5229       0.8630      2.6872
     Cohort (Col2 Risk)             0.7289       0.4584      1.1589

                        Sample Size = 66


                      Table 3 of type by fatal
                     Controlling for location=other
              type       fatal

                 Frequency|yes     |no      |  Total
                 ---------|--------|--------|
                 suicide  |    18  |    11  |    29
                 ---------|--------|--------|
                 accident |    11  |    29  |    40
                 ---------|--------|--------|
```

Figure 5.10 SAS output from conducting inferential tests for three-way tables using the data from Table 5.9.

```
            Total        29       40       69
              Statistics for Table 3 of type by fatal
                  Controlling for location=other
            Estimates of the Relative Risk (Row1/Row2)

    Type of Study                 Value      95% Confidence Limits
    -------------------------------------------------------------
    Case-Control (Odds Ratio)     4.3140      1.5526      11.9867
    Cohort (Col1 Risk)            2.2571      1.2662       4.0233
    Cohort (Col2 Risk)            0.5232      0.3163       0.8653

                    Sample Size = 69

            Summary Statistics for type by fatal
                  Controlling for location

       Cochran-Mantel-Haenszel Statistics (Based on Table Scores)

        Statistic   Alternative Hypothesis    DF     Value     Prob
        ------------------------------------------------------------
            1        Nonzero Correlation        1    21.8301   <.0001
            2        Row Mean Scores Differ     1    21.8301   <.0001
            3        General Association        1    21.8301   <.0001

            Estimates of the Common Relative Risk (Row1/Row2)
    Type of Study      Method             Value     95% Confidence Limits
    ------------------------------------------------------------------
    Case-Control       Mantel-Haenszel    3.5250     2.0615      6.0274
      (Odds Ratio)     Logit              3.5276     2.0554      6.0541

    Cohort             Mantel-Haenszel    1.9435     1.4421      2.6192
      (Col1 Risk)      Logit              1.9291     1.4312      2.6002

    Cohort             Mantel-Haenszel    0.5516     0.4233      0.7188
      (Col2 Risk)      Logit              0.5575     0.4276      0.7268

                      Breslow-Day Test for
                 Homogeneity of the Odds Ratios
                 -----------------------------
                 Chi-Square              1.4302
                 DF                           2
                 Pr > ChiSq              0.4891

                 Total Sample Size = 24
```

Figure 5.10 (Continued)

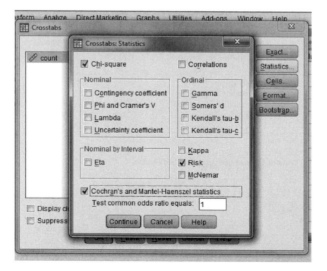

Figure 5.11 SPSS analysis window illustrating how to conduct inferential tests for three-way tables using the data from Table 5.9.

It should be noted that the test results for conditional independence that are obtained from SPSS differ somewhat from the results obtained from SAS. This is because SAS computes the Cochran–Mantel–Haenszel statistic to test for conditional association, whereas SPSS computes both the Cochran statistic (test statistic = 22.1, $df = 1$, $p < .0001$) and the Mantel–Haenszel statistic (test statistic = 20.6, $df = 1$, $p < .0001$) for this test. The results from these three tests differ slightly, as indicated in the output, but only in rare cases will the conclusions drawn on the basis of these tests differ.

type * fatal * location Crosstabulation

Count

location			fatal		
			yes	no	Total
home	type	suicide	45	20	65
		accident	15	29	44
	Total		60	49	109
friend/relative	type	suicide	13	12	25
		accident	14	27	41
	Total		27	39	66
other	type	suicide	18	11	29
		accident	11	29	40
	Total		29	40	69

Risk Estimate

location		Value	95% Confidence Interval	
			Lower	Upper
home	Odds Ratio for type (suicide / accident)	4.350	1.923	9.838
	For cohort fatal = yes	2.031	1.306	3.158
	For cohort fatal = no	.467	.306	.712
	N of Valid Cases	109		
friend/relative	Odds Ratio for type (suicide / accident)	2.089	.756	5.771
	For cohort fatal = yes	1.523	.863	2.687
	For cohort fatal = no	.729	.458	1.159
	N of Valid Cases	66		
other	Odds Ratio for type (suicide / accident)	4.314	1.553	11.987
	For cohort fatal = yes	2.257	1.266	4.023
	For cohort fatal = no	.523	.316	.865
	N of Valid Cases	69		

Tests of Homogeneity of the Odds Ratio

	Chi-Squared	df	Asymp. Sig (2-sided)
Breslow-Day	1.430	2	.489
Tarone's	1.430	2	.489

Figure 5.12 SPSS output from conducting inferential tests for three-way tables using the data from Table 5.9.

Tests of Conditional Independence

	Chi-Squared	df	Asymp. Sig (2-sided)
Cochran's	22.101	1	.000
Mantel-Haenszel	20.621	1	.000

Under the conditional independence assumption, Cochran's statistic is asymptotically distributed as a 1 df chi-squared distribution, only if the number of strata is. fixed, while the Mantel-Haenszel statistic is always asymptotically distributed as a 1 df chi-squared distribution. Note that the continuity correction is removed from the Mantel-Haenszel statistic when the sum of the differences between the observed and the expected is 0.

Mantel-Haenszel Common Odds Ratio Estimate

Estimate			3.525
ln(Estimate)			1.260
Std. Error of ln(Estimate)			.274
Asymp. Sig. (2-sided)			.000
Asymp. 95% Confidence Interval	Common Odds Ratio	Lower Bound	2.061
		Upper Bound	6.027
	ln(Common Odds Ratio)	Lower Bound	.723
		Upper Bound	1.796

The Mantel-Haenszel common odds ratio estimate is asymptotically normally distributed under the common odds ratio of 1.000 assumption. So is the natural log of the estimate.

Figure 5.12 (Continued)

5.6   Complete example

In this section we will demonstrate the analysis of a data set concerning University of California, Berkeley graduate admissions from the fall of 1973 (Freedman, Pisani, Purves, & Adhikari, 1991). The primary variables of interest involved the applicant's sex and admission to graduate school, and the data from six departments were used to investigate whether there was sex discrimination in admissions. The data are presented in Table 5.10 and the SAS syntax is shown in Figure 5.13. The first tables statement in the syntax provides the marginal table, which is shown in Figure 5.14, and the second tables statement provides the partial tables and conditional associations, shown in Figure 5.15, as well as the inferential tests involving conditional associations, shown in Figure 5.16.

If we wish to ignore the department variable, and analyze the aggregate data across departments, we would use the output in Figure 5.14 to conclude that the marginal association is significant and indicates that the odds of admission for females are significantly lower than the odds of admission for males (with a 95% confidence interval of [0.4792, 0.6156] for the marginal odds ratio). However, if the associations are examined by department, the Breslow–Day test indicates that there is a significant three-way association between gender, admission, and department ($\chi^2 = 18.8$, $df = 5$, $p = 0.002$). In fact, the conditional odds ratios range from a high of 2.86 (for Department A) to a low of 0.81 (for Department E). In addition, the only conditional odds ratio that is significant (i.e., corresponds to a confidence interval that excludes the value of 1) is that for Department A, and in Department A the odds of admission for females are significantly higher than the odds of admission

Table 5.10 Data on University of California, Berkeley Graduate Admissions (1973)

	Gender		Admitted		Odds ratio	95% CI for odds ratio
Overall		Yes	No	Total	0.54	[0.48, 0.62]
	Female	557	1278	1835		
	Male	1198	1493	2691		
	Total	1755	2771	4526		
By Department						
		Yes	No	Total	2.86	[1.71, 4.79]
A	Female	89	19	108		
	Male	512	313	825		
	Total	601	332	933		
B		Yes	No	Total	1.25	[0.53, 2.94]
	Female	17	8	25		
	Male	353	207	560		
	Total	370	215	585		
C		Yes	No	Total	0.88	[0.67, 1.17]
	Female	202	391	593		
	Male	120	205	325		
	Total	322	596	918		
D		Yes	No	Total	1.09	[0.81, 1.46]
	Female	131	244	375		
	Male	138	279	417		
	Total	269	523	792		
E		Yes	No	Total	0.81	[0.55, 1.21]
	Female	94	299	393		
	Male	53	138	191		
	Total	147	437	584		
F		Yes	No	Total	1.21	[0.66, 2.20]
	Female	24	317	341		
	Male	22	351	373		
	Total	46	668	714		

```
data admissions;
 input gender $ admitted $ count dept $;
 datalines;
 Female Yes 89 A
 Female No 19 A
 Male Yes 512 A
 Male No 313 A
 Female Yes 17 B
 Female No 8 B
 Male Yes 353 B
 Male No 207 B
 .
 .
 .
 Female Yes 24 F
 Female No 317 F
 Male Yes 22 F
 Male No 351 F
 ;
proc freq data=admissions order=data;
 weight count;
 tables gender*admitted /nocol norow nopercent relrisk;
 tables dept*gender*admitted /nocol norow nopercent relrisk cmh;
run;
```

Figure 5.13 SAS syntax for the UC Berkeley graduate admissions data.

for males. Therefore, we must conclude that if there is sex discrimination in admissions it occurs in only one department and appears to favor females.

Because Department A seems to present somewhat of an anomaly in the data set, we may wish to analyze the data without it. This would be a reasonable approach if there was sufficient theoretical justification for doing so; for example, we might determine that

```
                    The FREQ Procedure

               Table of gender by admitted

          gender      admitted

          Frequency|Yes     |No      |  Total
          ---------|--------|--------|
          Female   |   557  |  1278  |   1835
          ---------|--------|--------|
          Male     |  1198  |  1493  |   2691
          ---------|--------|------- |
          Total        1755     2771     4526


       Statistics for Table of gender by admitted

       Estimates of the Relative Risk (Row1/Row2)

   Type of Study              Value     95% Confidence Limits
   ----------------------------------------------------------
   Case-Control (Odds Ratio)   0.5432      0.4792      0.6156
   Cohort (Col1 Risk)          0.6818      0.6287      0.7395
   Cohort (Col2 Risk)          1.2553      1.1996      1.3136

                 Sample Size = 4526
```

Figure 5.14 Marginal table from SAS results for the UC Berkeley graduate admissions data.

```
                         The FREQ Procedure

                    Table 1 of gender by admitted
                       Controlling for dept=A

               gender      admitted

                 Frequency|Yes      |No       |  Total
                 ---------|---------|---------|
                 Female   |    89   |    19   |   108
                 ---------|---------|---------|
                 Male     |   512   |   313   |   825
                 ---------|---------|---------|
                 Total         601       332      933


              Statistics for Table 1 of gender by admitted
                       Controlling for dept=A

             Estimates of the Relative Risk (Row1/Row2)

Type of Study                        Value        95% Confidence Limits
-----------------------------------------------------------------------
Case-Control (Odds Ratio)           2.8636         1.7112        4.7921
Cohort (Col1 Risk)                  1.3279         1.1989        1.4707
Cohort (Col2 Risk)                  0.4637         0.3055        0.7039

                         Sample Size = 933


                    Table 2 of gender by admitted
                       Controlling for dept=B

               gender      admitted

                 Frequency|Yes      |No       |  Total
                 ---------|---------|---------|
                 Female   |    17   |     8   |    25
                 ---------|---------|---------|
                 Male     |   353   |   207   |   560
                 ---------|---------|---------|
                 Total         370       215      585


              Statistics for Table 2 of gender by admitted
                       Controlling for dept=B

             Estimates of the Relative Risk (Row1/Row2)

Type of Study                        Value        95% Confidence Limits
-----------------------------------------------------------------------
Case-Control (Odds Ratio)           1.2461         0.5285        2.9379
Cohort (Col1 Risk)                  1.0788         0.8183        1.4220
Cohort (Col2 Risk)                  0.8657         0.4839        1.5486

                         Sample Size = 585
```

Figure 5.15 Conditional tables from SAS output for the UC Berkeley graduate admissions data.

```
                    Table 3 of gender by admitted
                       Controlling for dept=C

              gender      admitted

              Frequency|Yes      |No      |  Total
              ---------|--------|--------|
              Female   |   202  |   391  |    593
              ---------|--------|--------|

              Male     |   120  |   205  |    325
              ---------|---------|---------|
              Total        322       596       918


              Statistics for Table 3 of gender by admitted
                       Controlling for dept=C

              Estimates of the Relative Risk (Row1/Row2)

Type of Study                    Value        95% Confidence Limits
--------------------------------------------------------------------
Case-Control (Odds Ratio)       0.8826         0.6656          1.1702
Cohort (Col1 Risk)              0.9226         0.7699          1.1055
Cohort (Col2 Risk)              1.0453         0.9446          1.1568

                     Sample Size = 918

                    Table 4 of gender by admitted
                       Controlling for dept=D

              gender      admitted

              Frequency|Yes      |No      |  Total
              ---------|--------|--------|
              Female   |   131  |   244  |    375
              ---------|--------|--------|
              Male     |   138  |   279  |    417
              ---------|--------|--------|
              Total        269       523       792

              Statistics for Table 4 of gender by admitted
                       Controlling for dept=D
              Estimates of the Relative Risk (Row1/Row2)


Type of Study                    Value        95% Confidence Limits
--------------------------------------------------------------------
Case-Control (Odds Ratio)       1.0854         0.8086          1.4570
Cohort (Col1 Risk)              1.0556         0.8693          1.2818
Cohort (Col2 Risk)              0.9725         0.8797          1.0751

                     Sample Size = 792
```

Figure 5.15 (Continued)

```
                 Table 5 of gender by admitted
                     Controlling for dept=E

            gender      admitted

            Frequency|Yes      |No       | Total
            ---------|--------|--------|
            Female   |     94 |    299 |   393
            ---------|--------|--------|
            Male     |     53 |    138 |   191
            ---------|--------|--------|
            Total         147      437      584

          Statistics for Table 5 of gender by admitted
                     Controlling for dept=E

          Estimates of the Relative Risk (Row1/Row2)

Type of Study                        Value        95% Confidence Limits
------------------------------------------------- --------------------
Case-Control (Odds Ratio)           0.8186         0.5529       1.2120
Cohort (Col1 Risk)                  0.8620         0.6457       1.1507
Cohort (Col2 Risk)                  1.0530         0.9491       1.1683

                     Sample Size = 584


                 Table 6 of gender by admitted
                     Controlling for dept=F

            gender      admitted

            Frequency|Yes      |No       | Total
            ---------|--------|--------|
            Female   |     24 |    317 |   341
            ---------|--------|--------|
            Male     |     22 |    351 |   373
            ---------|--------|--------|
            Total          46      668      714


          Statistics for Table 6 of gender by admitted
                     Controlling for dept=F

          Estimates of the Relative Risk (Row1/Row2)

Type of Study                        Value        95% Confidence Limits
------------------------------------------------- --------------------
Case-Control (Odds Ratio)           1.2079         0.6642       2.1968
Cohort (Col1 Risk)                  1.1933         0.6819       2.0881
Cohort (Col2 Risk)                  0.9879         0.9504       1.0269

                     Sample Size = 714
```

Figure 5.15 (Continued)

```
                        The FREQ Procedure

                Summary Statistics for gender by admitted
                         Controlling for dept

          Cochran-Mantel-Haenszel Statistics (Based on Table Scores)

          Statistic   Alternative Hypothesis    DF     Value      Prob
          --------------------------------------------------------------
              1        Nonzero Correlation        1     1.5246    0.2169
              2        Row Mean Scores Differ     1     1.5246    0.2169
              3        General Association        1     1.5246    0.2169


                Estimates of the Common Relative Risk (Row1/Row2)

          Type of Study    Method          Value    95% Confidence Limits
          --------------------------------------------------------------
          Case-Control     Mantel-Haenszel  1.1053     0.9431     1.2955
            (Odds Ratio)   Logit            1.0774     0.9171     1.2658

          Cohort           Mantel-Haenszel  1.0583     0.9704     1.1541
            (Col1 Risk)    Logit            1.1538     1.0712     1.2428

          Cohort           Mantel-Haenszel  0.9731     0.9307     1.0174
            (Col2 Risk)    Logit            0.9931     0.9617     1.0256


                         Breslow-Day Test for
                     Homogeneity of the Odds Ratios
                     -----------------------------
                     Chi-Square           18.8255
                     DF                         5
                     Pr > ChiSq            0.0021


                     Total Sample Size = 4526
```

Figure 5.16 Inferential results from SAS for the UC Berkeley graduate admissions data.

Department A is not representative of the campus as a whole or that the data obtained from it were inaccurate in some way. Supposing that there is justification for removing Department A from the analysis, the marginal table and the results of the inferential tests conducted on data from Departments B to F are provided in Figure 5.17 and Figure 5.18, respectively.

Without Department A, there is still a significant marginal association between sex and admission such that the odds of admission for females are significantly lower than the odds of admission for males (with a 95% confidence interval of [0.5549, 0.7368]). Conditional on department, the Breslow–Day test indicates that there is no significant three-way association ($\chi^2 = 2.56$, $df = 4$, $p = 0.634$) so the conditional association between gender and admission is the same for all departments (B through F). In fact, the conditional odds ratios for these departments (refer to Figure 5.15 or Table 5.8) range from a high of 1.25 (for Department B) to a low of 0.81 (for Department E), and the Mantel–Haenszel estimate of the common odds ratio is 0.97 (see Figure 5.18). Although the conditional odds ratios are not all larger or all smaller than one, they do not vary substantially from one in opposite directions and so the CMH test is appropriate. The CMH test statistic is not significant (CMH = 0.125, $df = 1$, $p = 0.724$), indicating conditional independence. This can

```
                    The FREQ Procedure

              Table of gender by admitted

          gender      admitted

            Frequency|Yes      |No      |  Total
            ---------|--------|--------|
            Female   |   468  |  1259  |   1727
            ---------|--------|--------|
            Male     |   686  |  1180  |   1866
            ---------|--------|--------|
            Total        1154     2439     3593


          Statistics for Table of gender by admitted

          Estimates of the Relative Risk (Row1/Row2)

  Type of Study                 Value      95% Confidence Limits
  ----------------------------------------------------------
  Case-Control (Odds Ratio)    0.6394      0.5549      0.7368
  Cohort (Col1 Risk)           0.7371      0.6686      0.8127
  Cohort (Col2 Risk)           1.1528      1.1021      1.2059

                Sample Size = 3593
```

Figure 5.17 Marginal table results from SAS for the UC Berkeley graduate admissions data without Department A.

```
                    The FREQ Procedure

            Summary Statistics for gender by admitted
                      Controlling for dept

        Cochran-Mantel-Haenszel Statistics (Based on Table Scores)

    Statistic    Alternative Hypothesis    DF    Value    Prob
    ----------------------------------------------------------
        1        Nonzero Correlation        1    0.1250   0.7237
        2        Row Mean Scores Differ     1    0.1250   0.7237
        3        General Association        1    0.1250   0.7237


        Estimates of the Common Relative Risk (Row1/Row2)

  Type of Study    Method          Value    95% Confidence Limits
  --------------------------------------------------------------
  Case-Control     Mantel-Haenszel  0.9699    0.8185     1.1493
   (Odds Ratio)    Logit            0.9689    0.8178     1.1481

  Cohort           Mantel-Haenszel  0.9800    0.8771     1.0951
   (Col1 Risk)     Logit            0.9855    0.8844     1.0981

  Cohort           Mantel-Haenszel  1.0076    0.9656     1.0515
   (Col2 Risk)     Logit            0.9977    0.9660     1.0304


              Breslow-Day Test for
          Homogeneity of the Odds Ratios
          ------------------------------
          Chi-Square              2.5582
          DF                           4
          Pr > ChiSq             0.6342
```

Figure 5.18 Inferential results from SAS for the UC Berkeley graduate admissions data without Department A.

also be verified by examining the individual confidence intervals for the conditional odds ratios (which all contain the value of 1). Therefore, we can conclude that (for Department B through F) there is no association between sex and admission conditional on department. In other words, without Department A there is conditional independence between sex and admission when examined by department. Therefore, although it may appear that overall there is some bias against females in admissions, there is in fact no gender bias in admission to the individual departments.

5.7   Summary

This chapter focused on investigating the association between three categorical variables. The concepts of marginal association or independence, conditional association or independence, and homogeneous association were introduced. Inferential procedures for testing which types of association are supported by the data were discussed.

The concepts discussed in this chapter provide a framework by which to evaluate the types of association that may exist among three categorical variables. Although this chapter builds on and extends some of the concepts discussed in the previous chapter, some of the methods discussed in this chapter are limited (e.g., in the number of categories the variables can have). Thus, the next chapter introduces a general modeling framework that allows for the investigation of associations between any number of variables with any number of categories.

Problems

5.1   Table 5.11 contains data obtained from the 2006 administration of the General Social Survey (GSS). Analyze the data and summarize the results. Include a discussion of any associations that exist. Specifically, discuss whether there appears to be a marginal association or a homogeneous association, and whether the data reflect a three-way interaction or only a two-way interaction. Is there conditional dependence present in the data? Is the data conditionally independent? Justify your response with the appropriate statistical tests, as well as the appropriate odds ratios. Be sure to include a substantive interpretation of any associations between the variables.

Table 5.11 Data for Problem 5.1 on Gender and Types of Employment From the 2006 General Social Survey (GSS)

		Work for someone else	Self-employed
Males	Work full-time	1051	199
	Work part-time	108	38
Females	Work full-time	978	87
	Work part-time	238	60

5.2   Answer the following questions using the data in Table 5.12, obtained from the 2006 administration of the GSS:
   a.   What is the marginal association between gender and belief in the afterlife? Interpret the value of the appropriate marginal odds ratio.
   b.   What are the conditional associations (odds ratios) between gender and belief in the afterlife (by religious beliefs group)?
   c.   Is there evidence that the conditional association between gender and belief in the afterlife depends on religious beliefs? Report the appropriate test statistic to support your answer.
   d.   Is there evidence for homogeneous association between gender and belief in the afterlife (conditional on religious beliefs)? Report the appropriate test statistic to support your answer.
   e.   Is there evidence for conditional independence between gender and belief in the afterlife (conditional on religious beliefs)? Report the appropriate test statistic to support your answer.
   f.   Write a brief (sentence or two) summary describing the nature of the associations present in this data set (including a substantive interpretation) based on your answers to parts (a)–(e).

Table 5.12 Data for Problem 5.2 on Gender and Types of Beliefs From the 2006 GSS

	Religious beliefs	Yes, believe in afterlife	No, do not believe in afterlife
Males	Fundamentalist	252	43
	Moderate	274	47
	Liberal	226	100
Females	Fundamentalist	420	50
	Moderate	415	50
	Liberal	273	83

5.3   Table 5.13 contains data obtained from the 2003 administration of the GSS. Analyze these data and summarize the results. Include a discussion of any associations that exist. Specifically, discuss whether there appears to be a marginal association or a homogeneous association, and whether the data reflect a three-way interaction or only

Table 5.13 Data for Problem 5.3 on Race, Gender, and Attitude Toward Discipline From the 2006 GSS

		Favor spanking to discipline a child?			
Race	Gender	Strongly agree	Agree	Disagree	Strongly disagree
Caucasians	Males	86	204	81	18
	Females	92	222	97	40
African-Americans	Males	12	19	3	3
	Females	27	32	6	1

a two-way interaction. Is there conditional dependence present in the data? Is the data conditionally independent? Justify your response with the appropriate statistical tests as well as the appropriate odds ratios. Be sure to include a substantive interpretation of any associations between the variables.

5.4 Answer the following questions using the data in Table 5.14, obtained from the 1993 administration of the GSS:

a. What is the marginal association between gender and attitude toward life? Interpret the value of the appropriate marginal odds ratio.

b. What is the marginal association between educational level and attitude toward life? Interpret the value of the appropriate marginal odds ratio.

c. What are the conditional associations between gender and attitude toward life (by educational level)?

d. What are the conditional associations between educational level and attitude toward life (by gender)?

e. Is there evidence that the conditional association between gender and attitude toward life depends on educational level? Report the appropriate test statistic to support your answer.

f. Is there evidence for homogeneous association between gender and attitude toward life (conditional on educational level)? Report the appropriate test statistic to support your answer.

g. Is there evidence for conditional independence between gender and attitude toward life (conditional on educational level)? Report the appropriate test statistic to support your answer.

h. Write a brief (sentence or two) summary describing the nature of the associations present in this data set (including a substantive interpretation) based on your answers to parts (c)–(g).

Table 5.14 Data for Problem 5.4 on Gender, Education, and Attitude Toward Life From the 1993 GSS

| Gender | Education | Think life is exciting or dull? | |
		Dull or routine	Exciting
Males	No college degree	178	130
	College degree	38	70
Females	No college degree	245	182
	College degree	37	69

5.5 Use the data in Table 5.15, obtained from the 1993 administration of the GSS. Analyze these data and summarize the results. Include a discussion of any associations that exist. Specifically, discuss whether there appears to be a marginal association or a homogeneous association, and whether the data reflect a three-way interaction or only a two-way interaction. Is there conditional dependence present in the data? Is the data conditionally independent? Justify your response with the appropriate statistical tests, as well as the appropriate odds ratios. Be sure to include a substantive interpretation of any associations between the variables.

Table 5.15 Data for Problem 5.5 on Political View, Age, and Attitude on Birth Control
From the 1993 GSS

Political view	Age category	Birth control should be given to teens (14–16 years)			
		Strongly agree	Agree	Disagree	Strongly disagree
Liberal Political View	18–29	31	22	5	4
	30–39	22	30	10	6
	40–49	17	16	12	5
	50+	20	19	21	7
Moderate Political View	18–29	31	22	19	10
	30–39	35	32	11	10
	40–49	17	23	22	9
	50+	24	33	29	30
Conservative Political View	18–29	17	9	17	9
	30–39	13	23	14	18
	40–49	10	26	15	12
	50+	25	35	47	53

5.6   Use the data in Table 5.16, obtained from the 2003 Programme for International Student Assessment (PISA) study. Come up with three specific research questions that can be answered using this data set. For each question, report the appropriate statistical tests and provide a substantive interpretation of the results that includes the appropriate odds ratios.

Table 5.16 Data for Problem 5.6 on Country, Gender, and Attitude Toward School From the 2003 PISA

Country	Gender	To what extent do you agree that school has been a waste of time?			
		Strongly agree	Agree	Disagree	Strongly disagree
United States	Females	38	125	1227	1253
	Males	102	249	1369	922
Korea	Females	26	199	1415	578
	Males	58	281	1942	897

5.7   Use the data in Table 5.17, obtained from the 2003 PISA study. Analyze these data and summarize the results. Include a discussion of any associations that exist. Specifically, discuss whether there appears to be a marginal association or a homogeneous association, and whether the data reflect a three-way interaction or only a two-way interaction. Is there conditional dependence present in the data? Is the data conditionally independent? Justify your response with the appropriate statistical tests, as well as the appropriate odds ratios. Be sure to include a substantive interpretation of any associations between the variables.

Table 5.17 Data for Problem 5.7 on Country, Owning a Computer, and Attitude Toward Learning Mathematics From the 2003 PISA

| Country | Computer ownership | To what extent do you agree that learning mathematics is worthwhile because it will improve your career prospects? | | | |
		Strongly agree	Agree	Disagree	Strongly disagree
United States	Own a computer	1230	2662	551	236
	Do not own a computer	159	373	95	41
Japan	Own a computer	204	776	803	361
	Do not own a computer	180	826	976	514

5.8 Answer the following questions using the data in Table 5.18, obtained from the 2003 PISA study:

a. Is there evidence that the association between self-efficacy in math and perception of teaching methods depends on country? Report the appropriate test statistic to support your answer.

b. Is there evidence for homogeneous association between self-efficacy in math and perception of teaching methods conditional on country? Report the appropriate test statistic to support your answer.

Table 5.18 Data for Problem 5.8 on Country and Attitudes About Mathematics From the 2003 PISA

| Country | I am just not good at math | In math class the teacher continues teaching until the students understand | | | |
		Every lesson	Most lessons	Some lessons	Never or hardly ever
United States	Strongly Agree	206	174	188	111
	Agree	366	390	321	115
	Disagree	873	870	439	131
	Strongly Disagree	500	319	176	51
Australia	Strongly Agree	299	347	326	193
	Agree	744	1074	749	241
	Disagree	2128	2585	1246	353
	Strongly Disagree	874	600	283	93
France	Strongly Agree	170	197	199	140
	Agree	237	299	238	122
	Disagree	516	623	433	185
	Strongly Disagree	283	226	175	66

c. Is there evidence for conditional independence between self-efficacy in math and perception of teaching methods (conditional on country)? Report the appropriate test statistic to support your answer.

d. Write a brief (sentence or two) summary describing the nature of the associations present in this data set (including a substantive interpretation) based on your answers to parts (a)–(c).

5.9   Use the data in Table 5.19, obtained from the 2003 PISA study. Five observations were added to each cell because of sparse data and only the results from China and the United States are presented. Come up with three specific research questions that can be answered using this data set. For each question, report the appropriate statistical tests and provide a substantive interpretation of the results.

Table 5.19 Data for Problem 5.9 on Country, Absenteeism, and Attitude Toward Teachers From the 2003 PISA

Country	In your school to what extent is student learning hindered by student absenteeism?	In your school to what extent is student learning hindered by students lacking respect for teachers?			
		Not at all	Very little	To some extent	A lot
China	Not at all	38	20	5	5
	Very little	18	35	15	8
	To some extent	7	14	15	6
	A lot	5	7	9	16
United States	Not at all	11	9	5	5
	Very little	17	54	9	5
	To some extent	15	80	30	5
	A lot	6	27	20	9

5.10 Using a substantive example, explain the difference between marginal and conditional associations.

5.11 Using a substantive example, explain the difference between homogeneous association and conditional independence.

5.12 Think of three categorical variables that theoretically should display homogeneous association and explain why you believe that to be the case.

5.13 Think of three categorical variables that theoretically should display conditional independence and explain why you believe that to be the case.

5.14 In a three-way contingency table, when any pair of the variables is conditionally independent is it necessary for the data to show homogeneous association? Explain your answer.

5.15 In a three-way contingency table, if there is no homogeneous association is it possible for any pair of the variables to be conditionally independent? Explain your answer.

chapter six

Modeling and the generalized linear model

A LOOK AHEAD

Chapters 4 and 5 discussed the analysis of several categorical variables and, specifically, methods by which the association between two or three categorical variables can be investigated. In this chapter, a more extensive framework for understanding the associations between categorical variables is described by introducing a class of prediction models called **generalized linear models**. This is analogous to the progression in the analysis of continuous variables, where we typically begin by learning how to describe relationships in terms of correlation coefficients and then extend these ideas to regression models, which allow for further investigation in terms of rates of change, model fit, and prediction of an outcome variable. In fact, the familiar linear regression model belongs to a class of models called general linear models, and these models are special cases of an even larger class of models, generalized linear models, which are the subject of this chapter. We will use the acronym **GLM** to refer to the generalized linear model.

Some of the advantages of using a model to understand the relationship between predictor variables (Xs) and an outcome variable (Y) are that a model allows us to gain insight about:

- Function: The structure of the association between the variables (e.g., linear or some other function).
- Parameters: How a change in a predictor variable, X, is expected to affect an outcome variable, Y.
- Partial parameters: How a change in one of the predictor variables affects the outcome variable while controlling for the effects of other predictor variables included in the model.
- Smooth prediction: What the expected (or predicted) value of the outcome variable might be for any given values of the predictor variables.

We will begin this chapter by discussing the components of a generalized linear model (GLM) followed by a general introduction to model estimation, fitting, and testing.

6.1 Components of a GLM

The GLM consists of three components: a random component, a systematic component, and a link function. The **random component** refers to the distribution of the outcome variable (*Y*), the **systematic component** refers to the predictor variables (*Xs*), and the **link function** refers to the way in which the outcome variable (or, more specifically, its expected value) is transformed so that a linear relationship can be used to model the association between the predictors (*Xs*) and the transformed outcome. These components are described in detail next.

6.1.1 The random component

The random component of a GLM is the probability distribution that is assumed to underlie the dependent or outcome variable. Recall from Chapter 2 that when we have continuous dependent or outcome variables we typically make the assumption that the values obtained for these variables are random observations that come from (or follow) a normal distribution. In other words, when the outcome or response variable is continuous, such as in simple linear regression or analysis of variance (ANOVA), we typically assume that the normal distribution is the random component or underlying probability distribution for the outcome variable.

However, when the dependent or outcome variable is categorical it can no longer be assumed that its values in the population are normally distributed. In fact, in a GLM the random component can be any known probability distribution and, as discussed in Chapter 2, with categorical outcome variables we typically assume that the random component underlying the outcome or response variable is a distribution such as the Poisson or binomial distribution. For example, if the outcome variable is whether a student passed (rather than failed) a test, we would assume that the underlying probability distribution of the outcome is the binomial distribution, not the normal distribution. As another example, if the outcome variable is the number of planes that land at a particular airport in an hour, we would assume that the underlying probability distribution is the Poisson distribution, not the normal distribution. The random component of a GLM thus allows us to model outcome variables (*Ys*) that are not necessarily normally distributed. In addition, as was shown in Chapter 2, the random component or distribution underlying the outcome variable (*Y*) is instrumental in computing its expected value (or mean),

$$E(Y) = \mu.$$

6.1.2 The systematic component

The systematic component of a GLM consists of the independent, predictor, or explanatory variables (*Xs*) that a researcher hypothesizes will predict (or explain) differences in the dependent or outcome variables. The predictors are considered to be the systematic component of the model because they systematically explain differences in the outcome variable and are treated as fixed, rather than random, variables. These variables may be subject to experimental control, or systematic manipulation, although this is not a necessary condition for the systematic component. These variables are combined to form the **linear predictor**, which is simply a linear combination of the predictors or the "right-hand side" of the model equation. In regression and ANOVA, as well as other GLMs, with a total of p predictors, $X_1, X_2, \ldots, X_p$, this linear combination is written as

$$\alpha + \beta_1 X_1 + \beta_2 X_2 + \cdots + \beta_p X_p,$$

where the coefficients of the model (α and βs) are estimated based on the observed data. The systematic component of a GLM thus specifies the way in which the explanatory variables or predictors are expected to linearly influence the predicted or expected value of the outcome, $E(Y)$. It should be noted that each of the predictors may be a combination of other predictors. For example, an interaction term can be represented by a predictor that is the product of two variables, such as $X_4 = X_1 X_3$, or a nonlinear trend can be represented by a predictor that is a function of a variable, such as using $X_2 = X_1^2$ to represent a quadratic trend by squaring a variable. The key is that the predictors are represented as a linear combination in the GLM, which is, after all, a generalized **linear** model.

6.1.3   The link function

The key to GLMs is to "link" the random and systematic components of the model with some mathematical function, call it $g(.)$, such that this function of the expected value of the outcome can be properly modeled using the systematic component:

$$g(E(Y)) = \alpha + \beta_1 X_1 + \beta_2 X_2 + \cdots + \beta_p X_p.$$

The link function is the mathematical function that is used to transform the dependent or outcome variable so that it can be modeled as a linear function of the predictors. In other words, the link function allows us to relate the systematic component (consisting of a linear predictor) to the random component (which is based on the probability distribution of the outcome variable) in a linear manner. More specifically, the predicted or expected value of the outcome is transformed by the link function to produce a transformed variable that is linearly related to the predictors.

For example, suppose that we would like to use family income (in thousands) as a predictor of a standardized test score (such as the ACT score). Figure 6.1 provides an illustration of a possible relationship between these variables. In this case, if the relationship depicted in Figure 6.1 provides a good representation of the actual relationship between

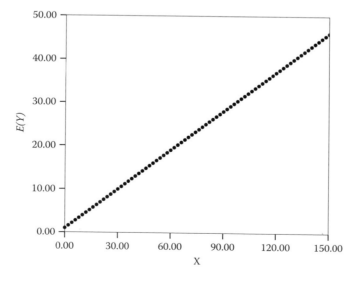

Figure 6.1 Example of a linear relationship between X and $E(Y)$.

these variables, the predicted outcome (ACT score) or the expected value of Y, denoted as $E(Y)$, can be written as

$$E(Y) = \alpha + \beta(X). \tag{6.1}$$

In Figure 6.1 it can be seen that as X increases by one unit the predicted outcome, $E(Y)$, also increases at a constant rate (represented by β in Equation 6.1). In this case, the predicted or expected outcome, $E(Y)$, does not need to be transformed to be linearly related to the predictor. More technically, if $g(\cdot)$ represents the link function, the transformation of $E(Y)$ by g in this case is $g(E(Y)) = E(Y)$. This is referred to as the **identity link function** because applying the $g(\cdot)$ function of $E(Y)$ in this case results in the same value, $E(Y)$. This function is usually reasonable, in that it represents the relationship appropriately, when the outcome variable is continuous. Thus, this is the link function that is used when the outcome or response variable is continuous and typically normally distributed, such as in regression and ANOVA models.

However, when the response variable is not assumed to follow a normal distribution, the predicted or expected outcome $E(Y)$ will not generally be linearly related to the predictors unless it is transformed. For example, suppose that the outcome variable was the probability that a student will pass (as opposed to fail) a specific test, so the predicted value is $E(Y) = \pi$. Using the same predictor as earlier (X = family income), the relationship depicted in Figure 6.2a illustrates a possible relationship between these two variables. Note that in this case the outcome variable, a probability, cannot (by definition) be lower than zero or greater than one no matter how high or low the value of the predictor gets. In addition, family income tends to be more strongly associated with the probability of passing the test for students in the middle of the family income range than at more extreme (very high or very low) income levels. In this case, using the identity link as in Equation 6.1 to link the random and systematic components of the GLM would amount to using the model $E(Y) = \pi = \alpha + \beta(X)$, or fitting a straight line to the points in Figure 6.2a. This would result in a poor representation of the association between the variables, especially for certain income ranges. It would also then be theoretically possible for the prediction obtained from the model to exceed one or fall below zero (for high or low enough values of X, respectively), which is nonsensical because probabilities must fall between zero and one. If, however, the predicted probability is transformed using the equation

$$g(E(Y)) = g(\pi) = \ln\left(\frac{\pi}{1-\pi}\right) = \text{logit of } \pi,$$

then the resulting relationship between the transformed value, $\ln(\pi/1-\pi)$, and income level (X) will be linear, as illustrated in Figure 6.2b. Therefore, the transformed outcome variable can be related (or linked) to the predictor, income, in a linear fashion by the following model:

$$g(E(Y)) = \ln\left(\frac{\pi}{1-\pi}\right) = \alpha + \beta(X).$$

This particular link function (or transformation) is called the **logit link function**, and the resulting GLM is called the **logistic regression model** (discussed in detail in

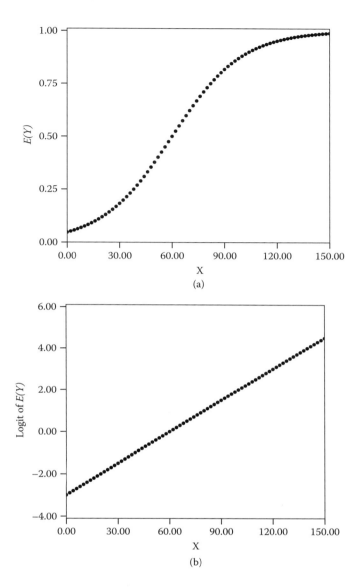

Figure 6.2 Example of a nonlinear (logistic) relationship between X and $E(Y)$, depicted with (a) the expected probability as outcome and (b) the logit of the expected probability as outcome.

Chapters 8, 9, and 10). The logit function typically works well with a binary outcome variable or a random component that is assumed to follow a binomial distribution.

The **probit link function** is a transformation that is closely related to the logit link function. These two link functions, or transformations, are closely related because either can be used to transform the relationship shown in Figure 6.2a to the one shown in Figure 6.2b. Therefore, either the logit link function or the probit link function can be used when the random component is binary and thus assumed to follow a binomial distribution. The probit link function is based on the idea that there is a continuous scale that underlies binary

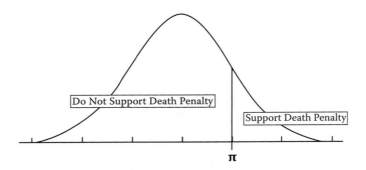

Figure 6.3 Illustration of a continuous distribution underlying responses when the probit link function is used.

or dichotomous variables. For example, assume that respondents are asked whether they support the death penalty. It is not unreasonable to assume that underlying the responses is a hypothetical continuous scale, which ranges from 0, for those who oppose the death penalty under any circumstances, to 1, for those who are strong advocates of the death penalty, with many different possible attitudes in between. Further, it is assumed that there is some threshold level on this continuous scale, π, at which respondents will shift from answering no to answering yes. This idea is illustrated in Figure 6.3. If we further assume that the theoretical response distribution is continuous and normal, the probit link function transforms the outcome or predicted probability, π, using the inverse cumulative normal distribution function as follows:

$$g(E(Y)) = g(\pi) = \frac{1}{\sqrt{2\pi^*}} \int_{-\infty}^{\pi} e^{-s^2/2} ds = \Phi^{-1}(\pi) = \text{probit of } \pi.$$

Note that π^* in this equation is used to represent the value of the π constant (i.e., $\pi^* \approx 3.14$) to distinguish it from the probability. Essentially, the probit link function transforms the predicted probability, π, to the z-score that corresponds to π in the cumulative normal distribution. For example, as illustrated in Figure 6.4, if $\pi = 0.50$ then

$$\text{probit}(\pi) = \Phi^{-1}(0.50) = 0$$

because 50% of the normal distribution falls at or below a z-score of 0. Similarly, if $\pi = 0.05$ then

$$\text{probit}(\pi) = \Phi^{-1}(0.05) = -1.645$$

because 5% of the normal distribution falls at or below a z-score of –1.645, and if $\pi = 0.975$ then

$$\text{probit}(\pi) = \Phi^{-1}(0.975) = 1.96$$

because 97.5% of the normal distribution falls at or below a z-score of 1.96.

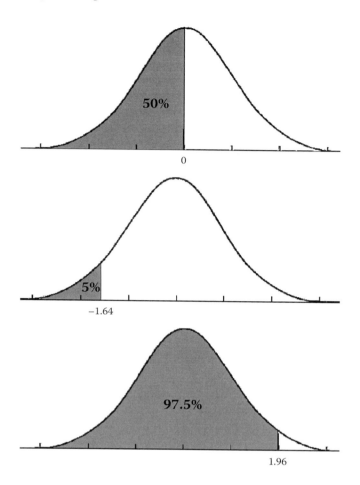

Figure 6.4 Illustration of cumulative normal probabilities used in the probit transformation.

Similar to the results obtained when using the logit link function to transform the hypothetical data presented in Figure 6.2a, use of the probit link function will result in a linear relationship between the transformed value, $\Phi^{-1}(\pi)$, and income level (X), as illustrated in Figure 6.2b. Therefore, the transformed outcome variable can be related (or linked) to the predictor in a linear fashion by the following model:

$$g(E(Y)) = \Phi^{-1}(\pi) = \alpha + \beta(X),$$

and the resulting GLM is called the **probit regression model**. When the random component is dichotomous or binary and thus is assumed to follow a binomial distribution, one advantage to using the probit link function, as opposed to the logit link function, is that the values obtained from fitting this model can be directly transformed into probabilities by using values from a standard normal table. One simply needs to look up the probability associated with the z-score obtained from the model. Conceptually, although either the logit or probit link function can be used to model the expected probability for a binary outcome, using the probit function makes sense when the outcome variable (random component) might have an underlying normal distribution where the probability represents a response threshold, whereas using the logit function makes sense when the outcome is more purely a dichotomous variable with an underlying binomial distribution. Practically, however, these two link functions typically produce similar results.

Yet another common case of a nonlinear relationship between an outcome and predictor variables arises when the outcome variable is a count variable, and thus the random component is assumed to follow a Poisson distribution. For example, suppose that we wished to predict, for each student, how many of his or her relatives attend college, λ. If family income was once again used as a predictor, it is plausible that the relationship between family income and the number of relatives who attend college may be fairly weak at lower income levels but stronger at higher incomes. This relationship is illustrated in Figure 6.5a. In this case, again, the relationship is nonlinear (i.e., not constant for all values of X), so using the identity link and fitting a simple linear regression model (i.e., a straight line as in Equation 6.1) will not reflect the data well. In addition, the outcome variable is a count so by definition it cannot be lower than zero, but if a linear regression model was fit using the untransformed outcome, nonsensical negative values could theoretically result as predictions for low values of X. On the other hand, when the predicted outcome, $E(Y)$, is transformed using the natural log function,

$$g(E(Y)) = \ln(E(Y)) = \ln(\lambda),$$

the resulting relationship between the transformed value, $\ln(\lambda)$, and income level (X) will be linear, as illustrated in Figure 6.5b. Therefore, the transformed outcome variable can be related (or linked) to the predictor, income, in a linear fashion by the following model:

$$g(E(Y)) = \ln(E(Y)) = \ln(\lambda) = \alpha + \beta(X).$$

This particular transformation is called the **log link function** and this model is called the **Poisson regression model**. The log function typically works well with outcome variables that represent counts or a random component that follows a Poisson distribution.

The aforementioned example used a continuous predictor (income) and thus resulted in a Poisson regression model. Another GLM that uses the log link function is the log-linear model (discussed extensively in Chapter 7), in which the predictor variables are typically categorical and the outcome variable, rather than representing yet another, separate variable, is the count or frequency obtained in each of the categories of the predictors. In other words, the predictors in log-linear models are categorical variables and the outcome is the count obtained for each category (or combination of categories) of these variables. Thus, the outcome is Poisson distributed and the log link function is used for these models as well.

As the previous examples demonstrate, the link function is usually determined according to the underlying probability distribution of the outcome variable, so the link function used for a GLM usually depends on the random component. The link function most typically used with certain random components (or specific probability distributions) is called the **canonical link function**. Using the canonical link function results in desirable mathematical and computational properties because the inverse of this function returns

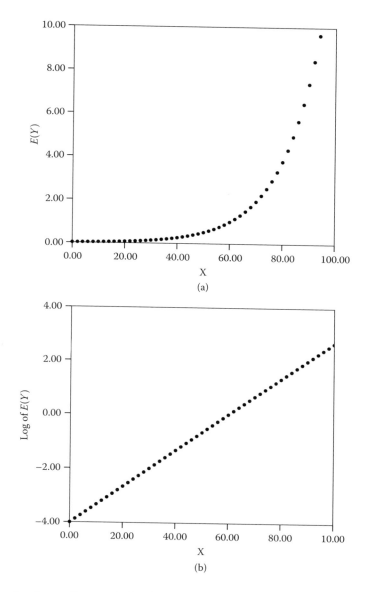

Figure 6.5 Example of a nonlinear relationship between X and E(Y), depicted with (a) the expected count as outcome and (b) the log of the expected count as outcome.

the same value (i.e., $g^{-1}(E(Y)) = E(Y)$). A summary of several canonical link functions and common models that use them is presented in Table 6.1. Note that general linear models (not to be confused with generalized linear models), such as regression, ANOVA, and ANCOVA (analysis of covariance), are a subset of GLMs that typically use the identity link. In other words, these are some of the simplest GLMs because the outcome variable, which is continuous and assumed to be normally distributed, does not require a transformation and thus utilizes the identity link in the GLM framework.

Table 6.1 Examples of Some Common Models and Their Properties in the GLM Context

Study example	Y (random component)	X (systematic component)	Canonical link function	Model
Predict standardized test score from family income	Continuous, normal	Continuous	Identity	Simple regression
Predict standardized test score from family income, IQ score, and GPA	Continuous, normal	Continuous	Identity	Multiple regression
Predict standardized test score from SES (low, medium, or high)	Continuous, normal	Categorical	Identity	ANOVA
Predict test score from IQ score and SES (low, medium, or high)	Continuous, normal	Continuous and categorical	Identity	ANCOVA
Predict standardized test performance (pass or fail) from IQ score and SES (low, medium, or high)	Categorical, binary	Continuous and categorical	Logit	Logistic regression
Predict number of relatives who graduate high school from IQ score and SES (low, medium, or high)	Categorical, Poisson	Continuous and categorical	Log	Poisson regression

6.2   *Parameter estimation*

As previously discussed, every GLM has the form

$$g(E(Y)) = \alpha + \beta_1 X_1 + \beta_2 X_2 + \cdots + \beta_p X_p, \tag{6.2}$$

where $g(\cdot)$ is the link function that provides the appropriate transformation of the expected value of Y to allow the relationship between the random and systematic components to be modeled in a linear fashion. The **model parameters** of the GLM are α, the intercept, and $\beta_1, \beta_2, \ldots, \beta_p$, the coefficients associated with the predictors $X_1, X_2, \ldots, X_p$, respectively. Using Equation 6.2 we can predict the outcome (expected value of Y, transformed) for any given value of the predictors. As is the case in linear regression, the intercept provides the predicted outcome value when all of the predictors take on the value zero, and the jth slope coefficient, β_j, provides the expected change in the predicted outcome that is associated with a one unit increase in the jth predictor, X_j, given that all other predictors are held constant. Later chapters that deal with specific GLMs will cover the interpretation of these coefficients in more detail. At this point, we discuss more broadly how to obtain estimates for these model parameters from sample data.

A common algorithm, or procedure, is used to estimate the GLM parameters for a variety of random components and link functions. In the case of linear regression, when the outcome variable is continuous, the algorithm or estimation procedure that is used to estimate the parameters of the model is known as **ordinary least squares** (OLS) estimation. This procedure minimizes the **sum of the squared errors** (SSE), which is simply the sum of the squared distances from the data points to their corresponding values generated by the regression model. This distance is also called the error or residual because it reflects the difference between the value of the actual or observed outcome and the value predicted by the regression model, and it is thus indicative of the relative inaccuracy of the model predictions. In other words, the higher the SSE, the larger the distances between observed and predicted values (errors) and the worse the accuracy of predictions generated by the model. However, OLS estimation does not work well when the outcome variable is discrete, so an alternative must be used. The most common approach to estimating models for which the response variable is discrete, and thus is assumed to follow a distribution other than the normal distribution, is a procedure (that was introduced in Chapter 3) known as **maximum likelihood estimation**. This procedure uses a function, called the **likelihood function**, that is based on the underlying probability distribution and provides the probability of obtaining the observed data over a range of parameter values. Likelihood functions allow the parameters of the model (e.g., π or λ) to vary while holding everything else constant. In Chapter 3, Section 3.1, we described this function (see Figure 3.1) in the context of finding the maximum likelihood estimate for a particular binomial distribution. Specifically, we demonstrated how to determine the maximum likelihood estimate for π, which reflected the probability of being proficient in mathematics, if we obtained a random sample of 10 students and found 4 of them to be proficient in mathematics. In this case, the likelihood function is expressed by

$$L(\pi|n = 10, k = 4) = \begin{pmatrix} 10 \\ 4 \end{pmatrix} \pi^4 (1 - \pi)^{(10-4)}.$$

The left hand of this equation can be read as "the likelihood for a specific value for π given a sample size of 10 in which we obtain 4 successes." By evaluating this function for different values of π we obtain the **maximum likelihood estimate** (MLE) of π, which is the value of π at which the probability (likelihood) is highest (maximized). In other words, the MLE is the value of the parameter that maximizes this function. Using calculus, this maximum value (or MLE) can be obtained by setting the partial derivative of the function with respect to π equal to zero and solving for π.

This procedure can also be used to estimate the parameters of more complicated models such as those that fit into the GLM framework presented in Equation 6.2. Most GLMs used with categorical outcome variables have multiple explanatory variables in the systematic component of the model, and these are used to predict an outcome variable, in the random component of the model, that must be transformed using a link function because it follows a distribution other than the normal distribution. The mathematics underlying the estimation procedure are somewhat intensive because calculus is used in conjunction with matrix algebra, which may be beyond the scope of the average reader of this book. However, for those familiar with calculus, conceptually what occurs when finding the MLE of a parameter for a more complicated model is identical to what has already been described. Basically, the partial derivative of the likelihood function, with respect to the parameters being estimated, is set to zero and solved while all of the other parameters of the model are held constant.

Maximum likelihood estimation of the multiple parameters of a GLM is typically accomplished using an iterative procedure or algorithm known as **Fisher scoring** (named after R. A. Fisher). When the random component of a GLM is assumed to follow either a binomial or Poisson distribution, this algorithm can be further simplified to an estimation algorithm procedure known as the **Newton–Raphson procedure**. Although we will not go into detail on the technical aspects of either of these procedures, we will describe how

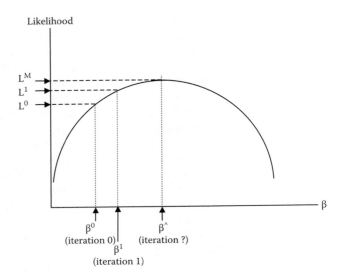

Figure 6.6 Illustration of an iterative estimation process.

these algorithms work conceptually. Both of these procedures use a likelihood function that expresses the probability of the observed data that would be obtained over a range of parameter values. These estimation algorithms are iterative in that they start with an initial estimate or "guess" for all of the parameters, then evaluate the likelihood function using these initial parameter estimates and the observed data. At this point, the likelihood function is further evaluated at a second set of parameter values that are close to the initial guess but adjusted so as to increase the value of the likelihood function, and a second estimate (or set of estimates) is obtained based on this information. The process continues until the estimates no longer change, which indicates that the likelihood is at its maximum and the iteration process has converged on the values of the final maximum likelihood estimates.

A simple illustration of the procedure is provided in Figure 6.6, where a hypothetical likelihood function is shown as a function of one parameter, β. Suppose that our initial guess is the value indicated by β^0 in Figure 6.6, and the value of the likelihood function at β^0 is L^0. At this stage, values of β close to β^0 are evaluated to see whether the likelihood might increase. Values lower (to the left) of β^0 will clearly decrease the likelihood, but values higher (to the right) of β^0 will increase the likelihood. Therefore, the procedure next selects a value that is higher than β^0, denoted by β^1 in Figure 6.6, with associated likelihood L^1. The procedure continues in this way until the likelihood function no longer increases, which is referred to as convergence. The final estimate, $\beta^\wedge$ in Figure 6.6, is thus obtained at the point where the likelihood is at its maximum value, L^M. The function depicted in Figure 6.6 is rather simple, but the estimation procedure is general in that it can be applied in a similar manner with more complex likelihood functions (and with several parameters).

6.3   Model fit

Once parameter estimates are obtained for a particular model, the fit of the model is evaluated by examining the discrepancy between the outcomes obtained from the model (predicted values) and the outcomes observed in the data (observed values). This is analogous to examining the difference between observed and predicted values in a linear regression model to describe how well the predicted values match the observed data overall. Specifically, predicted values of the dependent or response variable are obtained from the model using specific values for each of the independent variables or predictors, and these model generated outcomes are compared to the observed outcomes that are associated with the same predictor values in the data.

One way to evaluate model fit, based on the score method and the Pearson chi-squared test, was discussed in Chapters 3 and 4. Recall from Chapter 3 that the **Pearson chi-squared test statistic** is

$$X^2 = \sum_{i=1}^{n} \frac{(O_i - E_i)^2}{E_i},$$

where, O_i is used to represent the ith observed value and E_i is used to represent the ith expected value. A generalization of this procedure can be used to evaluate relative model fit for a GLM. Specifically, for the ith category (or set) of predictor values in a GLM, the observed outcome value is that obtained from the data and the corresponding predicted or expected outcome value is that generated by the model. Large discrepancies between predicted and observed values are indicative of poor model fit. On the other hand, if the model fit perfectly it would predict the outcome perfectly, thus predicted and observed values would be equal and $X^2 = 0$. As is the case in OLS regression, certain constraints or restrictions can be placed on the model parameters, such as that certain predictors are not needed in the model and thus their regression coefficient parameters are zero, to test specific null hypotheses and obtain the comparative fit of the model against a restricted model. Model fit is typically evaluated in relative terms by comparing the fit of one model with a restricted form of that model.

In OLS regression, the overall fit of a model that contains specific predictors is evaluated against the fit of a model that contains no predictors by comparing the sum of squared errors (SSE) of both models. Descriptively, this produces the familiar R^2 statistic, which is used to describe how much variability in the outcome or response variable is explained by the predictor variables included in the model. For inferential purposes, an F-test is conducted to compare the difference in SSE between the two models. Similarly, in GLMs the model containing the predictors of interest can be compared to the model that contains no predictors. However, rather than using the SSE of each model, we use other measures of model fit such as its X^2 or **maximum log-likelihood** because the parameter estimates are obtained using maximum likelihood (ML) as opposed to OLS estimation. The likelihood of the model is computed using the parameter estimates that are obtained as described in Section 6.2, which are commonly referred to as the maximum likelihood estimates. For example, in Figure 6.6 the maximum likelihood, which occurs at the value L^M, corresponds to the estimate $\hat{\beta}$. We have already seen how to compare two likelihoods in Section 3.2.3. Recall that we used L_0 to represent the likelihood obtained using the parameter values specified under the null hypothesis and L_1 to represent the likelihood obtained using the values of the parameters that are estimated from the data. In general, a model that includes no predictors is analogous to the null hypothesis that all β_j values in the GLM are equal to zero. Thus, L_0 represents the likelihood of a model that contains no predictors (or a model in which all β_j are restricted to be zero). Therefore, the model comparison we wish to test here is identical to that presented in Section 3.2.3 and is based on the **likelihood ratio test statistic**:

$$G^2 = -2 \ln\left(\frac{L_0}{L_1}\right) = -2 \left[\ln(L_0) - \ln(L_1)\right].$$

Recall that this test statistic follows a χ^2 distribution with degrees of freedom (df) equal to the number of parameters restricted under H_0, so when testing overall model fit the degree of freedom is equal to the number of predictors or independent variables that are included in the model. Large values of the G^2 statistic indicate that the log likelihood of the model with the predictors (where β_j values are estimated from the data) is significantly larger than the log likelihood of the model without predictors (where β_j values are restricted to be zero), and that using the predictors is advantageous to not using them in predicting the outcome. In other words, large values of this statistic indicate that the predictors included in the model explain a statistically significant amount of variability in the dependent variable, while small values of this statistic are indicative of poor model fit in that the predictors do not explain a statistically significant amount of variability in the dependent variable. Again, this is conceptually analogous to the omnibus F-test of a linear (OLS) regression model. Note, however, that the χ^2 distribution cannot be correctly used to evaluate the G^2 (or X^2) statistic when the model predictors are continuous. If that is the case, the observations must be grouped, as will be discussed in Chapter 8.

6.3.1   Residuals

Whereas overall model fit indicates whether the observed data follow a certain functional form as specified by the GLM, residuals allow us to evaluate how much specific observed values deviate from the corresponding outcome values generated from the model. As discussed in Chapters 3 and 4, a residual is the difference between the observed and expected (or model-generated) value of the outcome. For the ith observation (or set of predictor values) in a GLM, the observed outcome value obtained from the data is denoted by y_i and the corresponding predicted or expected outcome value generated by the model is denoted by $\hat{y}_i$. The residual for the ith observation (or set of predictor values) is thus computed as

$$(y_i - \hat{y}_i).$$

These residual values, typically referred to as **"raw" residuals**, are usually standardized or rescaled by dividing each residual by the standard error (SE) to obtain **standardized residuals**:

$$\frac{y_i - \hat{y}_i}{\text{SE}}.$$

Standardized residuals, like z-scores, indicate how far the observed and predicted values are in terms of standard errors and are easier to interpret because they typically follow an approximately normal distribution. Therefore, standardized residuals with absolute values greater than 2 are typically indicative of large discrepancies between the observed and expected values of the dependent or outcome variable (i.e., indicating that the predicted value is more than 2 standard errors from the observed value). Examples of residual computations were discussed in Chapters 3 (Section 3.4) and 4 (Section 4.3.4) and will be discussed in more detail in subsequent chapters in the context of specific GLMs. As is the case with linear regression, residuals can help in detecting outliers or influential observations.

6.3.2 Deviance

Yet another way to evaluate the fit of a model is to compare it to a model that fits the data perfectly. A model that fits the data perfectly is referred to as the **saturated model** because it contains as many parameters as observations and has thus reached saturation with respect to the number of parameters. In other words, the saturated model contains as many predictors as there are observations (or contingency table cells) in the data. Therefore, the saturated model is not very helpful as a model because it does not provide a parsimonious summary of the relationship between the outcome and predictor variables. However, its likelihood can be used as a "benchmark" to indicate the highest level of fit that can be attained.

Any model that restricts some of the parameters in the saturated model to be zero, referred to as a **restricted model**, will be more parsimonious but not fit as well as the saturated model because it will not fit the data perfectly. If the difference between the fit of this restricted model and the saturated model is not substantial (e.g., statistically significant), then the restricted model is preferred because it uses fewer parameters (and describes the relationships more parsimoniously, or efficiently) without sacrificing predictive ability to any significant extent. Denoting the likelihood of the saturated model by L_S and the likelihood of a restricted model of interest (model M) by L_M, the likelihood ratio statistic is called the **deviance** of model M:

$$\text{Deviance of model } M = -2\ln\left(\frac{L_M}{L_S}\right) = -2\left[\ln(L_M) - \ln(L_S)\right].$$

Small differences between L_S and L_M are indicative of good model fit for the restricted model (Model M) and suggest that this more parsimonious model explains almost as much variability in the outcome or dependent variable as the saturated model does. In other words, the restricted model is preferred because it is a more parsimonious model that achieves essentially the same fit as the saturated model but with fewer parameters. On the other hand, large differences are indicative of poor model fit for the restricted model because this more parsimonious model explains significantly less variability in the dependent or outcome variable than does the saturated model.

This approach can be generalized so that any two models of interest can be compared. Specifically, the log likelihood test can be conceptualized as the difference between the deviances of two models:

$$G^2 = -2\left[\ln(L_0) - \ln(L_1)\right]$$

$$= -2\left[\ln(L_0) - \ln(L_S) - \ln(L_1) + \ln(L_S)\right]$$

$$= (-2)[\ln(L_0) - \ln(L_S)] - (-2)[\ln(L_1) - \ln(L_S)]$$

$$= \text{Deviance of Model } 0 - \text{Deviance of Model } 1.$$

The deviance is often provided by computer software packages and can be used to compare the difference in fit between any two models, provided that one is a restricted version of the other. For example, suppose that Model 1, with a likelihood L_1, contains five predictors, while Model 2, with a likelihood L_2, contains only two of the five predictors in Model 1. In other words, Model 2 restricts three of the Model 1 coefficients to be zero, and thus the likelihood ratio test statistic comparing the two models is

$$G^2 = -2 \left[\ln(L_2) - \ln(L_1) \right]$$

$$= (-2)[\ln(L_2) - \ln(L_S)] - (-2)[\ln(L_1) - \ln(L_S)]$$

$$= \text{Deviance of Model 2} - \text{Deviance of Model 1}.$$

This test statistic follows a χ^2 distribution with degrees of freedom equal to the difference in the number of parameters between the two models. In this example, $df = 3$ since Model 1 contained five predictors and Model 2 contained only two of those five predictors for a difference of $5 - 2 = 3$. If G^2 is statistically significant then Model 1 performs significantly better than Model 2. On the other hand, if the difference is not significant then statistically the two models perform equally well and model 2 is preferred because it is a more parsimonious model that statistically achieves the same fit with fewer parameters. Comparing the deviance for two models, one of which is a restricted version of the other, is analogous to the F-test that is conducted to compare two nested models in linear regression. In fact, when comparing GLMs the more restricted model is also often referred to as being nested within the model that has the greater number of parameters.

6.4   Parameter inference

There are several general approaches to testing the GLM parameters, some of which have already been mentioned in previous chapters (as well as in this one). All of these tests are concerned with testing the null hypothesis H_0: $\beta_j = 0$, where β_j is the coefficient associated with a particular independent variable or predictor, X_j. Although the intercept parameter (α) can be similarly tested, it is usually not of interest because it does not describe the relationship between a predictor and the outcome variable. As is the case in linear regression, the primary focus is on testing and interpreting the "slope" parameters rather than the intercept.

As discussed in detail in the following section, one of the approaches to testing the significance of a GLM parameter is based on the deviance test discussed in the previous section. Specifically, the deviance difference or log-likelihood ratio is used to test whether the estimated parameter is statistically significantly different from zero. This should make sense intuitively because comparing the deviances of two models, one of which is nested within another, is simply evaluating whether the parameter estimates that are excluded in the more restricted model are equivalent to zero. Two other approaches can be used to determine if a given estimated parameter in a GLM is statistically significant. Both of these procedures are based on dividing a parameter estimate by its standard error but differ in the way in which the standard error is estimated.

In addition to conducting the statistical test, a confidence interval can be computed for the value of β_j. The confidence interval consists of a range of plausible values for β_j, any one of which might be the true value of β_j in the population. The construction of a confidence interval for β_j will also be discussed under each approach.

6.4.1   Deviance or likelihood-ratio test

The likelihood-ratio or deviance difference approach to testing the null hypothesis H_0: $\beta_j = 0$ uses the test statistic

$$G^2 = -2 \left[\ln(L_2) - \ln(L_1) \right] = \text{Deviance of Model 2} - \text{Deviance of Model 1},$$

where Model 1 contains one more predictor, X_j, than Model 2. Thus, this test statistic follows a χ^2 distribution with one degree of freedom. If this test is significant, then Model 1 performs significantly better than Model 2, and β_j is significantly different from zero. Otherwise, the null hypothesis cannot be rejected.

In addition, using the likelihood-ratio approach for testing parameters, the $100(1 - \alpha)\%$ confidence interval for β_j consists of all values of β that are not rejected under the null hypothesis H_0: $\beta_j = \beta$ at the α significance level. For example, a 95% confidence interval would contain all values of β that were *not* rejected by this test at the 0.05 significance level, and thus might be the true value of β_j in the population. The logic behind this approach is that the values of the parameter that cannot be rejected (at the 0.05 significance level) constitute legitimate, plausible values (with 95% confidence) of the population parameter. Some computer software packages (such as PROC GENMOD in SAS) can provide the upper and lower limits of this confidence interval.

6.4.2   Wald and score tests

The Wald and score tests for evaluating the significance of a parameter in a GLM are both based on dividing the parameter estimate, $\hat{\beta}_j$, by its standard error to form a test statistic that follows an approximately standard normal distribution. Specifically, under the null hypothesis (H_0: $\beta_j = 0$) the test statistic

$$z = \frac{\hat{\beta}_j - \beta_j}{\text{SE of } \hat{\beta}_j} = \frac{\hat{\beta}_j}{\text{SE of } \hat{\beta}_j} \tag{6.3}$$

follows approximately a standard normal distribution. Because squaring the standard normal distribution results in a χ^2 distribution with one degree of freedom, this test statistic could also be squared and evaluated using a χ^2 distribution.

In addition, a confidence interval can be formed for the value of β_j (in the population) using the formula

$$\hat{\beta}_j \pm z_{1-(\alpha/2)}(\text{SE of } \hat{\beta}_j), \tag{6.4}$$

where $z_{1-(\alpha/2)}$ is the critical value (or percentile rank) from the standard normal distribution corresponding to the desired confidence level, $100(1 - \alpha)\%$. For example, the critical value for a 95% confidence interval would be 1.96, because 95% implies $\alpha = 0.05$ and the value of the standard normal distribution corresponding to $1 - (0.05/2) = 0.975$, or the 97.5th percentile, is 1.96. Equations 6.3 and 6.4 are practically identical to those used for inference about a population mean (or linear regression coefficient) but are applied here to a population GLM coefficient instead.

The Wald and score tests differ in how they estimate the standard error, SE of $\hat{\beta}_j$, used in Equations 6.3 and 6.4. As you may recall from Chapter 3, the Wald test uses the maximum likelihood estimate of the parameter to estimate the standard error while the score test uses the null hypothesized value of the parameter to estimate the standard error. In the general case, described here, the Wald test uses information about the log-likelihood function at the maximum likelihood estimate to obtain the standard error, whereas the score test uses information about the log-likelihood function at the null hypothesis value (zero, here) to obtain the standard error (see Agresti, 2007, for a more detailed discussion). Typically, the standard error provided by the score test is larger than the standard error provided by the Wald test, which implies that (everything else being equal) the score test results in a larger range of values in confidence intervals and in smaller values for the test statistic (less power) than the Wald test. Moreover, the difference between the standard errors obtained from these two procedures becomes more pronounced as the MLE of the parameter deviates more from zero, which is the value of the parameter assumed under the null hypothesis. Thus, the Wald test is typically preferred to the score test, although the score test has the advantage of being able to provide an estimate for the standard error even when the maximum likelihood estimate of the parameter itself is infinite (in which case the Wald standard error cannot be estimated). This is not likely to occur in most cases, but could happen if the MLE procedure does not converge.

Finally, it should be noted that the likelihood-ratio (or deviance difference) approach to testing parameters combines information about the log-likelihood function at both the null and maximum likelihood values of the parameter (as is evident in its test statistic), so it essentially uses more information than either the score or Wald tests. Therefore, the likelihood ratio statistic is typically the most reliable of these three test statistics.

6.5   Summary

In this chapter we discussed a general framework for modeling an outcome (or dependent) variable based on values of predictor variables. Specifically, we showed how the GLM framework allows us to model a categorical outcome variable by using the appropriate random component, systematic component, and link function. This is useful when we wish to predict the values of a categorical outcome from the values of other variables, when we wish to examine and test the relationship between a categorical outcome and specific predictor variables, and when we wish to evaluate the fit of the model.

In the next several chapters we will examine specific GLMs in detail. Specifically, in Chapter 7 we discuss the log-linear model, used to predict the cell counts in contingency tables from the categories of the categorical variables that form these tables; in Chapter 8 we discuss the logistic regression model, used to predict a binary outcome from the values of continuous predictor variables; in Chapter 9 we extend the discussion of logistic regression models to include categorical predictor variables; and in Chapter 10 we discuss multinomial regression models, used to predict the probability of a multicategory outcome variable from continuous and/or categorical predictors.

Problems

6.1   What is the general purpose of a link function? Why is a link function other than the identity needed in some cases but not in others?

6.2   What advantages do GLMs (generalized linear models) have over general linear models (such as regression and ANOVA models)?

6.3   Suppose that a researcher would like to predict the number of students who are absent from a given classroom per day based on several predictors such as family income, race, and gender. Explain your reasoning for each of the following:
   a.   What is the random component of the GLM used in this study?
   b.   What is the systematic component of the GLM used in this study?
   c.   What is the most appropriate link function for the GLM used in this study?

6.4 Suppose that a researcher would like to predict the probability that a voter will vote for a particular candidate based on several characteristics of the voter such as family income, educational level, race, and gender. Explain your reasoning for each of the following:
  a. What is the random component of the GLM used in this study?
  b. What is the systematic component of the GLM used in this study?
  c. What is the most appropriate link function for the GLM used in this study?

6.5 Come up with an example of a study in which the outcome variable is likely to be Poisson distributed. Explain what the random component, systematic component, and link function would be in this case.

6.6 Use the data in Table 6.2, where X represents a continuous predictor and Y represents a probability.
  a. Create a scatter plot of the data (with values of X on the horizontal axis and values of Y on the vertical axis). Describe the shape of the relationship between X and Y. Is it linear throughout?
  b. Transform the values of Y using the natural log (ln) function and create a scatter plot with the original values of X plotted against the log of Y. Describe the shape of the relationship between X and the log of Y. Is it linear throughout?
  c. Transform the values of Y using the logit function and create a scatter plot with the original values of X plotted against the logit of Y. Describe the shape of the relationship between X and the logit of Y. Is it linear throughout?
  d. Would the log or logit link function be more appropriate for a GLM representing the relationship between X and Y? Explain.

Table 6.2 Hypothetical Data for Problem 6.6 (X Represents a Continuous Predictor and Y Represents a Probability)

X	Y
3	0.03
4	0.06
5	0.12
6	0.23
7	0.40
8	0.60
9	0.77
10	0.88
11	0.94
12	0.97

6.7 Suppose that a study was conducted to predict whether an individual regularly smoked, or the expected probability of smoking, based on four continuous predictors such as x_1 = smoking exposure, x_2 = healthy lifestyle (e.g., diet, exercise), x_3 = annual income, and x_4 = years of schooling. Further, suppose that the value of $-2\ln(\text{likelihood})$ for the model containing all four predictors is 558.

```
                          Model Fit Statistics


                                           Intercept
                             Intercept        and
             Criterion         Only        Predictor

             -2 Log L         672.023       652.504


             Analysis of Maximum Likelihood Estimates

                                  Standard         Wald
  Parameter    DF    Estimate      Error       Chi-Square    Pr > ChiSq

  Intercept     1     -2.8843      0.8667        11.0748        0.0009
  X4            1      0.4521      0.1043        18.8067        <.0001
```

Figure 6.7 SAS output for Problem 6.10.

a. If the value of –2ln(likelihood) for the model containing none of the predictors is 672, what is the value of the likelihood-ratio statistic for the overall fit of the model (containing all four predictors)?

b. Is the likelihood-ratio statistic for the overall fit obtained in part (a) significant? What conclusions (as related to this study) can be drawn based on this result?

6.8 Refer again to the study described in Problem 6.7. Suppose that the model containing only the "demographic" variables, x_3 = annual income and x_4 = years of schooling, results in –2ln(likelihood) = 574.

a. Is the difference between the model containing all four predictors and the model containing only the two "demographic" variables significant?

b. Based on these results, which of these models is preferred? What conclusions can be drawn (as related to these variables)? Explain.

6.9 Refer again to the overall model described in Problem 6.7. Explain your reasoning for each of the following:

a. What is the random component of the GLM used in this study?

b. What is the systematic component of the GLM used in this study?

c. What is the most appropriate link function for the GLM used in this study?

6.10 Suppose that the results shown in Figure 6.7 were obtained for the study described in Problem 6.7, using only x_4 = years of schooling as a predictor:

a. What are the estimated values of the intercept (α) and slope (β) for this GLM?

b. What is the likelihood ratio test statistic for the fit of this model?

c. What is the Wald test statistic for the fit of this model, based on Equation 6.3?

d. How was the (squared) Wald statistic shown in this output obtained?

e. What conclusions can be drawn from the likelihood ratio test of significance for the slope?

f. What conclusions can be drawn from the Wald test of significance for the slope?

chapter seven

Log-linear models

A LOOK AHEAD

In Chapters 4 and 5 we discussed how to measure and interpret the association between two and three categorical variables. In this chapter, we show how to accomplish this and more using a generalized linear model called the log-linear model. The difference between the material in those chapters and this one is analogous to the difference between measuring a correlation and fitting a regression model; while the two are related, a model allows for a wider range of possibilities and interpretations. In Chapter 5 we alluded to the fact that all of the inferential tests presented in that chapter, that are intended to help a researcher understand the associations between three categorical variables, could be better accomplished by modeling the associations between the categorical variables with a log-linear model. Using a log-linear modeling approach is advantageous to conducting inferential tests of the associations in contingency tables because the models can handle more complicated situations. For example, the Breslow–Day statistic is limited to $2 \times 2 \times K$ tables and estimates of common odds ratios cannot be obtained for tables larger than 2×2. Conversely, a log-linear modeling approach is not restricted to two- or three-way tables so it can be used for testing homogeneous association and estimating common odds ratios in tables of any size.

Log-linear models are used to model the cell counts in contingency tables. The ultimate goal of fitting a log-linear model is to estimate parameters that describe the relationships between categorical variables. Specifically, for a set of categorical variables, log-linear models do not really distinguish between explanatory and response variables but rather treat all variables as response variables by modeling the cell counts for all combinations of the levels of the categorical variables included in the model. Therefore, fitting a log-linear model is appropriate when all of the variables are categorical in nature and a researcher is interested in understanding how a count within a particular cell of the contingency table depends on the different levels of the categorical variables that define that particular cell. This dependency is, in turn, determined by the associations that either exist or do not exist among the categorical variables. Examples of research questions that can be addressed by log-linear modeling include the following:

- Is there a three-way association between gender, religious views, and beliefs about God? If not, are there any two-way associations between certain pairs of these variables? How can the associations be interpreted?
- Of the variables gender, IQ, SES, and college aspirations, which are associated and which are not? How can the associations help us understand the effect that one of these variables exerts on the others?

We will begin this chapter by discussing how to code the variables in a log-linear model and then proceed to specifically examine log-linear models for two-way contingency tables, which will elucidate the connection between log-linear modeling and the earlier approaches considered in Chapter 4. This will be followed by log-linear models for three-way tables, inference for log-linear models, and generalizations to higher-way tables. We conclude with a discussion of how to fit log-linear models using SAS and SPSS.

7.1   Coding of variables and notation in log-linear models

In general, the number of parameters in a log-linear model depends on the number of categories of the variables of interest. As is the case in regression models with categorical predictors, a log-linear model typically includes an intercept parameter as well as $(C - 1)$ unique parameters for each categorical variable represented in the model.

More specifically, in any log-linear model the effect of a categorical variable with a total of C categories requires $(C - 1)$ unique parameters. For example, if variable X is gender (with two categories), then $C = 2$ and only one predictor, thus one parameter, is needed to model the effect of X. This is due to the fact that the total number of observations is incorporated into the intercept parameter. Therefore, for the gender variable, once the number of males is known the number of females is predetermined as the difference between the total and the number of males. The number of females thus does not require its own parameter. On the other hand, if X represents the variable socioeconomic status with three categories (high, moderate, and low), then $C = 3$ and two parameters are needed to represent the SES variable.

There are several ways to "code" a categorical variable, or choose how to numerically reflect the $(C - 1)$ different categories of the variable. Moreover, the way in which the values of the estimated model parameters are interpreted depends on how the categories of a variable are coded. This is analogous to interpreting the values of the estimated parameters (regression coefficients) associated with categorical predictor variables in a linear regression model. In fact, the same multiple coding schemas that are used for categorical predictors in a linear regression model can also be used for the categorical variables in a log-linear model. One of the simplest and most intuitive ways to code categorical variables is called "**dummy coding**." For the sake of simplicity, and because we believe dummy coding to be easiest to interpret in the context of log-linear modeling, other coding methods are not discussed here but thorough discussions of these can be found in, for example, chapter 8 of Cohen, Cohen, West, and Aiken (2003) or chapter 11 of Pedhazur (1997).

7.1.1   Dummy coding

When dummy coding is used, the last category of the variable is used as a reference category. Therefore, the parameter associated with the last category is set to zero, and each of the remaining parameters of the model is interpreted relative to the last category. For example, if male is the last category of the gender variable, then the one gender parameter in the log-linear model will be interpreted as the difference between females and males because the parameter reflects the odds for females relative to the reference category, males. Thus, this one parameter will fully capture the effect of gender.

Table 7.1 General Representation of Dummy Coding a
Categorical Variable With C Categories Using C − 1 Indicators

Category	Indicator							
	X_1	X_2	...	X_{j-1}	X_j	X_{j+1}	...	X_{C-1}
1	1	0		0	0	0		0
2	0	1		0	0	0		0
⋮								
J	0	0		0	1	0		0
⋮								
C	0	0		0	0	0		0

In general, dummy coding involves a total of (C − 1) variables or "indicators" that together represent a categorical variable with C categories. Each indicator is assigned a value of 1 if the observation belongs to one of the categories and 0 otherwise. Formally, the value of the jth indicator is assigned such that

$$X_j = \begin{cases} 1 \text{ if the observation belongs to category } j \\ 0 \text{ otherwise} \end{cases}$$

and $j = 1, 2, \ldots, (C − 1)$.

The general system of dummy coding is represented in Table 7.1, which illustrates how C categories are coded using (C − 1) predictor variables. Note that the last category is indicated when all (C − 1) predictors take on the value of zero, whereas the other categories are indicated when one of the (C − 1) predictors takes on a value of one. We will use this dummy coding approach for all models presented in this chapter.

7.1.2 Notation

As discussed in Chapter 6, the log-linear model is a GLM for which the response variable is a cell count. Therefore, the random component follows a Poisson distribution and the log function is used to link the random and systematic components of the model. It is typical to use the natural log function for these models, and we (generically) use the notation "log" to represent this function in the model equations throughout this chapter.

In addition, the parameter notation for the systematic component discussed in Chapter 6 (and familiar from regression models) is somewhat different in the case of log-linear models. Instead of representing the parameter associated with the ith variable (X_i) as β_i, in log-linear models this parameter is represented by the Greek letter lambda, λ, with the variable indicated in the superscript and the (dummy-coded) indicator of the variable in the subscript. For example, if the variable X has a total of I categories $(i = 1, 2, \ldots, I)$, λ_i^X is the parameter associated with the ith indicator (dummy variable) for X. Similarly, if the variable Y has a total of J categories $(j = 1, 2, \ldots, J)$, then λ_j^Y is the parameter associated with the jth indicator for Y. This is the standard notation for log-linear models and it will be used throughout this chapter.

7.2   Log-linear models for two-way contingency tables

7.2.1   Log-linear model for independence for two-way contingency tables

For two categorical variables, the expected cell counts, denoted by μ_{ij} for the cell in the ith row and j^{th} column, are the outcome values from a log-linear model. Consider the data in Table 7.2, obtained from the 1996 General Social Survey (available online at www.norc.org) that cross-classifies respondents according to the choice for president in the 1992 presidential election and their political viewpoint. Recall that if the two categorical variables, choice for president and political viewpoint, are independent then the joint probability, π_{ij}, of observations falling into a particular cell is determined by the product of the row and column marginal probabilities. In other words, $\pi_{ij} = \pi_{i+}\pi_{+j}$ for all $i = 1, 2, \ldots, I$ and $j = 1, 2, \ldots, J$. Therefore, using n as the total sample size, under independence the expected cell counts or frequencies are computed as $\mu_{ij} = n\pi_{ij} = n\pi_{i+}\pi_{+j}$.

Taking the logarithms of the expected cell counts, used to link the random and systematic components of the model, results in the following log-linear model under independence:

$$\log(\mu_{ij}) = \log(n\pi_{ij}) = \log(n\pi_{i+}\pi_{+j}) = \log(n) + \log(\pi_{i+}) + \log(\pi_{+j}), \qquad (7.1)$$

which can be expressed more generally as

$$\log(\mu_{ij}) = \lambda + \lambda_i^X + \lambda_j^Y. \qquad (7.2)$$

In this representation, there are $(I-1)$ unique parameters for the X variable ($i = 1, 2, \ldots, I-1$) and $(J-1)$ unique parameters for the Y variable ($j = 1, 2, \ldots, J-1$).

For a two-way table, the model in Equation 7.2 is known as the **log-linear model of independence**. It is an ANOVA-like representation where:

1. λ represents an overall effect or constant. This term ensures that the sum of the expected cell counts is equal to the total sample size, n.
2. λ_i^X represents the "main" or marginal effect of the row variable, X. It represents the "effect" of classification in row i relative to the reference (e.g., last) row. This term ensures that the expected row marginal totals are equal to the observed row marginal totals (i.e., $\sum_j \mu_{ij} = \mu_{i+} = n_{i+}$).
3. λ_j^Y represents the "main" or marginal effect of the column variable, Y. It represents the "effect" of classification in column j relative to the reference (e.g., last) column. This term ensures that the expected column marginal totals are equal to the observed column marginal totals (i.e., $\sum_i \mu_{ij} = \mu_{+j} = n_{+j}$).

Table 7.2 Two-Way Contingency Table for Political Affiliation and Choice for President in 1992

Political viewpoint	Choice for president			
	Bush	Clinton	Perot	Total
Liberal	70 (0.16)	324 (0.72)	56 (0.12)	450
Moderate	195 (0.31)	332 (0.53)	101 (0.16)	628
Conservative	382 (0.55)	199 (0.29)	117 (0.17)	698
Total	647	855	274	1776

Note: Numbers in parentheses after the cell counts reflect the row proportions.

If this model fits the observed data in a two-way contingency table, then the two variables are independent and the null hypothesis of independence holds.

Using dummy coding, the following parameter estimates were obtained (using computer software) from fitting the model in Equation 7.2 to the data presented in Table 7.2:

$$\log(\mu_{ij}) = \lambda + \lambda_i^X + \lambda_j^Y = \lambda + \lambda_1^X + \lambda_2^X + \lambda_3^X + \lambda_1^Y + \lambda_2^Y + \lambda_3^Y$$

$$= 4.6792 - 0.4390 - 0.1057 + 0 + 0.8592 + 1.1380 + 0. \tag{7.3}$$

Because dummy coding was used, each of the parameter estimates corresponding to the last row and column of the table (i.e., λ_3^X and λ_3^Y) are zero. Note, for example, that there are only two unique parameters associated with X (political viewpoint) because it has a total of three categories. The last category of X, conservative, is considered the reference category and so its parameter is set to zero ($\lambda_3^X = 0$). The same is true in this case for Y (candidate choice), with the last category (Perot) used as the reference category ($\lambda_3^Y = 0$).

In general, main effects in log-linear models are interpreted as odds. However, to interpret the estimated parameters in Equation 7.3 as odds they must first be exponentiated because the natural log function was used to link the random and systematic components of the model. The (exponentiated) parameter values associated with X, λ_i^X, can be interpreted as the odds of being in the ith row versus being in the last row of the table regardless of the value of the other variable, Y.

For example, for political viewpoint the estimated model parameters are $\lambda_1^X = -0.4390$ for liberal and $\lambda_2^X = -0.1057$ for moderate, so their corresponding exponentiated values are $e^{-0.4390} = 0.6447$ and $e^{-0.1057} = 0.8997$, respectively. Therefore, regardless of one's choice for president, overall the odds of being liberal rather than conservative are 0.6447. Note, from Table 7.2, that the overall probability of being liberal is (450/1776) = 0.253 and the overall probability of being conservative is (698/1776) = 0.393 so the probability of being liberal is 0.253/0.393 = 0.6447 times the probability of being conservative. Similarly, the odds of being moderate rather than conservative are 0.8997.

Likewise, the (exponentiated) parameter values associated with Y, λ_j^Y, can be interpreted as the odds of being in the jth column versus being in the last column of the table regardless of the value of the other variable, X. For example, regardless of one's political affiliation, the odds of voting for Bush rather than Perot are $e^{0.8592} = 2.36$ and the odds of voting for Clinton rather than Perot are $e^{1.1380} = 3.12$. These parameters are, of course, based on a log-linear model of independence and thus could be used to accurately model the cell counts in the table only if there is independence between the two variables.

Table 7.3 depicts the fitted values obtained from the model. To illustrate how these values result from the model (Equation 7.3), we demonstrate how the expected value for

Table 7.3 Fitted Values Obtained From Fitting the Log-Liner Model of Independence to the Data in Table 7.2

Political viewpoint	Choice for president			
	Bush	Clinton	Perot	Total
Liberal	163.94	216.64	69.43	450
Moderate	228.78	302.33	96.89	628
Conservative	254.28	336.03	107.69	698
Total	647	855	274	1776

liberals who voted for Clinton, μ_{12}, was computed. Because this particular count refers to the cell in the first row (first category of X) and second column (second category of Y) in the table, only the parameters λ_1^X and λ_2^Y are involved in the computation of the expected value (in addition to the general "intercept" term, λ). Therefore, the predicted value based on the parameters in Equation 7.3 is

$$\log(\mu_{12}) = \lambda + \lambda_1^X + \lambda_2^Y = 4.6792 - 0.4390 + 1.1380 = 5.3782,$$

and its exponentiated value is

$$\mu_{12} = \exp\{\log(\mu_{12})\} = \exp(5.3782) = e^{5.3782} = 216.6.$$

As stated previously, the model parameters ensure that the row and column marginal totals of the fitted (expected) values sum to the observed values and, as Tables 7.2 and 7.3 illustrate, this is indeed the case (any deviations are due to rounding). Moreover, the fitted values from the log-linear model of independence must satisfy the property that the odds ratio of fitted values in every 2×2 subtable is exactly 1. For example, the odds ratio obtained for the 2×2 subtable formed from the first two rows and columns of Table 7.3 is

$$\theta = \frac{163.94(302.33)}{216.64(228.78)} = 1.$$

In fact, the fitted values or expected frequencies shown in Table 7.3 can also be calculated directly using the procedures described in Chapter 4 (and obtained from proc freq in SAS or crosstabs in SPSS).

7.2.2   Saturated log-linear model for two-way contingency tables

In the example discussed in the previous section, there is quite a large discrepancy between the observed values, depicted in Table 7.2, and the fitted values obtained from fitting the log-linear model of independence that are depicted in Table 7.3. This suggests that, as one might guess, the two categorical variables are not independent and there is an association between political affiliation and voter preference. Recall from Chapter 4 that the hypothesis of independence can also be tested using the Pearson chi-squared or the likelihood ratio test statistic. For Table 7.2 these two test statistics are both statistically significant ($X^2 = 238.54$, $df = 4$, $p < 0.001$ and $G^2 = 247.70$, $df = 4$, $p < 0.001$), which provides further evidence that the two variables are not independent.

When there is evidence for dependency between the row and column variables of a two-way table, the dependency is modeled using two-way interaction terms in the log-linear modeling framework. However, fitting a log-linear model with a two-way interaction to a two-way contingency table is analogous to fitting the saturated model, which, as stated in Chapter 6, will fit the data perfectly. When fitting log-linear models, we generally hope to find models that are simpler than the data itself (i.e., simpler than the saturated model). With three categorical variables, two-way interactions can be included in the model and it will not be saturated. In general, for N categorical variables, a model that includes the N-way interaction will be saturated and, therefore, is not very useful.

To illustrate the saturated model using the previous example, the parameter estimates obtained from fitting the saturated model to the data presented in Table 7.2 are as follows:

$$\log(\mu_{ij}) = \lambda = + \lambda_i^X + \lambda_j^Y + \lambda_{ij}^{XY} = \lambda + \lambda_1^X + \lambda_2^X + \lambda_3^X + \lambda_1^Y + \lambda_2^Y + \lambda_3^Y$$

$$+ \lambda_{11}^{XY} + \lambda_{12}^{XY} + \lambda_{13}^{XY} + \lambda_{21}^{XY} + \lambda_{22}^{XY} + \lambda_{23}^{XY} + \lambda_{31}^{XY} + \lambda_{32}^{XY} + \lambda_{33}^{XY}$$

$$= 4.762 - 0.74 - 0.157 + 0 + 1.18 + 0.53 + 0$$

$$- 0.96 + 1.22 + 0 - 0.525 + 0.66 + 0 + 0 + 0 + 0.$$

With two categorical variables, each interaction term, λ_{ij}^{XY}, reflects deviation from independence and in effect forces the fitted or expected cell counts to be equal to the observed cell counts. To interpret the interaction terms we again need to exponentiate them and, since dummy coding was used for estimation, these exponentiated values reflect the odds ratio obtained using the particular cell of the table that the parameter corresponds to and the cells obtained from the last row and column of the table. For example, $\lambda_{11}^{XY} = -0.96$ and $e^{-0.96} = 0.383$. This value is equivalent to the odds of voting for Bush, rather than Perot, if one were a liberal, as compared to a conservative. In fact, this is exactly the odds ratio that would be obtained from the observed data (in Table 7.2),

$$\theta = \frac{70(117)}{382(56)} = 0.383,$$

because the saturated model fits the data perfectly. Note that the saturated model in this case requires the estimation of nine distinct (nonzero) parameters, and, because there are nine observed cell counts, there is no advantage to fitting and using the saturated model over simply examining the observed table.

As illustrated earlier, if one is interested in determining whether there is an association between only two categorical variables there is really no advantage to fitting a log-linear model to the data rather than simply using the procedures described in Chapter 4. This is because, typically, only the log-linear model for independence and the saturated model would be fit to a two-way contingency table and there is not any additional information provided from fitting these models that cannot be obtained directly from utilizing the analytical techniques presented in Chapter 4. However, this is not the case with higher-way tables that involve more than two variables.

7.3   Log-linear models for three-way contingency tables

When fitting log-linear models to higher-way tables it is typical to only consider models that are hierarchical in nature. These are models that include all lower-order terms for variables involved in higher-order terms in the model. For three variables, if any two-way interactions are included in the model then the individual (main) effects of the variables involved in these interactions should also be included in the model. For example, the following log-linear model is hierarchical because it contains two interaction terms, one for X and Y and one for X and Z, as well as the main effects for all three variables:

$$\log(\mu_{ijk}) = \lambda + \lambda_i^X + \lambda_j^Y + \lambda_k^Z + \lambda_{ij}^{XY} + \lambda_{ik}^{XZ}. \tag{7.4}$$

On the other hand, if one of the main effect terms was not included in Equation 7.4, then the model would not be hierarchical. In models that are not hierarchical, the statistical significance and substantive interpretation of the interaction terms in the model depends on how the variables were coded. However, in hierarchical models the coding schema used for the variables may influence the actual values of the parameters but does not change the interpretation of the interaction terms because the interaction terms in hierarchical models represent *only* the association or dependency between the variables involved in the interaction. Moreover, restricting our attention to hierarchical models provides us with a framework for comparing models that decrease in complexity and allows us to fit log-linear models for three-way contingency tables that correspond to the types of associations described in Chapter 5.

7.3.1   Saturated log-linear model for three-way contingency tables

As stated in Chapter 6, the saturated model is the most complex model that can be fit to any contingency table. It has no degrees of freedom and will always fit the observed data perfectly, but it requires as many parameters as there are observed frequencies (cells) and is, therefore, not useful or informative. For a three-way contingency table, with variables X, Y, and Z, the saturated model includes all main effects, all two-way interactions and the three-way interaction, and is represented symbolically as follows:

$$\log(\mu_{ijk}) = \lambda + \lambda_i^X + \lambda_j^Y + \lambda_k^Z + \lambda_{ij}^{XY} + \lambda_{ik}^{XZ} + \lambda_{jk}^{YZ} + \lambda_{ijk}^{XYZ}. \tag{7.5}$$

The systematic component of this model is similar to a three-way factorial ANOVA. The main effects are denoted by the single-variable terms, λ_i^X, λ_j^Y, and λ_k^Z, the two-way interaction terms represent partial associations and are denoted by the terms with two variables, λ_{ij}^{XY}, λ_{ik}^{XZ}, and λ_{jk}^{YZ}, and the three-way interaction term is denoted by the term with three variables, λ_{ijk}^{XYZ}. As stated previously, the saturated model is not very useful as a model because it does not provide a parsimonious summary of the relationships among the variables but rather contains as many parameters as there are observations. Simpler models can be arrived at by setting higher interaction terms to zero. As one might suspect, in the case of a three-way table the first interaction term that would be eliminated (set to zero) from the saturated log-linear is the three-way interaction term.

In the saturated model, the three-way interaction term indicates that the odds ratio between *any* two variables could vary across the levels of the third variable. In other words, the way in which the odds ratio for any two variables depends on (or varies with) the level of the third variable is modeled or captured by the three-way interaction. Therefore, eliminating the three-way interaction from the saturated model (setting it to zero) restricts the association between any two variables to be the same across all levels of the third variable. This was referred to as homogenous association in Chapter 5 and it is discussed in the context of log-linear models in the next section.

7.3.2   Homogeneous association log-linear model for three-way contingency tables

For three categorical variables, the log-linear model that contains all two-way interactions (and main effects) but not the three-way interaction is a model of association, not of independence, and is referred to as the **homogeneous association model**. Recall from Chapter 5 that having a homogeneous association in a three-way table implies that the association

Table 7.6 Summary of Log-Linear Models Fit to the Data in Table 7.4

Model	Parameters	Deviance	Number of parameters	Degrees of freedom
Saturated	$\lambda + \lambda_i^X + \lambda_j^Y + \lambda_k^Z + \lambda_{ij}^{XY} + \lambda_{ik}^{XZ} + \lambda_{jk}^{YZ} + \lambda_{ijk}^{XYZ}$	0.00	18	$18 - 18 = 0$
Homogeneous association	$\lambda + \lambda_i^X + \lambda_j^Y + \lambda_k^Z + \lambda_{ij}^{XY} + \lambda_{ik}^{XZ} + \lambda_{jk}^{YZ}$ _Dropped_	6.52	14	$18 - 14 = 4$
Conditional association (on Z)	$\lambda + \lambda_i^X + \lambda_j^Y + \lambda_k^Z + \lambda_{ik}^{XZ} + \lambda_{jk}^{YZ}$ $\langle X Y \rangle$	256.75	10	$18 - 10 = 8$
Conditional association (on Y)	$\lambda + \lambda_i^X + \lambda_j^Y + \lambda_k^Z + \lambda_{ij}^{XY} + \lambda_{jk}^{YZ}$ $\langle X 2 \rangle$	17.61	12	$18 - 12 = 6$
Conditional association (on X)	$\lambda + \lambda_i^X + \lambda_j^Y + \lambda_k^Z + \lambda_{ij}^{XY} + \lambda_{ik}^{XZ}$ $\langle Y 2 \rangle$	28.19	12	$18 - 12 = 6$

Note: X = religious views, Y = belief about God, and Z = gender.

the χ^2 distribution with degrees of freedom equal to 4 (i.e., 8 – 4). This result implies that if this interaction is eliminated from the homogeneous association model, the fit of the model would be adversely affected (decrease significantly) and so the interaction should be retained rather than eliminated.

Similarly, eliminating only the interaction between religious view (X) and gender (Z) from the model of homogeneous association increases the deviance to 17.61 with 6 degrees of freedom, resulting in a test statistic value of $G^2 = (17.61 - 6.52) = 11.09$ with $(6 - 4) = 2$ *df,* and this is also a statistically significant decrease in model fit. Finally, eliminating the interaction between belief about God (Y) by gender (Z) from the homogeneous association model increases the deviance to 28.19 with 6 degrees of freedom, yielding a statistically significant decrease in model fit with a test statistic of $G^2 = (28.19 - 6.52) = 21.67$ and $(6 - 4) = 2$ *df.* Therefore, eliminating any of the two-way interactions would result in a significant decrease in model fit and so none of these interactions should be eliminated. The best fitting model for this data set is thus the homogeneous association model.

A summary of the models discussed thus far along with their deviance values, number of parameters, and degrees of freedom is presented in Table 7.6. Each of the tests discussed to this point can be easily obtained from this table. For example, to obtain the difference between the last conditional association model in the table (conditional on X) and the homogeneous association model, we simply take the difference in deviances, $28.19 - 6.52 = 21.67$, and compare it to a χ^2 distribution with 2 degrees of freedom. Note that the degrees of freedom for the test can be obtained from either the difference in the number of parameters or the difference in degrees of freedom of the two models.

Even though the homogeneous association model seems to be the most parsimonious model for the data depicted in Table 7.4, for illustrative purposes we consider the fitted values, shown in Table 7.7, for the conditional association model in which the religious view (X) by gender (Z) interaction term is eliminated:

$$\log(\mu_{ijk}) = \lambda + \lambda_i^X + \lambda_j^Y + \lambda_k^Z + \lambda_{ik}^{XY} + \lambda_{jk}^{YZ}.$$

Table 7.7 Fitted Values Obtained From Fitting the Conditional Association Log-Linear Model (With the Religious View and Gender Interaction Term Eliminated) to the Data in Table 7.4

| Gender | Religious views | Think God is judgmental? | | | |
		Yes	No	Unsure	Total
Male	Liberal	33.54	126.93	30.66	191.13
	Moderate	93.43	123.22	55.29	271.94
	Conservative	183.03	73.86	64.05	671.94
Female	Liberal	36.46	215.07	25.34	276.87
	Moderate	101.57	208.78	45.71	356.06
	Conservative	198.97	125.14	52.95	377.06
Total		647	873	274	1794

This particular conditional association model forces religious view and gender to be independent within each of the partial tables corresponding to the three different beliefs about God. Table 7.8 reorganizes the fitted values shown in Table 7.7 into the three two-way conditional tables, conditioning on belief about God. Conceptually, since eliminating the religious view by gender interaction term forces these two variables, conditioning on

Table 7.8 Partial Tables of Fitted Values (From Table 7.7), Obtained From Fitting the Conditional Association Log-Linear Model (With the Religious View and Gender Interaction Term Eliminated) to the Data in Table 7.4

Yes, God is judgmental

| Gender | Religious view | | | Total |
	Liberal	Moderate	Conservative	
Male	33.54	93.43	183.03	310
Female	36.46	101.57	198.97	337
Total	70	195	382	647

No, God is not judgmental

| Gender | Religious view | | | Total |
	Liberal	Moderate	Conservative	
Male	126.93	123.22	73.86	324
Female	215.07	208.78	125.14	549
Total	342	332	199	873

Not sure if God is judgmental

| Gender | Religious view | | | Total |
	Liberal	Moderate	Conservative	
Male	30.66	55.29	64.05	150
Female	25.34	45.71	52.95	124
Total	56	101	117	274

belief about God, to be conditionally independent, the odds ratio computed for any 2×2 subtable using the fitted values shown in Table 7.8 will be equivalent to one. For example, for respondents who believed that God is judgmental, the odds of a liberal religious view (as opposed to a moderate view) for males relative to females is

$$\theta = \frac{33.54(101.57)}{36.46(93.43)} = 1.0.$$

The same result would be obtained with similar computations using any of the 2×2 subtables in any of the three partial tables. This is because the conditional association model that was fit forces gender and religious view to be independent given one's belief in God.

7.3.4   Conditional independence versus marginal independence in log-linear models

Reread

Recall from Chapter 5 that conditional independence does not imply marginal independence. Therefore, when a conditional association model that excludes the XZ interaction term was fit to the data in Table 7.4 (see previous section), religious view (X) and gender (Z) were restricted to be conditionally independent (conditioning on belief about God) but this did not imply that religious view and gender are marginally independent (ignoring belief about God). To demonstrate this fact, Table 7.9 depicts the marginal table of fitted values (from either Table 7.7 or 7.8) for religious view and gender collapsing (i.e., summing) across belief about God. Using these fitted values to calculate the odds of males (versus females) having a liberal (versus moderate) religious view we get

$$\theta = \frac{191.13(356.06)}{276.87(271.94)} = 0.904.$$

Clearly, this conditional association model does not restrict these two variables to be marginally independent.

However, this particular conditional association model (that excludes the XZ interaction term) does force some of the marginal and conditional associations to be equivalent. Specifically, since this model has forced gender (Z) and religious view (X) to be

Table 7.9 Marginal Table, Collapsing Across Belief About God, of Fitted Values From Table 7.7 or Table 7.8, Obtained From Fitting the Conditional Association Log-Linear Model (With the Religious View and Gender Interaction Term Eliminated) to the Data in Table 7.4

Gender	Religious view			Total
	Liberal	Moderate	Conservative	
Male	191.13	271.94	320.94	784
Female	276.87	356.06	377.06	1010
Total	468	628	698	1767

Categorical data analysis for the behavioral and social sciences

conditionally independent controlling for belief about God (Y), the marginal and partial odds ratios for religious view (X) and belief about God (Y) will be identical as will the marginal and partial odds ratios for belief about God (Y) and gender (Z). For example, consider the rearrangement of the fitted values from Table 7.7 (or Table 7.8) showing the marginal table of fitted values for religious view (X) and belief about God (Y) collapsed across gender (Z), which are depicted in Table 7.10. If these values are used to calculate the (marginal) odds of a respondent with a liberal religious view (as opposed to a moderate religious view) believing that God is judgmental (as opposed to not believing God is judgmental) we get

$$\theta = \frac{70(332)}{195(342)} = 0.348,$$

which implies that liberal respondents are much less likely to believe that God is judgmental. Likewise, if the same odds ratio is computed from the partial table for males depicted in Table 7.7 we obtain

$$\theta = \frac{33.54(123.22)}{93.43(126.93)} = 0.348$$

for male respondents, and if we calculate the same odds ratio from the partial table (in Table 7.7) for females we obtain

$$\theta = \frac{36.46(208.78)}{101.57(215.07)} = 0.348$$

for female respondents. Therefore, the marginal association between X and Y is equal to the conditional associations between X and Y. The same equivalence would hold if we used these fitted values to compute the marginal and conditional associations for belief about God (Y) and gender (Z).

In general, a conditional association log-linear model used to model the relationships in a three-way contingency table restricts the marginal and partial odds ratios for the variables whose interactions are included in the model to be equivalent. So, for example, if the XY interaction is excluded but the XZ and YZ interactions are included in the model then the marginal and conditional associations for the XZ variables will be equivalent as

Table 7.10 Marginal Table, Collapsing Across Gender, of Fitted Values From Table 7.7 or Table 7.8, Obtained From Fitting the Conditional Association Log-Linear Model (With the Religious View and Gender Interaction Term Eliminated) to the Data in Table 7.4

Religious view	Belief about God			Total
	Liberal	Moderate	Conservative	
Liberal	70	342	56	468
Moderate	195	332	101	628
Conservative	382	199	117	698
Total	647	873	274	1794

will those for the *YZ* variables. Likewise, if only the *XZ* interaction is excluded (which was the case in our substantive example), then the marginal and conditional associations for the *XY* variables will be equivalent as will those for the *YZ* variables. Finally, if only the *YZ* interaction is excluded, then the marginal and conditional associations for the *XY* variables will be equivalent as will those for the *XZ* variables.

7.3.5 Joint independence and complete independence log-linear models for three-way contingency tables

Although none of the conditional association models were found to fit the data in Table 7.4 as well as the homogeneous association model, if one of these models were found to fit as well, then a researcher would typically be interested in seeing if an even simpler model could be used to model the relationships inherent in the data. The **joint independence** model is more parsimonious than the conditional association model, and it is a model that contains only one two-way interaction (so it is formed by eliminating two of the two-way interaction terms from the homogeneous association model). In the joint independence model, one of the categorical variables will not be involved in any interactions. For example, if the *XY* interaction is eliminated first from the homogeneous association model then the resulting conditional association model is

$$\log(\mu_{ijk}) = \lambda + \lambda_i^X + \lambda_j^Y + \lambda_k^Z + \lambda_{ik}^{XZ} + \lambda_{jk}^{YZ}.$$

From this model, either the *XZ* or the *YZ* interactions would, by process of elimination, have to be the next interaction to be eliminated. If the *XZ* interaction is eliminated next then the resulting joint independence model is

$$\log(\mu_{ijk}) = \lambda + \lambda_i^X + \lambda_j^Y + \lambda_k^Z + \lambda_{jk}^{YZ}$$

and the *X* variable is not involved in any of the interaction terms of the model. Similarly, if the *YZ* interaction term was eliminated from the initial conditional association model then the *Y* variable would not be involved in any interactions. The joint association model thus consists of the main effects for all three variables and only one two-way interaction. Continuing with our substantive example (Table 7.4) for illustrative purposes, suppose that after eliminating the Religious View (*X*) × Gender (*Z*) interaction from the homogeneous association model we found that we were also able to eliminate the belief about God (*Y*) × Gender (*Z*) interaction term from the model. Then gender would not be involved in any interaction terms and would be represented only as a main effect in the joint independence model:

$$\log(\mu_{ijk}) = \lambda + \lambda_i^X + \lambda_j^Y + \lambda_k^Z + \lambda_{ij}^{XY}.$$

Fitting this model restricts the partial odds ratios for religious view and gender, given belief about God, and the partial odds ratios for belief about God and gender, given religious view, to both be equal to one. In other words, this model implies that there is no association between religious view (*X*) and gender (*Z*) after controlling for belief about God (*Y*), and there is no association between belief about God (*Y*) and gender (*Z*) after controlling for religious view (*X*). However, there is a conditional association between religious view (*X*) and belief about God (*Y*) conditioning on (or controlling for) gender (*Z*), and this association (measured by the conditional odds ratio between these two variables) is equivalent across the two genders.

Finally, if the last interaction term is eliminated from the model, then this results in a model with no interactions terms, called the **complete independence** log-linear model:

$$\log(\mu_{ijk}) = \lambda + \lambda_i^X + \lambda_j^Y + \lambda_k^Z.$$

This model includes only main effects and implies, since it includes no interactions, that there are no associations among any of the categorical variables considered. Rather, all variables are independent of each other.

7.3.6   Summary of log-linear models for three-way contingency tables

Figure 7.1 summarizes the different log-linear models that can be fit to data from a three-way contingency table, in order of complexity, to illustrate the order in which a researcher would typically fit various log-linear models to find the most parsimonious model that can be used to describe the relationships inherent in the data. In this conceptualization, less complex models are nested within the more complex models, as each of the simpler models is a special case of a more complex model in which some parameters are eliminated (restricted to be zero).

Once the most parsimonious model is selected to explain the pattern of associations in a given data set, the highest-level terms (parameters) of this model are usually interpreted. Lower-level terms are interpreted only if the variables involved in these parameters are not involved in any higher-level terms. In general, the interpretation of parameters depends on their level of complexity: the lowest-level terms (involving only one variable) in a log-linear model are "main effects" and represent conditional odds; two-way interaction terms represent conditional odds ratios (i.e., the association between two variables); and three-way interaction terms represent the ratios of conditional odds ratios (i.e., a comparison of the association between two variables across levels of the third variable). In Sections 7.5 and 7.6, examples are discussed that further illustrate how these parameters can be interpreted.

7.4   Inference for log-linear models: model fit

A good fitting log-linear model provides a basis for describing the true associations among a set of categorical variables in the most parsimonious manner. As previously alluded to in this chapter (and in Chapter 6), one way to determine the best fitting model is to compare the deviance of nested models to establish which of the models provides the best fit. This is equivalent to conducting likelihood ratio tests and, typically, the order in which these tests are conducted is based on the hierarchy presented in Figure 7.1. However, as is usually the case in hypothesis testing, with a large sample a statistically significant difference between nested models can be weak and unimportant. Conversely, with small samples reality may be much more complex than indicated by the simplest model that is found by comparing the deviances of nested models. Therefore, it is important to examine the fit of the model and its residuals to ensure adequate fit.

In addition to comparing the deviance for hierarchical log-linear models to determine the best fitting model, the same tests that are used to test the association between categorical variables (i.e., X^2 and G^2) can be used to test the model fit of a particular model. The difference between using the deviance to compare the fit of nested models and using it to test the fit of a particular model is simply a difference in the hypothesis that is tested. In the

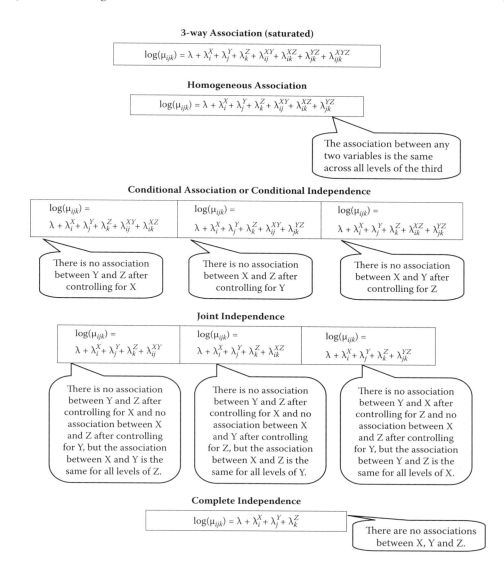

Figure 7.1 Summary of hierarchy of log-linear models for three-way contingency tables in order of complexity.

first case the hypothesis tested is whether the simpler nested model fits just as well as the more complex model, while in the latter case the hypothesis tested is whether the simpler model fits just as well as the (most complex) saturated model (i.e., the observed data).

To test the fit of a particular model, recall that both goodness-of-fit test statistics (i.e., X^2 and G^2) compare the expected values or fitted counts (E) to the observed counts (O). Specifically,

$$X^2 = \sum \frac{(O-E)^2}{E} \tag{7.8}$$

and

$$G^2 = 2\sum O\log\left(\frac{O}{E}\right),\tag{7.9}$$

where the sum is over all cells. The null hypothesis for either of these tests can be stated as:

> H_0: The observed data fit the model, or there is no difference between the expected (fitted) and observed (actual) counts.

The test statistics (in Equations 7.8 and 7.9) can be used to evaluate the overall global fit of a particular model; a significant result indicates poor fit (or poor correspondence between the data and the model), whereas a nonsignificant result indicates that the data adequately fit the model. Note that the saturated model is essentially the observed data, and so when the model is saturated the data fit the model perfectly and the test statistics will be zero. Note also that G^2 is thus the deviance of the model. These test statistics follow approximately a χ^2 distribution with degrees of freedom determined by the number of parameters estimated in the log-linear model that is fit. Specifically, the degrees of freedom are the difference between the number of cells in the table (or nonredundant parameters in the saturated model) and the number of nonredundant parameters in the model of interest. For example, when fitting the model of conditional independence for a 3×3 table (such as the data in Table 7.2), the degrees of freedom would be 4 because there are 9 cells in the table and 5 parameters estimated by the model of conditional independence (i.e., the intercept, two main effect parameters for the row variable and two main effect parameters for the column variable).

These global fit statistics are based on the overall difference between the observed cell counts and the expected cell counts (those that are predicted by the model), yet another way to assess the fit of a model is to analyze the residuals, which reflect local differences between the observed and expected cell counts. The adjusted residuals, which are approximately normally distributed, are especially useful in helping a researcher better understand why a particular model does not fit well. The residuals can be used to indicate which cells in the table are contributing most to the lack of fit, thereby helping the researcher identify an alternative model that might fit better.

Since all of the inferential procedures generalize to higher-way tables, their use will be illustrated in the next section, where log-linear modeling is used to model the data in a four-way contingency table.

7.5 Log-linear models for higher tables

All of the concepts presented for three-way tables extend to higher-way tables. However, as is the case in ANOVA, each additional categorical variable that is considered adds a great deal of complexity to the models that a researcher has to contend with. With a four-way table there is a four-way interaction term, as well as 4 three-way interaction terms, 6 two-way interaction terms, and four main effects. In fact, the number of parameters grows exponentially with the addition of each categorical variable and conducting all of the log-likelihood ratio tests for each of the hierarchical models is cumbersome. Therefore, it is best to make use of all the model-fitting procedures in concert to try and simplify the process of finding a model that best represents the data.

Consider the hypothetical four-way contingency table depicted in Table 7.11, which classifies high school students in terms of their gender, IQ, socioeconomic status (SES), and

Table 7.11 Four-Way Contingency Table of Gender,
IQ, SES, and College Aspirations

G Gender	I IQ	S SES	College plans A	
			Yes	No
Male	Above average	High	618	158
		Low	151	195
	Below average	High	130	225
		Low	76	579
Female	Above average	High	588	200
		Low	113	257
	Below average	High	129	227
		Low	53	809

college aspirations. Using the notation *G, I, S,* and *A* to represent the variables gender, IQ, SES and college aspirations, respectively, we can use the deviance of the following model (containing all three-way interactions)

$$\log(\mu_{ijkl}) = \lambda + \lambda_i^G + \lambda_j^I + \lambda_k^S + \lambda_l^A + \lambda_{ij}^{GI} + \lambda_{ik}^{GS} + \lambda_{il}^{GA} + \lambda_{jk}^{IS} + \lambda_{jl}^{IA} + \lambda_{kl}^{SA}$$
$$+ \lambda_{ijk}^{GIS} + \lambda_{ijl}^{GIA} + \lambda_{ikl}^{GSA} + \lambda_{jkl}^{ISA} \tag{7.10}$$

to compare its fit to that of the following saturated model (which, recall, fits the data perfectly)

$$\log(\mu_{ijkl}) = \lambda + \lambda_i^G + \lambda_j^I + \lambda_k^S + \lambda_l^A + \lambda_{ij}^{GI} + \lambda_{ik}^{GS} + \lambda_{il}^{GA} + \lambda_{jk}^{IS} + \lambda_{jl}^{IA} + \lambda_{kl}^{SA}$$
$$+ \lambda_{ijk}^{GIS} + \lambda_{ijl}^{GIA} + \lambda_{ikl}^{GSA} + \lambda_{jkl}^{ISA} + \lambda_{ijkl}^{GISA}.$$

To facilitate the discussion of model comparisons that follows, Table 7.12 lists the models that were fit (and are discussed) along with their deviances and degrees of freedom. For this data set, the deviance obtained from fitting the log-linear model that includes all interactions except for the four-way interaction (Equation 7.10) is 1.61 with 1 degree of freedom, which is not significant ($p = 0.204$). Thankfully, this implies that this model (Equation 7.10, without the four-way interaction) fits just as well as the saturated model and so there is a more parsimonious (simpler) model than the saturated model that can be used to describe the associations inherent in the data. Once the four-way interaction can be safely

Table 7.12 Models Fit to the Data in Table 7.11

Model equation	Three-way interaction terms included	Deviance	Degrees of freedom
7.10	GIS, GIA, GSA, ISA	1.61	1
7.11	None	14.60	5
7.12	GSA	3.09	4

eliminated, to determine which, if any, of the three-way interaction terms are needed in the model, there are two approaches that could be taken. One approach would be to eliminate each of the three-way interaction terms (from the model in Equation 7.10) one at a time and compare the deviance for each of the resulting models to the model that includes all of the three-way interaction terms (Equation 7.10). An alternative approach would be to eliminate all of the three-way interaction terms at once, resulting in the model

$$\log(\mu_{ijkl}) = \lambda + \lambda_i^G + \lambda_j^I + \lambda_k^S + \lambda_l^A + \lambda_{ij}^{GI} + \lambda_{ik}^{GS} + \lambda_{il}^{GA} + \lambda_{jk}^{IS} + \lambda_{jl}^{IA} + \lambda_{kl}^{SA}, \tag{7.11}$$

and look at the overall global fit of this model in addition to examining its residuals to determine which cells indicate a lack of fit. Using the second approach for this example, the deviance obtained from fitting a log-linear model with no three-way interaction terms (Equation 7.11) is 14.60, and with 5 degrees of freedom the *p*-value for the fit of this model (i.e., in comparison to the saturated model) is $p = 0.012$. This indicates that the model does not appear to fit the data well. In addition, the difference between the deviance of this model (Equation 7.11) and the deviance of the model with all of the three-way interaction terms (Equation 7.10) is 12.99, and with 4 degrees of freedom this indicates a statistically significant decrease in model fit ($p = 0.011$). Therefore, it does not appear that eliminating all three-way interactions is appropriate for these data.

However, the sample size in this example is quite large so the change in fit, although statistically significant, may not be indicative of substantive differences. Therefore, it makes sense to examine the adjusted residuals for the log-linear model without any three-way interaction terms to determine if there is a pattern to the lack of fit that may help us to understand which, if any, of the three-way interaction terms are needed. These residuals, obtained from fitting the model without any of the three-way interaction terms (Equation 7.11), are shown in Table 7.13. Examining the residuals, it appears that there may be an interaction between gender, SES, and college aspirations. Specifically, the cells that demonstrate the greatest lack of fit indicate that, compared to the observed counts, the model predicts more high SES males as not having college aspirations and less low SES males as not having college aspirations. Conversely, this model predicts less high SES

Table 7.13 Adjusted Residuals Obtained From Fitting a Log-Linear Model With No Three-Way Interaction Terms to the Data in Table 7.11

Gender	IQ	SES	College plans Yes	College plans No
Male	Above average	High	−1.918	0.215
		Low	2.276	−0.044
	Below average	High	−0.852	**2.833**
		Low	1.227	**−2.551**
Female	Above average	High	1.640	0.152
		Low	−1.917	−0.296
	Below average	High	1.266	**−3.074**
		Low	−1.726	**2.764**

females as not having college aspirations and more low SES females as not having college aspirations. If we now fit the model

$$\log(\mu_{ijkl}) = \lambda + \lambda_i^G + \lambda_j^I + \lambda_k^S + \lambda_l^A + \lambda_{ij}^{GI} + \lambda_{ik}^{GS} + \lambda_{il}^{GA} + \lambda_{jk}^{IS} + \lambda_{jl}^{IA} + \lambda_{kl}^{SA} + \lambda_{ikl}^{GSA} \tag{7.12}$$

that includes only the three-way interaction between gender, SES, and college aspirations (i.e., without the other 2 three-way interactions), to the data in Table 7.11, we obtain a deviance of 3.087 with 4 degrees of freedom, which is not statistically significant ($p = 0.543$) and therefore indicates that this model provides adequate fit. Moreover, the difference between the deviance obtained from this model and the deviance obtained from the model with all of the three-way interactions (Equation 7.10) is only 1.47, and with 3 degrees of freedom this difference in fit is not statistically significant ($p = 0.687$). Therefore, it appears that (at the very least) none of the other three-way interaction terms are needed to model the associations in the data.

Comparing the deviance for the model that includes the Gender × SES × College Aspiration interaction term (Equation 7.12) to the model without any three-way interaction terms (Equation 7.11) results in an increase in deviance of 11.51, and with 1 degree of freedom this is a statistically significant decrease in model fit ($p < 0.001$). Therefore, from a statistical perspective, this three-way interaction term is needed, as it contributes significantly to model fit. However, including a three-way interaction term in the model makes interpretation of the results more complex and, as stated previously, it is unclear whether this term is needed from a substantive perspective.

One way to further evaluate the need for the three-way interaction (in Equation 7.12) is to look at the similarity of the two models (Equations 7.11 and 7.12) in terms of the fitted odds ratios. The fitted (expected) odds ratios can be computed either from the fitted values for the model or by using the parameter estimates for the model. The former approach has been demonstrated in previous sections of this chapter to illustrate how the odds ratios are affected by different models and, as it also seems to be conceptually simpler, will be the approach demonstrated here.

Since the models that we are comparing do not include a four-way interaction term, we presume that the three-way association between gender, SES, and college aspiration is the same for every IQ level. Therefore, we need only look at the three-way tables for either the high IQ respondents or the low IQ respondents. The fitted values obtained from the two different models considered (Equations 7.11 and 7.12) for the high IQ respondents are presented in Table 7.14. The model with the three-way interaction term (Equation 7.12) assumes that the odds ratios for the two-way partial table that cross-classifies respondents by SES and college aspiration differs for males and females, while the model without this interaction term assumes that the odds ratios for the SES by college aspiration partial tables are equivalent for the two genders. Indeed, using the fitted values in Table 7.14 obtained from the model without any three-way interactions, the odds of having college aspirations for high (vs. low) SES respondents are the same for both males (M) and females (F):

$$\theta_M = \frac{635.71(195.34)}{156.41(134.53)} = \theta_F = \frac{573.05(259.42)}{126.70(198.83)} = 5.9. \tag{7.13}$$

Using the fitted values in Table 7.14 obtained from the model with the *GSA* three-way interaction term, the odds of having college aspirations for high (vs. low) SES male respondents is

$$\theta_M = \frac{615.88(189.21)}{166.63(150.27)} = 4.65, \tag{7.14}$$

Table 7.14 Fitted Values Obtained From Two Log-Linear Models Fit to Data in Table 7.11

		Log-linear model fit						
		No three-way interaction term				SES*gender*aspiration interaction		
		Males		Females		Males		Females	
	SES:	High	Low	High	Low	High	Low	High	Low
Plans for	Yes	635.71	134.53	573.05	198.83	615.88	150.27	593.01	110.84
college	No	153.41	195.34	126.70	259.42	166.63	189.21	188.47	265.68

whereas the same odds ratio for females is

$$\theta_F = \frac{593.01(265.68)}{188.47(110.84)} = 7.54. \tag{7.15}$$

So, when the *GSA* three-way interaction term is included in the model, the difference between the estimated odds ratios for males and females does not appear to be trivial. Therefore, there is both statistical and substantive evidence for including the three-way interaction term in the model.

At this point, however, it is unclear whether the model containing the three-way interaction term for *GSA* (Equation 7.12) is the most parsimonious model that can adequately fit the data in Table 7.11. Specifically, it is unclear whether any of the two-way interaction terms in this model, which are not nested within the three-way interaction term, can be eliminated from the model. In other words, because IQ is not involved in the three-way interaction in this model, any of the two-way interaction terms that include IQ can be eliminated from the model (Equation 7.12) to obtain a nested model that preserves the hierarchical structure. For example, eliminating the two-way interaction term for gender and IQ (*GI*) increases the deviance by only 0.133, which clearly is not statistically significant. However, the deviance increases to 141.81 or 602.94 when the IQ × SES (*IS*) or the IQ × College Aspiration (*IA*) two-way interactions, respectively, are eliminated from the model. Therefore, the most parsimonious model that can be fit to the data in Table 7.11 includes all two-way interaction terms with the exception of IQ × Gender, and only the three-way interaction term corresponding to gender, SES, and college aspirations:

$$\log(\mu_{ijkl}) = \lambda + \lambda_i^G + \lambda_j^I + \lambda_k^S + \lambda_l^A + \lambda_{ik}^{GS} + \lambda_{il}^{GA} + \lambda_{jk}^{IS} + \lambda_{jl}^{IA} + \lambda_{kl}^{SA} + \lambda_{ikl}^{GSA}. \tag{7.16}$$

The presence of the *GSA* term in this model indicates that

- the association between gender and SES differs for the two college aspiration levels;
- the association between gender and college aspiration differs for the two SES levels; and
- the association between SES and college aspiration differ for males and females.

Therefore, none of these two-way effects (*GS*, *GA*, or *SA*) should be interpreted. However, all of the two-way effects that that include IQ can be interpreted because these associations do not differ at different levels of the other variables. All of the estimated nonzero parameters for this log-linear model are presented in Table 7.15. The parameters of

Table 7.15 Estimated Parameters and Related Statistics for Most Parsimonious Log-Linear Model for Data in Table 7.11

Parameter estimate	df	Estimate	Std. error	Wald 95% confidence limits		Chi-squared	p-Value
Intercept	1	6.69	0.03	6.62	6.75	40850.90	<.001
Gender - Male	1	−0.32	0.05	−0.41	−0.23	45.95	<.001
IQ - High	1	−1.11	0.05	−1.21	−1.01	483.39	<.001
SES - High	1	−1.21	0.06	−1.33	−1.08	358.81	<.001
Aspire - Yes	1	−2.67	0.10	−2.86	−2.48	764.34	<.001
Gender*SES (Male - High)	1	0.21	0.08	0.05	0.38	6.22	.01
Gender*Aspire (Male - Yes)	1	0.63	0.11	0.41	0.85	31.66	<.001
IQ*SES (High - High)	1	0.87	0.07	0.72	1.01	141.24	<.001
IQ*Aspire (High - Yes)	1	1.80	0.08	1.65	1.95	557.40	<.001
SES*Aspire (High - Yes)	1	2.02	0.11	1.81	2.23	355.63	<.001
Gender*SES*Aspire (Male - High - Yes)	1	−0.48	0.14	−0.76	−0.20	11.42	<.001

the model that should be interpreted are the two-way interactions that include IQ as well as the three-way interaction between gender, SES, and college aspirations.

The three-way association parameter (see Table 7.15) is −0.48 and is interpreted as the ratio of two conditional odds ratios. The conditional odds ratios represent the association between two of the variables at each level of the third variable, and the parameter compares these conditional odds ratios to each other. In this data set, we could (for example) interpret this parameter as a gender comparison of the association between SES and college aspirations: for males, the odds ratio that compares the odds of having college aspirations among those of high SES and low SES is $e^{-0.48} = 0.62$ times the same odds ratio for females. In other words, this odds ratio is (significantly) higher for females than for males. In fact, using the fitted values from this model we can determine that for males the conditional odds ratio is 6.66 and for females it is 10.78 (and 6.66/10.78 = 0.62). Therefore, although for both genders there is an association such that the odds of having college aspirations are higher for those of high SES than for those of low SES, this association is stronger in females than in males. The same results and interpretation could also have been reached by computing the fitted (predicted) values from this model separately for males and females using the appropriate parameter estimates.

The two-way interaction between IQ and college aspirations (*IA*) should also be interpreted in this model. Because SES and gender are included in the model, the parameter estimate for this two-way association is a conditional odds ratio that controls for SES and gender. In other words, the association between IQ and college aspirations is considered to be equal for all levels of SES and gender, and this common association is represented by the *IA* parameter estimate of 1.80. This two-way parameter estimate represents an odds ratio and indicates that the odds of having college aspirations are $e^{1.80} = 6.0$ times higher for those with an above average IQ compared to those with below average IQ. This conditional odds ratio represents the *IA* association within each SES and gender combination.

Similarly, the two-way interaction between IQ and SES (*IS*) can also be interpreted in this model as the conditional association between IQ and SES within each aspiration and gender combination. The parameter estimate for this association is 0.87 and indicates that the odds of having an above average IQ are $e^{0.87} = 2.4$ times higher for high SES respondents than for low SES respondents. In other words, this is the association between IQ and SES controlling for aspiration level and gender.

7.6 Computer output: fitting log-linear models

To obtain computer output for the four-way log-linear models fit in this chapter, syntax and output for SAS, as well as menu instructions and output for SPSS, are discussed in this section. To our knowledge, neither software program automatically provides test results for model comparisons; however, these test results can be obtained by computing the difference between deviance values from two nested models and evaluating it using the chi-squared distribution. One useful online calculator for this purpose can be found at http://www.stat.tamu.edu/~west/applets/chisqdemo.html.

7.6.1 SAS

The SAS program used to fit the saturated log-linear model to the four-way contingency table depicted in Table 7.11 is provided in Figure 7.2. Note that the data set is entered in the usual manner. The SAS procedure genmod is used to request that a generalized linear model be fit to the data:

- The "dist=poisson" statement indicates that count data is being modeled, therefore a Poisson distribution should be used.

```
data fourway;
 input gender $ IQ $ SES $ aspire $ count;
 cards;
 M H H H 618
 M H H L 158
 M H L H 151
 M H L L 195
 M L H H 130
 M L H L 225
 M L L H 76
 M L L L 579
 F H H H 588
 F H H L 200
 F H L H 113
 F H L L 257
 F L H H 129
 F L H L 227
 F L L H 53
 F L L L 809
 ;

proc genmod order=data;
    class gender iq ses aspire;
    model count = gender iq ses aspire gender*iq gender*ses gender*aspire
        iq*ses iq*aspire ses*aspire gender*iq*ses gender*iq*aspire
        gender*ses*aspire iq*ses*aspire gender*iq*ses*aspire
        /dist=poisson link=log obstats;
    run;
```

Figure 7.2 SAS program to fit saturated model to four-way table depicted in Table 7.11.

- The "link=log" statement indicates that the link function that should be used is the log function.
- The "obstats" statement requests that the fitted values and the residuals be provided in the output.

To fit the model with only the three-way interactions, the four-way interaction term (i.e., gender*iq*ses*aspire) simply needs to be removed. Similarly, to fit the log-linear model with only two-way interactions all of the three-way interaction terms need to be removed.

The parameter estimates and test statistics obtained from fitting the log-linear model with all two-way interaction terms and the gender*ses*aspire three-way interaction term are depicted in Figure 7.3. Note that the deviance in the output is identical to that reported

```
                          The GENMOD Procedure

                          Model Information

                  Data Set              WORK.FOURWAY
                  Distribution               Poisson
                  Link Function                  Log
                  Dependent Variable           count


          Number of Observations Read          16
          Number of Observations Used          16


                     Class Level Information

                  Class      Levels    Values

                  gender         2     M F
                  IQ             2     H L
                  SES            2     H L
                  aspire         2     H L


              Criteria For Assessing Goodness Of Fit

         Criterion              DF        Value      Value/DF

         Deviance                4        3.0874      0.7719
         Scaled Deviance         4        3.0874      0.7719
         Pearson Chi-Square       4        3.0890      0.7723
         Scaled Pearson X2        4        3.0890      0.7723
         Log Likelihood                22166.6848


   Algorithm converged.


                  Analysis Of Parameter Estimates

                                    Standard      Wald 95%       Chi-
  Parameter          DF  Estimate    Error    Confidence Limits  Square  Pr > ChiSq

  Intercept           1    6.6850    0.0340    6.6185   6.7516  38749.4    <.0001
  gender      M       1   -0.3138    0.0502   -0.4122  -0.2153    39.02    <.0001
  gender      F       0    0.0000    0.0000    0.0000   0.0000      .        .
  IQ          H       1   -1.1027    0.0589   -1.2181  -0.9874   350.98    <.0001
  IQ          L       0    0.0000    0.0000    0.0000   0.0000      .        .
  SES         H       1   -1.2105    0.0642   -1.3363  -1.0848   355.86    <.0001
  SES         L       0    0.0000    0.0000    0.0000   0.0000      .        .
  aspire      H       1   -2.6747    0.0981   -2.8670  -2.4825   743.81    <.0001
  aspire      L       0    0.0000    0.0000    0.0000   0.0000      .        .
```

Figure 7.3 SAS output from fitting the log-linear model with all two-way interaction terms and the gender*SES*aspire three-way interaction term to the data in Table 7.11.

```
  gender*IQ           M  H     1    -0.0256    0.0694   -0.1616    0.1103    0.14     0.7117
  gender*IQ           M  L     0     0.0000    0.0000    0.0000    0.0000      .        .
  gender*IQ           F  H     0     0.0000    0.0000    0.0000    0.0000      .        .
  gender*IQ           F  L     0     0.0000    0.0000    0.0000    0.0000      .        .
  gender*SES          M  H     1     0.2163    0.0858    0.0481    0.3844    6.35     0.0117
  gender*SES          M  L     0     0.0000    0.0000    0.0000    0.0000      .        .
  gender*SES          F  H     0     0.0000    0.0000    0.0000    0.0000      .        .
  gender*SES          F  L     0     0.0000    0.0000    0.0000    0.0000      .        .
  gender*aspire       M  H     1     0.6438    0.1162    0.4160    0.8715   30.69    <.0001
  gender*aspire       M  L     0     0.0000    0.0000    0.0000    0.0000      .        .
  gender*aspire       F  H     0     0.0000    0.0000    0.0000    0.0000      .        .
  gender*aspire       F  L     0     0.0000    0.0000    0.0000    0.0000      .        .
  IQ*SES              H  H     1     0.8672    0.0729    0.7242    1.0102  141.33    <.0001
  IQ*SES              H  L     0     0.0000    0.0000    0.0000    0.0000      .        .
  IQ*SES              L  H     0     0.0000    0.0000    0.0000    0.0000      .        .
  IQ*SES              L  L     0     0.0000    0.0000    0.0000    0.0000      .        .
  IQ*aspire           H  H     1     1.8005    0.0764    1.6507    1.9503  554.99    <.0001
  IQ*aspire           H  L     0     0.0000    0.0000    0.0000    0.0000      .        .
  IQ*aspire           L  H     0     0.0000    0.0000    0.0000    0.0000      .        .
  IQ*aspire           L  L     0     0.0000    0.0000    0.0000    0.0000      .        .
  SES*aspire          H  H     1     2.0205    0.1071    1.8105    2.2305  355.58    <.0001
  SES*aspire          H  L     0     0.0000    0.0000    0.0000    0.0000      .        .
  SES*aspire          L  H     0     0.0000    0.0000    0.0000    0.0000      .        .
  SES*aspire          L  L     0     0.0000    0.0000    0.0000    0.0000      .        .
  gender*SES*aspire   M  H  H  1    -0.4828    0.1426   -0.7624   -0.2032   11.45     0.0007
  gender*SES*aspire   M  H  L  0     0.0000    0.0000    0.0000    0.0000      .        .
  gender*SES*aspire   M  L  H  0     0.0000    0.0000    0.0000    0.0000      .        .
  gender*SES*aspire   M  L  L  0     0.0000    0.0000    0.0000    0.0000      .        .
  gender*SES*aspire   F  H  H  0     0.0000    0.0000    0.0000    0.0000      .        .
  gender*SES*aspire   F  H  L  0     0.0000    0.0000    0.0000    0.0000      .        .
  gender*SES*aspire   F  L  H  0     0.0000    0.0000    0.0000    0.0000      .        .
  gender*SES*aspire   F  L  L  0     0.0000    0.0000    0.0000    0.0000      .        .
  Scale                        0     1.0000    0.0000    1.0000    1.0000

  NOTE: The scale parameter was held fixed.
```

Figure 7.3 (Continued)

earlier in this chapter (3.087 with 4 degrees of freedom). Note also that each of the parameter estimates has a Wald test statistic associated with it that reflects the importance of including that parameter estimate in the model. Recalling that the iq*gender interaction term was not needed in the most parsimonious model fit to the four-way table depicted in 7.11, it is not surprising that the Wald test statistic associated with this interaction term is not significant.

The residuals and fitted values obtained from invoking the obstats command are depicted in Figure 7.4:

- The fitted values are labled "pred"; the difference between the observed and fitted values is labeled "resraw" for raw residuals.
- Numerous other residuals are obtained from obstats, including:
  - the Pearson or chi-residual (labeled "reschi"),
  - the deviance residual (labeled "resdev"),
  - the likelihood residual (labeled "reslik"), and
  - standardized versions of each of these residuals, which use the same labels preceeded by "st" for standardized.
- These values or a subset of them can also be saved to a file in SAS by using the "output out=" statement options in PROC GENMOD.

```
                        The GENMOD Procedure
                        Observation Statistics

 Observation      count    gender   IQ   SES   aspire      Pred        Xbeta           Std
                           HessWgt       Lower       Upper     Resraw       Reschi
                           Resdev        StResdev    StReschi  Reslik
```

Observation	count	gender	IQ	SES	aspire	Pred	Xbeta	Std
1	618	M	H	H	H	615.88191	6.4230552	0.0385686
		615.88191		571.04161	664.24323	2.1180934	0.0853486	
		0.0852997		0.294574	0.2947427	0.2947286		
2	158	M	H	H	L	166.63474	5.1158042	0.0659365
		166.63474		146.43346	189.6229	-8.634741	-0.668908	
		-0.674814		-1.285567	-1.274317	-1.277427		
3	151	M	H	L	H	150.27047	5.0124368	0.0722243
		150.27047		130.43563	173.12151	0.7295315	0.0595124	
		0.0594643		0.1279061	0.1280095	0.1279871		
4	195	M	H	L	L	189.21309	5.2428738	0.0603623
		189.21309		168.10116	212.97648	5.7869121	0.4206988	
		0.4185813		0.7510892	0.7548889	0.7537109		
5	130	M	L	H	H	132.1181	4.8836962	0.0679002
		132.1181		115.65531	150.92425	-2.118098	-0.184274	
		-0.18477		-0.295536	-0.294743	-0.295053		
6	225	M	L	H	L	216.36549	5.3769691	0.060341
		216.36549		192.23198	243.52882	8.6345089	0.5870075	
		0.5831667		1.2659452	1.2742828	1.2725181		
7	76	M	L	L	H	76.729534	4.3402867	0.0866954
		76.729534		64.739193	90.940605	-0.729534	-0.083284	
		-0.083417		-0.128214	-0.12801	-0.128096		
8	579	M	L	L	L	584.78695	6.3712476	0.0392197
		584.78695		541.51918	631.51185	-5.786948	-0.239304	
		-0.239701		-0.756144	-0.754894	-0.755019		
9	588	F	H	H	H	593.00956	6.3852105	0.0393714
		593.00956		548.97011	640.58193	-5.00956	-0.205716	
		-0.206007		-0.724856	-0.723833	-0.723916		
10	200	F	H	H	L	188.47423	5.2389613	0.0622995
		188.47423		166.81019	212.95183	11.525767	0.8395448	
		0.8311989		1.6041363	1.620243	1.6159343		
11	113	F	H	L	H	110.83807	4.7080703	0.0826587
		110.83807		94.260501	130.33113	2.1619301	0.2053512	
		0.204689		0.4154862	0.4168304	0.4165045		
12	257	F	H	L	L	265.67844	5.5822867	0.0537675
		265.67844		239.10537	295.20472	-8.678442	-0.532431	
		-0.53537		-1.11165	-1.105547	-1.106966		
13	129	F	L	H	H	123.99046	4.8202046	0.0703528
		123.99046		108.01993	142.3222	5.0095373	0.449887	
		0.4469075		0.7190363	0.7238301	0.721982		
14	227	F	L	H	L	238.52623	5.4744793	0.0574716
		238.52623		213.11607	266.96609	-11.52623	-0.74631	
		-0.752445		-1.633628	-1.620308	-1.623143		
15	53	F	L	L	H	55.161948	4.0102734	0.096373
		55.161948		45.667444	66.630409	-2.161948	-0.291089	
		-0.293022		-0.419602	-0.416834	-0.418186		
16	809	F	L	L	L	800.32159	6.6850136	0.0339602
		800.32159		748.78579	855.40438	8.6784094	0.3067665	
		0.3062145		1.1035543	1.1055433	1.1053903		

Figure 7.4 SAS output obtained from invoking "obstats" option with proc genmod.

7.6.2   SPSS

To fit a log-linear model in SPSS one enters the data as described in previous chapters. However, when fitting a log-linear model we do not need to indicate weighting by counts. Be sure to indicate that all variables, with the exception of the count variable, are nominal variables. Then to use the menu options to fit the model:

- Choose Generalized Linear Model from the Analyze menu and then from the top tab titled Type of Model (which is the default tab that appears).

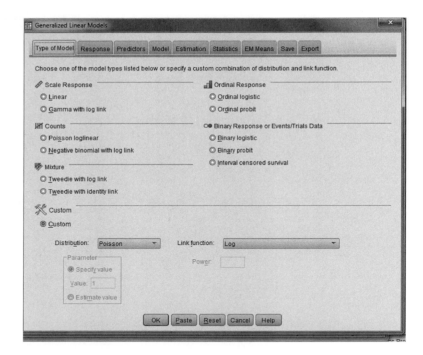

Figure 7.5 SPSS screenshot illustrating how to specify a log-linear model.

- Select the Custom button and then indicate that the Distribution is the Poisson distribution and the Link function is the Log function, as illustrated in Figure 7.5.
- Click on the Response tab at the top of the window and move the count variable into the Dependent variable box, as shown in Figure 7.6.
- Click on the predictors tab at the top of the window and move each of the categorical variables into the Factors box. Figure 7.7 illustrates this with only the variable gender selected as a factor. There is an Options button on this screen that can be selected to determine the category order for factors. This option allows a researcher to control which variable should be used as the last category, which is the reference category. For the purposes of this illustration, the option Use Data Order was selected so that the reference category would match the discussion in this chapter.
- Click on the Model tab at the top of the window to specify the model to be fit. To fit the log-linear model found to fit the data in Table 7.11, with all two-way interactions and the Gender × IQ × Aspire three-way interaction:
  - For the main effect terms, highlight all of the relevant factors (gender, IQ, and aspire) by holding down the Control key while clicking on them, and select Main effects under Build Term(s). Then click on the arrow to move these terms to the Model box.
  - For all two-way interaction terms, highlight all of the relevant factors (gender, IQ, and aspire) by holding down the Control key and select All 2-Way under the Build Term(s). Then click on the arrow to move the terms to the Model box.
  - For the three-way interaction term, highlight the gender, IQ, and aspire factors and select Interaction under Build Term(s). This is illustrated in Figure 7.8.

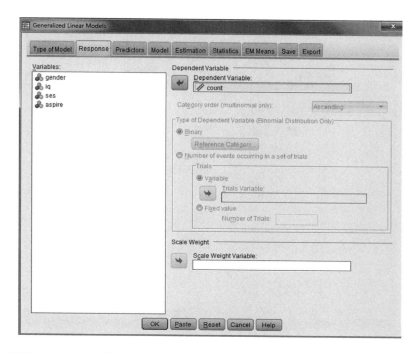

Figure 7.6 SPSS screenshot illustrating how to choose the response variable when fitting a log-linear model.

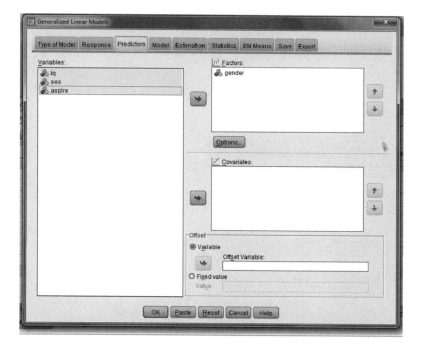

Figure 7.7 SPSS screenshot illustrating how to indicate the categorical variables when fitting a log-linear model.

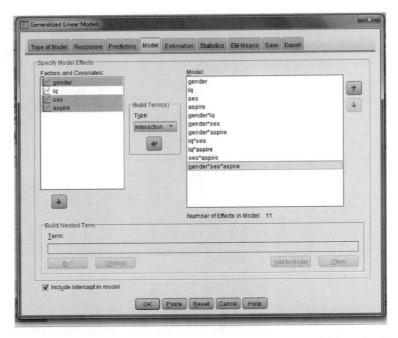

Figure 7.8 SPSS screenshot illustrating how to build the final log-linear model fit to the data in Table 7.11.

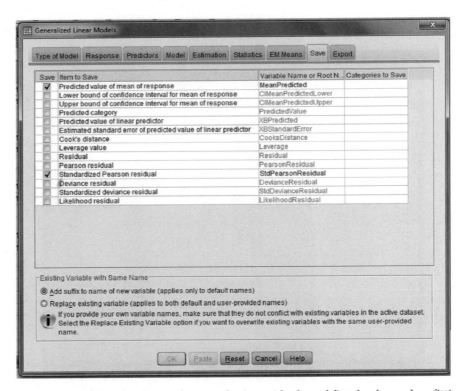

Figure 7.9 SPSS screenshot illustrating how to obtain residuals and fitted values when fitting a log-linear model.

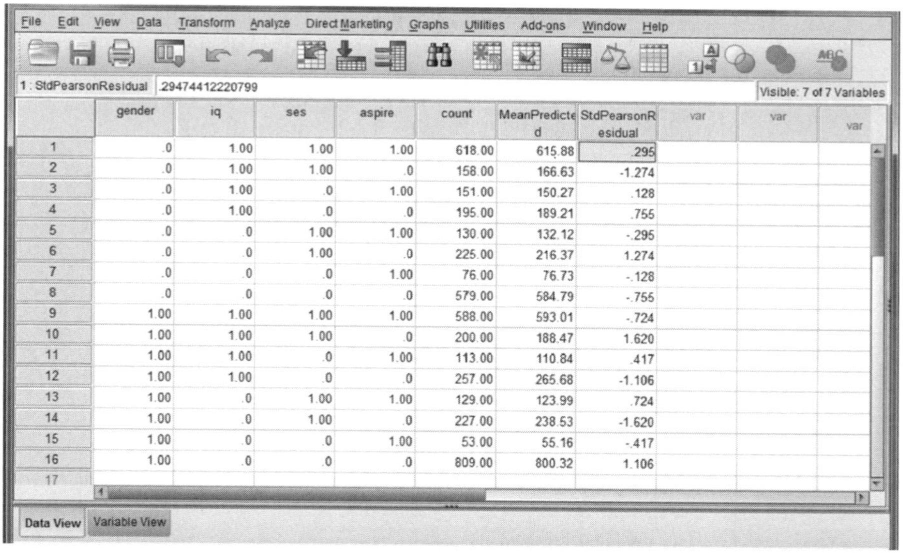

	gender	iq	ses	aspire	count	MeanPredicted	StdPearsonResidual	var	var	var
1	.0	1.00	1.00	1.00	618.00	615.88	.295			
2	.0	1.00	1.00	.0	158.00	166.63	-1.274			
3	.0	1.00	.0	1.00	151.00	150.27	.128			
4	.0	1.00	.0	.0	195.00	189.21	.755			
5	.0	.0	1.00	1.00	130.00	132.12	-.295			
6	.0	.0	1.00	.0	225.00	216.37	1.274			
7	.0	.0	.0	1.00	76.00	76.73	-.128			
8	.0	.0	.0	.0	579.00	584.79	-.755			
9	1.00	1.00	1.00	1.00	588.00	593.01	-.724			
10	1.00	1.00	1.00	.0	200.00	188.47	1.620			
11	1.00	1.00	.0	1.00	113.00	110.84	.417			
12	1.00	1.00	.0	.0	257.00	265.68	-1.106			
13	1.00	.0	1.00	1.00	129.00	123.99	.724			
14	1.00	.0	1.00	.0	227.00	238.53	-1.620			
15	1.00	.0	.0	1.00	53.00	55.16	-.417			
16	1.00	.0	.0	.0	809.00	800.32	1.106			
17										

Figure 7.10 SPSS data screenshot illustrating where fitted values and residuals can be found after fitting a log-linear model.

- In order to obtain the residuals and the predicted or fitted values select the Save tab at the top of the window and select the Standardized Pearson residual and the Predicted value of mean of response as depicted in Figure 7.9. These values will then be saved in your data file as depicted in Figure 7.10.
- Click the Run button to obtain the output depicted in Figures 7.11–7.13.

7.7 Complete example

In this section we will demonstrate the analysis of a data set obtained from the 2003 PISA (Programme for International Student Assessment) study. The data set consists of students' responses to two survey questions as well as the student's country (the United States, Australia, or France) and the student's sex. The two survey questions were: (1) "I am just not good at math" and (2) "In math class the teacher continues teaching until the students understand." This data set is depicted in Table 7.16. Given the large size of the table, the syntax and complete output are not provided, but pertinent results are interpreted.

Fitting a log-linear model with all three-way interaction terms, but not the four-way interaction term, resulted in a deviance of 13.85 and, with 18 degrees of freedom, this is not statistically significant ($p = 0.74$) so the four-way interaction term is not needed. Next, four models were fit to the data, each with one of the three-way interaction terms eliminated. The smallest change in the deviance of the model was obtained from the model that eliminated the Sex × Country × Question 2 interaction terms. For this model, the deviance was 24.96 with 24 degrees of freedom. Therefore, the change in fit was 12.11 with 6 degrees of freedom and, since this change is not statistically significant ($p = 0.06$), the Sex × Country × Question 2 interaction term was removed from the model. Removing any of the other three-way interaction terms (from the model that included all three-way interactions) resulted

Goodness of Fit[b]

	Value	df	Value/df
Deviance	3.087	4	.722
Scaled Deviance	3.087	4	
Pearson Chi-Square	3.089	4	.722
Scaled Pearson Chi-Square	3.089	4	
Log Likelihood[a]	−59.084		
Akaike's Information Criterion (AIC)	142.617		
Finite Sample Corrected AIC (AICC)	246.167		
Bayesian Information Criterion (BIC)	151.438		
Consistent AIC (CAIC)	163.438		

Dependent Variable: count
Model: (Intercept), gender, iq, ses, aspire, gender * iq, gender * ses, gender * aspire, iq * ses, iq * aspire, ses * aspire, gender * ses * aspire

    a. The full log likelihood function is displayed and used in computing information criteria
    b. Information criteria are in small-is-better form.

Omnibus Test[a]

Likelihood Ratio Chi-Square	df	Sig.
2489.932	11	.000

Dependent Variable: count
Model: (Intercept), gender, iq, ses, aspire, gender * iq, gender * ses, gender * aspire, iq * ses, iq * aspire, ses * aspire, Gender * ses * aspire

    a. Compares the fitted model against the intercept-only model.

Figure 7.11 SPSS output pertaining to model fit for a log-linear model.

in a statistically significant change in model fit, so the final model contains 3 three-way interaction terms. In addition, inspection of the standardized residuals from this model indicates that although six (of 96) cells had absolute standardized residuals greater than 2, none were greater than about 2.5 and there does not appear to be a particularly poor fit in any of the cells. Because all of the variables are involved in at least one three-way interaction in this final model, none of the lower interaction terms should be interpreted and only the three-way interaction terms should be interpreted.

In this final model there is a three-way association between students' responses to the first survey question (i.e., "I am just not good at math"), gender, and country. Because there is no four-way interaction, the three-way association between these three variables is the same for each level (response category) of the fourth variable (Question 2). There are multiple ways to interpret this three-way interaction because, in general, to interpret

Tests of Model Effects			
Source	Type III		
	Wald Chi-Square	df	Sig.
(Intercept)	75365.934	1	.000
gender	.233	1	.629
iq	36.490	1	.000
ses	36.958	1	.000
aspire	207.795	1	.000
gender * iq	.137	1	.712
gender * ses	.121	1	.728
gender * aspire	27.594	1	.000
Iq * ses	141.331	1	.000
Iq * aspire	554.992	1	.000
ses * aspire	539.051	1	.000
gender * ses * aspire	11.454	1	.001

Dependent Variable: count
Model: (Intercept), gender, iq, ses, aspire, gender * iq, gender * ses, gender * aspire, iq * ses, iq * aspire, ses * aspire, gender * ses * aspire

Figure 7.12 SPSS output pertaining to statistical significance of terms in the log-linear model.

a three-way interaction term one needs to consider the estimated odds ratio between any two variables at each level of the third variable. In this case, it seems to make the most sense to interpret the odds ratio between the first survey question and gender compared across the countries. Moreover, to completely interpret this interaction one would need to consider the odds ratios for each of the response categories of the survey item. However, interpreting the odds derived from the most extreme categories (i.e., strongly agree vs. strongly disagree) would be one approach to help explain what associations exist in the data. The nonzero parameter estimates and corresponding statistics for this three-way interaction term are provided in Table 7.17, and each represents a ratio of odds ratios.

The first parameter estimate represents a ratio of odds ratios equal to $e^{0.587} = 1.8$ and indicates that in Australia the odds ratio that compares the odds of strongly agreeing rather than strongly disagreeing with question 1 ("I am just not good in math") between females and males is 1.8 times the same odds ratio in the United States. The other relevant parameter estimate (to compare the strongly agree with strongly disagree categories) is a ratio of odds ratios equal to $e^{0.325} = 1.4$ and indicates that in France the odds ratio that compares the odds of strongly agreeing rather than strongly disagreeing with Question 1 between females and males is 1.4 times the same odds ratio in the United States. In fact, using the predicted values we can determine specifically that the odds ratio (comparing the odds of strongly agreeing rather than strongly disagreeing with question 1 between females and males) is 3.17 in Australia, 2.44 in France, and 1.75 in the United States. In addition, the tests for the three-way parameter estimates indicate that the odds ratio in Australia is significantly higher than the odds ratio in the United States (Wald $\chi_1^2 = 21.72$, $p < 0.0001$) and the odds ratio in France is also significantly higher than the odds ratio in the United States (Wald $\chi_1^2 = 4.79$, $p = 0.029$). In other words, the association between

Parameter Estimates

Parameter	B	Std. Error	95% Wald Confidence Interval Lower	95% Wald Confidence Interval Upper	Wald Chi-Square	df	Sig.
(Intercept)	6.685	.0340	6.618	6.752	38749.420	1	.000
[gender=.00]	-.314	.0502	-.412	-.215	39.025	1	.000
[gender=1.00]	0ª	.	.	.	.	.	.
[iq=1.00]	-1.103	.0589	-1.218	-.987	350.978	1	.000
[iq=.00]	0ª	.	.	.	.	.	.
[ses=1.00]	-1.211	.0642	-1.336	-1.085	355.864	1	.000
[ses=.00]	0ª	.	.	.	.	.	.
[aspire=1.00]	-2.675	.0981	-2.867	-2.483	743.811	1	.000
[aspire=.00]	0ª	.	.	.	.	.	.
[gender=.00] * [iq=1.00]	-.026	.0694	-.162	.110	.137	1	.712
[gender=.00] * [iq=.00]	0ª	.	.	.	.	.	.
[gender=1.00] * [iq=1.00]	0ª	.	.	.	.	.	.
[gender=1.00] * [iq=.00]	0ª	.	.	.	.	.	.
[gender=.00] * [ses=1.00]	.216	.0858	.048	.384	6.355	1	.012
[gender=.00] * [ses=.00]	0ª	.	.	.	.	.	.
[gender=1.00] * [ses=1.00]	0ª	.	.	.	.	.	.
[gender=1.00] * [ses=.00]	0ª	.	.	.	.	.	.
[gender=.00] * [aspire=1.00]	.644	.1162	.416	.872	30.694	1	.000
[gender=.00] * [aspire=.00]	0ª	.	.	.	.	.	.
[gender=1.00] * [aspire=1.00]	0ª	.	.	.	.	.	.
[gender=1.00] * [aspire=.00]	0ª	.	.	.	.	.	.
[iq=1.00] * [ses=1.00]	.867	.0729	.724	1.010	141.331	1	.000
[iq=1.00] * [ses=.00]	0ª	.	.	.	.	.	.
[iq=.00] * [ses=1.00]	0ª	.	.	.	.	.	.
[iq=.00] * [ses=.00]	0ª	.	.	.	.	.	.
[iq=1.00] * [aspire=1.00]	1.801	.0764	1.651	1.950	554.992	1	.000
[iq=1.00] * [aspire=.00]	0ª	.	.	.	.	.	.
[iq=.00] * [aspire=1.00]	0ª	.	.	.	.	.	.
[iq=.00] * [aspire=.00]	0ª	.	.	.	.	.	.
[ses=1.00] * [aspire=1.00]	2.020	.1071	1.810	2.230	355.578	1	.000
[ses=1.00] * [aspire=.00]	0ª	.	.	.	.	.	.
[ses=.00] * [aspire=1.00]	0ª	.	.	.	.	.	.
[ses=.00] * [aspire=.00]	0ª	.	.	.	.	.	.
[gender=.00] * [ses=1.00] * [aspire=1.00]	-.483	.1426	-.762	-.203	11.454	1	.001
[gender=.00] * [ses=1.00] * [aspire=.00]	0ª	.	.	.	.	.	.
[gender=.00] * [ses=.00] * [aspire=1.00]	0ª	.	.	.	.	.	.
[gender=.00] * [ses=.00] * [aspire=.00]	0ª	.	.	.	.	.	.
[gender=1.00] * [ses=1.00] * [aspire=1.00]	0ª	.	.	.	.	.	.
[gender=1.00] * [ses=1.00] * [aspire=.00]	0ª	.	.	.	.	.	.
[gender=1.00] * [ses=.00] * [aspire=1.00]	0ª	.	.	.	.	.	.
[gender=1.00] * [ses=.00] * [aspire=.00]	0ª	.	.	.	.	.	.
(Scale)	1ᵇ						

Dependent Variable: count

Model: (Intercept), gender, iq, ses, aspire, gender * iq, gender * ses, gender * aspire, iq * ses, iq * aspire, ses * aspire, gender * ses * aspire

a. Set to zero because this parameter is redundant.

b. Fixed at the displayed value.

Figure 7.13 SPSS output pertaining to model parameterization.

Table 7.16 Four-Way Contingency Table of Student Responses Obtained From the 2003 PISA Study

Sex	Country	I am just not good at math	In math class the teacher continues teaching until the students understand				
			Every lesson	Most lessons	Some lessons	Hardly or never	Total
Female	Australia	Strongly agree	208	211	223	116	758
		Agree	462	579	418	135	1594
		Disagree	1165	1139	552	150	3006
		Strongly disagree	350	209	86	40	685
		Total	2185	2138	1279	441	6043
	France	Strongly agree	110	128	137	84	459
		Agree	142	160	136	71	509
		Disagree	283	296	217	83	879
		Strongly disagree	130	88	86	28	332
		Total	665	672	576	266	2179
	United States	Strongly agree	123	108	108	64	403
		Agree	210	213	171	58	652
		Disagree	464	396	198	63	1121
		Strongly disagree	228	133	72	18	451
		Total	1025	850	549	203	2627
Male	Australia	Strongly agree	91	136	103	77	407
		Agree	282	495	331	106	1214
		Disagree	963	1446	694	203	3306
		Strongly disagree	524	391	197	53	1165
		Total	1860	2468	1325	439	6092
	France	Strongly agree	60	69	62	56	247
		Agree	95	139	102	51	387
		Disagree	233	327	216	102	878
		Strongly disagree	153	138	89	38	418
		Total	541	673	469	247	1930
	United States	Strongly agree	83	66	80	47	276
		Agree	155	177	150	57	539
		Disagree	409	474	241	68	1192
		Strongly disagree	272	186	104	33	595
		Total	919	903	575	205	2602

gender and Question 1 (using its extreme categories) is weakest in the United States and strongest in Australia.

In this model there is also a three-way association between the responses to the first survey question (i.e., "I am just not good at math"), the second survey question ("In math class the teacher continues teaching until the students understand"), and gender. In other

Table 7.17 Estimated Nonzero Parameters for the Sex by Country by First Survey Question (Q1) Three-Way Interaction Term and Related Statistics From the Most Parsimonious Log-Linear Model for the Data in Table 7.16

Parameter	df	Estimate	Std. error	Wald 95% confidence limits		Chi-squared	p-value
Sex*Country*q1 (Female – AUS – SA)	1	0.587	0.126	0.340,	0.834	21.72	<0.001
Sex*Country*q1 (Female – AUS – A)	1	0.348	0.105	0.141,	0.554	10.87	0.001
Sex*Country*q1 (Female – AUS – D)	1	0.235	0.093	0.053,	0.417	6.38	0.012
Sex*Country*q1 (Female – France – SA)	1	0.325	0.147	0.034,	0.611	4.79	0.029
Sex*Country*q1 (Female – France – A)	1	0.030	0.132	−0.229,	0.288	0.05	0.821
Sex*Country*q1 (Female – France – D)	1	0.032	0.116	−0.196,	0.260	0.08	0.783

words, the association between the responses to the two survey questions is different for males and females (but, because there is no four-way interaction, this three-way association is the same in each country). Once again, there are multiple ways to interpret the three-way interaction and it is somewhat more complicated to interpret this interaction term because there are several levels for each of the two survey questions. However, we could consider the association between the two survey questions by focusing on the odds ratio derived from the most extreme response options and compare these odds ratios across males and females. To interpret the three-way association in this way we need the three-way parameter estimates for the interaction terms pertaining to the two survey questions and sex, which are shown in Table 7.18. The first parameter indicates that, for females, the odds ratio computed from the two extreme categories of Question 1 (strongly agree vs. strongly disagree) and the two extreme categories of Question 2 (every lesson compared to never or hardly ever) is $e^{0.295} = 1.3$ times the same odds ratio for males. However, this is not a significant difference (Wald $\chi_1^2 = 2.31$, $p = 0.128$), indicating that some other categories of the two survey questions are responsible for this three-way association.

In fact, inspection of the p-values in Table 7.18 indicates that the only significant parameter is that corresponding to the comparison of odds ratios involving the two extreme categories of Question 1 (strongly agree vs. strongly disagree) and the last two categories of Question 2 (some lessons compared to never or hardly ever). The odds ratio computed using these categories for females is $e^{0.541} = 1.7$ times the same odds ratio for males, and this is significant (Wald $\chi_1^2 = 7.04$, $p = 0.008$). Therefore, the association between strongly agreeing rather than strongly disagreeing with the statement "I am just not good in math" and reporting that the teacher continues teaching until the students understand in some lessons rather than never or hardly ever is significantly stronger for females than for males. Using the predicted values from the model, we can more specifically examine the conditional odds ratios representing the odds of strongly agreeing rather than strongly disagreeing with the statement "I am just not good in math" for those who reported that the teacher continues teaching until the students understand in some lessons compared with the same odds for those who reported that the teacher never or hardly ever continues teaching until

Table 7.18 Estimated Nonzero Parameters for the Sex by First Survey Question (q1) by Second Survey Question (q2) Three-Way Interaction Term and Related Statistics From the Most Parsimonious Log-Linear Model for the Data in Table 7.16

Parameter	df	Estimate	St. error	Wald 95% confidence limits	Chi-Squared	p-Value
Sex*q1*q2 (Female – SA – Every lesson)	1	0.295	0.194	−0.086, 0.676	2.31	0.128
Sex*q1*q2 (Female – SA – Most lessons)	1	0.358	0.196	−0.026, 0.741	3.34	0.068
Sex*q1*q2 (Female – SA – Some lessons)	1	0.541	0.204	0.142, 0.941	7.04	0.008
Sex*q1*q2 (Female – A – Every lesson)	1	0.114	0.185	−0.247, 0.476	0.38	0.536
Sex*q1*q2 (Female – A – Most lessons)	1	0.064	0.186	−0.300, 0.427	0.12	0.732
Sex*q1*q2 (Female – A – Some lessons)	1	0.109	0.195	−0.274, 0.491	0.31	0.578
Sex*q1*q2 (Female – D – Every lesson)	1	0.316	0.172	−0.022, 0.654	3.37	0.066
Sex*q1*q2 (Female – D – Most lessons)	1	0.155	0.175	−0.188, 0.499	0.79	0.375
Sex*q1*q2 (Female – D – Some lessons)	1	0.165	0.189	−0.199, 0.529	0.79	0.373

the students understand. We can think of this odds ratio as representing the association between low self-efficacy in math and a tendency to report that the teacher does, at least sometimes, try to teach all students. The relevant conditional odds ratios, computed from the fitted values of this model, are 0.70 for females and 0.41 for males in Australia, 0.63 for females and 0.37 for males in France, and 0.51 for females and 0.30 for males in the United States. Therefore, in each country the odds ratio is 1.7 times higher for females than for males (which is what the three-way association parameter indicated). In addition, all of the conditional odds ratios are below one, indicating that the odds of low self-efficacy in math are smaller among those who report that the teacher continues teaching until the students understand in some lessons than among those who report that the teacher never or hardly ever continues teaching until the students understand.

Finally, the last three-way association is between the responses to the two survey questions and country, indicating that the association between the two survey questions is not the same for all three countries. However, this three-way association is the same for both males and females because there is no four-way interaction. Once again, although there are multiple ways to interpret the three-way interaction, it seems to make sense to focus on the odds ratio between the two survey questions using their most extreme response options and compare these odds ratios across the countries. The parameter estimates for this three-way interaction are shown in Table 7.19. The pertinent odds ratios compare the odds of strongly agreeing rather than strongly disagreeing with the statement "I am just not good in math" for students who reported that the teacher continues teaching until the students understand for every lesson with the same odds for students who reported that the teacher never or hardly ever continues teaching until the students understand. The

Table 7.19 Estimated Nonzero Parameters for the Country by First Survey Question (q1) by Second Survey Question (q1) Three-Way Interaction Term and Related Statistics From the Most Parsimonious Log-Linear Model for the Data in Table 7.16

Parameter	df	Estimate	St. error	Wald 95% confidence limits	Chi-squared	p-value
Country*q1*q2 (AUS – SA – Every lesson)	1	0.041	0.233	−0.416, 0.498	0.03	0.861
Country*q1*q2 (AUS – SA – Most lessons)	1	0.311	0.238	−0.155, 0.777	1.71	0.191
Country*q1*q2 (AUS – SA – Some lessons)	1	0.312	0.246	−0.171, 0.794	1.60	0.206
Country*q1*q2 (AUS – A – Every lesson)	1	0.003	0.225	−0.438, 0.444	0.00	0.989
Country*q1*q2 (AUS – A – Most lessons)	1	0.250	0.227	−0.195, 0.696	1.21	0.271
Country*q1*q2 (AUS – A – Some lessons)	1	0.239	0.239	−0.229, 0.707	1.00	0.317
Country*q1*q2 (AUS – D – Every lesson)	1	−0.062	0.214	−0.481, 0.357	0.09	0.770
Country*q1*q2 (AUS – D – Most lessons)	1	0.074	0.217	−0.352, 0.500	0.12	0.734
Country*q1*q2 (AUS – D – Some lessons)	1	0.184	0.231	−0.268, 0.636	0.64	0.425
Country*q1*q2 (France – SA – Every lesson)	1	0.585	0.256	0.083, 1.088	5.21	0.022
Country*q1*q2 (France – SA – Most lessons)	1	0.688	0.260	0.178, 1.198	6.98	0.008
Country*q1*q2 (France – SA – Some lessons)	1	0.212	0.267	−0.312, 0.736	0.63	0.427
Country*q1*q2 (France – A – Every lesson)	1	0.333	0.253	−0.164, 0.829	1.72	0.189
Country*q1*q2 (France – A – Most lessons)	1	0.277	0.255	−0.223, 0.777	1.18	0.278
Country*q1*q2 (France – A – Some lessons)	1	−0.097	0.265	−0.617, 0.424	0.13	0.716
Country*q1*q2 (France – D – Every lesson)	1	−0.052	0.238	−0.518, 0.413	0.05	0.826
Country*q1*q2 (France – D – Most lessons)	1	−0.079	0.241	−0.552, 0.393	0.11	0.742
Country*q1*q2 (France – D – Some lessons)	1	−0.099	0.253	−0.594, 0.397	0.15	0.697

first parameter estimate indicates that in Australia this odds ratio is $e^{0.041} = 1.0$ times the same odds ratio in the United States and, not surprisingly, this is not significant (Wald $\chi_1^2 = 0.03$, $p = 0.861$). The other relevant parameter estimate indicates that in France this odds ratio is $e^{0.585} = 1.8$ times the same odds ratio in the United States and this is significant (Wald $\chi_1^2 = 5.21$, $p = 0.022$). Again, we can use the fitted values from the model to obtain the conditional odds ratios, each comparing the odds of strongly agreeing rather than strongly disagreeing with the statement "I am just not good in math" for students who reported that the teacher continues teaching until the students understand for every lesson with the same odds for students who reported that the teacher never or hardly ever continues teaching until the students understand. For females these conditional odds ratios are 0.18 in Australia, 0.31 in France, and 0.17 in the United States, whereas for males these odds ratios are 0.13 in Australia, 0.23 in France, and 0.13 in the United States. Thus, within each gender, the odds ratios in Australia and the United States are almost identical, whereas in France they are 1.8 times higher than in either Australia or the United States. Note also that the odds ratios in France are closer to one than in either Australia or the United States, indicating a weaker association in France. Therefore, we can conclude that although there is no difference between Australia and the United States in terms of this particular odds ratio, the association between these two survey questions (using their extreme categories) is significantly weaker in France. In addition, as was the case with the previous three-way association, all of the conditional odds ratios are below one, indicating that the odds of low self-efficacy in math are smaller among those who report that the teacher continues teaching until the students understand in every lesson than among those who report that the teacher never or hardly ever continues teaching until the students understand.

7.8   Summary

This chapter introduced the log-linear model, a GLM used to examine the associations that exist between categorical variables using the contingency table frequencies as the outcomes of the model. In this chapter we discussed strategies for selecting the most parsimonious log-linear model for a data set and the interpretations of the parameters of log-linear models for the purpose of understanding the associations present among the categorical variables.

The purpose of this chapter was to explain how the significance of the deviance of a log-linear model can be interpreted and used to evaluate model fit, how to test the comparative fit of nested log-linear models, and how to use these tests as well as model residuals to choose the most appropriate model for the data. In addition, we discussed how to obtain the fitted values and parameters for the selected log-linear model and use these to fully interpret the associations that are present (or absent) among the categorical variables.

In the next several chapters we will discuss variations on the logistic regression model, another GLM that is commonly used in the social sciences. In particular, Chapter 9 covers logistic regression models that use only categorical variables as predictors and as such the material in that chapter will be related back to the material on log-linear models discussed in this chapter.

Problems

7.1 Table 7.20 depicts data that was obtained from the 1994 administration of the General Social Survey (GSS) on respondents' sex, level of fundamentalism, and whether they favor or oppose the death penalty for murder. Fit and interpret the most parsimonious log-linear model to this data. Describe the process you went through to determine the best fitting, most parsimonious model. What types of associations exist? Demonstrate how the fitted values obtained from the model depict these associations.

Table 7.20 Data for Problem 7.1 on Fundamentalism, Sex, and
Opinion on the Death Penalty Obtained From the 1994
Administration of the General Social Survey (GSS)

| Fundamentalism | Sex | Favor or oppose death penalty for murder | | |
		Favor	Oppose	Total
Fundamentalist	Male	128	32	160
	Female	123	73	196
	Total	251	105	356
Moderate	Male	182	56	238
	Female	168	105	273
	Total	350	161	511
Liberal	Male	119	49	168
	Female	111	70	181
	Total	230	119	349

7.2 Table 7.21 depicts data that was obtained from the 1994 administration of the GSS on respondents' sex, race, and level of agreement with spanking to discipline a child. Fit and interpret the most parsimonious log-linear model to this data. Describe the process you went through to determine the best fitting, most parsimonious model. What types of associations exist? Demonstrate how the fitted values obtained from the model depict these associations.

Table 7.21 Data for Problem 7.2 Sex, Race, and Attitude Toward Disciplining
Children Obtained from the 1994 Administration of the GSS

| Favor spanking to discipline child | Sex | Race | | | |
		White	Black	Other	Total
Strongly agree	Male	96	16	3	115
	Female	71	30	6	107
	Total	167	46	9	222
Agree	Male	172	17	23	212
	Female	174	34	13	221
	Total	346	51	36	433
Disagree	Male	59	1	13	73
	Female	96	3	10	109
	Total	155	4	23	182
Strongly disagree	Male	15	2	1	18
	Female	35	2	5	42
	Total	50	4	6	60

Table 7.22 Data for Problem 7.3 on Ability to Use the Internet Obtained From the 1994 Administration of the GSS

U.S. Born	Sex	Ability to Use the Internet					
		Excellent	Good	Fair	Poor	Very Poor	Total
Yes	Male	72	98	53	15	11	249
	Female	94	166	69	16	6	351
	Total	166	264	122	31	17	600
No	Male	15	11	8	3	1	38
	Female	11	14	9	2	3	39
	Total	26	25	17	5	4	77

7.3 Table 7.22 depicts data that was obtained from the 1994 administration of the GSS on whether the respondent was born in the United States, respondent's sex, and the respondent's ability to use the Internet. Fit and interpret the most parsimonious log-linear model to this data. Describe the process you went through to determine the best-fitting most parsimonious model. What types of associations exist? Demonstrate how the fitted values obtained from the model depict these associations.

7.4 Table 7.23 depicts data that was obtained from the 1994 GSS on respondents' sex, whether separating from spouse/partner, ability to afford needed medical care, and condition of home. Fit and interpret the most parsimonious log-linear model to this data. Describe the process you went through to determine the best fitting, most parsimonious model. What types of associations exist? Demonstrate how the fitted values obtained from the model depict these associations.

Table 7.23 Data for Problem 7.4 Obtained From the 1994 Administration of the GSS

Sex	Separating from spouse/ partner	Unable to afford needed medical care	Home in poor condition		
			Yes	No	Total
Male	Yes	Yes	1	16	17
		No	1	41	42
	No	Yes	15	40	55
		No	24	481	505
Female	Yes	Yes	7	12	19
		No	1	35	36
	No	Yes	10	58	68
		No	25	559	584

7.5 Table 7.24 depicts data obtained from the 1994 administration of the GSS. Fit and interpret the most parsimonious log-linear model to this data. Describe the process you went through to determine the best fitting, most parsimonious model. What types of associations exist? Demonstrate how the fitted values obtained from the model depict these associations.

Table 7.24 Data for Problem 7.5 Obtained From the 1994 Administration of the GSS

Sex	Looking for work over a month	Currently in relationship with last sex partner		
		Yes	No	Total
Male	Yes	27	11	38
	No	391	55	446
Female	Yes	26	0	26
	No	467	26	493

7.6 What are the advantages and disadvantages of fitting a log-linear model rather than using the procedures described in Chapter 5? When would a researcher be more likely to fit a log-linear model than to use the tests of association described in Chapter 5? When would a researcher be more likely to use the tests of association described in Chapter 5 than to fit a log-linear model?

chapter eight

Logistic regression with continuous predictors

A LOOK AHEAD

Whereas Chapter 7 showed how to model the association between two or more categorical variables, this chapter is concerned with predicting a categorical response from a set of continuous predictors. Specifically, in this chapter we discuss the logistic regression model, a generalized linear model appropriate for binary outcomes. The logistic regression model is similar to the more familiar linear regression model in that both models predict an outcome (also known as a response or dependent) variable, from a set of predictor variables (also known as explanatory or independent variables). In the case of linear regression, the response or dependent variable is a continuous variable (typically measured on an interval or ratio scale). In the case of logistic regression, however, the response variable is a binary or dichotomous variable, which means it can only take on one of two possible values. For example, whether a student is proficient in mathematics would be an appropriate dependent variable for logistic regression. Both logistic and linear regression models allow for predictor variables that can be continuous or categorical. Because there are interpretational similarities between the logistic and the more familiar linear regression model with continuous predictors, in this chapter we focus on the logistic model with continuous predictor variables.

Logistic regression models can be used to address a variety of research questions. Some common uses of these types of models are:

- To **model the probabilities** of certain conditions or states (e.g., divorce, disease, resilience, etc.) as a function of some predictor variables. For example, one might want to model whether an individual has diabetes as a function of weight, plasma insulin, and fasting plasma glucose.
- To describe differences between individuals from separate groups as a function of some predictor variables, also known as **descriptive discriminant analysis**. For example, one might want to describe the difference between students who attend public versus private schools as a function of achievement test scores, desired occupation, and socioeconomic status (SES).
- To classify individuals into one of two categories on the basis of the predictor variables, also known as **predictive discriminant analysis**. This is closely related to

descriptive discriminant analysis, but the descriptive information is used to predict group membership or classify individuals into one of two groups. For example, one may want to predict whether a student is more likely to attend a private school (as opposed to a public school) as a function of achievement test scores, desired occupation, and SES.

- In the psychometric field, there are specific applications that are closely tied to predictive discriminant analysis. For example, one might want to predict the probability that an examinee will correctly answer a test item as a function of race and gender. These types of studies are known in the psychometric literature as **differential item functioning** analyses.

In this chapter, we focus on the first of these uses; namely, modeling the probability or predicting the outcome of a binary variable from a set of continuous predictors.

8.1 The logistic regression model

As was discussed in Chapter 6, for a binary outcome, the generalized linear model has the following components:

1. **Random component:** The response variable (Y) is **dichotomous** or **binary** such that, for the ith individual, $Y_i = 1$ or 0. The distribution of Y_i is **binomial** and we are interested in modeling the probability that $Y_i = 1$ as a function of the predictor variables, $X_1, X_2, ..., X_p$.
2. **Systematic component:** The predictor variables may be quantitative (continuous), qualitative (discrete), or both, and the systematic component consists of a linear predictor of the form $\alpha + \beta_1(X_{1i}) + \beta_2(X_{2i}) + \cdots + \beta_p(X_{pi})$, where α and $\beta_1, ..., \beta_p$ are fixed coefficients, and X_{ji} is value of the jth predictor variable for the ith individual.
3. **Link function:** For logistic regression models, the link function (canonical link) is the natural log of the odds that $Y_i = 1$, otherwise known as the "logit" of the probability that $Y_i = 1$: $\text{logit}[P(Y_i = 1)] = \text{logit}(\pi) = \ln(\pi/1 - \pi)$, where π is the probability that $Y_i = 1$.

Putting these components together, the logistic regression model is

$$\text{logit}[P(Y_i = 1)] = \alpha + \beta_1(X_{1i}) + \beta_2(X_{2i}) + \cdots + \beta_p(X_{pi}).$$

To simplify the notation, we will drop the individual (i) subscripts and write the model more generally (across all individuals) as

$$\text{logit}(\pi) = \ln\left(\frac{\pi}{1 - \pi}\right) = \alpha + \beta_1 X_1 + \beta_2 X_2 + \cdots + \beta_p X_p = \alpha + \boldsymbol{\beta}\mathbf{X}. \tag{8.1}$$

The bold notation indicates vectors; in other words, $\boldsymbol{\beta}$ is a (row) vector containing all the regression coefficients and $\mathbf{X}$ is a vector containing all of the predictor variables. Thus, we use $\boldsymbol{\beta}\mathbf{X}$ as shorthand to denote the linear combination of the predictors multiplied by their corresponding coefficients. Note that this model (Equation 8.1) is very similar to the linear regression model in that the outcome is predicted from a linear function of the predictor variables. However, the difference between this model and the linear regression model is that we are predicting a binary—rather than a continuous—outcome, and so the distribution of the random component is not the normal distribution, as it is in linear regression, but instead is the binomial distribution. Therefore, instead of using the identity link, as we do in linear regression, we use the logit function, which is the canonical link for the binomial distribution, in formulating the logistic regression model. This provides a function that relates the systematic component to the outcome more accurately because, unlike the linear regression model, the relationship between the predictor(s) and the outcome is not linear and the predicted values of the outcome are bounded between 0 and 1.

Using the logistic regression model (Equation 8.1) results in a model in which the predicted response is the **natural log of the odds** that $Y_i = 1$ (rather than the predicted value of Y_i itself, as is the case in linear regression when the identity link is used). Although the natural log of the odds changes linearly with X, the natural log of the odds is not an intuitively easy or common scale to interpret. Therefore, Equation 8.1 can be rearranged to predict the **odds** that $Y_i = 1$ (rather than the natural log of the odds) by making use of the exponential function, $\exp(x) = e^x$, where e is a constant (equal to approximately 2.718) and $\exp[\ln(x)] = x$. In other words, the exponentiation of each side of Equation 8.1 results in

$$\exp\left[\ln\left(\frac{\pi}{1-\pi}\right)\right] = \left(\frac{\pi}{1-\pi}\right) = \exp(\alpha + \boldsymbol{\beta X})$$

$$= \exp(\alpha + \beta_1 X_1 + \cdots + \beta_p X_p) = e^\alpha e^{\beta_1 X_1} \cdots e^{\beta_p X_p}. \tag{8.2}$$

Rewriting Equation 8.1 in this way facilitates interpretation because using the odds, $\pi/(1 - \pi)$, as the outcome allows us to determine the effect of each independent variable on the odds that $Y_i = 1$. For a single predictor, X, the odds increase multiplicatively (rather than linearly) such that a one unit increase in X results in an increase of e^β times in the odds that $Y_i = 1$. When $\beta = 0$, $e^0 = 1$, so as X increases the odds are multiplied by one and, consequently, do not change as a function of X.

Further, recall that probability is related to the odds by the formula

$$\text{Probability} = \frac{\text{Odds}}{1 + \text{Odds}}.$$

Therefore, the logistic model can also be written in terms that directly predict the **probability** that $Y_i = 1$ (or π) using the equation

$$\pi = \frac{\exp(\alpha + \boldsymbol{\beta X})}{1 + \exp(\alpha + \boldsymbol{\beta X})}. \tag{8.3}$$

Although the parallels between logistic and linear regression are less apparent in Equation 8.3, this form of the logistic model can be used to facilitate interpretation because it allows us to determine the effect of the independent variable(s) on the probability that $Y_i = 1$ rather than on the odds or natural log of the odds that $Y_i = 1$. Graphically, in the case of a single predictor variable, X, if one were to graph the function in Equation 8.1 with X on the horizontal axis and the natural log of the odds on the vertical axis, one would obtain a straight line (e.g., see Figure 6.2b). On the other hand, if one were to graph the function in Equation 8.3 with X on the horizontal axis and the probability on the vertical axis, one would obtain an S-shaped curve, commonly referred to as a logistic or sigmoid curve (e.g., see Figure 6.2a).

Table 8.1 Probability Values, Their Corresponding Odds, and the Natural Log of the Odds

Probability	1-Probability	Odds	ln(Odds)
0.001	0.999	0.001	−6.907
0.1	0.9	0.111	−2.197
0.2	0.8	0.25	−1.386
0.3	0.7	0.429	−0.847
0.4	0.6	0.667	−0.405
0.5	0.5	1	0
0.6	0.4	1.5	0.405
0.7	0.3	2.333	0.847
0.8	0.2	4	1.386
0.9	0.1	9	2.197
0.999	0.001	999	6.907

To further clarify the relationship between probabilities, odds, and the natural log of the odds, Table 8.1 includes probability values along with their corresponding odds as well as the natural log of the odds, ln(odds). Table 8.1 demonstrates that as the probability gets smaller and approaches 0, the odds also approach 0 while the log odds approach −∞ (negative infinity), and as the probability gets larger and approaches 1, the odds also get larger while the log odds approach +∞ (positive infinity). Therefore, while probabilities can theoretically vary from 0 to 1 with a midpoint of 0.5, the corresponding odds can theoretically vary from 0 to +∞ with 1 corresponding to the probability midpoint, and the natural log of the odds can theoretically vary from −∞ to +∞ with 0 corresponding to the probability midpoint. Thus, the range of the ln(odds) more closely resembles the standard normal distribution in that it is unbounded, has a midpoint of 0, and is symmetric around the midpoint. This helps to explain why the log odds scaling (or logit link function) is a reasonable choice for this generalized linear model (Equation 8.1). We now turn to examples of logistic regression models and explain how to fit them, interpret them, and use them to answer a variety of research questions.

8.2 Parameter interpretation

To begin with the simplest model, consider the case of a binary outcome and a single predictor variable (X). For example, suppose that the dependent variable for the ith student is measured as $Y_i = 1$ if the student is proficient in mathematics and 0 if the student is not, while the predictor variable is the student's science achievement test score. Because the predicted outcome in logistic regression is different from the predicted outcome in linear regression, the interpretations of the intercept, α, and slope, β, are also somewhat different as they must be interpreted in the context of the predicted response.

8.2.1 The intercept in logistic regression models

Using Equation 8.2, the exponentiated intercept, e^α, can be interpreted as the predicted odds that $Y_i = 1$ (as opposed to $Y_i = 0$) when the predictor variable, X, is zero. Using our example, the value of e^α can be interpreted as the predicted odds that a student who obtained a score of 0 on the science achievement test is proficient (as opposed to not proficient) in mathematics. For example, if the intercept was $\alpha = -2$, then the odds that a student who obtained a score of 0 on the science achievement test is proficient in mathematics would be $e^{-2} \approx (2.718)^{-2} = 0.14$. Similarly, if the intercept was $\alpha = 2$ then the odds that a student who obtained a score of 0 on the science achievement test is proficient in mathematics would be $e^2 \approx (2.718)^2 = 7.39$. Graphically, the meaning of the intercept can be illustrated by referring to the regression curve obtained using the form of the logistic regression function presented in Equation 8.3. In linear regression, the value of the intercept is the value of Y at which the regression line "intercepts" the vertical or y-axis (i.e., the point on the y-axis at which $X = 0$). In logistic regression, this interpretation is identical in that the value of the intercept is the value of the response at which the logistic curve "intercepts" the response axis. Figure 8.1 shows three examples of logistic curves graphed using Equation 8.3, all with the same slope (of 0.3) but with intercepts of –2, 0, and 2. Note that the higher the value of the intercept, the higher the point at which the curve intercepts the y-axis. Moreover, as the figure demonstrates, using Equation 8.3 the intercept can be interpreted as the probability that a student who obtained a score of 0 on the science achievement test is proficient in mathematics. For example, substituting $\alpha = 2$ and $X = 0$ into Equation 8.3 we obtain

$$\pi = \frac{\exp(2+0)}{1+\exp(2+0)} = \frac{e^2}{1+e^2} = \frac{7.4}{8.4} = 0.88,$$

so the predicted probability that a student with a test score of zero is proficient in mathematics is 88%. Note that when the science test score is $X = 0$ in Figure 8.1 the logistic curve with $\alpha = 2$ indeed intercepts the probability axis at the value of 0.88. The meaning of the intercept can be easily extended to the case of several predictor variables, where the value of the intercept is interpreted as the predicted response when *all* of the predictors take on a value of zero.

8.2.2   *The slope in logistic regression models*

With one predictor variable, the slope, β, is interpreted in simple linear regression as the predicted change in the response variable, Y, when the predictor variable, X, increases by one unit. Likewise, using Equation 8.1, in a logistic regression with one predictor, the

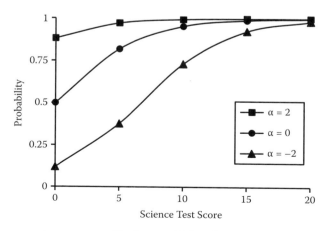

Figure 8.1 Logistic regression curves with slopes of 0.3 and various intercepts.

slope can be interpreted as the predicted change in the natural log of the odds that $Y_i = 1$ (as opposed to $Y_i = 0$) when X increases by one unit. However, the slope is more typically interpreted using Equation 8.2, just as the intercept was, because it is somewhat awkward to interpret the change in the outcome using the natural log odds scale. This results in a multiplicative relationship, rather than an additive relationship, between the predictor and the outcome (odds that $Y_i = 1$). Specifically, a one unit increase in X leads to an increase of e^β times in the odds that $Y_i = 1$.

For example, if $\beta = 0.5$, then as X increases by one unit the odds that $Y_i = 1$ are multiplied by $e^{0.5} = 1.65$. In the context of our previous substantive example, predicting mathematics proficiency from science test scores, if $\beta = 0.5$ then the odds of being proficient in mathematics are increased 1.65 times for each additional point a student obtains on the science test. In other words, for every 1 point increase in a student's science test score the odds of being proficient in mathematics increase by 165%. To further clarify this interpretation, consider three science test scores—10, 11, and 12—and suppose, for the sake of this example, that the intercept is $\alpha = -4$ and the slope is $\beta = 0.5$. Then, using Equation 8.2, the predicted odds associated with each science score are computed as follows:

$$\text{For } X = 10, \text{ predicted odds} = \left(\frac{\pi}{1-\pi}\right) = \exp(\alpha + \beta X) = e^\alpha e^{\beta X}$$

$$= \exp(-4 + 0.5(10)) = e^{-4} e^{0.5(10)} = (0.018)(148.41) = 2.72;$$

$$\text{For } X = 11, \text{ predicted odds} = \left(\frac{\pi}{1-\pi}\right)$$

$$= \exp(-4 + 0.5(11)) = e^{-4} e^{0.5(11)} = (0.018)(244.69) = 4.48;$$

$$\text{For } X = 12, \text{ predicted odds} = \left(\frac{\pi}{1-\pi}\right)$$

$$= \exp(-4 + 0.5(12)) = e^{-4} e^{0.5(12)} = (0.018)(403.43) = 7.39.$$

Using these predicted values, note that the increase from a science score of 10 to 11 (an increase of 1 unit in X) results in an increase of 165% in the predicted odds because $(2.72)(1.65) = 4.48$ and $4.48/2.72 = 1.65 = 165\%$. Similarly, an increase from a science score of 11 to 12 (an increase of 1 unit in X) results in an increase of 165% in the predicted odds because $(4.48)(1.65) = 7.39$ and $7.39/4.48 = 1.65 = 165\%$. Therefore, for every 1 unit increase in X, the odds increase by $e^{0.5} = 1.65 = 165\%$.

In general, as X increases by any constant number of units (or points), c, the expected (predicted) odds are multiplied $e^{c\beta}$ times. For example, if $\beta = 0.5$ then for a 3 point increase in X the odds of being proficient in mathematics increase (or are multiplied) by $e^{3(0.5)} = e^{0.5} e^{0.5} e^{0.5} = (1.65)(1.65)(1.65) = 4.5$ times. In terms of our example, if a student obtained a science test score of 13 then the odds that he or she is proficient in mathematics would be 4.5 times greater than the odds for a student who obtained a science test score of 10 (and 4.5 times smaller than the odds for a student who obtained a score of 16). Note that when $\beta = 0$, $e^\beta = 1$, thus the odds are multiplied by 1 (or do not change) as X increases. Similarly, when $\beta > 0$, $e^\beta > 1$, thus the odds increase as X increases, and when $\beta < 0$, $e^\beta < 1$, thus the odds decrease as X increases.

Graphically, the slope, β, can be generally interpreted as the rate of change of the logistic curve provided by Equation 8.3. Figure 8.2 depicts logistic curves that all have the same intercept (of -2) but different slope parameters. This figure illustrates that the magnitude

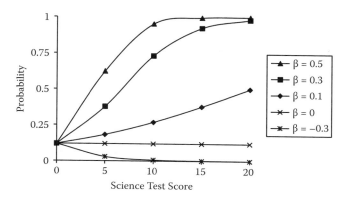

Figure 8.2 Logistic regression curves with intercepts of –2 and various slopes.

of β determines the "steepness" of the logistic curve and the sign of β determines the direction of the curve. As is the case in linear regression, when the slope is positive (β > 0) the curve increases as X increases, and when the slope is negative (β < 0) the curve decreases as X increases. If the slope is zero (β = 0) then the graph is a flat (horizontal) line, indicating that the response value is identical regardless of the value of X.

The steepest slope of a logistic curve occurs when the probability is 50%, or π = 0.5, and the odds are one. The value of X at which the probability is 50% is sometimes referred to as the **median effective level**. This can be thought of as the point of inflection on the logistic curve, or the value of X for which it is just as likely that $Y_i = 1$ as it is that $Y_i = 0$. Using Equation 8.1 with one predictor and solving for the value of X when π = 0.5, we obtain:

$$\ln(0.5/(1-0.5)\,) = \alpha + \beta X$$

$$\ln(1) = \alpha + \beta X$$

$$0 = \alpha + \beta X$$

$$-\alpha = \beta X$$

$$X = -\alpha/\beta.$$

Therefore, the median effective level, or the value of X at which the probability is 50% and the logistic curve is steepest, is given by –α/β. From Figure 8.2, it is apparent that in our example higher science test scores are needed to achieve 50% probability as the value of β decreases. For example, when β = 0.3 the value of X needed to achieve 50% probability is –(–2)/0.3 = 6.67. In other words, using our example with β = 0.3 and α = –2, a student who received a science test score of 6.67 would be just as likely to be proficient as not proficient in mathematics. On the other hand, when β = 0.5 the test score needed to achieve 50% probability is –(–2)/0.5 = 4.

Because the relationship between the probability that $Y_i = 1$ and the value of X is nonlinear (e.g., see Figure 8.2), the rate of change in the predicted probability that $Y_i = 1$ (which can be thought of as the change in the predicted probability for a one unit increase in X) is not constant, but rather varies depending on the value of X. The value of the slope can be used to compute the rate of change of the curve at a particular value of X by using the formula

$$\text{Rate of change in the predicted probability} = \beta \pi (1 - \pi),$$

which reflects the linear approximation to the logistic curve. For example, consider the logistic curve in Figure 8.2 with $\beta = 0.3$ (and $\alpha = -2$). For a science test score of 10, the rate of change or slope of that curve at $X = 10$ can be computed as follows:

$$\pi = \frac{\exp(\alpha + \beta x)}{1 + \exp(\alpha + \beta x)} = \frac{\exp(-2 + 0.3(10))}{1 + \exp(-2 + 0.3(10))} = \frac{e^1}{1 + e^1} = \frac{2.72}{3.72} = 0.731,$$

$$1 - \pi = 1 - 0.731 = 0.269,$$

$$\text{Rate of change} = \beta\pi(1 - \pi) = 0.3(0.731)(0.269) = 0.06.$$

Repeating the same calculation at, say, $X = 15$, the slope would be considerably less steep with a rate of change of only 0.02. Therefore, for students with science test scores of 10, the predicted probability of being proficient in mathematics increases at a rate of about 0.06 for a 1 point increase in science test scores, but for students with science tests scores of 15 the predicted probability increases at a rate of only about 0.02 for a 1 point increase in test scores. This formula can thus be used to compute the rate of change at different values of X to get a more complete understanding of the effect of X on the predicted probability at different points on the predictor scale.

The interpretation of the slope can be easily extended to the case of several predictors, as is the case in extending the interpretation of the slope in simple regression to partial slopes in multiple linear regression. In other words, the value of the partial slope β_j associated with a specific predictor, X_j, is interpreted as the rate of change in the response (e.g., log odds) when X_j increases by one unit and all other predictors are held constant.

8.3   Inference

The notation we have used for the model parameters, α and β, are indicative of values that are obtained from the population of interest. In other words, in the examples presented up to this point we were assuming that we had access to students' science test scores from all schools of interest and were able to determine the odds of proficiency in mathematics given a particular science test score using these data. However, this assumption is quite unrealistic in practice. Typically a researcher would only have access to a sample of students' science test scores from a sample of schools that is, in the best case scenario, representative of the population, and the parameters of the model must be estimated using the sample data. When the parameters of the model are estimated from sample data, they are commonly represented using the "hat" notation; that is, α and β are estimated by $\hat{\alpha}$ and $\hat{\beta}$, respectively. The inferential methods we discuss in this section generalize sample information to the population of interest. To properly use these methods, the sample should be a random sample drawn from the population or at the very least be representative of the population of interest. As is the case in linear regression, we are typically only interested in making inferential statements about the slope parameter(s), not the intercept, because the intercept typically does not reflect a relationship between the response and predicted variables, whereas the slope (i.e., rate of the change of the response as the predictor increases) does reflect such a relationship and is therefore substantively meaningful.

In logistic regression, parameter estimates are obtained from sample data using maximum likelihood (ML) estimation (see Chapters 3 and 6). When ML estimation is used to obtain the slope, $\hat{\beta}$, the sampling distribution of $\hat{\beta}$ will be approximately normal for large samples.

In other words, if the sample size, n, is reasonably large, then the distribution of $\hat{\beta}$ values obtained from all possible random samples of size n drawn from a given population will be approximately normal, with mean β and standard deviation $\sigma_{\hat{\beta}}$. This standard deviation is a parameter (since it is based on all possible random samples of size n), so when estimated from the data the estimate of the standard deviation (or the standard error of $\hat{\beta}$) is denoted by $s_{\hat{\beta}}$. These concepts are virtually identical to those involved in the sampling distribution of many common and familiar statistics. For example, the sampling distribution of the sample mean, $\overline{X}$, is also normally distributed for reasonably large samples. It is centered around its parameter (the population value, μ), and its standard deviation is measured using the standard error of the mean, $\sigma_{\overline{X}}$, or the estimated standard error, $s_{\overline{X}}$.

In the case of the sample slope, $s_{\hat{\beta}}$ represents the estimated standard deviation of the sampling distribution of $\hat{\beta}$ and is called the standard error of $\hat{\beta}$. It is obtained using the delta method, which is a general approach used to derive the standard error of a parameter when ML estimation is used to obtain the parameter estimate. Details about the delta method can be found in many other sources, including Agresti (1990). Because this estimate of the standard error, $s_{\hat{\beta}}$, becomes more accurate as the sample size used to obtain the parameter estimates increases, it is called an asymptotic standard error, or ASE. As is the case with other inferential procedures, the standard error indicates the degree of variability associated with the estimate of the parameter. This variability can be interpreted as the level of imprecision associated with the estimated parameter, or how far from the true population parameter any given sample estimate is expected to be. Therefore, large standard errors indicate that any one given sample estimate, $\hat{\beta}$, is likely to be an imprecise estimate of the parameter, β, whereas small standard errors indicate that the estimate is likely to be a relatively precise estimate of β.

8.3.1 Hypothesis testing for the slope

There are two general approaches to testing the null hypothesis that the predictor does not affect the response, or H_0: $\beta = 0$. These two approaches are analogous to the two approaches that exist in linear regression—namely, the t-test and the F-test—where, when there are multiple predictors, the t-test can be used for testing one parameter at a time, whereas the F-test is more general and can be used to test any number of parameters in one test. In logistic regression, the Wald test is analogous to the t-test, as it is designed to test one slope parameter at a time, whereas the likelihood ratio test is analogous to the F-test as it can test several slope parameters at once. When there is a single predictor the two tests are identical in linear regression ($t^2 = F$), but this is not necessarily the case in logistic regression.

The **Wald test** follows the typical formula (from basic statistics) for evaluating the likelihood that an estimated parameter, or sample statistic, was obtained from the population hypothesized under the null hypothesis. Specifically, the Wald test statistic, X^2, is the squared form of the z-statistic:

$$X^2 = \left(\frac{\hat{\beta} - \beta}{s_{\hat{\beta}}} \right)^2 \sim \chi^2 \quad \text{with} \quad df = 1.$$

(8.4)

The X^2-test statistic will follow a χ^2 distribution for large samples, and has only one degree of freedom because it tests a single parameter.

Another way to test this hypothesis is with the **likelihood ratio test**. This test compares the likelihoods of two logistic regression models: one that restricts β to be zero, reflecting the null hypothesis, and one that uses the ML estimate (from the data), $\hat{\beta}$, for β. In the case of one predictor, the two logistic regression models compared are

$$\text{Nonrestricted model:} \quad \text{logit}(\pi) = \ln\left(\frac{\pi}{1-\pi}\right) = \alpha + \beta X, \text{ and}$$

$$\text{Restricted model:} \quad \text{logit}(\pi) = \ln\left(\frac{\pi}{1-\pi}\right) = \alpha$$

This is conceptually analogous to the F-test in linear regression in that it compares the amount of error, or model fit, of the two models: if the fit of the restricted (simpler) model to the data is as good as the fit of the nonrestricted (more complex) model, then the restricted model (reflecting the null hypothesis) is retained because it is more parsimonious (simpler). On the other hand, if the fit of the restricted model to the data is significantly worse than the fit of the nonrestricted model, then the restricted model is rejected in favor of the nonrestricted model, reflecting support for the alternative hypothesis and a nonzero slope (i.e., H_1: $\beta \neq 0$). The maximum likelihood of the restricted model (under H_0) is denoted by L_0 and the maximum likelihood of the nonrestricted model (under H_1) is denoted by L_1. The ratio L_0/L_1 represents the likelihood ratio. If the likelihood of the nonrestricted model is much larger than the likelihood of the restricted model, then the likelihood ratio will be much smaller than 1 and will provide evidence against the null hypothesis. The likelihood ratio test statistic, G^2, is obtained by taking the (natural) log of the likelihood ratio and multiplying it by -2 as was discussed in previous chapters. Specifically,

$$G^2 = -2\ln\left(\frac{L_0}{L_1}\right) = -2\left[\ln(L_0) - \ln(L_1)\right] = \left[-2\ln(L_0)\right] - \left[-2\ln(L_1)\right]. \tag{8.5}$$

At the extreme, when the likelihoods of the restricted and nonrestricted models are equivalent, the likelihood ratio will be one and the test statistic will be zero. As the likelihood of the nonrestricted model becomes larger relative to the likelihood of the restricted model, the likelihood ratio will become smaller than one, its natural log will become more negative, and the test statistic will become more positive. Therefore, a larger (more positive) test statistic indicates stronger evidence against H_0, as is typically the case with positive test statistics. Under H_0 this test statistic follows a χ^2 distribution, as did the Wald test statistic, with degrees of freedom equal to the number of parameters restricted under H_0 (i.e., $df = 1$ in the case of a single predictor). Note that any two models can be compared using the likelihood ratio test (see Chapter 6), as long as one is a restricted version of the other, making this a much more general test than the Wald test. For example, the likelihood ratio test can be used to compare a model with three predictors to a model where two of the predictors are restricted to be zero (or are excluded from the model), whereas the Wald test statistic cannot. Moreover, there is some evidence that the likelihood ratio test is more powerful and accurate than the Wald statistic (Hauck & Donner, 1977) in testing the significance of a single predictor.

To illustrate the use of these hypothesis tests, we used student data from the Programme for International Student Assessment (PISA) for 2006. The data were obtained from the Institute of Education Sciences's Web site, http://nces.ed.gov/surveys/pisa/index.asp.

Specifically, we used the students' mathematics self-efficacy scores to predict whether a student is proficient in mathematics. For this example only the 5,251 students from the United States that had a valid mathematics self-efficacy score were considered. Of these students 4,614 were proficient in mathematics and 637 were not. The predictor variable was obtained by scaling responses to eight items measuring students' confidence with various mathematical tasks. Higher values indicate higher levels of self-efficacy in mathematics, and scores on this measure ranged from –3.89 to 2.53, with a mean of 0.24 and a standard deviation of 1.05. For students in the United States the reliability of this measure was 0.86. We will investigate whether there is evidence for a relationship between mathematics self-efficacy and proficiency in mathematics using these sample data. The results, shown in Table 8.2, were obtained using computer software, and the model for these data is

$$\ln\left(\frac{\hat{\pi}}{1-\hat{\pi}}\right) = \hat{\alpha} + \hat{\beta}X = 1.99 + 0.72X.$$

In this example $\hat{\pi}$ denotes the estimated probability of achieving math proficiency, X denotes the self-efficacy score, and the ML estimates of the intercept and slope are $\hat{\alpha} = 1.99$ and $\hat{\beta} = 0.72$, respectively. The estimated intercept of $\hat{\alpha} = 1.99$ indicates that when students' self-efficacy in mathematics is zero (or slightly below average), the expected natural log odds of being proficient (rather than not proficient) in math will be 1.99 and the expected odds of being proficient (rather than not proficient) in math will be $e^{1.99} = 7.3$. Therefore, a student is 7.3 times more likely to be proficient in math than not when his or her level of self-efficacy in mathematics is slightly below average. The slope estimate indicates that when students' mathematics self-efficacy scores increase by one, the natural log odds of being proficient (rather than not proficient) in math increase by 0.72 and the odds of being proficient (rather than not proficient) in math are multiplied by $e^{0.72} = 2.05$ (i.e., increase by 205%) or are approximately doubled.

To test the significance of the slope estimate using the Wald test we use the estimated ASE of the slope (obtained from computer software) provided in Table 8.2, which is 0.049. Therefore, to test whether the slope is significantly different from zero (H_0: $\beta = 0$), we use Equation 8.4 to obtain the Wald test statistic:

$$X^2 = \left(\frac{\hat{\beta} - \beta}{s_{\hat{\beta}}}\right)^2 = \left(\frac{.72 - 0}{.049}\right)^2 = 215.91.$$

The Wald test statistic value of 215.91 deviates slightly from the value provided in Table 8.2 due to rounding. Using the χ^2 distribution with 1 degree of freedom, the test statistic $X^2 = 215.91$ indicates that if the null hypothesis was true (i.e., $\hat{\beta}$ was obtained from

Table 8.2 Results From Logistic Regression Predicting the Probability of Mathematics Proficiency (Yes/No) From Mathematics Self-Efficacy Scores for Students From the United States

Parameter	Parameter estimate	ASE of estimate	Wald test statistic	*p*-Value (Wald Test)	LR test statistic	*p*-Value (LR Test)
Intercept	1.99	0.045	1973.01	<.0001		
Slope (matheff)	0.72	0.049	215.61	<.0001	260.94	<.0001

a sample that was drawn from a population in which $\beta = 0$), the probability of obtaining this estimated slope is less than 0.0001 (see p-value of the Wald test in Table 8.2). Therefore, the null hypothesis is rejected and we can conclude that there is a significant relationship between students' self-efficacy in mathematics and the probability of being proficient in mathematics. More specifically, as self-efficacy increases, the probability of being proficient in mathematics increases as well.

Alternatively, to test the significance of the slope using the likelihood ratio test, we need to find the difference between -2 times the log of the likelihood ratio for the restricted (intercept only) and unrestricted models. This information (model likelihood or deviance) is readily provided by most statistical software programs. For our example, the log likelihood of the restricted model multiplied by -2 is 3880.777 (which is the value of $-2\ln(L_0)$, where L_0 represents the restricted model) and the log likelihood of the unrestricted model multiplied by -2 is 3619.840 (which is the value of $-2\ln(L_1)$, where L_1 represents the unrestricted model). Therefore, the likelihood ratio test statistic using Equation 8.5 is

$$G^2 = -2\ln\left(\frac{L_0}{L_1}\right) = -2\ln(L_0 - L_1)$$

$$= -2\ln(L_0) - (-2\ln(L_1)) = 3880.777 - 3619.840 = 260.94.$$

As can be seen in Table 8.2, using the χ^2 distribution with 1 degree of freedom, the test statistic $G^2 = 260.94$ has a p-value that is less than 0.0001, indicating that the null hypothesis is rejected (as was the case with the Wald test) and thus there is a significant positive relationship between mathematics self-efficacy scores and the probability of being proficient in mathematics.

For large samples, the Wald and likelihood ratio tests of model parameters will typically produce very similar results. While the Wald test is valid with large samples, the likelihood ratio test appears to be more powerful and reliable with the kind of sample sizes typically used in practical applications (Agresti, 2007).

8.3.2   Confidence intervals for the slope

Although hypothesis tests are useful for determining whether there is a relationship between the predictor and outcome (i.e., whether the slope is significantly different from zero), we need confidence intervals to obtain more specific information on the actual value of the slope in the population. Confidence intervals achieve this by providing an interval estimate for the slope parameter with a desired level of confidence. We will consider three types of confidence intervals: (1) for the effect of the predictor on the natural log odds that $Y_i = 1$; (2) for the effect of the predictor on the odds that $Y_i = 1$; and (3) for the effect of the predictor on the probability that $Y_i = 1$ at a given value of the predictor. The parameter that measures the effect of the predictor on the natural log odds in the population is β, and the confidence interval for β can be obtained using the general formula

$$\hat{\beta} \pm z_{CL} s_{\hat{\beta}} = [\text{LL}_\beta, \text{UL}_\beta],$$

where $\hat{\beta}$ is the ML estimate of the effect of the predictor, $s_{\hat{\beta}}$ is its estimated asymptotic standard error, and z_{CL} is the critical value of the standard normal distribution corresponding to a given confidence level. In most applications $z_{CL} = z_{0.95} = 1.96$, which corresponds to the nominal α-level of 0.05 and a 95% confidence level. LL_β and UL_β refer to the lower and upper limits of the confidence interval for β, respectively. The formula and interpretation of this confidence interval is analogous to the confidence interval of most parameters in basic statistics, such as the population mean or the slope parameter in linear regression. Using the example presented previously (see Table 8.2), in which $\beta = 0.72$ and $s_\beta = 0.049$, the 95% confidence interval would be

$$0.72 \pm 1.96(0.049) = 0.72 \pm 0.096 = [0.62, 0.82].$$

This indicates that *in the population* (from which the sample data was obtained)—for our example, high school students in the United States—we can be 95% confident that the true value of the slope is somewhere between 0.62 and 0.82. Therefore, in the case of our example the true (population) value of the slope or rate of change appears to be positive and is somewhere between 0.62 and 0.82 at the 95% confidence level. In other words, while *in the sample* the natural log odds increase at a rate of 0.72 for every one unit increase in mathematics self-efficacy score, we can be 95% confident that *in the population* the natural log odds of being proficient in mathematics increases somewhere between 0.62 and 0.82 for every one unit increase in a student's mathematics self-efficacy score.

The parameter that measures the true (or population) effect of the predictor on the odds is e^β, so the confidence interval for e^β can be obtained by exponentiation of the limits of the confidence interval for β. Using the numerical example just presented, the 95% confidence interval for e^β is

$$[\exp(LL_\beta), \exp(UL_\beta)] = [e^{0.62}, e^{0.82}] = [1.86, 2.27].$$

Therefore, we can be 95% confident that *in the population* (from which the sample was obtained) the odds of being proficient in mathematics are multiplied by a value between 1.86 and 2.27 for every 1 unit increase in a student's mathematics self-efficacy score. Note that the true (population) value thus appears to be above 1 (i.e., it is between 1.86 and 2.27, with 95% confidence), indicating that the odds of being proficient in mathematics increases as one's mathematics self-efficacy increases. This confidence interval (for the odds) is often automatically provided by computer software programs (e.g., PROC LOGISTIC in SAS).

Recall that the parameter that measures the true or population effect on the probability at a given value of X is $\beta\pi(1 - \pi)$, which is the linear approximation to the logistic curve at X. Therefore, the confidence interval for this parameter can be obtained by multiplying the limits of the confidence interval for β by $\pi(1 - \pi)$. For example, suppose that we would like to estimate the rate of change in the probability of being proficient in mathematics at the median effective level, or at the point where the logistic curve is at its steepest. This would occur when $\pi = 0.5$, which corresponds to

$$X = -\alpha/\beta = -1.99/0.72 = -2.76$$

in this example. Thus the confidence interval for the rate of change at this point would be:

$$[\pi(1 - \pi)LL_\beta, \pi(1 - \pi)UL_\beta] = [(0.5)(1 - 0.5)(0.62), (0.5)(1 - 0.5)(0.82)] = [0.16, 0.21].$$

Therefore, we can be 95% confident that *in the population*, as mathematics self-efficacy score increases by 1 unit, the steepest increase in the probability of being proficient in mathematics will be between 0.16 and 0.21. Note that in this case the true (population) value of $(0.5)(1 - 0.5)\,\beta = 0.25\,\beta$ appears to be positive (i.e., above 0), indicating that at this point on the curve the probability of being proficient in mathematics increases as self-efficacy in mathematics increases. This confidence interval can, of course, be computed at any specific point on the logistic curve (given by X or π).

8.3.3 Other topics in inference

There are some other issues, mostly related to sample size, that affect hypothesis testing. Although these topics are certainly important, we will not discuss them in detail here but refer the reader to other sources for more information. First, as with other hypothesis testing procedures, when one is able to estimate various parameters or effect sizes for a study ahead of time, it is possible to compute the approximate sample size needed to achieve a given level of power for hypothesis testing in logistic regression. In general, as is the case with other statistics, for a given power level the stronger the effect size for the association between the predictor and outcome variables, the smaller the sample size needed to detect that effect or association. Alternatively, for given parameter values, the larger the sample size used the larger the expected power of the test. Detailed information on power and sample size computations is provided in Agresti (1996) and Fleiss (1981).

Second, we mentioned earlier that hypothesis testing in logistic regression relies on large sample approximations to the χ^2 distribution. Specifically, the tests discussed in this chapter work best when the sample size is large relative to the number of parameters in the model. When the sample size is small (at least relative to the number of parameters), exact inference methods are available to obtain exact p-values rather than p-values that rely on an approximation to the χ^2 distribution. Further information on exact inference is available in Agresti (1990, 1996).

8.4 Model fit, residuals, and diagnostics of fit

In logistic regression, evaluating the fit of the model can be accomplished using a procedure similar to that which is used to assess the fit of log-linear (and other generalized linear) models. Specifically, the fit of a logistic model is evaluated by comparing the results **predicted** by the logistic model to the results actually **observed** in the data set using X^2 or G^2 as a test statistic (see Chapter 6). Since the logistic model predicts the probability that $Y_i = 1$, the test of fit involves comparing, at each value of X, the number of individuals predicted by the model to be in the $Y_i = 1$ category to the number of individuals observed to be in the $Y_i = 1$ category in the data set. As discussed in previous chapters, the test statistics are given by

$$X^2 = \sum \frac{(\text{Observed} - \text{Predicted})^2}{\text{Predicted}}$$

and

$$G^2 = \sum \text{Observed} \times \ln\left(\frac{\text{Observed}}{\text{Predicted}}\right),$$

with the summation occurring over all values of the predictor, X. Both of these test statistics follow approximately a χ^2 distribution with degrees of freedom equal to the difference between the number of possible values of the predictor, X, and the number of parameters estimated by the model. Predicted counts of at least five for each possible value of the predictor are necessary for the χ^2 approximation of the test statistic to hold. The null hypothesis tested by these fit statistics is that the observed and predicted values are the same, indicating that the model fits with the observed data. A large test statistic (and thus a rejection of the null hypothesis) indicates that the model predictions do not provide a good fit to the observed data.

To illustrate how these fit statistics work, 389 individuals in our sample obtained a mathematics self-efficacy score of $X = -0.4317$ and 325 of these individuals were proficient in mathematics (i.e., they were in the $Y_i = 1$ category) while 64 were not. Using the estimated logistic model presented earlier, where $\hat{\alpha} = 1.99$ and $\hat{\beta} = 0.72$, the predicted probability that a student would be proficient in mathematics if he or she had a mathematics efficacy score of -0.4317 is

$$\hat{\pi} = \frac{\exp(1.99 + 0.72(-0.4317))}{1 + \exp(1.99 + 0.72(-0.4317))} = \frac{\exp(1.68)}{1 + \exp(1.68)} = \frac{e^{1.68}}{1 + e^{1.68}} = \frac{5.366}{6.366} = 0.84.$$

Therefore, the number of individuals with a score of $X = -0.4317$ who are predicted by the model to be proficient is $389(0.84) = 326.76$. So, for this particular value of X, the predicted count is 326.76 and the observed count is 325. If we repeat this computation for each unique value of X, and no predicted count is smaller than 5, then we can test the fit of the model using either the X^2 or G^2 test statistic.

8.4.1   Model fit statistics for continuous predictors

When X is a continuous variable with many potential values, there may be values of X for which counts are quite low, in which case the χ^2 approximation of the test statistics will not hold and these tests of fit will not be valid. In our example we have many unique values for X (mathematics self-efficacy score) so it is not feasible to use either the X^2 or G^2 test statistic to evaluate model fit. In this case, it is sometimes preferable to group the observations into categories based on ranges of the predictor values. For example, if we have 50 unique values of X, we can group individuals into 10 categories (each based on a unique range of X-values). For each category, we can use the number of individuals in the X category who obtained a value of $Y_i = 1$ in the sample as our observed count. The fitted count can be obtained (most optimally for the test statistic) by using the logistic model to compute the predicted probability of $Y_i = 1$, $\hat{\pi}$, for each individual in the category based on his or her X value, and then adding the values of $\hat{\pi}$ for all individuals in the category to obtain the predicted count. In this case, we would be much less likely to obtain small predicted counts for any category (or X value). The degrees of freedom would now be the total number of grouped X categories (e.g., 10) minus the number of model parameters (e.g., 2 for one intercept and one slope).

A quick way to obtain the goodness-of-fit statistic in the case of continuous predictors is to use the Hosmer and Lemeshow goodness-of-fit test (Hosmer & Lemeshow, 1989). This test partitions the X values into 10 unique categories and computes a test statistic based on the observed and expected values for these 10 groups using the following formula:

$$G_{HL}^2 = \sum_{j=1}^{10} \frac{(\text{Observed}_j - \text{Expected}_j)^2}{\text{Expected}_j(1 - \text{Expected}_j/n_j)},$$

where n_j is the number of total observations in the jth group (or X category). Table 8.3 depicts the partitions (obtained in SAS by using the option "lackfit" in the model statement of proc logistic) used to compute the Hosmer and Lemeshow goodness-of-fit test statistic for our example, which resulted in a test statistic of 26.53 with 8 degrees of freedom (and a p-value of 0.0009). This indicates a lack of fit between the model and the data, likely due to the

Table 8.3 Partitions Used to Compute the Hosmer and Lemeshow Goodness-of-Fit Test Statistic for the Math Proficiency Example (PISA Data)

Partition	Total n_j	Proficient in mathematics		Not proficient in mathematics	
		Observed$_j$	Expected$_j$	Observed$_j$	Expected$_j$
1	525	376	382.21	149	142.79
2	524	412	430.05	112	93.95
3	409	337	344.87	72	64.13
4	425	368	364.60	57	60.40
5	664	567	578.66	97	85.34
6	381	353	337.06	28	43.94
7	669	620	604.28	49	64.72
8	640	607	594.03	33	45.97
9	553	529	527.07	24	25.93
10	461	445	451.12	16	9.88

omission of other predictor variables that would explain more of the variability in whether a student is proficient in mathematics.

Note that if a model fits the data relatively well, this in itself does not indicate that other models (for example, with more predictors) will not provide a significantly better fit. To compare models based on their fit is analogous to using the likelihood ratio test discussed in Section 8.3.1. In addition, if a model does not provide good fit to the data, one may wish to further investigate the lack of fit to understand where and why this lack of fit may be occurring from a substantive perspective. To do this, residuals and diagnostic measures can be used, and so we turn to a discussion of these next.

8.4.2   *Residuals and other diagnostic measures*

The X^2 statistic (see Section 8.4) can be expressed as a sum of squared **Pearson residuals**, where, for the jth X value (or grouped category, as discussed in the previous section), the residual has the form

$$\text{Residual}_j = \frac{y_j - n_j \hat{\pi}_j}{\sqrt{n_j \hat{\pi}_j (1 - \hat{\pi}_j)}}.$$

In this formula, y_j represents the observed count (or number of individuals in the jth X category who obtained a value of $Y = 1$) and $n_j \hat{\pi}_j$ represents the predicted count (or number of individuals in the jth X category predicted by the model to have a value of $Y = 1$). The Pearson residual is analogous to a z-score because the expected value of this residual is zero if the correct model has been fit to the data. Furthermore, because the observed counts follow a binomial distribution, the denominator of the Pearson residual is in fact the standard deviation of the observed count and thus (using the normal approximation to the binomial distribution) when n_j is large these residuals follow approximately a standard normal distribution.

Therefore, residuals with absolute values larger than two indicate a potential lack of fit at the jth X value, and residuals can be examined across X values to determine, from a substantive perspective, at which values the model tends to produce optimal and suboptimal fit. For example, we may find that the model provides good fit for individuals with intermediate X scores, but does not fit as well for individuals with very low or very high scores. In this case, the model may not fit the data well overall, but we might conclude that the model would still be valuable in predicting outcomes for students with intermediate scores. Similarly, the likelihood or deviance-based measure of fit, G^2, can also be decomposed into a sum of squared residuals and those residuals can be examined for lack of fit in the same manner.

As is the case in linear regression, other useful measures of fit are generally concerned with how much any one observation influences the model. Measures of influence usually include, in part, the **leverage** of an observation, which is a measure of the distance (for an individual observation) from the mean of the predictor variable (i.e., the observation's deviation on the X scale). Those observations that are found to be extreme outliers in terms of leverage could potentially influence the final logistic model that is obtained, in the same way that an outlier can influence the final regression model that is obtained in simple linear regression. The most common notation for the leverage of the jth X value is h_j, because leverage is computed based on the jth diagonal of what is called the "hat matrix" (if this terminology is not familiar to you from linear regression, suffice it to say that it is a measure of how extreme the observation is on the X scale). Leverage values vary between 0 and 1, with larger values indicating more extreme observations, and can be used to compute an **adjusted residual** using the formula

$$\frac{\text{Residual}_j}{\sqrt{1-h_j}} = \frac{y_j - n_j \hat{\pi}_j}{\sqrt{n_j \hat{\pi}_j (1 - \hat{\pi}_j)(1 - h_j)}}.$$

These adjusted residuals still approximately follow a standard normal distribution, so again absolute values larger than about 2 indicate a lack of fit. Note that large leverage values would reduce the denominator and thus increase the value of the adjusted residual. In some sense, whereas the unadjusted residuals measure whether a particular observation might be an outlier in terms of the response variable, the adjusted residuals incorporate information on whether the observation might also be an outlier in terms of the predictor variable.

Another measure of the **influence** of an observation is the degree to which the intercept and slope estimates would change if that observation was to be deleted. In other words, the intercept and slope are estimated with and without the observation, and the standardized difference between the two estimates is a measure of influence called **dfBeta**. If the observation is not influential, then the parameter estimate should not change when the observation is deleted and dfBeta will be small. However, if the observation is highly influential, then the estimate will change when the observation is deleted and dfBeta will be relatively large. The dfBeta value pertaining to the slope is usually more informative than that pertaining to the intercept since we are typically most interested in the slope parameter. The dfBeta values are evaluated somewhat subjectively and are usually compared to each other (across observations) to determine what value might be considered relatively large in a given data set. Along the same lines as dfBeta, measures of overall model fit, X^2 and G^2, can be computed with and without a particular observation thought to be an outlier. Influential observations would produce a large change in the measure of fit when deleted. These measures of influence are referred to as **delta chi-squared** and **delta deviance** for the change in X^2 and G^2, respectively.

For our example, these measures (obtained from SAS by using the option "influence" in the model statement of proc logistic; see also the example at the end of this chapter) are depicted in Figure 8.3 for a subset of the observations. As the table illustrates, the 310th and the 314th observations have relatively large residuals compared to the other observations

```
                                      Pearson Residual                    Deviance Residual
              Covariates
     Case                              (1 unit = 0.85)                    (1 unit = 0.35)
     Number    MATHEFF      Value      -8  -4  0 2 4 6 8      Value       -8  -4  0 2 4 6 8

       309     -0.8891     0.5093       |       |*       |     0.6791      |          |*    |
       310      0.2459    -2.9604       |  *    |        |    -2.1348      |  *       |     |
       311      0.0632     0.3609       |       |*       |     0.4948      |        |*      |
       312      0.9179     0.2649       |       |*       |     0.3683      |        |*      |
       313     -0.1088     0.3840       |       |*       |     0.5245      |         |*     |
       314      0.2459    -2.9604       |  *    |        |    -2.1348      |  *       |     |
       315      0.9179     0.2649       |       |*       |     0.3683      |         |*     |

                          Hat Matrix Diagonal                        Intercept
     Case                  (1 unit = 5.E-04)                         DfBeta     (1 unit = 9.E-03)
     Number     Value      0 2 4 6 8  12  16                         Value      -8  -4  0 2 4 6 8

       309     0.000485     |*            |                         0.00703      |        |*    |
       310     0.000223     |*            |                        -0.0429       |  *     |     |
       311     0.000213     |*            |                         0.00526      |        |*    |
       312     0.000310     |*            |                         0.00367      |       *|     |
       313     0.000215     |*            |                         0.00560      |        |*    |
       314     0.000223     |*            |                        -0.0429       |  *     |     |
       315     0.000310     |*            |                         0.00367      |       *|     |

     Case      DfBeta       (1 unit = 0.02)                                     (1 unit = 0.48)
     Number     Value       -8  -4  0 2 4 6 8           Value                   0 2 4 6 8  12  16

       309    -0.00676      |       *|     |            0.4614                   |*         |
       310    -0.0208       |     *| |     |            4.5594                   |       *  |
       311     0.00163      |       |*     |            0.2449                   |*         |
       312     0.00369      |       |*     |            0.1357                   |*         |
       313     0.000726     |       |*     |            0.2752                   |*         |
       314    -0.0208       |     *| |     |            4.5594                   |       *  |
       315     0.00369      |       |*     |            0.1357                   |*         |

                                              Delta Chi-Square
                       Case                   (1 unit = 2.86)
                       Number     Value       0 2 4 6 8  12  16

                         309     0.2595        |*          |
                         310     8.7660        |   *       |
                         311     0.1303        |*          |
                         312     0.0702        |*          |
                         313     0.1475        |*          |
                         314     8.7660        |   *       |
                         315     0.0702        |*          |
                         316     0.1303        |*          |
```

Figure 8.3 Measures of influence obtained for a subset of the observations used in the math proficiency example (PISA data).

considered. However, the dfBeta values suggest that these observations are influencing the intercept of the logistic regression model, as opposed to the slope coefficient pertaining to math efficacy scores. Therefore, even though the delta chi-squared and delta deviance measures indicate that eliminating these two observations would substantially improve the overall measures of fit, it is likely that these two observations would be retained in the final model.

8.5   Complete example and computing

In this section we work through a complete example of a logistic regression analysis, including the SAS and SPSS commands, output, and interpretation of the results. The "impeachment" data set, which we obtained from the Web site of the *Journal for Statistics Education*, consists of census data on the impeachment votes as well as other information from 100 U.S. senators in 1999. For this example, we used the senator's vote on whether President Clinton is guilty of perjury (0 = not guilty, 1 = guilty) as the dependent variable and a measure of the senator's conservatism (on a 0–100 scale) as well as the percent of the State's votes Clinton received in the 1996 presidential election as predictor variables. More information on the data and the variables is available from http://www.amstat.org/publications/jse/datasets/impeach.txt.

This particular data set can be treated as either a population (because it consists of all senators in 1999) or as a sample of 100 senators that represents the population of all senators throughout the years. If one is interested only in the 1999 Senate, and wishes to treat the data as the population, inferential procedures are unnecessary. However, if one is interested in generalizing the results from this data set to infer the general voting behavior of U.S. senators, the data could be treated as a sample and inferential procedures may be used to generalize the results. We acknowledge that one can argue for either approach in this case, but we choose to treat the data set as a sample for both theoretical and illustrative purposes. We begin with instructions for SAS and SPSS followed by an interpretation of the results and some overall conclusions.

8.5.1 SAS

In this example, we would like to determine whether a senator's vote on perjury (vote1) can be predicted from degree of conservatism (conservatism) and the percentage of the senator's state voters who voted for the president (votepct). The SAS syntax for fitting this model (with various options) is shown in Figure 8.4:

- The first line of the program is used to specify that we are using the logistic regression procedure and analyzing a data set called "impeach" (which has been previously read into SAS using data steps). The "descending" command is used to specify that we would like to model the probability of $Y_i = 1$ (guilty) rather than $Y_i = 0$ (not guilty).
  - By default, SAS arranges the values of Y in order from smallest to largest, and predicts the odds or probability of the first value.
  - In our case, this would mean that the probability of $Y_i = 0$ (not guilty) would be modeled by default, so the "descending" command is used to specify that the Y values should be arranged in descending order such that $Y_i = 1$ (guilty) is the outcome modeled.
- The second line of the syntax specifies that we would like to model the dependent variable (vote1) from two independent variables (votepct and conservatism). Some optional commands appear after the slash:
  - the "expb" option requests that the exponentiated values of the parameters be provided in the output;
  - the "lackfit" command is used to request that the lack of fit test be included in the output; and
  - the "iplots" command requests plots of the values of various diagnostic measures (on the vertical axis) for each observation (on the horizontal axis).

```
proc logistic data=impeach descending;
   model vote1 = votepct conservatism /expb lackfit iplots;
   output out=results PREDICTED=pihat DFBETAS=_ALL_
   DIFCHISQ=x2 DIFDEV=g2 RESCHI=x2res RESDEV=g2res;
run;
```

Figure 8.4 SAS program syntax for logistic regression example.

- The third line requests that an output data set (called "results" in our program) be created. Following the out=results command, a list of variables to be included in the results data set is provided; for example:
  - PREDICTED=pihat provides the value of the model's predicted probability (that $Y_i = 1$) in the results data set under the name "pihat".
  - DFBETAS=_ALL_ DIFCHISQ=x2 DIFDEV=g2 RESCHI=x2res RESDEV=g2 res similarly request, respectively, values for each of the DfBetas, the delta chi-squared value, the delta deviance value, the X^2 residual, and the G^2 residual for each observation.

- The run statement closes out the syntax and requests the execution of the program.

The model output (i.e., parameter estimates and tests) from SAS is shown in Figure 8.5, and contains the parameter estimates:

- The intercept estimate is −4.216.
- The slope estimate for vote percentage is −0.040.
- The slope estimate for conservatism is 0.105.

The exponentiated values of these estimates are provided in the last column:
  - The exponentiated intercept is $e^{-4.216} = 0.015$.
  - The exponentiated slope for vote percentage is $e^{-0.040} = 0.961$.
  - The exponentiated slope for conservatism is $e^{0.105} = 1.111$.

The output shown in Figure 8.6 provides information on the likelihood ratio test. Specifically, the output shows that

- for the model with only an intercept, $-2\log(L_0) = 137.63$,
- for our model with both predictors, $-2\log(L_1) = 36.77$, and
- the difference between these values, shown under Likelihood Ratio in the "Testing Global Null Hypothesis: BETA=0" portion of the output in Figure 8.6, is 137.63 − 36.77 = 100.86.

```
                          The LOGISTIC Procedure

                  Analysis of Maximum Likelihood Estimates

                                   Standard        Wald
   Parameter      DF    Estimate      Error    Chi-Square    Pr > ChiSq    Exp(Est)

   Intercept       1     -4.2160     3.7738       1.2481        0.2639       0.015
   votepct         1     -0.0396     0.0696       0.3242        0.5691       0.961
   conservatism    1      0.1051     0.0242      18.8922       <.0001        1.111


                          Odds Ratio Estimates

                             Point            95% Wald
           Effect          Estimate       Confidence Limits

           votepct           0.961        0.839      1.102
           conservatism      1.111        1.059      1.165
```

Figure 8.5 Parameter estimate output for the impeachment example from the logistic procedure in SAS.

```
                        Model Fit Statistics

                                              Intercept
                              Intercept            and
              Criterion            Only      Covariates

              AIC               139.628          42.771
              SC                142.233          50.587
              -2 Log L          137.628          36.771


          Testing Global Null Hypothesis: BETA=0

  Test                     Chi-Square        DF      Pr > ChiSq

  Likelihood Ratio           100.8565         2         <.0001
  Score                       75.2578         2         <.0001
  Wald                        20.6693         2         <.0001
```

Figure 8.6 Log likelihood output for the impeachment example from the logistic procedure in SAS.

- The degrees of freedom of 2 for the likelihood ratio test are also shown; these represent the difference between the 3 parameters in the full model (intercept and two slopes) and the 1 parameter in the intercept only model (intercept).
- The *p*-value provided for the likelihood ratio test is less than .0001, indicating a significant difference between the log-likelihoods of these two models.

Therefore, because this test evaluates the inclusion of both predictors simultaneously, the results indicate that the model containing both predictors fits the data significantly better than a model containing neither predictor. To obtain a likelihood ratio test for one predictor at a time, we would need to fit a model containing just one of the predictors and compare its likelihood to that of the model containing both predictors (in the same way that an *F*-test is conducted in linear multiple regression). This test was demonstrated in detail in the chapter on log-linear models (and is also demonstrated in the next chapter on logistic regression with categorical predictors).

Figure 8.7 shows the Hosmer and Lemeshow partitions and test of fit for this logistic regression model:

- In our case, with a test statistic of 12.99 and a *p*-value of 0.11, the null hypothesis (that the residuals are zero) is not rejected, indicating that the model fits the data adequately.
- In other words, modeling the odds of a guilty vote on perjury using these two predictors results in reasonably small residuals overall.

Figure 8.8 demonstrates just one of the plots of diagnostic measures provided by SAS. We chose to show the plot of the Pearson residuals, but plots of other measures (including influence measures) are provided in the SAS output as well. In Figure 8.8:

- the observation number (on the horizontal axis) is plotted against its Pearson residual (on the vertical axis), and
- a few observations do appear to have very large residuals; for example, observation 1 seems to have a Pearson residual that is well below –2, as do observations 84 and 92.

To examine these more closely, the "results" data set created in the syntax can be printed; a portion of this output for this data set is summarized in Table 8.4 for observations 1, 84, and 92, where we provide pertinent information for these three observations (i.e., senators). Using Senator Shelby (Observation 1) as an example, in his state (Alabama)

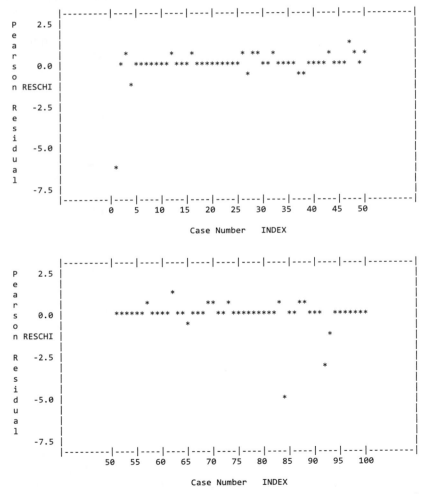

```
                Partition for the Hosmer and Lemeshow Test

                                vote1 = 1                vote1 = 0
        Group     Total   Observed    Expected    Observed    Expected

          1         11        0         0.02          11       10.98
          2         10        0         0.03          10        9.97
          3         10        0         0.06          10        9.94
          4         11        0         0.14          11       10.86
          5         10        1         1.85           9        8.15
          6         10        9         7.03           1        2.97
          7         10       10         8.61           0        1.39
          8         10        8         9.54           2        0.46
          9         10        9         9.80           1        0.20
         10          8        8         7.92           0        0.08

            Hosmer and Lemeshow Goodness-of-Fit Test

            Chi-Square        DF       Pr > ChiSq

             12.9877           8          0.1123
```

Figure 8.7 Model fit output for the impeachment example from the logistic procedure in SAS.

Figure 8.8 Pearson residual plots for the impeachment example from the logistic procedure in SAS.

Table 8.4 Diagnostic Measures for Observations 1, 84, and 95 From the Impeachment Example

Observation	Senator	Vote1	Votepct	Conservatism	Pihat	DFBETA_ intercept	DFBETA_ votepct	DFBETA_ conservatism	x2res
1	Shelby	0	43	92	.977	.171	.054	-.650	-6.52
84	Thompson	0	48	88	.958	.427	-.272	-.607	-4.79
92	Warner	0	45	80	.917	.130	-.033	-.367	-3.34

43% of voters voted for Clinton in 1996 and his conservatism score is 92. We will discuss the results summarized in Table 8.4 in more detail in Section 8.5.3.

8.5.2 SPSS

To obtain the model parameter estimates and tests using menus, after reading the data into SPSS:

- Choose Regression from the Analyze menu.
- Select Binary logistic….
  - In the Logistic Regression window that opens up, the outcome variable (vote1) is moved into the Dependent box and the predictors (conservatism and votepct) are moved into the Covariates box as illustrated in Figure 8.9.
- To obtain residuals and other diagnostic measure, click on the Save… button at the bottom of the Logistic Regression window.
  - For this analysis, we checked the boxes for all influence measures as well as the Standardized box under Residuals as illustrated in Figure 8.10.
  - Click on the Continue button to return to the Logistic Regression window.
- Click on the Options… button to select more options. As illustrated in Figure 8.11, for this analysis we selected:
  - the Hosmer-Lemeshow statistics;
  - a casewise listing of residuals that were greater than 2;
  - the confidence intervals for the exponentiated parameter values, "CI for exp(B)";
  - that output be displayed "At last step" rather than at each step.
- Click on Continue and then OK to obtain the output.

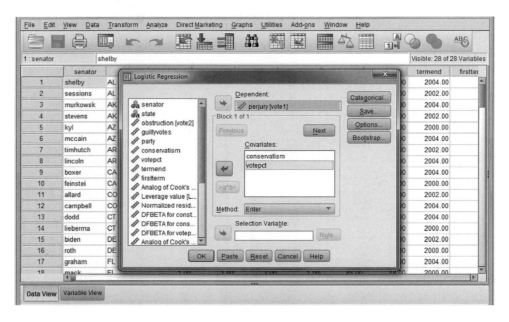

Figure 8.9 SPSS screenshot illustrating how to fit a logistic regression model.

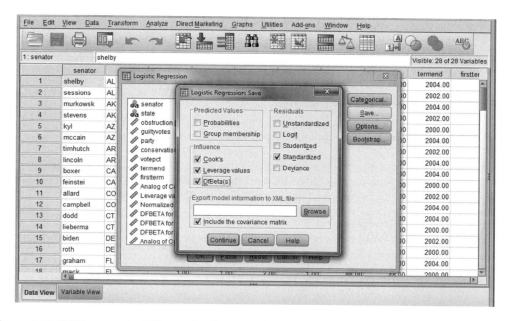

Figure 8.10 SPSS screenshot illustrating how to obtain residuals and other diagnostic measures when fitting a logistic regression model.

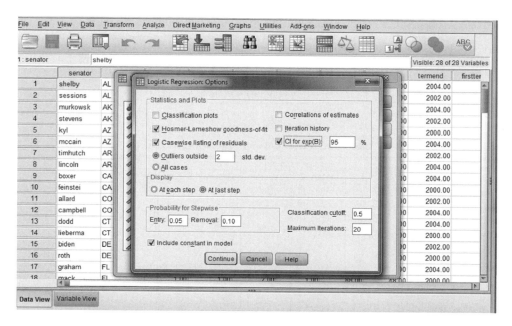

Figure 8.11 SPSS screenshot illustrating options available when fitting a logistic regression model.

Variables in the Equation

	B	S.E.	Wald	df	Sig.	Exp(B)	95.0% C.I.for EXP(B) Lower	Upper
Step 1[a] conservatism	.105	.024	18.892	1	.000	1.111	1.059	1.165
votepct	-.040	.070	.324	1	.569	.961	.839	1.102
Constant	-4.216	3.774	1.248	1	.264	.015		

a. Variables(s) entered on step 1: conservatism, votepct.

Figure 8.12 Parameter estimate output for the impeachment example from SPSS.

The relevant output from SPSS is presented in Figures 8.12–8.16. SPSS first fits an inter-cept-only model in a step it calls "Step 0," and then fits the model with both predictors in a step called "Step 1." In Figure 8.12, the results (under "Step 1"), include

- the parameter estimates; and
- their associated Wald tests of significance, their exponentiated values, and the 95% confidence intervals for the exponentiated values.

These values are identical to those in Figure 8.5 (from SAS; see previous section).

Omnibus Tests of Model Coefficients

		Chi-Square	df	Sig.
Step 1	Step	100.856	2	.000
	Block	100.856	2	.000
	Model	100.856	2	.000

Figure 8.13 Likelihood ratio test output for the impeachment example from SPSS.

Hosmer and Lemeshow Test

Step	Chi-Square	df	Sig.
1	12.988	8	.112

Contingency Table for Hosmer and Lemeshow Test

		Perjury = not guilty Observed	Expected	Perjury = guilty Observed	Expected	Total
Step 1	1	11	10.979	0	.021	11
	2	10	9.965	0	.035	10
	3	10	9.943	0	.057	10
	4	11	10.862	0	.138	11
	5	9	8.146	1	1.854	10
	6	1	2.973	9	7.027	10
	7	0	1.388	10	8.612	10
	8	2	.464	8	9.536	10
	9	1	.196	9	9.804	10
	10	0	.084	8	7.916	8

Figure 8.14 SPSS output of Hosmer and Lemeshow partitions and test of fit for the impeachment example.

Casewise List[b]

Case	Selected Status[a]	Observed perjury	Predicted	Predicted Group	Temporary Variable	
					Resid	ZResid
1	S	n**	.977	g	-.997	-6.525
84	S	n**	.958	g	-.958	-4.789
92	S	n**	.918	g	-.918	-3.338

a. S = Selected, U = Unselected cases, and** = Misclassified cases.
b. Cases with studentized residuals greater than 2.000 are listed.

Figure 8.15 SPSS output of observations with standardized residuals greater than 2 for the impeachment example.

The other SPSS output provides the following results:

- Figure 8.13 shows the SPSS output of the likelihood ratio test (shown in Figure 8.6 for SAS).
- Figure 8.14 shows the Hosmer and Lemeshow partitions and test of fit for this logistic regression model (shown in Figure 8.7 for SAS).
- Figure 8.15 shows a table of the observations that resulted in standardized residuals greater than 2, and also includes, for each observation,

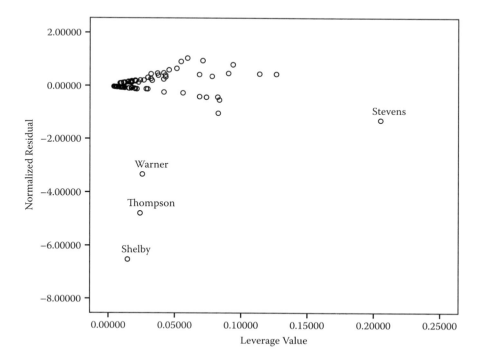

Figure 8.16 SPSS plot of residuals against leverage values for the impeachment example.

- the observed group (n = not guilty, g = guilty),
- the predicted probability of a guilty vote (e.g., 0.977 for Observation 1), and
- the predicted outcome (n = not guilty, g = guilty) based on the predicted probability.
- The measures of influence requested from SPSS appear in the data window, and can thus be examined in this window or plotted using the plotting procedures (under the Graphs menu) in SPSS.
    - For example, a plot of the standardized residuals (saved in the data window under the name ZRE_1) against the leverage values (saved in the data window under the name LEV_1) is shown in Figure 8.16 with outliers on either axis identified with the senator's name.
    - Thus, for example, we see that the leverage value for Stevens is relatively high and the standardized residuals for Warner, Thompson, and Shelby are rather large as well.

8.5.3   Interpretations

The parameter values are shown in Figures 8.5 (SAS) and 8.12 (SPSS). The exponentiated value of the intercept, $e^{-4.2} = 0.015$, indicates that the odds that a senator would vote to accuse the president of perjury is 0.015 (or the probability is $0.015/1.015 = 0.01$) if his or her conservatism score is zero and zero percent of voters in his or her state voted for Clinton. Note that in this example, as is the case in many applied contexts, the intercept value is not very meaningful because we do not expect that realistically a senator exists who would both score zero on conservatism (i.e., is very liberal) and represent a state where zero percent of voters voted for Clinton in 1996. Therefore, we focus our interpretation on the slope values.

The slope estimates (exponentiated) can be interpreted as follows: For every 1% increase in the state's votes for Clinton, when holding conservatism constant, the odds of voting guilty on perjury increase $e^{-0.04} = 0.96$ times (i.e., the odds decrease slightly); for every 1 point increase in conservatism, when holding vote percentage constant, the odds of voting guilty on perjury increase $e^{0.105} = 1.11$ times (i.e., the odds increase slightly). Using the Wald tests, the slope associated with conservatism reaches statistical significance ($\chi_1^2 = 18.89$, $p < .0001$), whereas the slope associated with vote percentage does not ($\chi_1^2 = 0.32$, $p = .5691$).

In addition, the part of the output pertaining to odds ratio estimates again shows the exponentiated slopes along with their 95% confidence intervals; note that the confidence interval for vote percentage includes one, indicating that statistically vote percentage is not associated with the odds of voting guilty (rather than not guilty), whereas the confidence interval for conservatism does not include one and, with both limits greater than one, indicates that degree of conservatism is positively associated with the odds of voting guilty (rather than not guilty). Therefore, in the population (which might consist of all senators over the years, represented by this sample of 100), we can be 95% confident that when holding vote percentage constant the odds of voting guilty on perjury increase somewhere from 1.06 to 1.17 times for each one point increase in conservatism.

Because both predictors in our example are continuous, it may not be appropriate to examine residuals for individual observations (senators) unless they share predictor values and produce reasonably large predicted counts. For illustrative purposes, however, we discuss how to interpret the Pearson residuals for this example. From Figure 8.8 (SAS) and Figure 8.16 (SPSS), as well as Table 8.4, we can examine the residuals more closely. Using Senator Shelby (Observation 1) as an example, in his state (Alabama) 43% of voters voted for Clinton in 1996 and his conservatism score is 92. Therefore, the predicted probability that Shelby would vote guilty on perjury according to this logistic regression model is (see Equation 8.3)

$$\hat{\pi} = \frac{\exp\{-4.216 - .0396(43) + .1051(92)\}}{1 + \exp\{-4.216 - .0396(43) + .1051(92)\}} = \frac{42.54}{43.54} = 0.977,$$

which is indeed the predicted probability value (pihat) shown in Table 8.4 for this senator. Because most senators from conservative states who have a high degree of conservatism tended to vote guilty, the predicted probability that Shelby would vote guilty is 97.7%. However, Senator Shelby actually voted not guilty (vote1 = 0), and thus his Pearson residual is

$$\frac{y_j - n_j\hat{\pi}_j}{\sqrt{n_j\hat{\pi}_j(1 - \hat{\pi}_j)}} = \frac{0 - 1(.977)}{\sqrt{1(.977)(1 - .977)}} = -6.52,$$

which is indeed the Pearson residual (x2res) for Shelby shown in Table 8.4.

In addition to this large (in absolute sense) residual for Senator Shelby, the DFBeta values of the intercept and votepct for this senator are quite reasonable but the DFBeta of conservatism is relatively high (see Table 8.4). This indicates that if Shelby's data were removed from the analysis, the slope associated with conservatism in the logistic regression model would most likely change. A similar pattern of results is seen for Senators Thompson (Observation 84) and Warner (Observation 92). It is clear that while all three of these senators have a high degree of conservatism, and all represent conservative states (where fewer than 50% of voters voted for Clinton in 1996), they nevertheless voted not guilty on perjury, counter to the model's predictions that are based on the overall trends in the data. Therefore, given their conservatism scores, these three senators represent "outliers" for this model.

8.5.4   Conclusions

In general, it is possible to predict senators' votes on perjury relatively well using their conservatism scores and state vote percentage. When holding vote percentage constant there is a significant positive relationship between senators' conservatism and the odds (or probability) of voting guilty on perjury ($\beta = .105$, $\chi_1^2 = 18.89$, $p < .0001$). Specifically, we can be 95% confident that when holding vote percentage constant the odds of voting guilty on perjury charges increase somewhere from 1.06 to 1.17 times for each one point increase in conservatism. On the other hand, holding the degree of conservatism constant, there is a negative but insignificant relationship between senators' state votes for Clinton and the odds (or probability) of voting guilty on perjury ($\beta = -.034$, $\chi_1^2 = 0.32$, $p = .5691$).

At this point, if vote percentage is removed as a predictor (due to its statistical insignificance), all of the results previously discussed (including model fit, residuals, diagnostics, and so forth) might change. Moreover, it is possible that this new model, with only conservatism as predictor, may not fit the data as well. Therefore, if vote percentage was removed as a predictor, the model would need to be refit and the results reinterpreted. In addition, if vote percentage is a substantively meaningful predictor that was included based on theoretical considerations, one could argue that it should not be removed from the model on the basis of statistical insignificance alone. Therefore, for this example, we choose to leave both predictors in the model.

This logistic regression model with both predictors fits the data (i.e., predicts voting outcomes) reasonably well ($G_{HL}^2 = 12.99$, $df = 8$, $p = 0.11$), although a few outliers do exist; namely, some conservative senators from conservative states voted not guilty on perjury. Although we do not recommend that these observations be removed from the data set, as they are representative of a segment of the senator population, we acknowledge that the slope of conservatism in this model is likely affected by inclusion of these senators.

8.6   Summary

In this chapter we introduced the logistic regression model to predict a dichotomous (or binary) response variable from continuous predictor variables. Our aim was to help the reader develop a conceptual understanding by explicitly making the connections between logistic regression modeling components and their analogous counterparts in linear regression modeling, which presumably are more familiar to the reader.

Specifically, we discussed general ideas such as parameter estimation and interpretation, overall model fit, tests to compare nested models, and diagnostic procedures for model fit. As is the case in linear regression, all of these statistical procedures, coupled with substantive judgment, can be used to make decisions regarding the predictors that should be included in the final prediction model.

Finally, it should be noted that both continuous and categorical variables can be used when fitting logistic regression models, just as they can when fitting linear regression models. However, the use of categorical predictors involves some different concepts in model fitting and interpretation. Therefore, this topic was intentionally omitted from this chapter and is the subject of the next chapter. Taken together, this chapter and the next should provide researchers with the necessary tools to fit and interpret logistic regression models that contain both continuous and categorical predictor variables.

Problems

8.1. Consider a logistic regression model with two predictors, and the following parameters: the intercept is $\alpha = 2$, and the slopes are $\beta_1 = 0.5$ and $\beta_2 = -0.3$.
   a. Compute the predicted logit of the probability when $X_1 = 0$ and $X_2 = 0$.
   b. Compute the predicted odds when $X_1 = 0$ and $X_2 = 0$.
   c. Based on your answers to (a) and (b), explain how the value of the intercept can be interpreted.
   d. Compute the predicted logit of the probability when $X_1 = 1$ and $X_2 = 5$.
   e. Compute the predicted odds when $X_1 = 1$ and $X_2 = 5$.
   f. Compute the predicted probability when $X_1 = 1$ and $X_2 = 5$.

8.2. Consider a logistic regression model with two predictors, and the following parameters: the intercept is $\alpha = 1.5$, and the slopes are $\beta_1 = 0.4$ and $\beta_2 = -0.1$.
   a. Compute the predicted logit of the probability when $X_1 = 0$ and $X_2 = 0$.
   b. Compute the predicted odds when $X_1 = 0$ and $X_2 = 0$.
   c. Based on your answers to (a) and (b), explain how the value of the intercept can be interpreted.
   d. Compute the predicted logit of the probability when $X_1 = 1$ and $X_2 = 5$.

    e. Compute the predicted odds when $X_1 = 1$ and $X_2 = 5$.
    f. Compute the predicted probability when $X_1 = 1$ and $X_2 = 5$.

8.3. Consider a logistic regression model with two predictors, and the following parameters: the intercept is $\alpha = 2$, and the slopes are $\beta_1 = 0.5$ and $\beta_2 = -0.3$.
    a. Compute the predicted odds when $X_1 = 2$ and $X_2 = 5$.
    b. Compute the predicted odds when $X_1 = 3$ and $X_2 = 5$.
    c. Based on your results to parts (a) and (b), explain how the value of β_1 can be interpreted.

8.4. Consider a logistic regression model with two predictors, and the following parameters: the intercept is $\alpha = 1.5$, and the slopes are $\beta_1 = 0.4$ and $\beta_2 = -0.1$.
    a. Compute the predicted odds when $X_1 = 2$ and $X_2 = 4$.
    b. Compute the predicted odds when $X_1 = 2$ and $X_2 = 5$.
    c. Based on your results to parts (a) and (b), explain how the value of β_2 can be interpreted.

Use the ADD data set described next for Problems 8.5 to 8.8:

> In 1965, second-grade teachers in a number of schools in Vermont were asked to complete a questionnaire indicating the extent to which each student exhibited behaviors associated with attention deficit disorder (ADD). Based on the questionnaire, an ADD "score" was computed for each student (with higher scores indicating more ADD-like behaviors). The questionnaires for the same children were again completed when the children were in fourth and fifth grades. The children were followed through high school, and in 1985 Howell and Huessy reported some data from this study. (Howell, 2007)

The variables in the data set are as follows:

ID	ID number
ADDSC	Average of the three ADD scores
SEX	1 = male; 2 = female
REPEAT	1 = repeated at least one grade; 0 = did not repeat a grade
IQ	IQ obtained from a group-administered test
ENGL	Level of English in ninth grade: 1 = college prep; 2 = general; 3 = remedial
ENGG	Grade in English in ninth grade: 4 = A; 3 = B; etc.
GPA	Grade point average in ninth grade
SOCPROB	Social problems in ninth grade: 1 = yes; 0 = no
DROPOUT	1 = dropped out before completing high school; 0 = did not drop out

Source: Obtained from http://www.uvm.edu/~dhowell/methods6/DataFiles/Add.dat.

8.5. Use the ADD data set and fit a logistic regression model to predict whether a student dropped out before completing high school from average ADD score (ADDSC) and ninth grade GPA.
   a. Does the model appear to have adequate overall fit (i.e., do the two predictors, together, provide better prediction than a model with no predictors)?
   b. Fully interpret the value, direction, and statistical significance of each of the slope estimates in this model.

8.6. Use the ADD data set and fit a logistic regression model to predict whether a student dropped out before completing high school from average ADD score (ADDSC) only.
   a. Fully interpret the value, direction, and statistical significance of the slope estimate in this model.
   b. Does the model appear to have adequate overall fit (i.e., does the predictor provide better prediction than a model with no predictors)? Conceptually, how does this test compare to the test conducted in part (a)?

8.7. Compare the models fit in Problems 8.5 and 8.6:
   a. Conduct the likelihood ratio (G^2) test to compare the two models. Is there a significant difference between these two models in terms of fit? What conclusions can you draw from these results?
   b. Report the Wald test statistic that corresponds to the test you conducted in part (a). How does it compare to the likelihood ratio test statistic and conclusions?

8.8. Pick an outcome measure and at least two predictors from the ADD data set that can be modeled using logistic regression.
   a. Fit the model and report its fit.
   b. Conduct the appropriate tests to determine if any predictors can or should be dropped from the model. Explain your process and conclusions.
   c. Using your final model, examine the residuals and report any apparent problems.
   d. Fully interpret the value, direction, and statistical significance of each of the slope estimates in your final model.

8.9. Use the 2006 GSS data set (e.g., at http://sda.berkeley.edu/archive.htm) to predict whether a respondent favors sex education in the public schools (SEXEDUC) from the respondent's age (AGE), highest year of school completed (EDUC), and socioeconomic index (SEI). Note: For valid model comparisons, make sure that you eliminate all observations with missing values on any of the relevant variables before running the analyses.
   a. Conduct the likelihood ratio test to compare the model with all three predictors to a model with the predictors of AGE and EDUC only. Report and (substantively) interpret the results of this test.
   b. Conduct the likelihood ratio test to compare the model with the predictors of AGE and EDUC to the model with AGE only. Report and (substantively) interpret the results of this test.
   c. Based on the results from parts (a) and (b), which model (of the three) is most parsimonious? Explain
   d. Fully interpret the values, signs, and significance tests of the parameter estimates in the most parsimonious model.

e. While a model may be the most parsimonious of a given set of models, it may or may not fit the observed data well. Conduct the test of fit (that compares observed and predicted values) for the most parsimonious model and interpret the results.

f. Based on the model with the predictors of AGE and EDUC only, what is the predicted probability that a respondent would favor sex education in the public schools if that respondent is 40 years old and has completed 12 years of education?

8.10. Pick your own research question that can be addressed using variables from the 2006 GSS data set and a logistic regression analysis. You should include at least two predictors.

a. State your research question and expectations regarding the findings.

b. Explain why a logistic regression analysis is appropriate to your research question.

c. Conduct the appropriate tests to determine if any predictors or terms can or should be dropped from the model. Explain your process and conclusions.

d. Fully interpret the value, direction, and statistical significance of each of the parameter estimates in your final model.

e. Summarize the results substantively: What does the model tell you about any associations between the variables? Do these results conform to your expectations?

8.11. The diabetes data set (http://www.psych.yorku.ca/friendly/lab/files/psy6140/examples/logistic/logidiab.sas) contains 145 observations on 4 measures of glucose or insulin levels, relative weight, and diabetic status (group). Use this data set to predict whether a patient is normal or diabetic from the other variables. Fully interpret the results of the analysis, including the process you used to select a final model and substantive interpretations of the parameter estimates.

chapter nine

Logistic regression with categorical predictors

> **A LOOK AHEAD**
>
> In this chapter we discuss logistic regression models in which the predictors are categorical or qualitative variables (such as gender, location, and socioeconomic status). This chapter builds on the previous chapter in that all of the material on logistic regression modeling remains the same, but the coding of the predictors and interpretation of the regression coefficients changes due to the categorical nature of the predictors. In addition, the similarities and differences between logistic regression with categorical predictors and log-linear models will be discussed in this chapter.

9.1   Coding categorical predictors

The logistic model has the same basic form that we discussed in Chapter 8, namely,

$$\text{logit}(\pi) = \ln\left(\frac{\pi}{1-\pi}\right) \alpha + \beta_1 X_1 + \beta_2 X_2 + \dots + \beta_p X_p.$$

Recall that in this model π is used to represent the probability of "success" or the probability that the (binary) outcome $Y_i = 1$, α represents the intercept parameter, and β_j represents the coefficient associated with the jth predictor, X_j. Fortunately, the interpretation of the model parameters (intercept, slope) discussed for continuous predictor variables in the previous chapter does not change fundamentally for categorical predictor variables. The main difference between quantitative or continuous predictors and qualitative or categorical predictors is that the latter need to be coded such that $(C-1)$ indicator variables are required to represent a total of C categories, as discussed in Chapter 7 (see Section 7.1 for a detailed description). In this chapter, **dummy coding** of the categorical predictors will once again be applied.

For example, suppose that gender was used as a predictor of whether a student attends an academic or nonacademic high school program. In this case, to "dummy code" the gender variable only one indicator variable, X, is needed (because $C = 2$ and so $C - 1 = 1$). Thus, coding is simply a matter of choosing for which of the two genders X will be assigned a value of zero and for which it will be assigned a value of one. Suppose that we decide to represent males with a value of zero and females with a value of one. In this case, using π to represent the probability of attending an academic program (i.e., a success), the logistic model predicts the logit of π (or the log odds of attending an academic program) from the predictor, gender, as follows:

$$\ln\left(\frac{\pi}{1-\pi}\right) = \alpha + \beta X = \alpha + \beta(0) = \alpha, \qquad \text{if the student is male; and}$$

$$\ln\left(\frac{\pi}{1-\pi}\right) = \alpha + \beta X = \alpha + \beta(1) = \alpha + \beta, \quad \text{if the student is female.}$$

Using the form of the logistic function presented in Equation 8.2, in which both sides of the equation are exponentiated,

$$\left(\frac{\pi}{1-\pi}\right) = e^{(\alpha+\beta X)} = e^{(\alpha+\beta(0))} = e^{\alpha}, \qquad \text{if the student is male; and}$$

$$\left(\frac{\pi}{1-\pi}\right) = e^{(\alpha + \beta X)} = e^{(\alpha+\beta(1))} = e^{(\alpha+\beta)} = e^{\alpha}e^{\beta}, \quad \text{if the student is female.}$$

Therefore, the exponentiated value of the intercept, e^{α}, can be interpreted as the predicted odds that a male student attended an academic program, and the exponentiated value of the slope, e^{β}, can be interpreted as the difference between the odds of attending an academic program for male and female students. From the previous equations, we can see that e^{α} would be the expected odds of attending an academic program for males and $e^{\alpha+\beta} = e^{\alpha}e^{\beta}$ would be the expected odds of attending an academic program for females. Therefore, the odds of attending an academic program for females are e^{β} times the odds for males. For example, suppose that $\alpha = 2$ and $\beta = 0.5$. Then for male students

$$\ln\left(\frac{\pi}{1-\pi}\right) = \alpha + \beta X = 2 + 0.5(0) = 2,$$

and

$$\left(\frac{\pi}{1-\pi}\right) = e^{(2+0.5(0))} = e^2 = 7.4;$$

and for female students

$$\ln\left(\frac{\pi}{1-\pi}\right) = \alpha + \beta X = 2 + 0.5(1) = 2.5,$$

and

$$\left(\frac{\pi}{1-\pi}\right) = e^2 e^{0.5} = 12.2.$$

Therefore, in this example, the effect of gender is such that females are more likely to attend academic programs than males. Specifically, the odds of attending an academic program are $e^{0.5} = 1.65$ times higher for females than for males, and indeed $1.65(7.4) = 12.2$. In terms of probabilities, the probability of having attended an academic program can be computed (see Equation 8.3) as

$$\pi = \left(\frac{e^\alpha}{1+e^\alpha} \right) = \left(\frac{e^2}{1+e^2} \right) = \left(\frac{7.4}{8.4} \right) = 0.88 \quad \text{for male students; and}$$

$$\pi = \left(\frac{e^{\alpha+\beta}}{1+e^{\alpha+\beta}} \right) = \left(\frac{e^{2.5}}{1+e^{2.5}} \right) = \left(\frac{12.2}{13.2} \right) = 0.92 \quad \text{for female students.}$$

In a model with a single categorical predictor variable that is dummy coded, the exponentiated intercept can always be interpreted as the predicted odds that $Y_i = 1$ for the reference group or the category that is coded as zero (i.e., the category for which all of the indicators take on the value zero). The exponentiated slope, corresponding to the particular group or category that is coded as one, can always be interpreted as the change in the odds that $Y_i = 1$ *relative to the reference category*. For instance, consider the use of SES as a categorical predictor, where students are categorized as either belonging to high, moderate or low SES. In this case, two variables are needed to reflect the three levels of SES. For example, if low SES is coded as the reference (or zero) group, then the two variables needed would be

$$X_1 = \begin{cases} 1 \text{ if SES level is moderate} \\ 0 \text{ otherwise} \end{cases}$$

$$X_2 = \begin{cases} 1 \text{ if SES level is high} \\ 0 \text{ otherwise} \end{cases}.$$

In this case, low SES is indicated when both X_1 and X_2 are zero. The logistic model would then be

$$\ln\left(\frac{\pi}{1-\pi} \right) = \alpha + \beta_1 X_1 + \beta_2 X_2 = \alpha + \beta_1(0) + \beta_2(0) = \alpha, \qquad \text{for low SES;}$$

$$\ln\left(\frac{\pi}{1-\pi} \right) = \alpha + \beta_1 X_1 + \beta_2 X_2 = \alpha + \beta_1(1) + \beta_2(0) = \alpha + \beta_1, \quad \text{for moderate SES; and}$$

$$\ln\left(\frac{\pi}{1-\pi} \right) = \alpha + \beta_1 X_1 + \beta_2 X_2 = \alpha + \beta_1(0) + \beta_2(1) = \alpha + \beta_2, \quad \text{for high SES.}$$

In this example, the value of α would be interpreted as the predicted log odds of attending an academic program for a student with low SES, and e^α would indicate the predicted odds of attending an academic program for a student with low SES. Similarly, the value of β_1 would be interpreted as the difference between the predicted log odds for students with low and moderate SES, and β_2 would be interpreted as the difference between the predicted log odds for students with low and high SES. Therefore, the difference between β_1 and β_2 indicates the

Table 9.1 Hypothetical Results From a Logistic Regression Model With a Predictor, SES, That Has Three Categories and Parameters: $\alpha = 0.5$, $\beta_1 = 0.2$, and $\beta_2 = 0.3$

SES	Predicted log(odds)	Predicted odds	Predicted probability
Low	$\alpha = 0.5$	$e^\alpha = e^{0.5} = 1.65$	$1.65/2.65 = 0.62$
Moderate	$\alpha + \beta_1 = 0.5 + 0.2 = 0.7$	$e^{\alpha + \beta_1} = e^{0.7} = 2.01$	$2.01/3.01 = 0.67$
High	$\alpha + \beta_2 = 0.5 + 0.3 = 0.8$	$e^{\alpha + \beta_2} = e^{0.8} = 2.23$	$2.23/3.23 = 0.69$

difference between the predicted log odds for students with moderate and high SES, and these parameters together completely represent the effect of SES on the response variable.

To illustrate this numerically, consider the example shown in Table 9.1, where $\alpha = 0.5$, $\beta_1 = 0.2$, and $\beta_2 = 0.3$. In this example, for the reference category (low SES) the predicted odds would be $e^\alpha = e^{0.5} = 1.65$, which are the predicted odds for low SES shown in Table 9.1. In addition, for this example the predicted odds of having attended an academic program for a student of moderate SES are $e^{\beta_1} = e^{0.2} = 1.22$ times the predicted odds for low SES, and indeed the predicted odds in Table 9.1 show that $(1.22)(1.65) = 2.01$. Similarly, the predicted odds of having attended an academic program for a student of high SES are $e^{\beta_2} = e^{0.3} = 1.35$ times the predicted odds for low SES, and indeed $(1.35)(1.65) = 2.23$. Finally, the difference between the two β parameters reflect the difference in the predicted log odds between those of moderate and high SES. In terms of predicted odds, the predicted odds of having attended an academic program for a student of moderate SES are $e^{\beta_1 - \beta_2} = e^{0.2 - 0.3} = e^{-0.1} = 0.90$ times the predicted odds of having attended an academic program for a student of high SES and, as can be seen in the Table 9.1, $(0.90)(2.23) = 2.01$. Taking the inverse of this value (i.e., $1/0.9$) provides the odds of having attended an academic program for a student of high SES as compared to a student of moderate SES.

9.2   Parameter interpretation

As discussed in the last section, when categorical predictors are dummy coded the logistic regression parameters can be interpreted relative to the **reference category**, where the choice of reference category is somewhat arbitrary. In this section, we discuss how the values of the parameters for logistic regression models with categorical predictors are related to odds and odds ratios as computed in earlier chapters for contingency tables.

Consider, for example, the data discussed in Chapter 4, Table 4.1, where we examined the relationship between voter's gender and candidate choice. In that example, using data from the 2008 Wisconsin Democratic Primary, we saw that the odds of a female voting for Clinton are 2 times (or 200% of) the odds of a male voting for Clinton. In the case of a logistic regression model, one of the variables is to be predicted from the other so, for example, we may wish to predict candidate choice from the voter's gender. Further, if we are to predict the odds of a vote for Clinton and let the predictor be coded as 1 for females and 0 for males, we would expect that the slope parameter of the logistic regression model would represent the difference between females and males in the log odds of voting for Clinton. In other words, the slope parameter would measure the effect gender has on the log odds of voting for Clinton, and the exponentiated slope parameter would indicate the effect that gender has on the odds of voting for Clinton. In fact, the logistic model in this case would be:

$$\ln\left(\frac{\pi}{1-\pi}\right) = \alpha + \beta X = -0.71 + 0.71X,$$

where π is the probability of voting for Clinton and $X = 1$ when the voter is female (so $X = 0$ when the voter is male). Note that the intercept of -0.71 represents the log odds of a male voting for Clinton, and its exponentiated value of $e^{-0.71} = 0.49$ represents the odds that a male voted for Clinton as predicted by this model. In addition, the slope of 0.71 represents the difference between males and females in the log odds of voting for Clinton, so its exponentiated value, $e^{0.71} = 2.03$, indicates that the odds of a female voting for Clinton are twice the odds of a male voting for Clinton. In other words, e^{β} represents the odds ratio.

In general, then, for one categorical predictor (with $C - 1$ indicators) the slope parameter β_j in the logistic regression model represents the difference between category j and the reference category (where all predictor values are zero) in terms of the log odds that the outcome $Y = 1$ (or success). Further, exponentiating β_j provides the value of the odds ratio comparing the odds of success for category j and the odds of success for the reference category. The intercept simply represents the log odds of success for the reference category, and its exponentiated value represents the odds of success for the reference category.

9.3   Inferential procedures

Methods for testing the parameters of logistic regression models were discussed in the previous chapter and also apply in this chapter. The results of tests of the slope parameters need to be interpreted in light of the material in this chapter; that is, if β_j is significantly different from zero, this indicates that there is a significant difference between the log odds (of $Y = 1$) for category j and the reference category. For example, in testing whether SES affects the school program attended (academic or not), suppose that $Y = 1$ corresponds to an academic program and the three levels of SES (low, moderate, high) are coded as described earlier:

$$X_1 = \begin{cases} 1 \text{ if SES level is moderate} \\ 0 \text{ otherwise} \end{cases}$$

$$X_2 = \begin{cases} 1 \text{ if SES level is high} \\ 0 \text{ otherwise} \end{cases}.$$

In this case, β_1 represents the difference between students of moderate (represented by X_1) and low (reference category) SES levels in the log odds of attending an academic program. Thus, if β_1 is significantly different from zero, we can conclude that there is a significant difference between moderate and low SES levels in the log odds (of attending an academic program). Similarly, a significant value of β_2 in this example would indicate a significant difference between high and low SES levels in the log odds. However, researchers are often interested in first answering the more global question of whether the categorical predictor variable (e.g., SES) affects the outcome (attending an academic program) overall. To answer this question, the null hypothesis would state that all three SES levels produce the same outcome, and this is equivalent to showing that there is no difference in outcome between moderate and low SES levels as well as no difference between high and low SES levels. Therefore, to test the null hypothesis of no SES effect we would need to test that both β_1 and β_2 are zero simultaneously:

$$H_0: \beta_1 = \beta_2 = 0$$

or

H_0: difference in log odds between moderate and low SES

= difference in log odds between high and low SES = 0

or

H_0: log odds are equal for all three SES levels.

These null hypotheses are equivalent and can be tested using model comparison proce-dures as discussed in the next section.

9.4 Model testing

In previous chapters we discussed the likelihood ratio test for comparing the likelihood of a logistic model that includes all desired effects (predictors) to the likelihood of a restricted form of this model, where the restrictions are typically based on the null hypothesis. Recall that the maximum likelihood of the restricted model (specified under H_0) is denoted by L_0 and the maximum likelihood of the nonrestricted model (specified under H_1) is denoted by L_1. The ratio L_0/L_1 represents the likelihood ratio, and the **likelihood ratio test statistic** is

$$G^2 = -2\log\left(\frac{L_0}{L_1}\right) = -2\log(L_0 - L_1) = [-2\log(L_0)] - [-2\log(L_1)].$$

Under H_0, for adequate sample sizes, this test statistic follows a χ^2 distribution with degrees of freedom equal to the number of parameters restricted under H_0.

Returning to our example, where we used SES (with three levels) as a categorical pre-dictor, two dummy coded variables were required. In this case, to test whether SES affects the outcome (i.e., attending an academic program rather than a nonacademic program), one needs to compare a model where the coefficients for both SES dummy variables are simulta-neously restricted to be zero (i.e., H_0: $\beta_1 = \beta_2 = 0$), indicating that all three SES levels affect the outcome equally, against a model where neither parameter is restricted. This can be achieved with a likelihood ratio test comparing the likelihood (L_1) of the nonrestricted model,

$$\text{Model 1: } \ln\left(\frac{\pi}{1-\pi}\right) = \alpha + \beta_1 X_1 + \beta_2 X_2,$$

with the likelihood (L_0) of the restricted model (under H_0: $\beta_1 = \beta_2 = 0$),

$$\text{Model 0: } \ln\left(\frac{\pi}{1-\pi}\right) = \alpha + (0)X_1 + (0)X_2 = \alpha.$$

The test statistic, G^2, would be compared to the χ^2 distribution with 2 degrees of free-dom in this case because two parameters were restricted under the null hypothesis. If the null hypothesis is rejected, we can conclude that the two likelihoods, and thus these two models, are significantly different from each other such that model 1 fits significantly bet-ter than model 0. Therefore, rejection of H_0 would indicate that the three SES levels do not all yield the same outcome or that SES level affects the outcome.

Conducting the likelihood ratio test to determine whether a categorical predictor affects the outcome is analogous to the omnibus test of a main effect in analysis of variance (ANOVA). In rejecting the null hypothesis, we are finding support for the notion that our predictor (factor in ANOVA terms) has an overall effect on the outcome because the out-come is not the same across all levels of the predictor. When several categorical predictors are used, an approach similar to a factorial ANOVA is used in that interactions between the predictors are tested before individual ("main") effects are examined. We turn to a discussion of interactions in the next section.

9.5 Interactions

When several categorical predictors (e.g., both SES and gender) are included in a logistic regression model, the **interactions** between these predictors can, and usually should, be included as well. If we were to predict the probability that a student attended an academic (rather than a nonacademic) program from SES and gender, the interaction between SES and gender would indicate the joint effects that these two predictors exert on the outcome beyond any individual ("main") effects that each predictor exerts individually. For example, an interaction would indicate that the effect of gender (on the outcome) differs from one SES level to another. This is analogous to the interpretation of an interaction in ANOVA models.

Suppose, for example, that the dummy coding system from Section 9.1 is applied to the variables of gender and SES. Table 9.2 summarizes the coding of each variable individually as well as the coding of the indicators that represent the interaction between these variables. In this case, X_1 represents the gender variable (0 for males and 1 for females), and X_2 and X_3 together represent the SES variable (X_2 is 1 for moderate SES and 0 otherwise, and X_3 is 1 for high SES and 0 otherwise). The indicator variables representing the interaction effect are formed by multiplying each gender indicator by each SES indicator. Therefore, the number of indicators needed to represent the interaction effect is equal to the product of the number of indicators needed for each of the variables involved in the interaction. In our example, for one gender indicator (X_1) and two SES indicators (X_2 and X_3), a total of $(1)(2) = 2$ interaction indicators are created and these are represented by X_4 ($=X_1 X_2$) and X_5 ($=X_1 X_3$) in Table 9.2. This results in a logistic regression model with five predictor variables:

$$\ln\left(\frac{\pi}{1-\pi}\right) = \alpha + \beta_1 X_1 + \beta_2 X_2 + \beta_3 X_3 + \beta_4 X_4 + \beta_5 X_5 \tag{9.1}$$

In this model (Equation 9.1) the intercept (α) represents the expected outcome for a male student from low SES because, using our coding scheme, all indicator variables are zero for this case (see Table 9.2). In addition, for example, the expected outcome for a female student ($X_1 = 1$) from moderate SES ($X_2 = 1$) would be

$$\ln\left(\frac{\pi}{1-\pi}\right) = \alpha + \beta_1(1) + \beta_2(1) + \beta_3(0) + \beta_4(1) + \beta_5(0) = \alpha + \beta_1 + \beta_2 + \beta_4.$$

Table 9.2 Dummy Coding of Two Categorical Variables and Their Interaction

Gender	SES	Gender X_1	SES X_2	X_3	Interaction $X_4 = (X_1)(X_2)$	$X_5 = (X_1)(X_3)$
Male	Low	0	0	0	0	0
	Moderate	0	1	0	0	0
	High	0	0	1	0	0
Female	Low	1	0	0	0	0
	Moderate	1	1	0	1	0
	High	1	0	1	0	1

Each combination of gender and SES will thus result in a different combination of the parameters. (Try this for yourself: For example, which parameters would be involved in determining the outcome for a female from high SES? How about the outcome for a male from high SES?)

Note that because the predictors X_4 and X_5 (in Equation 9.1) represent the interaction, to test whether SES and gender interact in affecting the outcome we would test the null hypothesis H_0: $\beta_4 = \beta_5 = 0$ using the likelihood ratio test described in the previous section. If this null hypothesis is rejected (i.e., the test statistic is significant), we would attempt to interpret the interaction by examining how the effect of gender on the outcome differs across SES levels. However, if this null hypothesis test is not significant, we can proceed to test the individual effects of SES and gender separately. This would be accomplished by testing the null hypothesis H_0: $\beta_2 = \beta_3 = 0$ for SES, and the null hypothesis H_0: $\beta_1 = 0$ for gender.

If the interaction is significant, the regression parameters must be interpreted carefully. It is typically sufficient to interpret the parameters that represent interaction terms, but for the sake of completeness we discuss the interpretation of all parameters. For example, in Equation 9.1, if the interaction between SES and gender is significant then the coefficient β_1 is interpreted as the effect of the gender category represented by X_1 (female) relative to the effect of the reference gender category (male) *within the reference category* of SES (low SES). Thus, the exponentiated value exp(β_1) or e^{β_1} is the odds ratio for gender (females vs. males attending rather than not attending the academic program) within the low SES level. In general, then, when X_j is an indicator of one of the predictors (rather than an interaction indicator), the interpretation of exp(β_j) or e^{β_j} is as the odds ratio of the category represented by X_j relative to the reference category of the predictor in question conditional on the reference category of the other predictor. This is somewhat analogous to a "simple effect" in ANOVA; that is, it is the effect of one of the factors at a specific level of the other (rather than overall).

In addition, in Equation 9.1 the interaction coefficient β_4 represents the difference between the effect of gender in the SES category represented by X_4 (moderate) and the effect of gender in the reference SES category (low). In other words, exp(β_4) or e^{β_4} is a ratio of two odds ratios and represents how many times larger the odds ratio for gender (females vs. males) in the moderate SES category is compared to the odds ratio for gender in the low SES category. If we define θ_G as the odds ratio for gender (females vs. males, where the odds are for attending rather than not attending the academic program), then the exponentiated value of β_4 is

$$e^{\beta_4} = \frac{\theta_G \text{ for moderate SES}}{\theta_G \text{ for low SES}}.$$

Similarly, exp(β_5) or e^{β_5} would represent how many times larger the odds ratio for gender (females vs. males) in the high SES category is compared to the low SES category, or

$$e^{\beta_5} = \frac{\theta_G \text{ for high SES}}{\theta_G \text{ for low SES}}.$$

We would typically interpret only these two interaction parameters if the interaction effect is significant. A numerical example of these concepts is provided in Section 9.7.

9.6   The relationship between logistic regression and log-linear models

Logistic regression models with categorical predictors essentially analyze the relationships among a set of categorical variables, as do **log-linear models** (see Chapter 7). Therefore, the two modeling procedures are related to each other, and in this section we explain the nature of this relationship.

The model shown in Equation 9.1,

$$\ln\left(\frac{\pi}{1-\pi}\right) = \alpha + \beta_1 X_1 + \beta_2 X_2 + \beta_3 X_3 + \beta_4 X_4 + \beta_5 X_5,$$

is sometimes written in a short-hand form similar to that used in representing log-linear models. For example, we might represent the two substantive predictors used in Equation 9.1 as X for gender and Z for SES, and write the logistic model as

$$\ln\left(\frac{\pi}{1-\pi}\right) = \alpha + \beta_i^X + \beta_k^Z + \beta_{ik}^{XZ}. \tag{9.2}$$

In this model (Equation 9.2), the superscript for the β parameter indicates the predictor and the subscript indicates the level of the predictor, which varies from 1 to $C - 1$ where C is the total number of categories of the predictor. For example, the notation β_i^X in equation 9.2 is used to represent the overall effect of the predictor X on the outcome (log odds of π) where $i =$ 1, … $C - 1$ and C is the total number of categories of X. In our example, because there are only two categories for X (gender), $i = 1$ and β_1^X would be equivalent to the term $\beta_1 X_1$ in Equation 9.1. Similarly, β_k^Z is used to represent the overall effect of the predictor Z on the outcome variable, and, because there are three categories for Z (SES), $k = 1$ or 2. Therefore, β_1^Z and β_2^Z are equivalent to the terms $\beta_2 X_2$ and $\beta_3 X_3$ in Equation 9.1, respectively. Last, β_{ik}^{XZ} is used to represent the overall effect of the XZ interaction on the outcome variable, with i and k as defined earlier. Therefore, β_{11}^{XZ} and β_{12}^{XZ} are equivalent to the terms $\beta_4 X_4$ and $\beta_5 X_5$ in Equation 9.1, respectively. In general, then, each of the parameters in Equation 9.2 represents all dummy variables needed to completely code the corresponding effect. We use this short-hand notation in this section to facilitate the discussion of the equivalence between log-linear and logistic models.

The logistic regression model that includes only categorical (or qualitative) predictor variables is related to the log-linear model if one of the variables in the log-linear model is binary. For example, consider the case in which we have three categorical variables, X, Y, and Z, where Y is binary (i.e., has only two categories). While the log-linear model does not distinguish between predictor and response variables, but rather models the frequencies of a contingency table formed by the categories of all variables, the logistic model treats Y as the outcome variable with X and Z as predictors. Table 9.3 shows the relevant log-linear models and their equivalent logistic regression models. Not surprisingly, model testing and conclusions regarding associations in the data also follow the equivalences shown in Table 9.3.

To illustrate these concepts with a numerical example, consider the data in Table 9.4, obtained from the 2006 General Social Survey (GSS; through the Web site http://sda. berkeley.edu/archive.htm), on the variables of whether the respondent has at least a bachelor's degree, the respondent's sex, and whether the respondent's mother has at least a bachelor's degree. In conducting a log-linear analysis, we would use the three variables to model the counts in the three-way contingency table and determine which variables are associated and which are not. In conducting a logistic regression analysis, we would predict one of the variables—in our example, whether the respondent has at least a bachelor's

Table 9.3 Equivalence Between Log-Linear and Logistic Regression Models

Model	Log-linear model: $\log(\mu_{ijk}) =$	Logistic Model: $\ln\left(\dfrac{\pi}{1-\pi}\right) =$
1	$\lambda + \lambda_i^X + \lambda_j^Y + \lambda_k^Z + \lambda_{ik}^{XZ}$	α
2	$\lambda + \lambda_i^X + \lambda_j^Y + \lambda_k^Z + \lambda_{ij}^{XY} + \lambda_{ik}^{XZ}$	$\alpha + \beta_i^X$
3	$\lambda + \lambda_i^X + \lambda_j^Y + \lambda_k^Z + \lambda_{ik}^{XZ} + \lambda_{jk}^{YZ}$	$\alpha + \beta_k^Z$
4	$\lambda + \lambda_i^X + \lambda_j^Y + \lambda_k^Z + \lambda_{ij}^{XY} + \lambda_{ik}^{XZ} + \lambda_{jk}^{YZ}$	$\alpha + \beta_i^X + \beta_k^Z$
5	$\lambda + \lambda_i^X + \lambda_j^Y + \lambda_k^Z + \lambda_{ij}^{XY} + \lambda_{ik}^{XZ} + \lambda_{jk}^{YZ} + \lambda_{ijk}^{XYZ}$	$\alpha + \beta_i^X + \beta_k^Z + \beta_{ik}^{XZ}$

degree—from the other two variables, and determine which predictor is related to the outcome as well as whether the predictors interact in predicting the outcome variable.

We begin by fitting a logistic regression model that predicts the respondent's degree attainment (Y) from the predictors of mother's degree attainment (X) and respondent's sex (Z) as well as their interaction. Because X, Z and their interaction are all postulated to influence Y in this model, the equivalent log-linear model in this case is the saturated model, represented in Table 9.3 as Model 5. In fact, the parameter β_{ik}^{XZ} in the logistic model is identical to the parameter λ_{ijk}^{XYZ} in the log-linear model, and in our example both analyses (log-linear and logistic) obtain an estimate of -0.0648 for this parameter with an associated p-value of 0.77. Therefore, both analyses indicate that the parameter is not significantly different from zero and that the interaction between X and Z does not significantly affect Y. Another way of stating this result is that the effect of X on Y is independent of the effect of Z on Y (although X and Z may still be associated with each other), suggesting that the three-way association term in the log-linear model in not needed and, equivalently, that the two-way interaction term in the logistic regression model is not needed.

The next model to fit would thus be either a log-linear model with all two-way associations (interaction terms for XY, YZ, XZ) or, equivalently, a logistic model with only the main effects. These are shown as Model 4 in Table 9.3. In addition, the values of the log-likelihood multiplied by -2 (or $-2LL$) for all models are shown in Table 9.5. Comparing Models 4 and 5 (using a likelihood ratio test) is another way to test whether the last term

Table 9.4 Data on Educational Achievement from the 2006 General Social Survey

Sex	Bachelor's for respondent	Bachelor's for mother		
		No	Yes	Total
Male	No	782	84	866
	Yes	255	111	367
	Total	1038	195	1233
Female	No	1018	108	1126
	Yes	273	110	383
	Total	1291	218	1508

of Model 5 is significantly different from zero. Note that the difference in the values of –2LL between Models 4 and 5 is nearly identical regardless of whether one examines the log-linear or logistic models (see Table 9.5). In fact, in either case the comparison of Models 4 and 5 shows that the log-likelihood barely changes when the last term is dropped from Model 5, thus the change in fit is not significant and Model 4 (which is more parsimonious) is more desirable with either analysis.

At this point, we may want to test the incremental or unique effects of mother's degree attainment (X) and sex (Z) on the respondent's degree attainment (Y). Note, from Table 9.3, that all log-linear models having corresponding equivalent logistic models contain the association between X and Z (the predictors). This association is modeled implicitly in all logistic models but must be modeled explicitly in the equivalent log-linear models. Be aware that the interaction between X and Z in a logistic regression model is indicative of the effect that the association between X and Z has on the outcome variable, Y, and is thus different than the term representing the association between X and Z in a log-linear model. Therefore, to determine whether the effect of X (mother's degree attainment) is significant once the effect of Z (sex) is used to predict the outcome (Y), Models 3 and 4 are compared in Table 9.5. In fact, an examination of the difference between Models 3 and 4 (in Table 9.5) should make it clear that the parameter β_i^X in Model 4 for logistic regression is equivalent to the parameter λ_{ij}^{XY} in Model 4 for log-linear analysis. This should not be surprising, as both parameters represent the association between X and Y (once the effect of Z is accounted for). In other words, we compare Models 3 and 4 to determine whether the association between X and Y is significant after controlling for the effect of Z. In our example (see Table 9.5) we see a very large difference (of about 151) between the –2LL values of Models 3 and 4, indicating that mother's degree attainment is significant even after the effect of sex is accounted for in predicting the respondent's degree attainment. Similarly, we compare Models 2 and 4 to determine whether the effect of Z (sex) is significant once the effect of X (mother's degree attainment) is used to predict the outcome. In this case, the difference between Models 2 and 4 (in –2LL) is about 5.5 (with 1 degree of freedom), which is significant and thus indicates that sex is significant even after the effect of mother's degree attainment is accounted for in predicting the respondent's degree attainment.

Table 9.5 The Log-Likelihood Multiplied by –2 (–2LL) for Log-Linear and Logistic Regression Models Fit to the Data in Table 9.4

Model	Log-Linear Model: $\log(\mu_{ijk}) =$	–2LL	Logistic Model: $\ln\left(\dfrac{\pi}{1-\pi}\right) =$	–2LL
1	$\lambda + \lambda_i^X + \lambda_j^Y + \lambda_k^Z + \lambda_{ik}^{XZ}$	–28604.416	α	3215.680
2	$\lambda + \lambda_i^X + \lambda_j^Y + \lambda_k^Z + \lambda_{ij}^{XY} + \lambda_{ik}^{XZ}$	–28756.200	$\alpha + \beta_i^X$	3063.772
3	$\lambda + \lambda_i^X + \lambda_j^Y + \lambda_k^Z + \lambda_{ik}^{XZ} + \lambda_{jk}^{YZ}$	–28610.794	$\alpha + \beta_k^Z$	3209.369
4	$\lambda + \lambda_i^X + \lambda_j^Y + \lambda_k^Z + \lambda_{ij}^{XY} + \lambda_{ik}^{XZ} + \lambda_{jk}^{YZ}$	–28761.722	$\alpha + \beta_i^X + \beta_k^Z$	3058.303
5	$\lambda + \lambda_i^X + \lambda_j^Y + \lambda_k^Z$ $+\lambda_{ij}^{XY} + \lambda_{ik}^{XZ} + \lambda_{jk}^{YZ} + \lambda_{ijk}^{XYZ}$	–28761.808	$\alpha + \beta_i^X + \beta_k^Z + \beta_{ik}^{XZ}$	3058.214

Note: Y = respondent's degree attainment, X = mother's degree attainment, Z = sex.

Finally, we may want to test the individual, separate effects of mother's degree attainment (X) and sex (Z) on the respondent's degree attainment (Y). In other words, in Table 9.5 we would compare Models 1 and 2 to determine whether mother's degree attainment (X) affects respondent's degree attainment and we would compare Models 1 and 3 to determine whether sex (Z) affects respondent's degree attainment. In this example, the comparison of Models 1 and 2 proves to be significant (difference of about 152 in –2LL), indicating that mother's degree attainment by itself significantly affects the respondent's degree attainment. In addition, the comparison of Models 1 and 3 also proves to be significant (difference of about 6 in –2LL), indicating that the respondent's sex by itself significantly affects the respondent's degree attainment. In conclusion, then, we can say that Model 4 is most appropriate for these data regardless of whether a log-linear or logistic regression analysis is conducted. In fact, it turns out that using either of the two analysis approaches results in parameter estimates (or odds ratios) for Model 4 that indicate the odds of obtaining at least a bachelor's degree are 1.2 higher for males than for females and these odds are also 3.9 times higher for respondents whose mother obtained at least a bachelor's degree than for those whose mothers did not.

In general, when all variables in the analysis are categorical and at least one variable is binary, the data could potentially be modeled using either log-linear or logistic regression models. The choice depends on the research question and conclusions one wishes to draw about the data: if one is interested in predicting the response on one of the (binary) variables, then a logistic regression model is more appropriate, but if there is no obvious response variable and interest is in the associations between variables, then log-linear modeling is sufficient.

9.7   Computing

In this section we will analyze a data set with SAS and SPSS to show how to obtain and interpret computer output for a logistic regression analysis with categorical predictors. The data set, obtained from the 2006 GSS (through the Web site http://sda.berkeley.edu/archive.htm), is used to model the probability that the respondent has at least a bachelor's degree (i.e., bachelor's or graduate degree) using the predictors of respondent's sex (X) and educational attainment of the respondent's mother (Z). The mother's educational attainment was measured using five categories: less than high school, high school, junior college, bachelor's degree, graduate degree. The data are shown in Table 9.6, which also includes the odds ratio (the odds that females attain a bachelor's relative to the odds that males attain a bachelor's) by mother's educational level. In this example we chose to code the respondent's sex as $X_1 = 0$ for males and $X_1 = 1$ for females, and to code the mother's educational level (using less than high school as the reference category) as

$$X_2 = \begin{cases} 1 \text{ if education level is graduate} \\ 0 \text{ otherwise} \end{cases}$$

$$X_3 = \begin{cases} 1 \text{ if education level is bachelor's} \\ 0 \text{ otherwise} \end{cases}$$

$$X_4 = \begin{cases} 1 \text{ if education level is junior college} \\ 0 \text{ otherwise} \end{cases}$$

$$X_5 = \begin{cases} 1 \text{ if education level is high school} \\ 0 \text{ otherwise} \end{cases}$$

Table 9.6 General Social Survey (2006) Frequency Data
for Respondent's Sex, Whether Respondent Attained a
Bachelor's Degree, and Mother's Educational Level

Mother's Education	Sex	Bachelor's Yes	No	Odds Ratio
<High school				0.516
	Female	52	457	
	Male	71	322	
High school				0.905
	Female	183	518	
	Male	164	420	
Junior college				1.683
	Female	38	43	
	Male	21	40	
Bachelor's				0.687
	Female	80	82	
	Male	71	50	
Graduate				0.981
	Female	30	26	
	Male	40	34	

The full logistic regression model, containing all relevant effects, is

$$\ln\left(\frac{\pi}{1-\pi}\right) = \alpha + \beta_1 X_1 + \beta_2 X_2 + \beta_3 X_3 + \beta_4 X_4 + \beta_5 X_5 + \beta_6 X_6 + \beta_7 X_7 + \beta_8 X_8 + \beta_9 X_9,$$

where the last four terms represent the interaction such that $X_6 = (X_1)(X_2)$, $X_7 = (X_1)(X_3)$, $X_8 = (X_1)(X_4)$, and $X_9 = (X_1)(X_5)$. Equivalently, we can write this model as

$$\ln\left(\frac{\pi}{1-\pi}\right) = \alpha + \beta_i^X + \beta_k^Z + \beta_{ik}^{XZ},$$

where β_i^X represents the effect of respondent's sex (with one dummy variable, so $i = 1$), β_k^Z represents the effect of mother's educational attainment (with four dummy variables, so $k = 1, 2, 3, 4$), and β_{ik}^{XZ} represents the interaction effect (with four dummy variables, where i and k are as defined earlier).

9.7.1   SAS

Figure 9.1 shows the SAS syntax for this example, including the data used in the analysis. The number of respondents is represented by the variable "count" and entered for each category of the three variables: respondent's sex, respondent's education level (ba_degree), and mother's educational level (mother_ed).

```
data GSS;
 input sex $ ba_degree $ mother_ed $ count;
 datalines;
 f n <hs 457
 f n hs 518
 f n jc 43
 f n ba 82
 f n >ba 26
 f y <hs 52
 f y hs 183
 f y jc 38
 f y ba 80
 f y >ba 30
 m n <hs 322
 m n hs 420
 m n jc 40
 m n ba 50
 m n >ba 34
 m y <hs 71
 m y hs 164
 m y jc 21
 m y ba 71
 m y >ba 40
 ;
proc logistic data=GSS;
 freq count;
 class sex (param=ref ref ='m') mother_ed (param=ref ref ='<hs')   /order=data;
 model ba_degree(event='y') = sex|mother_ed /expb;
run;
```

Figure 9.1 SAS syntax for logistic regression with categorical predictors using the data from Table 9.6.

In the "proc logistic" syntax:

- The statement "freq count;" is used to indicate that the count variable represents the frequency (number of respondents) in each category.
- The class statement indicates which variables must be coded as categorical.
  - The defaults in SAS are to arrange the values of each categorical variable in alphabetical order and to code the predictors using effect coding. To change these defaults, we use options (in parentheses) after each variable name.
  - Specifically, because we discussed dummy coding in this chapter and because we believe that it is easier to interpret, we use the option param = ref in the class statement to request dummy coding for the variables.
  - In addition, the option ref= is used to specify the reference category for each variable (i.e., male for sex and less than high school for mother's education level).
  - We also used the option (after a slash) of order=data so that the variable categories are sorted in the order in which they appear in the data set.
- The model statement specifies the respondent's education (ba_degree) as the response variable, and the option (in parentheses) event = 'y' specifies that the probability of a yes response (or ba_degree = 'y') should be modeled (or that $Y = 1$ for yes and $Y = 0$ for no).
  - The predictors in the model statement are separated with a "pipe," the vertical line symbol, to indicate that their interaction should be included in the model as well as their individual effects. Alternatively, each of the effects can be separated with a space and the interaction term can be specified as sex*monther_ed.
  - Finally, the option expb is used to request that the exponentiated parameter estimates be provided in the output.

The output, showing descriptive information as well as the coding scheme used for the categorical variables, is presented in Figure 9.2. The output includes:

```
                        Response Profile

              Ordered                          Total
              Value        ba_degree        Frequency

                1            n                  1992
                2            y                   750

            Probability modeled is ba_degree='y'.


                     Class Level Information

      Class           Value          Design Variables

      sex              f         1
                       m         0

      mother_ed       <hs        0     0     0     0
                      hs         1     0     0     0
                      jc         0     1     0     0
                      ba         0     0     1     0
                      >ba        0     0     0     1
                      <hs        0     0     0     0
```

Figure 9.2 SAS output showing the coding of categorical predictors in logistic regression.

- A summary of the number of cases in each of the outcome categories under Response Profile.
- The coding of the predictors, under Design Variables in the Class Level Information, showing that
  - sex was coded using one variable with males represented by 0 and females represented by 1, and
  - mother's education level was coded using four variables with the lowest level (less than high school) used as the reference category (where all four variables are zero).

The remaining output will be discussed in detail in Section 9.7.3.

9.7.2   SPSS

The data are entered into SPSS in the usual manner. Specifically, each cell in the table is represented by a row in the data set and there are four columns representing the variables sex, whether the respondent obtained a bachelor's degree, mother's educational level, and count. This is illustrated in Figure 9.3.

To conduct the analyses using SPSS menus (after weighting the cases by count) the same procedures are followed as outlined in Chapter 8 with some slight modifications. Specifically:

- Select Regression under the Analyze menu and then choose Binary Logistic.
- Move the outcome variable (whether respondent obtained a bachelor's degree) to the Dependent variable box, then move both predictors (sex and mother's education) to the Covariates box, as illustrated in Figure 9.4
- Click on the Categorical button at the top of the window and move both predictors over to the Categorical Covariates box (if they are not already there) to indicate that these are categorical variables. Note that SPSS uses the last category of each predictor as the reference category by default.

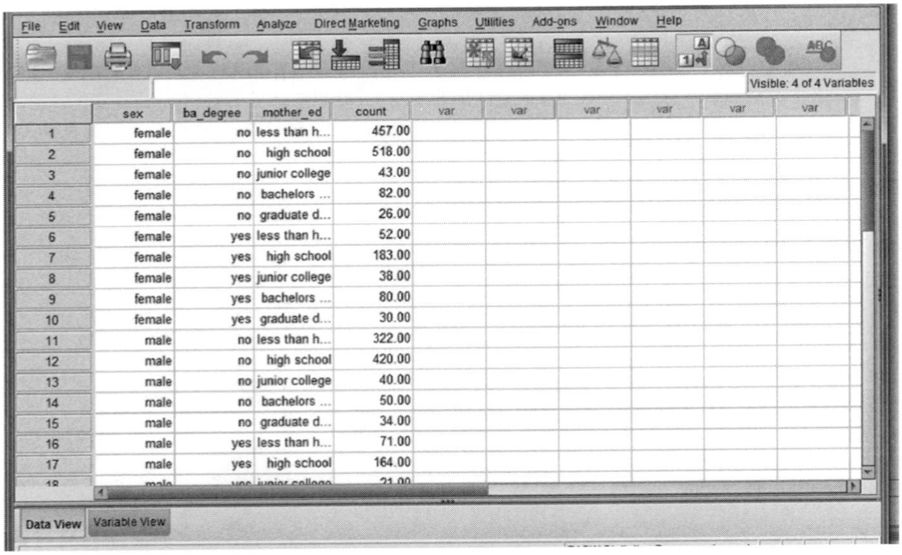

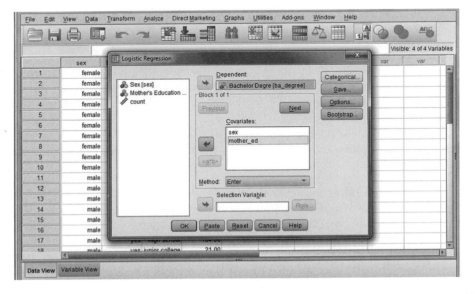

Figure 9.3 SPSS data screenshot illustrating how to enter the data from the three-way table depicted in Table 9.6.

- To change this default, choose the predictor (e.g., mother's education) in the Categorical Covariates box, and under Change Contrast select whether the reference category should be the first or last category of the predictor, as illustrated in Figure 9.5.
- Because we wanted Less than High School to be the reference category for mother's education, and it is the category that appears first in the data set, we chose

Figure 9.4 SPSS screenshot illustrating how to fit a logistic regression model to the data in Table 9.6.

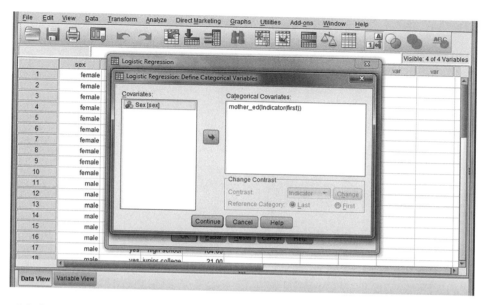

Figure 9.5 SPSS screenshot illustrating the window in which the reference category can be changed for a categorical variable in logistic regression.

> First for this variable and then clicked on the Change button. Note that this will change the text in the parenthesis following the variable to (Indicator(first)).
> - The Continue button is clicked to return to the Logistic Regression window.
> - To add the interaction and test for its significance, it should be added as a second "block" in SPSS.
> - To create a second block, click on the Next button located just above the Covariates box in the Logistic Regression window.
>   - Click on both predictors while holding down the Control key.
>   - The >a*b> button will then become active and clicking on it will add the interaction term to the covariates box. This is illustrated in Figure 9.6.
> - Click OK to run the analysis.

Figure 9.7 shows the SPSS output that indicates the coding used by SPSS for the variables. Note that, as desired in this example, the yes category of the response variable (bachelor's degree) is coded as 1, whereas the no category is coded as 0. Also note that, as was desired, the reference category of the sex variable is males (coded as 0) and the reference category of the mother's education variable (where all four indicators are 0) is less than high school. The remaining output will be discussed in the next section.

9.7.3   *Interpretation of output*

The first thing to determine about the "full" model, that contains both predictors and their interaction, is whether a simpler model might be more appropriate. This can be accomplished using either a Wald test for the interaction parameter in the full model or a likelihood ratio test comparing this model to a model that contains only the two predictors without their interaction.

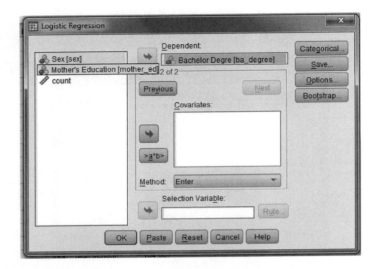

Figure 9.6 SPSS screenshot illustrating how to include an interaction term when fitting a logistic regression model.

Case Processing Summary

Unweighted Cases[a]		N	Percent
Selected Cases	Included in Analysis	20	100.0
	Missing Cases	0	.0
	Total	20	100.0
Unselected Cases		0	.0
Total		20	10.00

a. If weight is in effect, see classification table for the total number of cases.

Dependent Variable Encoding

Original Value	Internal Value
no	0
yes	1

Categorical Variables Codings

		Frequency	Parameter coding			
			(1)	(2)	(3)	(4)
Mother's Education	less than high school	4	.000	.000	.000	.000
	high school	4	1.000	.000	.000	.000
	junior college	4	.000	1.000	.000	.000
	bachelors degree	4	.000	.000	1.000	.000
	graduate degree	4	.000	.000	.000	1.000
Sex	female	10	1.000			
	male	10	.000			

Figure 9.7 SPSS coding for logistic regression model fit to data in Table 9.6.

Type 3 Analysis of Effects			
Effect	DF	Wald Chi-Square	Pr > ChiSq
sex	1	11.3360	0.0008
mother_ed	4	87.9288	<.0001
sex*mother_ed	4	11.1653	0.0248

Figure 9.8 SAS output for testing the interaction term.

Figure 9.8 shows the Wald test output from SAS and indicates that the test of the interaction results in a test statistic of 11.2 and has a p-value of 0.0248. These same results appear in the SPSS output in Figure 9.9 (see the test for the overall interaction term, mother_ed*sex, with a Wald test statistic of 11.165 and a p-value of 0.025).

The test results using the likelihood ratio approach are provided by SPSS in Figure 9.10 (see the test for Block) and provide a test statistic of 11.3 with a p-value of 0.023. These likelihood ratio test results can also be obtained from SAS by fitting the main effects model and using the options "scale=none" and "aggregate" in the model statement (not shown here). This test has 4 degrees of freedom because four dummy variables were needed to represent the interaction in this example.

The results of the (Wald or likelihood ratio) test for the interaction effect indicate that the interaction is significant so it should be retained in the model, and a simpler model, without the interaction, is not more appropriate. However, had this test yielded an insignificant result, the main effects model, which is considerably simpler, would be fit and interpreted.

The presence of a significant interaction in this example indicates that the effect of sex on whether the respondent obtained a bachelor's degree depends on the mother's educational level. This can be seen in Table 9.6, where the odds ratio (effect of sex on obtaining a bachelor's degree) favors males when mother's educational level is less than high school (odds ratio is about 0.52), but favors females when the mother attends junior college

Variables in the Equation

		B	S.E.	Wald	df	Sig.	Exp(B)
Step 1[a]	sex(1)	−.662	.196	11.336	1	.001	.516
	mother_ed			87.929	4	.000	
	mother_ed(1)	.571	.160	12.723	1	.000	1.771
	mother_ed(2)	.868	.300	8.380	1	.004	2.381
	mother_ed(3)	1.863	.226	67.656	1	.000	6.440
	mother_ed(4)	1.674	.268	39.155	1	.000	5.336
	mother_ed * sex			11.165	4	.025	
	mother_ed(1) by sex(1)	.561	.233	5.786	1	.016	1.753
	mother_ed(2) by sex(1)	1.182	.401	8.693	1	.003	3.262
	mother_ed(3) by sex(1)	.286	.312	.841	1	.359	1.331
	mother_ed(4) by sex(1)	.642	.406	2.502	1	.114	1.901
	Constant	−1.512	.131	132.969	1	.000	.220

a. Variable(s) entered on step 1: mother_ed * sex.

Figure 9.9 SPSS output of parameter estimates (including the Wald test for the interaction term).

Omnibus Tests of Model Coefficients

		Chi-square	df	Sig.
Step 1	Step	11.312	4	.023
	Block	11.312	4	.023
	Model	253.541	9	.000

Figure 9.10 SPSS output for testing the interaction term.

(odds ratio is about 1.68) and does not favor either sex when the mother obtains a graduate degree (odds ratio is about 0.98). Residuals and diagnostic measures can be obtained (as shown in the previous chapter) to find cases or cells in which observed counts deviate most markedly from predicted counts. We now proceed to examine and interpret the parameter estimates of this model.

The parameter estimates from SAS are provided in the part of the output shown in Figure 9.11 and the same estimates from SPSS are provided in Figure 9.9. Parameters that represent interaction indicators are interpreted as ratios of odds ratios. The relevant odds ratios here are those comparing females to males in the odds of obtaining a bachelor's degree, and ratios of these are computed across mother's education levels. For example, the estimate of β_6 (or, equivalently, β_{11}^{XZ}) is 0.56 and its exponentiated value of 1.75 indicates that the odds ratio shown in Table 9.6 for those whose mother's education level is high school (i.e., 0.905) is 1.75 times larger than the odds ratio for those whose mother's education level is less than high school (i.e., 0.516), the reference category. Similarly, the estimate of β_9 (or, equivalently, β_{14}^{XZ}) is 0.64 and its exponentiated value of 1.90 indicates that the odds ratio for those whose mothers obtained a graduate degree (i.e., 0.981) is 1.90 times the odds ratio for those whose mother's educational level is less than high school (i.e., 0.516). In other words, the interaction parameters measure and test the ratios of each odds ratio in Table 9.6 relative to the odds ratio of the reference category (<high school). Thus, it is important to select the reference categories so that they make sense from a substantive or theoretical perspective.

As discussed in Section 9.5, the interpretation of the other parameters in the presence of an interaction effect can be somewhat tricky because they represent "simple effects" rather than "main effects." For example, the parameter estimate for the effect of sex (i.e., β_1 or β_1^X) is –0.66, and when exponentiated the value of $\exp(-0.66) = 0.516$ is interpreted as the odds ratio for sex (odds for females over males, because $X_1 = 1$ for females) *at the reference category* for mother's education (less than high school). This can be confirmed by

```
                    Analysis of Maximum Likelihood Estimates

                                      Standard      Wald
Parameter              DF   Estimate    Error    Chi-Square   Pr > ChiSq   Exp(Est)

Intercept               1    -1.5119    0.1311    132.9693     <.0001       0.220
sex            f        1    -0.6616    0.1965     11.3360      0.0008       0.516
mother_ed      hs       1     0.5715    0.1602     12.7234      0.0004       1.771
mother_ed      jc       1     0.8675    0.2997      8.3798      0.0038       2.381
mother_ed      ba       1     1.8625    0.2264     67.6556     <.0001       6.440
mother_ed      >ba      1     1.6744    0.2676     39.1552     <.0001       5.336
sex*mother_ed f  hs     1     0.5615    0.2334      5.7862      0.0162       1.753
sex*mother_ed f  jc     1     1.1823    0.4010      8.6932      0.0032       3.262
sex*mother_ed f  ba     1     0.2862    0.3121      0.8412      0.3591       1.331
sex*mother_ed f  >ba    1     0.6421    0.4060      2.5019      0.1137       1.901
```

Figure 9.11 SAS output of parameter estimates.

examining Table 9.6; note that when mother's education level is less than high school the odds that a female will obtain a bachelor's degree are about half (or 0.516 times) the odds that a male will obtain a bachelor's degree. Similarly, the parameter estimate for the effect of high school education, β_2 (because X_2 is 1 for high school) or β_1^Z, is 0.57 and its exponentiated value of 1.77 indicates the odds ratio (odds of obtaining a bachelor's) for high school as compared to less than high school (the reference category in mother's education) *at the reference category* for sex (males). In other words, the odds that a male respondent whose mother achieved a high school education will obtain a bachelor's degree are 1.77 times the odds for a male whose mother achieved less than a high school education.

9.8 *Complete example of logistic regression using both categorical and continuous predictors*

In this section we use an example to demonstrate how the material discussed in Chapters 8 and 9 can be combined to fit a logistic regression model with both categorical and continuous predictors. In general, when a categorical variable is included in the model its interactions with all other predictors are examined; therefore, the interaction between categorical and continuous predictors is included in the model. If the interaction is significant, it can be interpreted as a "moderation" effect; that is, the interaction indicates that the effect of the continuous predictor on the outcome depends on (or varies with) the level of the categorical predictor.

We again use data from the GSS, this time to predict the probability that respondents will favor the death penalty for murder using their race (coded as White, Black, or Other) and their level of education (highest year of school completed, treated as continuous with values ranging from 0 to 20) as predictors.

The SAS statements are provided in Figure 9.12 and the relevant output is shown in Figure 9.13. Note that only race appears in the class statement (because it is the only categorical predictor), it is dummy coded (using the param option), and White is specified as the reference category (using the ref option).

The output shows that overall there is a significant interaction between race and education in their effect on favoring capital punishment (Wald $X^2 = 30.5$, $df = 2$, $p < 0.0001$). Therefore, the effect of education on endorsing capital punishment depends on the race of the respondent. To explore this further, we examine the parameter estimates for the interaction terms.

Using the parameter estimates from the output shown in Figure 9.13, with $\hat{\pi}$ representing the estimated probability of favoring capital punishment, the model is

$$\ln\left(\frac{\hat{\pi}}{1-\hat{\pi}}\right) = 2.415 - 3.415(\text{Black}) - 2.684(\text{Other}) - 0.101(\text{Educ}) + 0.154(\text{Educ})(\text{Black})$$

$$+ 0.145(\text{Educ})(\text{Other}).$$

For example, in the above model, if the respondent's race is Black, then Black = 1, whereas if the respondent's race is Other or White, then Black = 0. Similarly if the respondent's race

```
proc logistic;
 class race (param=ref ref ='WHITE') ;
 model CAPPUN = race|educ  /expb;
run;
```

Figure 9.12 SAS syntax for predicting endorsement of capital punishment from education, race, and their interaction.

```
                              Response Profile
                    Ordered                        Total
                    Value        CAPPUN         Frequency

                       1         FAVOR              1882
                       2         OPPOSE              929

               Probability modeled is CAPPUN='FAVOR'.


                        Class Level Information

                                               Design
                   Class       Value         Variables

                   RACE        BLACK         1       0
                               OTHER         0       1
                               WHITE         0       0


                       Model Fit Statistics
                                               Intercept
                                  Intercept       and
                Criterion          Only        Covariates

                   AIC            3569.290      3388.640
                   SC             3575.231      3424.287
                   -2 Log L       3567.290      3376.640


                    Type 3 Analysis of Effects

                                         Wald
                  Effect       DF     Chi-Square    Pr > ChiSq

                  RACE          2       65.6901       <.0001
                  EDUC          1       31.1196       <.0001
                  EDUC*RACE     2       30.5180       <.0001


                Analysis of Maximum Likelihood Estimates

                                     Standard      Wald
       Parameter          DF  Estimate  Error  Chi-Square  Pr > ChiSq  Exp(Est)

       Intercept          1    2.4149   0.2605   85.9406     <.0001     11.189
       RACE      BLACK    1   -3.4145   0.5244   42.3924     <.0001      0.033
       RACE      OTHER    1   -2.6839   0.4028   44.3874     <.0001      0.068
       EDUC               1   -0.1007   0.0181   31.1196     <.0001      0.904
       EDUC*RACE BLACK    1    0.1542   0.0390   15.6210     <.0001      1.167
       EDUC*RACE OTHER    1    0.1453   0.0303   23.0425     <.0001      1.156
```

Figure 9.13 SAS output for predicting endorsement of capital punishment from education, race, and their interaction.

is Other, then Other = 1, whereas if the respondent's race is Black or White, then Other = 0. To interpret the overall interaction, note that we obtain three different models depending on the race of the respondent, namely,

for White respondents,

$$\ln \frac{\hat{\pi}}{1-\hat{\pi}} = 2.415 - 0.101(\text{Educ});$$

for Black respondents,

$$\ln\left(\frac{\hat{\pi}}{1-\hat{\pi}}\right) = 2.415 - 3.415 - 0.101(\text{Educ}) + 0.154\,(\text{Educ})$$

$$= -1.00 + 0.053(\text{Educ}); \text{ and}$$

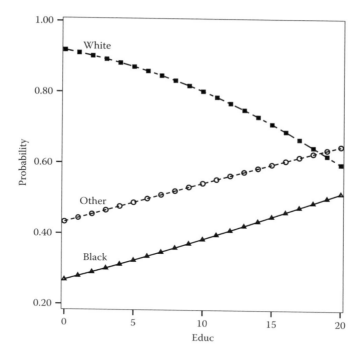

Figure 9.14 Graphical representation of the logistic regression model predicting the probability of endorsing capital punishment from education, race, and their interaction.

for Other respondents,

$$\ln\left(\frac{\hat{\pi}}{1-\hat{\pi}}\right) = 2.415 - 2.684 - 0.101(\text{Educ}) + 0.145(\text{Educ})$$

$$= -0.269 + 0.044(\text{Educ}).$$

Therefore, the effect of education on the outcome depends on one's race: for White respondents the effect of education is represented with a slope parameter of −0.101, for Black respondents the effect of education is represented with a slope parameter of 0.053, and for Other respondents the effect of education is represented with a slope parameter of 0.044. The overall significance of the interaction term indicates that there is a significant difference between the three slopes (−0.101, 0.053, and 0.044). These logistic regression equations are shown graphically in Figure 9.14 using the predicted probability (rather than the log odds) as outcome.

Note that the parameter estimates associated with the interaction terms in the model (i.e., 0.154 and 0.145) reflect the difference between Whites and each of the other race groups in terms of the effect of education on the outcome. For example, the parameter estimate 0.154 represents the difference between Black and White respondents in the education slope parameter: for Black respondents it is 0.053 and for White respondents it is −0.101 for a difference of 0.053 − (−0.101) = 0.154. Therefore, the test of this parameter estimate indicates whether the effect of education on the outcome is significantly different between

Black and White respondents. Note that for White respondents, as education increases by 1 year the log odds decrease by 0.101 or the odds are multiplied by $e^{-0.101} = 0.904$, thus indicating that for Whites higher levels of education are associated with lower odds of endorsing capital punishment. For Black respondents, as education increases by 1 year the log odds increase by 0.053 or the odds are multiplied by $e^{0.053} = 1.05$. Although this rate of change may not be significant in itself, the test of the interaction parameter provided in the output (Wald $X^2 = 15.6$, $df = 1$, $p < 0.0001$) indicates that the rate of change for Black respondents is significantly different from the rate of change for White respondents. The same interpretation can be similarly made for respondents of "Other" races.

Finally, if the interaction was not significant we could say that the effect of education (i.e., the slope) is the same for all three races. In this case, we could delete the interaction term from the model, resulting in a model with one slope parameter. The effect of race would thus impact only the intercept and the interpretation of the model would be similar to that of an analysis of covariance (ANCOVA) model. Although it would be inappropriate to do so in this case, due to the significant interaction, for illustrative purposes we fit a model without the interaction term to these data. The output from this model is shown in Figure 9.15. In this case, using $\hat{\pi}$ to denote the estimated probability (of endorsing capital punishment), the model for each race is:

for White respondents,

$$\ln\left(\frac{\hat{\pi}}{1-\hat{\pi}}\right) = 1.484 - 0.03(\text{Educ});$$

for Black respondents,

$$\ln\left(\frac{\hat{\pi}}{1-\hat{\pi}}\right) = 1.484 - 1.365 - 0.03(\text{Educ}) = 0.12 - 0.03(\text{Educ}); \text{ and}$$

for Other respondents,

$$\ln\left(\frac{\hat{\pi}}{1-\hat{\pi}}\right) = 1.484 - 0.801 - 0.03(\text{Educ}) = 0.67 - 0.03(\text{Educ}).$$

Note that the effect of education on the outcome (i.e., the slope) is the same for all three race groups in this case, reflecting the lack of interaction with race. The significant main effect of race in this model (Wald $X^2 = 155.9$, $df = 2$, $p < 0.0001$) indicates that, controlling for education, there is a significant difference between the three race groups in terms of the outcome (i.e., probability of endorsing capital punishment). In fact, by examining the values of the intercept estimates we can see that after controlling for education White respondents are most likely to endorse capital punishment and Black respondents are least likely to endorse capital punishment. However, this interpretation would only be appropriate if we could assume that education affects the outcome equally for all three race groups (and we know that this is not the case given that the interaction was significant in the previous model).

An examination of Figure 9.14 should further clarify why it would be inappropriate to discuss the main effect of race: At certain (low) education levels Whites are more likely to endorse capital punishment, but at other (high) education levels Whites may be less likely to endorse capital punishment. Thus, the way in which the interaction between race and

```
                            Response Profile

                    Ordered                    Total
                      Value       CAPPUN     Frequency

                          1       FAVOR         1882
                          2       OPPOSE         929

            Probability modeled is CAPPUN='FAVOR'.


                     Class Level Information

                                          Design
                    Class     Value     Variables

                    RACE      BLACK      1      0
                              OTHER      0      1
                              WHITE      0      0


                     Model Fit Statistics

                                             Intercept
                               Intercept         and
                    Criterion     Only       Covariates

                    AIC         3569.290      3415.874
                    SC          3575.231      3439.640
                    -2 Log L    3567.290      3407.874


                   Type 3 Analysis of Effects

                                     Wald
                    Effect    DF   Chi-Square    Pr > ChiSq

                    RACE       2    155.8858       <.0001
                    EDUC       1      6.9282       0.0085


              Analysis of Maximum Likelihood Estimates

                                   Standard      Wald
 Parameter         DF   Estimate     Error    Chi-Square   Pr > ChiSq   Exp(Est)

 Intercept          1     1.4838    0.1885     61.9744       <.0001      4.410
 RACE     BLACK     1    -1.3649    0.1170    135.9739       <.0001      0.255
 RACE     OTHER     1    -0.8097    0.1200     45.5280       <.0001      0.445
 EDUC               1    -0.0344    0.0131      6.9282       0.0085      0.966
```

Figure 9.15 SAS output for predicting endorsement of capital punishment from education and race (without their interaction).

education impacts the endorsement of capital punishment should be discussed in this case to fully understand and properly interpret the data.

9.9   Summary

In this chapter we extended the logistic model introduced in Chapter 8 to include the interpretation of categorical predictor variables. Specifically, we discussed dummy coding of categorical predictors and how to interpret the parameter estimates associated with these variables. In addition, this chapter discussed the interpretation of interaction terms, formed by the joint effects of categorical predictors on the (binary) outcome. We also showed that logistic models with categorical predictors are closely related—and in some cases actually equivalent—to log-linear models (which were discussed in Chapter 7).

Finally, we concluded this chapter by demonstrating an application of logistic regression that included both categorical and continuous predictors. However, all of the logistic regression models discussed thus far were appropriate for modeling a binary outcome, or an outcome variable with two categories. In the next chapter we discuss an extension of logistic regression that allows for the modeling of a categorical outcome variable with multiple categories.

Problems

9.1 Suppose that a logistic regression model contains one categorical predictor with three categories: A, B, and C. Using dummy coding with category A as the reference category for the predictor, the model has the following parameters: $\alpha = -1.0$, $\beta_1 = 2.0$, and $\beta_2 = 1.0$.
   a. What does each of the parameter values represent? Interpret these values fully.
   b. If Category C was used as the reference category, would the parameter values change? What would each of the parameter values represent if category C was used as the reference category?
   c. If Category B was used as the reference category, would the parameter values change? What would each of the parameter values represent if Category B was used as the reference category?

9.2 Using the data in Table 7.1 from the 1992 United States presidential election, logistic regression was used to model voting for Clinton (yes or no) from the voter's political view (liberal, moderate, or conservative). Using dummy coding with conservative as the reference category for political view, the following parameter estimates were obtained: $\hat{\alpha} = -0.92$, $\hat{\beta}_1 = 1.86$, and $\hat{\beta}_2 = 1.03$.
   a. Use a computer software package to fit a logistic regression model to these data and obtain these parameter estimates.
   b. What does each of the parameter values represent? Interpret these values fully and substantively.
   c. Change the reference category to liberal and report if and how the parameter estimates change. What does each of the parameter values represent using liberal as the reference category?
   d. Change the reference category to moderate and report if and how the parameter estimates change. What does each of the parameter values represent using moderate as the reference category?

9.3 In Chapter 7 we discussed the log-linear regression model used to fit the data in Table 7.1. Using the appropriate logistic regression model (from Problem 9.2), discuss the differences and similarities between the logistic and log-linear models fit to this data set. Include an interpretation of the parameter estimates of both models in your discussion.

9.4 Use the 2006 GSS data set to predict whether a respondent favors the death penalty for murder (CAPPUN) from the respondent's sex (SEX) and race (RACE) as well as their interaction.
   a. Conduct the likelihood ratio test of the interaction between SEX and RACE. Report and fully interpret the results from a substantive perspective.

b. If one were to fit a log-linear model using all three variables (CAPPUN, SEX, and RACE), what model comparison would be equivalent to the one performed in part (a)? Explain why these model comparisons are conceptually equivalent: What does the model comparison represent in each case (logistic/log-linear)?

c. Fully interpret all of the parameter estimates in the logistic regression model that contains only the main effects of SEX and RACE.

d. What log-linear model is equivalent to the logistic regression model fit in part (c)? Fit this log-linear model and show which of its parameter estimates are equivalent to those obtained from the logistic model in part (c).

e. Based on the logistic regression model with the interaction between SEX and RACE, what is the predicted probability that a Black male would favor the death penalty? What is this predicted probability from the model without the interaction term?

9.5 Table 9.7 provides data (obtained from the York University Web site) pertaining to the relationship between a treatment for diabetes (treated or placebo), sex (male or female), and improvement status (improved or not improved).

a. Fit the logistic regression model to predict improvement from treatment, sex, and their interaction. Conduct the likelihood ratio test of the interaction between treatment and sex. Report and fully interpret the results from a substantive perspective.

b. If one were to fit a log-linear model using all three variables (improvement, treatment, and sex), what model comparison would be equivalent to the one performed in part (a)? Explain why these model comparisons are conceptually equivalent: What does the model comparison represent in each case (logistic/log-linear)?

c. Fully interpret all of the parameter estimates in the logistic regression model that contains only the main effects of treatment and sex.

d. What log-linear model is equivalent to the logistic regression model fit in part (c)? Fit this log-linear model and show which of its parameter estimates are equivalent to those obtained from the logistic model in part (c).

e. Based on the logistic regression model with the interaction between treatment and sex, what is the predicted probability that a treated male would improve? What is this predicted probability from the model without the interaction term?

Table 9.7 Data for Problem 9.5 on the Relationship Between Treatment for Diabetes, Improvement Status, and Sex

Sex	Treatment	Improvement	
		No	Yes
Female	Placebo	19	13
	Treated	6	21
Male	Placebo	10	1
	Treated	7	7

9.6 Use the data from Problem 7.1 to predict the probability that a respondent will favor the death penalty from the respondent's fundamentalism level and sex as well as their interaction. Fully interpret the results of the analysis, including substantive interpretations of the model's fit and parameter estimates.

9.7   Using the data from Problem 7.3, choose one variable as the response and the other two as predictors. Explain your research question and choice of the response variable as well as how you would code it. Fit the logistic regression model to address your research question. Fully interpret the results of the analysis, including substantive interpretations of the model's fit and parameter estimates.

9.8   Using the data from Problem 7.4, choose a research question that can be addressed with these data using a logistic regression analysis. Explain which of the variables is to be used as the outcome and which as predictors. Fit the logistic regression model to address your research question. Fully interpret the results of the analysis, including the process you used to select a final model and substantive interpretations of its parameter estimates.

9.9   Use the data set on arthritis (from http://www.psych.yorku.ca/friendly/lab/files/ psy6140/examples/logistic/logist1a.sas) to predict whether the patient improves based on the patient's sex, treatment group, and age (a continuous variable). Be sure to include all interactions. Fully interpret the results of the analysis, including the process you used to select a final model and substantive interpretations of its parameter estimates.

9.10 Pick your own research question that can be addressed using variables from the 2006 GSS data set and a logistic regression model with at least two predictors.
      a. State your research question and expectations regarding the findings.
      b. Explain why a logistic regression model is more appropriate to your research question than a log-linear model.
      c. Conduct the appropriate tests to determine if any predictors or terms can or should be dropped from the model. Explain your process and conclusions.
      d. Fully interpret the value, direction, and statistical significance of each of the parameter estimates in your final model.
      e. Summarize the results substantively: What does the model tell you about any associations between the variables? Do these results conform to your expectations?

chapter ten

Logistic regression for multicategory outcomes

A LOOK AHEAD

In the last two chapters we discussed logistic regression models for a binary outcome; that is, an outcome variable that consists of two categories. In this chapter, we extend our discussion of logistic regression to multicategory outcomes, or outcome variables with several categories. For example, in the previous chapter we discussed an outcome variable measured as whether the respondent obtained at least a bachelor's degree. However, the original variable (from the General Social Survey) in fact consisted of several educational attainment levels for the respondent: less than high school, high school, junior college, bachelor's degree, and graduate degree. The models discussed in this chapter would allow us to predict the probability of any of these outcome categories, so we would not need to dichotomize the outcome as we did previously. The multicategory logistic model can still accommodate several predictor (or explanatory) variables, and these can be either continuous, categorical, or both. We will start this chapter by discussing a model that treats the outcome variable as nominal and then extend this discussion to a model that can incorporate the ordering of the categories when the outcome variable is ordinal.

10.1   The multicategory logistic regression model

In this section we focus on models used for predicting an outcome variable that is treated as nominal. In general, multicategory logistic regression models are used to predict the log odds of any outcome category relative to another outcome category. In that sense, they do not differ conceptually from the logistic models previously discussed because only two outcome categories are compared at a time. However, when the outcome variable consists of more than two categories, and thus more than one comparison of (or logit formed by) the categories, multicategory models can be used to efficiently estimate and interpret the parameters for all pairs of logits simultaneously.

In logistic regression models the response variable was binary so it consisted of two outcome categories and followed the binomial distribution. The response variable in a multicategory logistic model follows a multinomial distribution, with the total number of outcome categories denoted by J and each individual category indexed by j. Thus, the probability associated with the jth outcome category is $\pi_j, j = 1, 2, \ldots, J$. The multicategory logistic model consists of $(J-1)$ logits, with one outcome category serving as the reference category and the logits formed as the log odds of the jth outcome relative to the reference category. Typically, the last (or J^{th}) category is used to denote the reference category, so the jth logit (for the jth category) is

$$\ln(\pi_j/\pi_J),$$

and the $j = 1, 2, \ldots, (J–1)$ logits for all categories are

$$\ln(\pi_1/\pi_J), \ln(\pi_2/\pi_J), \ldots, \ln(\pi_{(J-1)}/\pi_J).$$

In general, the jth logit, $\ln(\pi_j/\pi_J)$, represents the log odds of outcome j relative to the baseline or reference outcome, J. If $J = 2$ (indicating a total of two outcome categories), the only logit would be

$$\ln(\pi_1/\pi_2) = \ln(\pi_1/(1 - \pi_1)),$$

which is exactly the outcome that we modeled in the previous two chapters. In other words, the typical logistic regression model discussed previously is a special case of the multicategory logistic model when $J = 2$.

The multicategory logistic regression model used to predict the odds of outcome j relative to outcome J using the predictor variables $X_1, X_2, \ldots, X_p$ is

$$\ln\left(\frac{\pi_j}{\pi_J}\right) = \alpha_j + \beta_{j1} X_1 + \beta_{j2} X_2 + \ldots + \beta_{jp} X_p. \tag{10.1}$$

There are $(J - 1)$ such models, and each of these models is essentially a logistic regression model of the form that was discussed in the previous two chapters. Note that if J (rather than $J - 1$) logits were used, the last logit would be rather meaningless because $\ln(\pi_J/\pi_J) = \ln(1) = 0$ and so the model parameters for this logit would have to be zero.

The j subscript on the parameters (intercept and slopes) of the model in Equation 10.1 is needed because it is likely that the model parameters would differ depending on the outcome category being modeled. For example, suppose that we were to use the age at which a respondent got married as a predictor of the respondent's highest level of education, where education level is measured as either less than high school, high school, junior college, bachelor's degree, or graduate degree. If we use the less than high school category as the reference category, then the relationship between age at marriage and the odds of completing high school (as opposed to less than high school) is likely to be different than the relationship between the age at marriage and the odds of completing a bachelor's degree (as opposed to less than high school). Therefore, by allowing different parameters for each logit, each outcome category is allowed to have its own prediction equation.

Although there are many similarities in the form and interpretation of the multicategory logistic models (in Equation 10.1) and the logistic models covered in previous chapters, estimation algorithms for multicategory models (implemented in software packages) estimate all $(J - 1)$ models simultaneously to ensure the smallest standard errors for the parameters. Therefore, the parameter estimates obtained from a simultaneous fitting of all $(J - 1)$ models is advantageous to fitting $(J - 1)$ separate logistic regression models. Another advantage of simultaneous estimation is that the odds involving any two outcomes can be directly modeled using the estimated parameters; for example, to predict the odds of outcome a relative to outcome b we can simply take the difference between the logit for outcome a and the logit for outcome b:

$$\ln\left(\frac{\pi_a}{\pi_b}\right) = \ln\left(\frac{\pi_a/\pi_J}{\pi_b/\pi_J}\right) = \ln\left(\frac{\pi_a}{\pi_J}\right) - \ln\left(\frac{\pi_b}{\pi_J}\right)$$

$$= (\alpha_a + \beta_{a1}X_1 + \beta_{a2}X_2 + \ldots + \beta_{ap}X_p) - (\alpha_b + \beta_{b1}X_1 + \beta_{b2}X_2 + \ldots + \beta_{bp}X_p)$$

$$= (\alpha_a - \alpha_b) + (\beta_{a1} - \beta_{b1})X_1 + (\beta_{a2} - \beta_{b2})X_2 + \ldots + (\beta_{ap} - \beta_{bp})X_p.$$

This allows us to obtain the parameters and interpret the results for any logit of interest from the parameter estimates for the initial set of $(J-1)$ logits that use the last category as the reference category.

For a numerical example of multicategory logistic models, we use data from the 2006 General Social Survey (GSS) to predict a respondent's highest educational level (less than high school, high school, junior college, bachelor's degree, or graduate degree) from age at which the respondent first got married. Note that, although the categories of the outcome variable in this example can be ordered (by level of educational attainment), at this point we treat this variable as nominal and ignore the ordering of the categories for illustrative purposes. The SAS output of this analysis is shown in Figure 10.1. Note that less than high school was used as the reference category and the estimated logistic regression models (presented in the order given in the output) are as follows:

Predicted ln(odds of bachelor's degree rather than less than high school) =
$-1.44 + 0.06$(AgeWed),

Predicted ln(odds of graduate degree rather than less than high school) =
$-2.22 + 0.07$(AgeWed),

Predicted ln(odds of high school rather than less than high school) =
$0.76 + 0.02$(AgeWed),

Predicted ln(odds of junior college rather than less than high school) =
$-1.76 + 0.04$(AgeWed).

In addition, for the last or reference category (less than high school), the logistic model would always be

Predicted ln(odds of less than high school rather than less than high school) =
Predicted $\ln(1) = 0$.

This last logit is typically not shown but is needed when probabilities are computed, as will be discussed shortly.

Note that in this example the values of the intercepts are not conceptually meaningful because they refer to the odds (or log odds) when age at marriage is zero, which is nonsensical. The values of the slopes, however, indicate the rate of change in the log odds

```
                          The LOGISTIC Procedure

                          Model Information

Data Set                      WORK.IN             General Social Surveys, 2006
Response Variable             DEGREE              RS HIGHEST DEGREE
Number of Response Levels     5
Model                         generalized logit
Optimization Technique        Fisher's scoring


                  Number of Observations Read      4510
                  Number of Observations Used      1160


                          Response Profile

          Ordered                              Total
          Value       DEGREE               Frequency

             1        BACHELOR                   185
             2        GRADUATE                   104
             3        HIGH SCHOOL                590
             4        JUNIOR COLLEGE              86
             5        LT HIGH SCHOOL             195


     Logits modeled use DEGREE='LT HIGH SCHOOL' as the reference category.

 NOTE: 3350 observations were deleted due to missing values for the response or
       explanatory variables.


                       Model Convergence Status

            Convergence criterion (GCONV=1E-8) satisfied.


                        Model Fit Statistics

                                            Intercept
                               Intercept       and
               Criterion         Only       Covariates

               AIC             3129.600      3114.768
               SC              3149.824      3155.217
               -2 Log L        3121.600      3098.768



               Testing Global Null Hypothesis: BETA=0

       Test                Chi-Square      DF     Pr > ChiSq

       Likelihood Ratio      22.8319        4       0.0001
       Score                 23.9811        4      <.0001
       Wald                  21.4571        4       0.0003


                     Type 3 Analysis of Effects

                                   Wald
               Effect     DF    Chi-Square    Pr > ChiSq

               AGEWED      4      21.4571       0.0003
```

Figure 10.1 SAS output from modeling the relationships between the probability of educational achievement and the age at first marriage for respondents of the General Social Survey.

```
                    Analysis of Maximum Likelihood Estimates

                                               Standard        Wald
       Parameter    DEGREE          DF  Estimate   Error   Chi-Square  Pr > ChiSq

       Intercept    BACHELOR         1   -1.4390   0.4335    11.0187     0.0009
       Intercept    GRADUATE         1   -2.2158   0.4779    21.5000     <.0001
       Intercept    HIGH SCHOOL      1    0.7576   0.3822     3.9293     0.0475
       Intercept    JUNIOR COLLEGE   1   -1.7592   0.5417    10.5480     0.0012
       AGEWED       BACHELOR         1    0.0593   0.0182    10.6455     0.0011
       AGEWED       GRADUATE         1    0.0674   0.0196    11.8029     0.0006
       AGEWED       HIGH SCHOOL      1    0.0154   0.0165     0.8693     0.3512
       AGEWED       JUNIOR COLLEGE   1    0.0408   0.0227     3.2416     0.0718


                             Odds Ratio Estimates

                                        Point         95% Wald
              Effect     DEGREE        Estimate   Confidence Limits

              AGEWED     BACHELOR        1.061     1.024      1.100
              AGEWED     GRADUATE        1.070     1.029      1.112
              AGEWED     HIGH SCHOOL     1.016     0.983      1.049
              AGEWED     JUNIOR COLLEGE  1.042     0.996      1.089
```

Figure 10.1 (Continued)

for a 1-year increase in age at first marriage. For example, for every 1-year increase in the age at first marriage, the log odds of completing high school rather than completing less than high school increase by 0.02. Thus, the odds of completing high school relative to less than high school increase with the age at marriage; in other words, the older one is when first married, the more likely it is that he or she completed high school rather than not. Note that the slopes are positive for the remaining logits as well, indicating that as age at first marriage increases, the odds of completing an educational level greater than high school increase relative to not completing high school.

The intercept and slope estimates together can be used to compute the (expected) odds for any two categories. For example, if one wished to predict the log odds of completing a bachelor's degree rather than completing high school, these two logits (given above) can be subtracted as follows:

Predicted ln(odds of bachelor's degree rather than high school)

$$= [-1.44 + 0.06(\text{AgeWed})] - [0.76 + 0.02(\text{AgeWed})]$$

$$= -2.2 + 0.04(\text{AgeWed}).$$

The positive coefficient for AgeWed indicates that as the age at marriage increases, the odds of completing a bachelor's degree rather than completing high school increase as well.

As is the case with binary logistic regression, the linear equation predicts the log odds of the response variable but one may wish to predict the odds or probability of an outcome category rather than its log odds. To predict the **odds** of the jth outcome relative to the reference category, J, we can exponentiate the jth logit in equation 10.1 to obtain

$$\left(\frac{\pi_j}{\pi_J}\right) = \exp(\alpha_j + \beta_{j1}X_1 + \beta_{j2}X_2 + \ldots + \beta_{jp}X_p). \tag{10.2}$$

To predict the **probability** of the jth outcome, π_j, note that the sum of all odds (or exponentiated logits) including that from the Jth logit is

$$(\pi_1/\pi_J) + (\pi_2/\pi_J) + \ldots + (\pi_{(J-1)}/\pi_J) + (\pi_J/\pi_J)$$

$$= (\pi_1 + \pi_2 + \ldots + \pi_J)/\pi_J$$

$$= 1/\pi_J = \sum_{j=1}^{J} \pi_j/\pi_J,$$

whereas the odds (or exponentiated logit) of the jth outcome is π_j/π_J. Therefore, using Equation 10.2, the predicted probability of the jth outcome is

$$\pi_j = \left(\frac{\pi_j/\pi_J}{1/\pi_J} \right) = \frac{\pi_j/\pi_J}{\displaystyle\sum_{j=1}^{J} \pi_j/\pi_J} = \frac{\exp(\alpha_j + \beta_{j1}X_1 + \beta_{j2}X_2 + \cdots + \beta_{jp}X_p)}{\displaystyle\sum_{j=1}^{J} \exp(\alpha_j + \beta_{j1}X_1 + \beta_{j2}X_2 + \cdots + \beta_{jp}X_p)}. \tag{10.3}$$

Equation 10.3 indicates that to compute the predicted probability for category j, π_j, the prediction equation of the jth logit is used in the numerator and the sum of the prediction equations over all logits (including the reference category) is used in the denominator. For example, using the output in Figure 10.1 once again, the following equations can be used to predict the probabilities associated with each educational level from age at marriage (X):

$$P(\text{Less than high school}) = \frac{e^0}{e^0 + e^{-1.44 + 0.06X} + e^{-2.22 + 0.07X} + e^{0.76 + 0.02X} + e^{-1.76 + 0.04X}},$$

$$P(\text{Junior college}) = \frac{e^{-1.76 + 0.04X}}{e^0 + e^{-1.44 + 0.06X} + e^{-2.22 + 0.07X} + e^{0.76 + 0.02X} + e^{-1.76 + 0.04X}},$$

$$P(\text{High school}) = \frac{e^{0.76 + 0.02X}}{e^0 + e^{-1.44 + 0.06X} + e^{-2.22 + 0.07X} + e^{0.76 + 0.02X} + e^{-1.76 + 0.04X}},$$

$$P(\text{Bachelor's degree}) = \frac{e^{-1.44 + 0.06X}}{e^0 + e^{-1.44 + 0.06X} + e^{-2.22 + 0.07X} + e^{0.76 + 0.02X} + e^{-1.76 + 0.04X}}, \text{ and}$$

$$P(\text{Graduate degree}) = \frac{e^{-2.22 + 0.07X}}{e^0 + e^{-1.44 + 0.06X} + e^{-2.22 + 0.07X} + e^{0.76 + 0.02X} + e^{-1.76 + 0.04X}}.$$

So, for example, for a respondent who first got married at the age of 20 the predicted probability of obtaining a high school degree is

$$P(\text{High school}) = \frac{e^{0.76 + 0.02(20)}}{1 + e^{-1.44 + 0.06(20)} + e^{-2.22 + 0.07(20)} + e^{0.76 + 0.02(20)} + e^{-1.76 + 0.04(20)}} = 0.53.$$

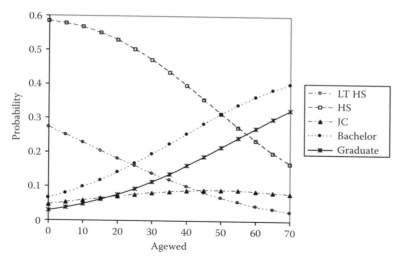

Figure 10.2 Graphical representation of the relationships between the predicted probability of educational achievement (LS HS = Less than high school; HS = High school; JC = Junior college; Bachelor = Bachelor's degree; Graduate = Graduate degree) and the age at first marriage (AgeWed) for respondents of the General Social Survey.

Similarly, for a respondent who first got married at the age of 20 it can be shown that the predicted probability of obtaining a bachelor's degree is 0.14, it is 0.08 for a graduate degree, 0.07 for junior college, and 0.18 for less than high school. Note that these probabilities do and will always sum to 1, because each respondent must fall into one and only one of the outcome categories. The relationship between age at first marriage and the predicted probabilities (obtained from the previous equations) is depicted graphically in Figure 10.2.

In the next section we will discuss inference for the parameter estimates of a multicategory logistic model and then discuss an extension of the model that incorporates the ordering of these outcome categories in the following section.

10.2   Parameter testing and interpretation

To test the statistical significance of predictors in a multicategory logistic model we can again use either the Wald test or likelihood ratio test as discussed in previous chapters. The Wald test is typically limited to testing one parameter at a time, whereas the likelihood ratio test allows us to test several parameters simultaneously by comparing nested models that differ only by the parameters we wish to test. In the case of the multicategory logistic model, we can also use the likelihood ratio test to test whether a predictor (or set of predictors) is significant across all $(J-1)$ logits.

To illustrate these tests, consider again our example shown in Figure 10.1, where there is only one predictor (AgeWed). In this case, we can use a likelihood ratio test to test whether age at marriage affects all $(J-1)$ logits simultaneously (i.e., H_0: age at marriage has no effect for all $(J-1)$ logits), or we can use a Wald test to test whether age at marriage affects any one specific logit (i.e., H_0: age at marriage has no effect for the jth logit). If we had several predictors, each one could be similarly tested for its effect on all $(J-1)$ logits or on any one of the logits. In Figure 10.1 (under Testing Global Null Hypothesis: BETA=0) we first see that the difference in log likelihood values between the model with and without the predictor is

22.83. For five outcome categories, the degrees of freedom for the likelihood ratio test are $(J - 1) = (5 - 1) = 4$, and with an associated p-value of 0.0001 this test indicates that there is a statistically significant relationship between age at first marriage and level of education. Therefore, we reject the omnibus null hypothesis that age at first marriage has no effect in any of the $(J - 1)$ logits.

The individual tests (or 95% confidence intervals) are also shown in Figure 10.1, and can be used to test the effect of age at first marriage for each of the $(J - 1)$ logits. These results indicate that age at first marriage is a significant predictor of the logits for those with a bachelor's degree ($p = 0.0011$) or a graduate degree ($p = 0.0006$) when compared to those who have not completed high school. For both of these educational levels, note also that the value of 1 is not included in the 95% confidence interval for the odds ratio. On the other hand, age at first marriage is not a significant predictor of the logits for those with a high school degree ($p = 0.3512$) or junior college degree ($p = 0.0718$) when compared to those who have not completed high school, and for both of these educational levels the value of 1 is included in the 95% confidence interval for the odds ratio. These results make sense conceptually, because those who have completed high school or junior college are relatively closer (in terms of educational achievement) to those that have not completed high school than are those who have completed a bachelor's or graduate degree. However, it is important to note that these tests should not be interpreted as tests of the slopes in Figure 10.2, but rather as comparisons (of sorts) of each slope in Figure 10.2 to the less than high school slope in the same figure. In general, in order for the results to be interpreted in the most meaningful way, the reference category should be appropriately selected such that it makes substantive sense as a baseline category. For example, in our case it would have also made substantive sense to use the graduate degree category as the reference or baseline category.

Tests involving more than one predictor will be illustrated and discussed in the last (computing and complete example) section of this chapter.

10.3   *Multicategory logistic regression with ordinal outcome variables*

The multicateogry models discussed thus far presumed no specific ordering of the outcome categories and are most appropriate when no such ordering is indicated or when one wishes to treat the outcome as a nominal variable. In the example discussed earlier in this chapter we used the outcome variable of educational attainment, with five outcome categories: less than high school, high school, junior college, bachelor's degree, and graduate degree. Although we previously treated it as a nominal variable for illustrative purposes, the categories of the educational attainment variable have an inherent ordering, as is the case with many categorical variables that consist of multiple categories. Therefore, this variable can be treated as ordinal, as opposed to nominal, using an extension of multi-category logistic models that is appropriate for ordinal response variables. These models typically provide more powerful tests and simpler interpretations by accounting for the inherent ordering of the response categories.

The main feature of these ordinal logistic models is that they predict the log odds, odds, or probability of a response occurring at or below any given outcome category. For example, ordering the educational attainment categories from lowest to highest—less than high school, high school, junior college, bachelor's degree, graduate degree—we can use this model to predict the probability of being (for example) at the bachelor's level or below from age at first marriage. Thus, the outcome of interest is generally defined as the probability of being at or below the jth category and is denoted by

$$P(Y \le j) = \pi_1 + \pi_2 + \cdots + \pi_j. \tag{10.4}$$

Equation 10.4 is called the jth **cumulative probability**. The probability of being above the jth category is thus the complement of the cumulative probability:

$$P(Y > j) = 1 - P(Y \le j).$$

The odds of the jth cumulative probability are defined as the probability of being at or below the jth category relative to being above the jth category, and the logistic model predicts the log odds of the jth cumulative probability as follows:

$$\text{logit}[P(Y \le j)] = \ln\left(\frac{P(Y \le j)}{1 - P(Y \le j)}\right) = \ln\left(\frac{P(Y \le j)}{P(Y > j)}\right) = \alpha_j + \beta_1 X_1 + \beta_2 X_2 + \cdots + \beta_p X_p. \tag{10.5}$$

Note that we fit this model only for the first $(J-1)$ outcome categories (i.e., $j = 1, 2, \ldots, J-1$), because for the last outcome category (i.e., $j = J$) the cumulative probability must always be 1.0 as it contains all possible outcomes. For example, using the outcome variable of educational attainment from the GSS, the probability of attaining a graduate degree or less must be 1.0 regardless of the values of the predictors because there is no higher educational attainment category for this variable in this data set. In other words, as defined in this data set, any educational level attained necessarily meets the condition of being a graduate degree or less.

The definition of the cumulative probability (Equation 10.4) also allows us to compute the probability for a specific category, j, as the difference between two adjacent cumulative probabilities:

$$\begin{aligned} P(Y = j) = \pi_j &= (\pi_1 + \pi_2 + \ldots + \pi_{j-1} + \pi_j) - (\pi_1 + \pi_2 + \ldots + \pi_{j-1}) \\ &= P(Y \le j) - P(Y \le j - 1). \end{aligned} \tag{10.6}$$

For example, if the predicted probability of obtaining a bachelor's degree or less is $P(Y \le 4) = 0.7$ and the predicted probability of obtaining a junior college degree or less is $P(Y \le 3) = 0.4$ then the probability of obtaining a bachelor's degree is

$$P(Y = 4) = P(Y \le 4) - P(Y \le 3) = 0.7 - 0.4 = 0.3.$$

In comparing the model in Equation 10.5 with the model in Equation 10.1, note that while the intercept in both models can vary with the outcome category (as indicated by its j subscript), the slopes in Equation 10.5 are assumed to be the same for all outcome categories, which was not the case in Equation 10.1. The main reason for "forcing" or restricting the slopes to be the same across the different logits is due to the ordinal and cumulative nature of the outcome variable. Specifically, the ordering of the categories must be preserved in the predicted cumulative outcomes for any given value of the predictor(s). For example, suppose that for a given value of the predictor (age at first marriage) we found that the predicted probability of attaining a bachelor's degree or less is 0.70. In this case, the lower educational attainment categories are subsumed by this value and, therefore, the model (using the same value of the predictor) must ensure that the predicted probability of attaining a lower educational level or less (e.g., junior college or less) is smaller than 0.70, whereas the predicted probability of attaining a higher educational level (i.e., a graduate degree or less) is larger than 0.70. It would be nonsensical to predict that (at a given value of the predictor) the probability of obtaining a high school diploma or less is greater than 0.70 if the probability of obtaining a bachelor's degree or less is 0.70. However, if the slopes were allowed to vary according to the predicted logit (as in Equation 10.1) then this kind of nonsensical result could occur. Therefore, the slopes are assumed to be the same for all logits and, under this assumption, the model is known as the **proportional odds model**. The underlying assumption of equivalent slopes across all logits can, and should, be tested to verify that this model is appropriate. If this assumption appears to be violated, then one could fit the nominal, baseline-reference model discussed at the beginning of this chapter (Equation 10.1) or more complicated alternative models.

10.3.1   Evaluating the proportional odds assumption

One approach to testing the proportional odds (or equivalent slopes) assumption involves either a score test (provided by SAS output) or a likelihood ratio test (provided by SPSS output), which tests the null hypothesis that the slope parameter (β, associated with a given predictor variable) is the same across all logit models ($j = 1, 2,\ldots, J - 1$). A rejection of this null hypothesis thus implies that the assumption is violated, whereas failure to reject this null hypothesis provides support for the assumption. The models compared for this test are

$$\text{Restricted model:}\quad \text{logit}[P(Y \leq j)] = \alpha_j + \beta_1 X_1 + \beta_2 X_2 + \cdots + \beta_p X_p;\text{ and}$$

$$\text{Unrestricted model:}\quad \text{logit}[P(Y \leq j)] = \alpha_j + \beta_{j1} X_1 + \beta_{j2} X_2 + \cdots + \beta_{jp} X_p.$$

Unfortunately, even when the estimated slopes may appear to be rather similar across the ($J - 1$) logit models, these tests often tend to reject the null hypothesis (and indicate lack of support for the proportional odds assumption), especially when the number of predictors is large, the sample size is large, or when continuous predictors are included in the model (O'Connell, 2006).

Thus, alternative strategies to evaluating the proportional odds assumption can be used. One such strategy is to simply fit ($J - 1$) separate models, one for each cumulative probability, and examine the slope parameters across these models. Although somewhat subjective, this approach can be used to judge whether the slopes appear to vary substantially or are relatively stable across the models. If all of the slopes are in the same direction (i.e., all positive or all negative), and if the average value of these slopes is close to that obtained from the overall proportional odds model, this lends further support to the proportional odds assumption. A second strategy involves fitting the partial proportional odds model, which involves an interaction between the logit category (i.e., j) and the predictor(s). If the interaction is significant, this indicates that the effect of the predictor(s) on the outcome depends or varies with the logit under consideration, and the proportional odds assumption is most likely violated. O'Connell (2006) provides examples of these strategies.

10.3.2   Alternative models

If the proportional odds assumption appears to be violated, alternative models can be used. Alternatives to the proportional odds model include the **continuation ratio** (or proportional hazards) model and the **adjacent-categories** model. These models also have assumptions regarding the equivalency of parameters over all logits, but can be used as alternatives to the proportional odds model if the research questions of interest can be better addressed using these modeling approaches.

The continuation ratio model essentially uses predictor variables to predict the logit of $P(Y > j | Y \geq j)$ relative to $P(Y = j | Y \geq j)$, or the log odds of being beyond category j relative to being in category j given that one is in category j or above:

$$\ln\left(\frac{P(Y > j | Y \geq j)}{P(Y = j | Y \geq j)}\right) = \alpha_j + \beta_1 X_1 + \beta_2 X_2 + \cdots + \beta_p X_p.$$

In other words, these models use only those observations that fall into category j or above for each logit. For instance, if j = high school in our example, we could use this model with age at first marriage as a predictor to predict the log odds of attaining an educational level beyond high school (relative to just high school) given that one at least graduated from high school.

The adjacent-categories model uses predictor variables to predict the log odds of being at a given category relative to being in an adjacent category (i.e., the category just below). This model thus uses the logit of $P(Y = j + 1)$ relative to $P(Y = j)$:

$$\ln\left(\frac{P(Y = j + 1)}{P(Y = j)}\right) = \alpha_j + \beta_1 X_1 + \beta_2 X_2 + \cdots + \beta_p X_p.$$

In our example, we could use this model (with age at first marriage as a predictor) to predict the odds of being in the high school category relative to the less than high school category, the odds of attaining a graduate degree relative to attaining a bachelor's degree, and so forth. Currently, however, software packages are limited to estimating this model with categorical predictors only and as such this analysis is not optimal for continuous predictor variables (O'Connell, 2006).

Although a detailed discussion of these models is beyond the scope of this book, further information on these models can be found in sources such as Agresti (1984, 2007), Clogg and Shihadeh (1994), and O'Connell (2006). An illustrative example of fitting and interpreting the proportional odds model is presented in the final section of this chapter.

10.4 Computing and complete example using a nominal outcome variable

In this section we use data obtained from the 2006 GSS to predict a respondent's marital status (measured as either married, widowed, divorced, separated, or never married) from the respondent's level of education (measured as highest year of education completed by the respondent) and the respondent's race (measured as White, Black, or Other). Because one of the predictors (race) is categorical, we also consider its interaction with the other predictor, educational level. We present the syntax and output for SAS as well as the menu commands and output for SPSS and conclude this section with an interpretation of the results.

10.4.1 SAS

The SAS syntax that should be used following a data step (to read in the data set) is shown in Figure 10.3. The logistic procedure is invoked in the proc logistic statement and specifies:

```
proc logistic data=in desc;
 class race /param=ref;
 model marital = educ race educ*race /link=glogit;
 output out=predicted predprobs=individual;
run;

proc gplot data=predicted;
 title1 ;
 symbol1 value=dot;
 symbol2 value=triangle;
 symbol3 value=star;
 plot (IP_NEVER_MARRIED IP_MARRIED IP_SEPARATED IP_DIVORCED IP_WIDOWED)*educ = race;
run;
```

Figure 10.3 SAS syntax for the nominal multicategory logistic model predicting the probability of marital status categories from educational level and race for respondents of the General Social Survey.

- the data set to be analyzed, which here was called "in," and
- the descending (desc) option, used to indicate that the outcome variable categories should be ordered in descending alphabetical order because ascending alphabetical order is the default.
  - This ordering results in the "divorced" category serving as the reference (last) category, which seems to make sense from a substantive perspective.
  - If one wishes to change the order, or the reference category, then categories of the outcome variable should be labeled in a data step so that the desired category is last (or first) alphabetically.
  - Alternatively, the reference category for the response variable can be specified in the model statement as discussed below.

The class statement specifies any categorical independent variables; in this case, race.

- The param=ref option specifies that the race variable should be dummy coded (effect coding is the default).
- In this case, because White is last alphabetically, it will serve as the reference category for dummy coding.

The model statement specifies the outcome variable (marital) as well as any model predictors.

- In this example, we use education (educ), race, and their interaction as predictors.
- The link=glogit (for generalized logit) option is used to specify a multicategory logistic model.
- The reference category for the response can also be specified in this statement.
  - For example, to use married as the reference category, the syntax (ref='MARRIED') would be inserted after the name of the outcome variable (marital) in the model statement.

Finally, the output statement is used to save predicted (and other) values from the model.

- The name of the output file is given after the out= command (in this case we called it "predicted").

- The predprobs=individual command requests that predicted probabilities be computed and saved for each level (category) of the outcome variable.
  - To view these predicted probabilities, the output data set ("predicted") would need to be printed using proc print.

To aid in the interpretation of any interaction between the two predictors, race and education, on the probability of marital status, we used the gplot procedure syntax shown in Figure 10.3 to plot the relationship between education and the predicted probabilities, by race, for each marital status.

10.4.2   SPSS

To fit a multicategory logistic regression model with SPSS:

- Select Regression under the Analyze menu and then choose Multinomial Logistic.
- Move the outcome variable (i.e., Marital status) into the Dependent box, any categorical predictors (i.e., Race) into the Factor(s) box, and any continuous predictors (i.e., Education) into the Covariate(s) box. This is illustrated in Figure 10.4.
- To specify the reference category for the outcome variable, click on the Reference Category... button underneath the Dependent box, where you can choose the first, last, or another (custom) category as the reference category. This is illustrated in Figure 10.5.
- Back in the main Multinomial Logistic Regression window (shown in Figure 10.4), click on Model... to specify the model parameters. Select the Custom button to fit a model with the two main effects and their interaction. This is illustrated in Figure 10.6.

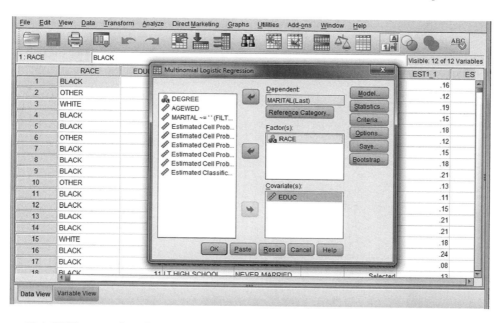

Figure 10.4 SPSS screenshot illustrating how to fit a nominal multinomial logistic model predicting the probability of marital status categories from educational level and race for respondents of the General Social Survey.

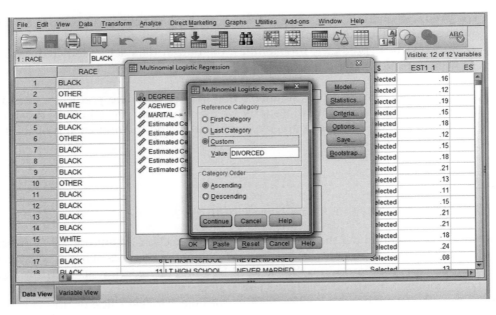

Figure 10.5 SPSS screenshot illustrating how to chose the reference category when fitting a nominal multinomial logistic regression model.

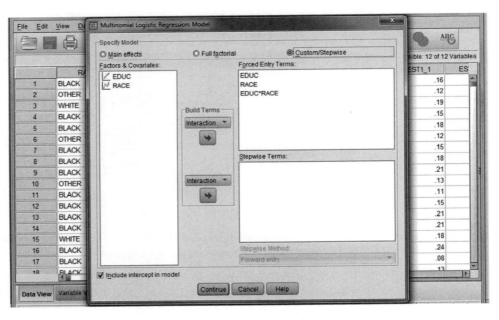

Figure 10.6 SPSS screenshot illustrating how to specify the terms to include in a multinomial regression model.

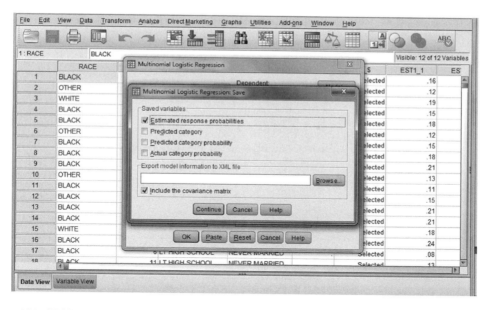

Figure 10.7 SPSS screenshot illustrating how to save the predicted probabilities so that the results from fitting a multinomial logistic regression model can be graphically depicted.

- To be able to plot the relationships between the predictor(s) and the outcome probabilities, click on the Save... button in the main Multinomial Logistic Regression window (shown in Figure 10.4) and choose Estimated response probabilities, as depicted in Figure 10.7. The probabilities will then appear as variables in the data window.

10.4.3   Interpretation

The omnibus tests are provided in Figure 10.8 (under Testing Global Null Hypothesis: BETA=0) for SAS and Figure 10.9 (under Model Fitting Information) for SPSS. These tests show that, overall, the model with both predictors and their interaction fits significantly better than an "empty" model (with no predictors) as indicated by the likelihood ratio test statistic of 368.35, $df = 20$, $p < .0001$. To test the individual effects, starting with the interaction effect, recall that one can test the effects using either Wald or likelihood ratio statistics. In SAS the test is conducted using a Wald statistic and the results ($X^2 = 25.19$, $df = 8$, $p = 0.0014$) are shown in Figure 10.8 (under Type 3 Analysis of Effects). In SPSS the test is conducted using a likelihood ratio statistic and the results ($G^2 = 25.75$, $df = 8$, $p = 0.001$) are shown in Figure 10.9 (under Likelihood Ratio Tests). Both test statistics obtain statistical significance and thus indicate that a model with the interaction fits significantly better than a model without it. Therefore, regardless of the statistical package (or test) used, we conclude that the Race × Education interaction effect is needed in the model and so only the parameter estimates associated with the interaction should be interpreted. As we have indicated previously, the main (or individual) effects, in this case of race and education, should not be interpreted in the presence of a significant interaction.

```
                              The LOGISTIC Procedure

                                Response Profile

                    Ordered                              Total
                    Value      MARITAL              Frequency

                       1       WIDOWED                    366
                       2       SEPARATED                  155
                       3       NEVER MARRIED             1076
                       4       MARRIED                   2169
                       5       DIVORCED                   729

          Logits modeled use MARITAL='DIVORCED' as the reference category.


                           Class Level Information

                                              Design
                    Class      Value      Variables

                    RACE       BLACK        1     0
                               OTHER        0     1
                               WHITE        0     0


                        Model Convergence Status
             Convergence criterion (GCONV=1E-8) satisfied.

                           Model Fit Statistics

                                                  Intercept
                                   Intercept            and
                    Criterion           Only      Covariates

                    AIC            11777.798       11449.452
                    SC             11803.441       11603.309
                    -2 Log L       11769.798       11401.452


                  Testing Global Null Hypothesis: BETA=0

          Test                   Chi-Square      DF    Pr > ChiSq

          Likelihood Ratio         368.3464      20       <.0001
          Score                    378.0815      20       <.0001
          Wald                     346.4385      20       <.0001

                      Type 3 Analysis of Effects

                                         Wald
          Effect          DF      Chi-Square    Pr > ChiSq

          EDUC             4        83.3557        <.0001
          RACE             8        43.1919        <.0001
          EDUC*RACE        8        25.1920        0.0014
```

Figure 10.8 SAS output (omnibus tests) for the nominal multicategory logistic model predicting the probability of marital status categories from educational level and race.

The parameter estimates, shown in both Figure 10.10 (SAS) and Figure 10.11 (SPSS), provide the models for each of the $(J-1) = (5-1) = 4$ logits in this analysis. For example, the estimated model to predict the logit comparing married and divorced individuals is

$$\ln\left(\frac{P(\text{married})}{P(\text{divorced})}\right) = 0.40 + 0.05(\text{Educ}) + 1.16(\text{Black}) + 1.64(\text{Other})$$
$$- 0.13(\text{Black})(\text{Educ}) - 0.09(\text{Other})(\text{Educ}).$$

Case Processing Summary

		N	Marginal Percentage
Marital status	DIVORCED	729	16.2%
	MARRIED	2169	48.3%
	NEVER MARRIED	1076	23.9%
	SEPARATED	155	3.4%
	WIDOWED	366	8.1%
RACE	BLACK	630	14.0%
	OTHER	591	13.1%
	WHITE	3274	72.8%
Valid		4495	100.0%
Missing		9	
Total		4504	
Subpopulation		61[a]	

a. The dependent variable has only one value observed in 4 (6.6%) subpopulations.

Model Fitting Information

Model	Model Fitting Criteria	Likelihood Ratio Tests		
	−2 Log Likelihood	Chi-Square	df	Sig.
Intercept Only	1262.47			
Final	894.127	368.346	20	.000

Likelihood Ratio Tests

Effect	Model Fitting Criteria	Likelihood Ratio Tests		
	−2 Log Likelihood of Reduced Model	Chi-Square	df	Sig.
Intercept	894.127	.000	0	.
EDUC	894.127	.000	0	.
RACE	940.935	46.808	8	.000
RACE * EDUC	919.877	25.750	8	.001

The Chi-square statistic is the difference in -2 log-likelihoods between the final model and a reduced model. The reduced model is formed by omitting an effect from the final model. The null hypothesis is that all parameters of the effect are 0.

a. This reduced model is equivalent to the final model because omitting the effect does not increase the degrees of freedom.

Figure 10.9 SPSS output (omnibus tests) for the nominal multicategory logistic model predicting the probability of marital status categories from educational level and race.

```
                        Analysis of Maximum Likelihood Estimates

                                              Standard      Wald
      Parameter          MARITAL       DF  Estimate  Error  Chi-Square  Pr > ChiSq

      Intercept          WIDOWED        1    0.8901  0.3116    8.1600      0.0043
      Intercept          SEPARATED      1   -0.4232  0.4851    0.7610      0.3830
      Intercept          NEVER MARRIED  1   -0.4836  0.2828    2.9241      0.0873
      Intercept          MARRIED        1    0.3995  0.2369    2.8441      0.0917
      EDUC               WIDOWED        1   -0.1188  0.0236   25.3898     <.0001
      EDUC               SEPARATED      1   -0.1166  0.0373    9.7571      0.0018
      EDUC               NEVER MARRIED  1    0.0453  0.0202    5.0055      0.0253
      EDUC               MARRIED        1    0.0513  0.0170    9.0856      0.0026
      RACE      BLACK    WIDOWED        1    1.6748  0.7901    4.4929      0.0340
      RACE      BLACK    SEPARATED      1    2.0077  0.9736    4.2529      0.0392
      RACE      BLACK    NEVER MARRIED  1    2.6005  0.6573   15.6515     <.0001
      RACE      BLACK    MARRIED        1    1.1582  0.6747    2.9465      0.0861
      RACE      OTHER    WIDOWED        1   -0.7008  0.7118    0.9693      0.3249
      RACE      OTHER    SEPARATED      1    0.4437  0.7594    0.3414      0.5590
      RACE      OTHER    NEVER MARRIED  1    1.3303  0.5367    6.1434      0.0132
      RACE      OTHER    MARRIED        1    1.6442  0.4798   11.7417      0.0006
      EDUC*RACE BLACK    WIDOWED        1   -0.1360  0.0614    4.9139      0.0266
      EDUC*RACE BLACK    SEPARATED      1   -0.0935  0.0757    1.5256      0.2168
      EDUC*RACE BLACK    NEVER MARRIED  1   -0.1322  0.0478    7.6468      0.0057
      EDUC*RACE BLACK    MARRIED        1   -0.1286  0.0493    6.8174      0.0090
      EDUC*RACE OTHER    WIDOWED        1   -0.0111  0.0611    0.0330      0.8559
      EDUC*RACE OTHER    SEPARATED      1    0.0737  0.0598    1.5169      0.2181
      EDUC*RACE OTHER    NEVER MARRIED  1   -0.0383  0.0407    0.8860      0.3466
      EDUC*RACE OTHER    MARRIED        1   -0.0943  0.0369    6.5520      0.0105
```

Figure 10.10 SAS output (model parameters) for the nominal multicategory logistic model predicting the probability of marital status categories from educational level and race.

In this model the indicator variables are specified such that Black = 1 if the respondent's race is Black and Black = 0 if the respondent's race is White or Other. Similarly, Other = 1 if the respondent's race is Other and Other = 0 if the respondent's race is Black or White. Thus, for example, the predicted log odds for a White respondent would be

$$\ln\left(\frac{P(\text{married})}{P(\text{divorced})}\right) = 0.40 + 0.05(\text{Educ}) + 1.16(0) + 1.64(0) - 0.13(0)(\text{Educ}) - 0.09(0)(\text{Educ})$$

$$= 0.40 + 0.05(\text{Educ}).$$

Similarly, the predicted log odds for a Black respondent would be

$$\ln\left(\frac{P(\text{married})}{P(\text{divorced})}\right) = 0.40 + 0.05(\text{Educ}) + 1.16(1) + 1.64(0) - 0.13(1)(\text{Educ}) - 0.09(0)(\text{Educ})$$

$$= 1.56 - 0.08(\text{Educ}).$$

   Due to the significant interaction, both the intercept and slope of the regression equation that is used to predict the odds of marital status from education change with, or depend on, the respondent's race. In other words, the relationship between education and marital status depends on one's race. The estimated intercepts in the previous equations indicate that the expected odds of being married rather than divorced are higher for Blacks than for Whites when one has zero years of education, whereas the estimated slopes show that as one's education increases the odds of being married rather than divorced increase

Parameter Estimates

Marital status[a]		B	Std. Error	Wald	df	Sig.	Exp(B)	95% Confidence Interval for Exp (B)	
								Lower Bound	Upper Bound
MARRIED	Intercept	.399	.237	2.844	1	.092			
	EDUC	.051	.017	9.086	1	.003	1.053	1.018	1.088
	[RACE=BLACK]	1.158	.675	2.946	1	.086	3.184	.849	11.948
	[RACE=OTHER]	1.644	.480	11.742	1	.001	5.177	2.021	13.258
	[RACE=WHITE]	0[b]	.	.	0	.	.	.	.
	[RACE=BLACK] * EDUC	−.129	.049	6.817	1	.009	.879	.798	.968
	[RACE=OTHER] * EDUC	−.094	.037	6.552	1	.010	.910	.847	.978
	[RACE=WHITE] * EDUC	0[b]	.	.	0	.	.	.	.
NEVER MARRIED	Intercept	−.484	.283	2.924	1	.087			
	EDUC	.045	.020	5.005	1	.025	1.046	1.006	1.089
	[RACE=BLACK]	2.600	.657	15.652	1	.000	13.470	3.714	48.853
	[RACE=OTHER]	1.330	.537	6.143	1	.013	3.782	1.321	10.830
	[RACE=WHITE]	0[b]	.	.	0	.	.	.	.
	[RACE=BLACK] * EDUC	−.132	.048	7.647	1	.006	.876	.798	.962
	[RACE=OTHER] * EDUC	−.038	.041	.886	1	.347	.962	.889	1.042
	[RACE=WHITE] * EDUC	0[b]	.	.	0	.	.	.	.
SEPARATED	Intercept	−.423	.485	.761	1	.383			
	EDUC	−.117	.037	9.757	1	.002	.890	.827	.957
	[RACE=BLACK]	2.008	.974	4.253	1	.039	7.446	1.105	50.194
	[RACE=OTHER]	.444	.759	.341	1	.559	1.559	.352	6.904
	[RACE=WHITE]	0[b]	.	.	0	.	.	.	.
	[RACE=BLACK] * EDUC	−.093	.076	1.526	1	.217	.911	.785	1.056
	[RACE=OTHER] * EDUC	.074	.060	1.517	1	.218	1.076	.957	1.210
	[RACE=WHITE] * EDUC	0[b]	.	.	0	.	.	.	.
WIDOWED	Intercept	.890	.312	8.160	1	.004			
	EDUC	−.119	.024	25.390	1	.000	.888	.848	.930
	[RACE=BLACK]	1.675	.790	4.493	1	.034	5.338	1.134	25.113
	[RACE=OTHER]	−.701	.712	.969	1	.325	.496	.123	2.002
	[RACE=WHITE]	0[b]	.	.	0	.	.	.	.
	[RACE=BLACK] * EDUC	−.136	.061	4.914	1	.027	.873	.774	.984
	[RACE=OTHER] * EDUC	−.011	.061	.033	1	.856	.989	.877	1.115
	[RACE=WHITE] * EDUC	0[b]	.	.	0	.	.	.	.

a. The reference category is: DIVORCED.

b. This parameter is set to zero because it is redundant.

Figure 10.11 SPSS output (model parameters) for the nominal multicategory logistic model predicting the probability of marital status categories from educational level and race.

for Whites but decrease for Blacks. Thus, for example, the predicted log odds for a White respondent with 12 years of education would be

$$\ln\left(\frac{P(\text{married})}{P(\text{divorced})}\right) = 0.40 + 0.05(12) = 1.0,$$

and the predicted log odds for a Black respondent with 12 years of education would be

$$\ln\left(\frac{P(\text{married})}{P(\text{divorced})}\right) = 1.56 - 0.08(12) = 0.6.$$

The significance tests of the individual interaction parameters (shown in Figures 10.10 and 10.11 for SAS and SPSS, respectively) compare the education slopes between White and either the Black or Other race category for each logit (using divorced as the reference category). For example, the interaction parameter estimate of –0.129, corresponding to the Black and Married categories, indicates that in predicting the married versus divorced logit the effect of education is about 0.13 units lower for Blacks than for Whites. Note that this was also shown in the previous equations, where the slope for Whites is 0.05 and the slope for Blacks is –0.08 (for a difference of 0.13 units). The *p*-value associated with this parameter estimate is 0.009, indicating that this is a significant difference. Similarly, we can see that the slope is significantly lower for Blacks than for Whites in predicting the widowed (vs. divorced) logit and the never married (vs. divorced) logit, but there is no significant difference between Blacks and Whites in the effect of education on the separated (vs. divorced) logit. We also see that in comparing the effect of education on the four logits between Whites and Other races, the only significant difference occurs for the married versus divorced logit ($p = 0.0105$), where the effect of education is significantly lower for Other races than for Whites (because the parameter estimate is –0.094).

To fully understand a significant interaction it is often best to examine the results graphically, and the graphs in Figure 10.12 (obtained from SPSS) show how the relationship between education and the predicted probability vary by race for each marital status category. Note that the relationship between education and the probability for each marital status category depends on race, and the nature of the effect of race varies with marital status. For example, the relationship between education and the probability of being in the never married category (see Figure 10.12a) is generally positive for all three race groups, indicating that more education is related to a higher probability of being never married, but the relationship is strongest (i.e., the slope tends to be steepest) for Blacks and weakest for Whites. On the other hand, the relationship between education and the probability of being in the married category (see Figure 10.12b) is strong and positive for Whites, generally weak and positive for Blacks, and actually negative for those of other races. Furthermore, the relationship between education and the probability of being separated (see Figure 10.12c) is negative for all three race groups, though the relationship is stronger for Blacks and Whites than for those of other races. The relationship between education and the probability of being divorced (see Figure 10.12d) is a relatively strong positive relationship for Blacks, a generally weak negative relationship for Whites, and a relatively weak positive relationship for those of other races. Finally, the relationship between education and the probability of being widowed (see Figure 10.12e) is negative for all three race groups, is virtually identical for Blacks and Whites, and relatively weaker for those of other races.

10.5 Computing and complete example using an ordinal outcome variable

In this section we use data from the 2006 GSS to predict a respondent's educational attainment level (degree), measured as either less than high school, high school, junior college, bachelor's degree, or graduate degree, from the respondent's age when first married (agewed). The outcome variable (educational attainment level) is treated as ordinal, so the proportional odds model is used. We present the syntax and output for SAS as well as the menu options and output for SPSS and conclude this section with an interpretation of the results.

10.5.1 SAS

The SAS syntax used to fit the proportional odds model (after reading in the data set in a data step) is shown in Figure 10.13. The proc logistic statement specifies:

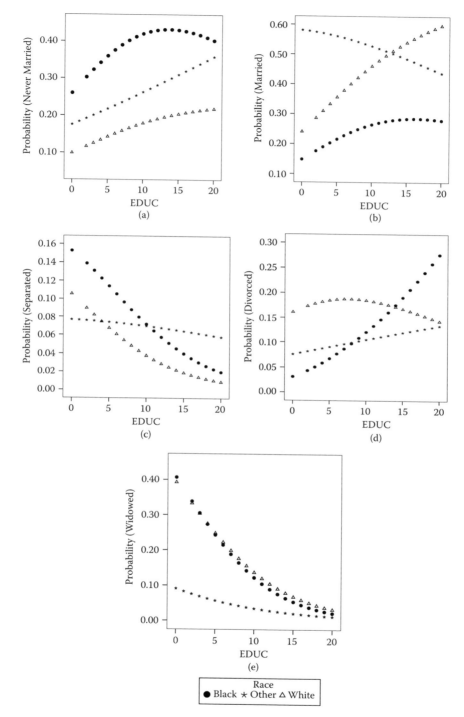

Figure 10.12 Graphs (from SPSS) depicting the relationship between education and the predicted probability, by race, of each marital status category: (a) never married, (b) married, (c) separated, (d) divorced, and (e) widowed.

```
proc logistic data=in order=internal;
model degree = agewed;
 output out=predicted predprobs=cumulative;
run;

proc gplot data=predicted;
 title1 ;
 symbol1 value=dot color=black;
 symbol2 value=triangle color=black;
 symbol3 value=star color=black;
 symbol4 value=square color=black;
 symbol5 value=circle color=black;
 axis2 label=('cumulative probability');
 legend1 frame label=(justify=l 'Degree')
  value=(tick=1 justify=l 'Less than HS'
         tick=2 justify=l 'HS'
         tick=3 justify=l 'Junior College'
         tick=4 justify=l 'Bachelors'
         tick=5  justify=l 'Graduate');
 plot (CP_LT_HIGH_SCHOOL CP_HIGH_SCHOOL CP_JUNIOR_COLLEGE CP_BACHELOR
       CP_GRADUATE)*agewed /overlay legend=legend1 vaxis=axis2;
run;
```

Figure 10.13 SAS syntax for the proportional odds model predicting a respondent's educational attainment level (degree) from the respondent's age when first married (agewed) using the General Social Survey data set.

- the name of the data set, here called "in"; and
- the order=internal option to specify that the response categories should be ordered according to their unformatted values, or as numerically coded, rather than by their formatted values (i.e., labels).

The model statement then specifies

- the response variable (degree), and
- the predictor (agewed), which is continuous in this case (and thus does not require a class statement).

The output statement options are used to request that

- the fitted values be saved to a file named "predicted" (out=predicted) and
- this file should contain the predicted cumulative probabilities (predprobs=cumulative).

The gplot command is used to plot the predicted cumulative probabilities as a function of the predictor (agewed).

10.5.2   SPSS

In SPSS we must first ensure that the response variable is ordered from lowest to highest category. One can, for example, obtain the frequencies for the response variable (using the Frequencies option from Descriptive Statistics under the Analyze menu) to determine how its categories are ordered in SPSS. If the ordering is not from lowest to highest, the response variable should be recoded (e.g., using the Transform menu) to achieve the desired ordering. We did so in this example so that the outcome variable categories are in order from 1 (less than high school) to 5 (graduate degree).

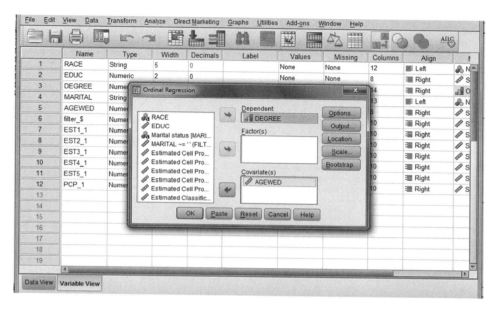

Figure 10.14 SPSS menu illustrating how to fit the proportional odds model predicting a respondent's educational attainment level (degree) from the respondent's age when first married (AGEWED) using the General Social Survey data set.

To fit the proportional odds model in SPSS:

- Select Regression under the Analyze menu and then choose Ordinal Regression
- Move the (ordered) response variable (Degree in this example) to the Dependent box. Move any categorical predictors (none in this example) to the Factor(s) box, and any continuous predictors (agewed in this example) to the "Covariate(s)" box, as illustrated in Figure 10.14.
- Click on the Output… button in the Ordinal Regression window, then select
  - Test of parallel lines (to test the proportional odds assumption), and
  - Estimated response probabilities (to save the predicted probabilities, which can be used to produce graphs).
  - This is depicted in Figure 10.15.
- Click Continue (in the Ordinal Regression: Output window) and then OK (in the Ordinal Regression window) to produce the output.
- Under the Graphs menu, the Overlay Scatterplot chart type can be used to graph the results.

10.5.3   Interpretation

First we need to examine the test of the common slopes or proportional odds assumption, testing the null hypothesis that the slope associated with the predictor (agewed) is the same for all four logits. This test is shown in Figure 10.16 (under Score Test for the Proportional Odds Assumption) for SAS and in Figure 10.17 (under Test of Parallel Line) for SPSS. This

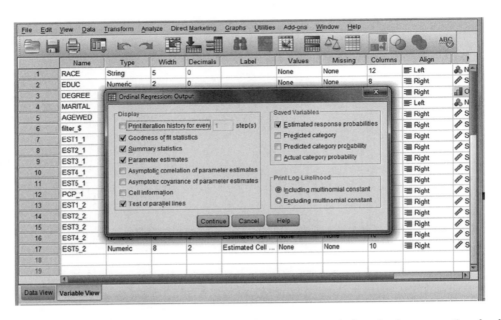

Figure 10.15 SPSS menu illustrating how to select options needed to fit the proportional odds model predicting a respondent's educational attainment level (degree) from the respondent's age when first married.

test compares the fit of the model that restricts all slopes to be equal (and thus estimates one slope) for all four logits with the fit of the model that allows a separate slope to be estimated for each of the four logits. The results of these tests from SAS ($X^2 = 4.2$, $df = 3$, $p = 0.24$) and SPSS ($G^2 = 3.7$, $df = 3$, $p = 0.29$) differ slightly because SAS uses a score test, whereas SPSS uses a likelihood ratio test, but in both cases the results lead to the same conclusion: The assumption of a common slope for all logits is appropriate since the test is not statistically significant and, therefore, the null hypothesis is not rejected. We can thus proceed with fitting the proportional odds model.

The output of the likelihood ratio test for the fit of the proportional odds model with one predictor (agewed) is shown in Figure 10.18 (under Testing Global Null Hypothesis: BETA=0) for SAS and in Figure 10.19 (under Model Fitting Information) for SPSS. The results ($G^2 = 25.4$, $df = 1$, $p < 0.0001$) indicate that the model with this predictor fits significantly better than the model without this predictor. Therefore, the age at which one was first married is a significant predictor of the cumulative probability of educational attainment.

The parameter estimates, shown in Figure 10.18 for SAS and Figure 10.19 for SPSS, provide the logistic models for all four logits. Note that while both software packages produce the same intercepts, the direction of the slopes is reversed due to the way in which the model is specified. Whereas in SAS the model is specified as discussed in this chapter (see Equation 10.5), in SPSS the model is specified as

$$\text{logit}[P(Y \le j)] = \ln\left(\frac{P(Y \le j)}{1 - P(Y \le j)}\right) = \ln\left(\frac{P(Y \le j)}{P(Y > j)}\right) = \alpha_j + (-\beta_1 X_1 - \beta_2 X_2 - \ldots - \beta_p X_p). \quad (10.7)$$

```
                        The LOGISTIC Procedure

                        Model Information

     Data Set                    WORK.IN          General Social Surveys, 2006
     Response Variable           DEGREE           RS HIGHEST DEGREE
     Number of Response Levels   5
     Model                       cumulative logit
     Optimization Technique      Fisher's scoring


               Number of Observations Read       4510
               Number of Observations Used       1160


                        Response Profile

               Ordered                          Total
               Value      DEGREE             Frequency

                  1    LT HIGH SCHOOL           195
                  2    HIGH SCHOOL              590
                  3    JUNIOR COLLEGE            86
                  4    BACHELOR                 185
                  5    GRADUATE                 104

        Probabilities modeled are cumulated over the lower Ordered Values.

NOTE: 3350 observations were deleted due to missing values for the response or explanatory
      variables.


                     Model Convergence Status

             Convergence criterion (GCONV=1E-8) satisfied.


             Score Test for the Proportional Odds Assumption

                Chi-Square      DF      Pr > ChiSq

                  4.2238         3        0.2383
```

Figure 10.16 SAS output showing the test of the common slopes assumption for the proportional odds model predicting a respondent's educational attainment level (degree) from the respondent's age when first married.

Liu (2007) and O'Connell (2006) provide an explanation of the different specification approaches used by SAS and SPSS when fitting the proportional odds model, but suffice it to say that although the slope estimates have different signs the meaning remains the same and the model specification presented in this chapter (Equation 10.5) is consistent with the SAS output. For example, using the first logit, the slope associated with the predictor (agewed) is −0.051 in the SAS output and 0.051 in the SPSS output. Thus, using either the SAS formulation (i.e., Equation 10.5) with the SAS slope estimate of −0.051, or the SPSS formulation (Equation 10.7) with the SPSS slope estimate of 0.051, we obtain

logit[P(at or below less than high school)]

= ln[P(at or below less than high school)/P(above less than high school)]

= −0.455 − 0.051(agewed).

Case Processing Summary

		N	Marginal Percentage
DEGREE	Less than High School	195	16.8%
	High School	590	50.9%
	Junior College	86	7.4%
	Bachelor	185	15.9%
	Graduate	104	9.0%
Valid		1160	100.0%
Missing		3344	
Total		4504	

Test of Parallel Lines[c]

Model	−2 Log Likelihood	Chi-Square	df	Sig.
Null Hypothesis	566.636			
General	562.901[a]	3.734[b]	3	.292

The null hypotheis is states that the location parameters (slope coefficients) are the same across response categories.

a. The log-likelihood value cannot be further increased after maximum number of step-halving.

b. The Chi-Square statistic is computed based on the log-likelihood value of the last iteration of the general model. Validity of the test is uncertain.

c. Link function: Logit.

Figure 10.17 SPSS output showing the test of the common slopes assumption for the proportional odds model predicting a respondent's educational attainment level (degree) from the respondent's age when first married.

Therefore, the odds of attaining an education level that is at or below the less than high school category are negatively associated with the age at first marriage; the younger the individual at first marriage, the higher the probability that he or she will be in the category less than high school or below it rather than above it. For example, for an individual who got married at the age of 20:

$$\ln[P(\text{at or below less than high school})/P(\text{above less than high school})]$$
$$= -0.455 - 0.051(20) = -1.475,$$

$$P(\text{at or below less than high school})/P(\text{above less than high school})$$
$$= \exp(-1.475) = 0.229, \text{ and}$$

$$P(\text{at or below less than high school}) = 0.229/1.229 = 0.186.$$

```
                        The LOGISTIC Procedure

                       Model Fit Statistics

                                              Intercept
                                  Intercept      and
                    Criterion       Only      Covariates

                    AIC           3129.600      3106.156
                    SC            3149.824      3131.437
                    -2 Log L      3121.600      3096.156


             Testing Global Null Hypothesis: BETA=0

        Test                  Chi-Square      DF     Pr > ChiSq

        Likelihood Ratio        25.4435       1        <.0001
        Score                   21.4718       1        <.0001
        Wald                    30.8520       1        <.0001


              Analysis of Maximum Likelihood Estimates

                                           Standard      Wald
  Parameter                DF   Estimate     Error    Chi-Square   Pr > ChiSq

  Intercept LT HIGH SCHOOL  1    -0.4553    0.2203      4.2703       0.0388
  Intercept HIGH SCHOOL     1     1.9221    0.2249     73.0451       <.0001
  Intercept JUNIOR COLLEGE  1     2.2935    0.2281    101.0954       <.0001
  Intercept BACHELOR        1     3.5237    0.2461    205.0148       <.0001
  AGEWED                    1    -0.0506    0.00910    30.8520       <.0001


                      Odds Ratio Estimates

                        Point          95% Wald
          Effect      Estimate     Confidence Limits

          AGEWED        0.951       0.934      0.968
```

Figure 10.18 SAS output (including model parameters) for the proportional odds model predicting a respondent's educational attainment level (degree) from the respondent's age when first married (AGEWED).

Model Fitting Information

Model	−2 Log Likelihood	Chi-Square	df	Sig.
Intercept Only	592.079			
Final	566.636	25.444	1	.000

Link function: Logit.

Parameter Estimates

		Estimate	Std. Error	Wald	df	Sig.	95% Confidence Interval	
							Lower Bound	Upper Bound
Threshold	[DEGREE = 1]	−.455	.220	4.260	1	.039	−.887	−.023
	[DEGREE = 2]	1.923	.225	73.083	1	.000	1.482	2.363
	[DEGREE = 3]	2.294	.228	101.137	1	.000	1.847	2.741
	[DEGREE = 4]	3.524	.246	205.061	1	.000	3.042	4.007
Location	AGEWED	.051	.009	30.881	1	.000	.033	.068

Link function: Logit.

Figure 10.19 SPSS output (including model parameters) for the proportional odds model predicting a respondent's educational attainment level (degree) from the respondent's age when first married (AGEWED).

Similarly, for an individual who got married at the age of 20, the probabilities for each of the other three logits are

P(at or below high school) = 0.71,

P(at or below junior college) = 0.78, and

P(at or below bachelor's degree) = 0.92.

Note that we do not need to compute the last cumulative probability (at or below graduate degree) because we know that it must be one. In addition, using these probabilities with Equation 10.6 we can determine (for example) that the probability of obtaining a bachelor's degree for an individual who got married at the age of 20 is

P(bachelor's degree)

= P(at or below bachelor's degree) – P(at or below junior college)

= 0.92 – 0.78 = 0.14.

The significance tests (shown in Figure 10.18 for SAS and Figure 10.19 for SPSS) for the estimated intercept parameters in this model are not particularly meaningful, as each indicates whether the predicted value of the logit is significantly different from zero when agewed = 0. For example, for the first outcome category (i.e., an education level of less than high school rather than any level above it) we see that when agewed = 0 the predicted logit will be –0.455 (the estimate of the intercept) and the predicted odds will be exp(–0.455) = 0.63. The significance test for this intercept indicates that the value of the predicted log odds from this first logit is significantly different from zero, or that the predicted odds are significantly different from one, when an individual gets married at age zero, a nonsensical value.

However, the significance test for the slope parameter (also shown in Figure 10.18 for SAS and Figure 10.19 for SPSS) is the Wald test of the null hypothesis that the slope parameter is zero or that the predictor is not associated with the outcome. In this case, the results show that the slope estimate of –0.051 is significantly different from zero (X^2 = 30.9, df = 1, p < .0001) and indicate that the predictor (agewed) is significantly associated with educational attainment or that age at first marriage is a significant predictor of the cumulative probability of educational attainment.

Whereas SAS saves the predicted cumulative probabilities, SPSS saves the differences between adjacent cumulative probabilities as shown in Equation 10.6; for example, using the age of 20 again, SAS saves the probability values as computed earlier (0.19, 0.71, 0.78, 0.92, 1.00), whereas SPSS would save the differences between each probability value and the one below it: 0.19, 0.52, 0.07, 0.14, and 0.08. A graph (from SAS) of the predicted cumulative category probabilities as a function of the predictor (agewed) is shown in Figure 10.20, and a graph (from SPSS) of the predicted category probabilities as a function of the predictor (agewed) is shown in Figure 10.21. Note, for example, that in the graph of the category probabilities produced by SPSS (Figure 10.21), at the agewed value of 20 the most probable outcome by far is high school, and this is in fact the most probable outcome up until about the age of 50, although its likelihood relative to the other categories diminishes as agewed increases.

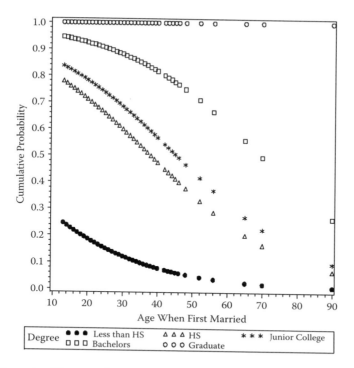

Figure 10.20 SAS graph of the cumulative category probabilities from the proportional odds model predicting a respondent's educational attainment level as a function of age at first marriage.

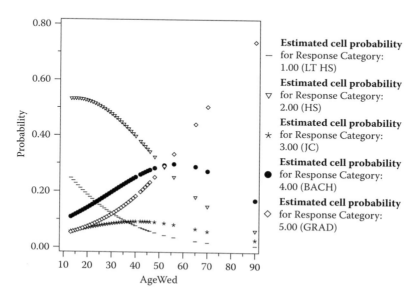

Figure 10.21 SPSS graph of the individual category probabilities from the proportional odds model predicting a respondent's educational attainment level as a function of age at first marriage.

10.6   Summary

In this chapter we extended the logistic regression model used for binary outcome variables to the case of an outcome variable with several categories. We first discussed models in which the outcome variable was treated as nominal, with J outcome categories, where there is no inherent ordering of the J categories. In this case, $(J - 1)$ logits are formed where each represents the log of the odds of one of the outcome categories relative to a reference category.

We then discussed models in which the outcome variable can be treated as ordinal, so the J outcome categories do have a meaningful ordering. To incorporate this ordering into the model, $(J - 1)$ logits are formed where each represents the log of the odds of being at or below a given category relative to being above the category. The model we discussed in detail is called the proportional odds model because it assumes that the effect of each predictor on the outcome is the same for all $(J - 1)$ logits.

These models should allow researchers greater flexibility in predicting categorical outcome variables that may consist of more than two categories as well as the option to make use of the inherent ordinal properties of outcome variables.

Problems

10.1   Use the logidiab data from http://www.psych.yorku.ca/lab/psy6140/ex/logistic.htm to fit a logistic regression model predicting the type of diabetes from the four glucose (or insulin) level predictors. Use the normal group as the reference category. Describe your model selection process and fully interpret the results of the final model selected.

10.2   Suppose that we would like to investigate whether gender has a significant effect on the choice of ice cream flavor. Data, available at http://www.ats.ucla.edu/stat/Spss/output/mlogit.htm, were collected on 200 high school students and include each student's favorite ice cream flavor as well as gender. Strawberry was treated as the reference ice cream flavor category, and the gender variable, female, was coded such that 0 indicates a male and 1 indicates a female. The parameter estimate output (from SPSS) is shown in Figure 10.22.
   a.   Interpret the value of 0.469 in the Exp(B) column. What specifically does this number represent for this analysis?
   b.   What is the logistic regression model to predict the preference of chocolate over strawberry ice cream? What are the predicted odds of this preference for males? What are the predicted odds of this preference for females?

10.3   Refer to the information in Problem 10.2 to answer the following questions (show your work):
   a.   What is the logistic regression model to predict the preference of vanilla over strawberry ice cream? What is the predicted probability of this preference for males? What is the predicted probability of this preference for females?
   b.   What is the logistic regression model to predict the preference of chocolate over vanilla ice cream? What is the predicted probability of this preference for males and for females?

Parameter Estimates

favorite flavor of ice cream[a]		B	Std. Error	Wald	df	Sig.	Exp(B)	95% confidence Interval for Exp (B)	
								Lower Bound	Upper Bound
Chocolate	Intercept	0.98	-256	.147	1	.701			
	[female=.00]	-.758	-409	3.440	1	.064	.469	.210	1.044
	[female=1.00]	0°	.	.	0	.	.	.	.
Vanilla	Intercept	.504	-235	4.590	1	.032			
	[female= 00]	-.021	-333	.004	1	.950	.979	.510	1.882
	[female=1.00]	0°	.	.	0	.	.	.	.

a. The reference category is: strawberry.

b. This parameter is set to zero because it is redundant.

Figure 10.22 SPSS output for Problem 10.2 (using gender as a predictor of ice cream flavor preference).

10.4 Use the logist1 data from http://www.psych.yorku.ca/lab/psy6140/ex/logistic.htm to fit a logistic regression model predicting the level of improvement from the patient's sex and treatment. Assume that the level of improvement is a nominal variable.

10.5 Use the logist1 data from http://www.psych.yorku.ca/lab/psy6140/ex/logistic.htm to fit a logistic regression model predicting the level of improvement from sex and treatment. Assume that the level of improvement is ordinal, with categories representing 0 = no improvement, 1 = some improvement, 2 = marked improvement.

10.6 Explain what the proportional odds assumption requires in general. Use the variables from the model in Problem 10.4 to illustrate your answer specifically and explain whether the assumption is satisfied for this model.

10.7 O'Connell (2006) used data from the Early Childhood Longitudinal Study to examine how gender affects literacy proficiency for first-grade children. The outcome variable of literacy proficiency consisted of six categories, level 0 to level 5, ordered in terms of the level of proficiency attained by the child. Gender was dummy coded such that 0 = girls and 1 = boys. The proportional odds model resulted in approximately the parameter estimates shown in Table 10.1 (which were all significant).
   a. What is the logistic regression equation to predict the odds that the child reached the second proficiency level (level 1) or less?
   b. What are the predicted odds that a boy would reach the second proficiency level (level 1) or less? What are the same predicted odds for a girl?

Table 10.1 Parameter Estimates for Problem 10.7

Parameter	Estimate
Intercept 0	−4.1
Intercept 1	−2.4
Intercept 2	−1.1
Intercept 3	0.8
Intercept 4	2.0
GENDER	0.4

   c. Explain how your answers to parts (a) and (b) relate to the interpretation of the parameter estimate for gender.

   d. Repeat parts (a), (b), and (c) above for the odds that a child reached the first proficiency level (level 0) or less.

10.8   Use the information from Problem 10.7 to answer the following (show your work):

   a. What is the predicted cumulative probability for a boy to reach the fourth proficiency level (level 3) or less? What is the predicted cumulative probability for a boy to reach the third proficiency level (level 2) or less?

   b. What is the probability that a boy would be at the fourth proficiency level (level 3)? What is the same predicted probability for a girl?

   c. What is the probability that a boy would be at the highest proficiency level (level 4)? What is the same predicted probability for a girl?

10.9   Explain what the proportional odds assumption means in the context of the study described in Problem 10.7.

10.10 Pick your own research question that can be addressed using variables from the 2006 GSS data set and a logistic regression model with at least two predictors and a response variable containing at least three categories.

   a. State your research question and expectations regarding the findings.

   b. Explain whether a multicategory logistic regression or a proportional odds model is more appropriate to your research question.

   c. Fully interpret the value, direction, and statistical significance of each of the parameter estimates in your final model.

   d. Summarize the results substantively: What does the model tell you about any associations between the variables? Do these results conform to your expectations?

References

Agresti, A. (1984). *Analysis of ordinal categorical data*. New York: Wiley.

Agresti, A. (1990). *Categorical data analysis*. New York: Wiley.

Agresti, A. (1996). *An introduction to categorical data analysis*. New York: Wiley.

Agresti, A. (2007). *An introduction to categorical data analysis* (2nd ed.). Hoboken, NJ: Wiley.

Agresti, A., & Coull, B. A. (1998). Approximate is better than "exact" for interval estimation of binomial proportion. *American Statistician, 52*, 119–126.

Byrt, T., Bishop, J., & Carlin, J. B. (1993). Bias, prevalence and kappa. *Journal of Clinical Epidemiology, 46*, 423–429.

Cheng, T. (1949). The normal approximation to the Poisson distribution and a proof of a conjecture of Ramanujan. *Bulletin of the American Mathematical Society, 55*, 396–401.

Clogg, C. C., & Shihadeh, E. S. (1994). *Statistical models for ordinal variables*. Thousand Oaks, CA: Sage.

CNN Election Center. (2008). Retrieved March 18, 2008 from http://www.cnn.com/ELECTION/2008/primaries/results/epolls/#WIDEM

Cohen, J. (1960). A coefficient of agreement for nominal scales. *Educational and Psychological Measurement, 20*, 37–46.

Cohen, J. (1968). Weighted kappa: Nominal scale agreement with provision for scaled disagreement or partial credit. *Psychological Bulletin, 70*, 213–220.

Cohen, J., Cohen, P., West, S., & Aiken, L. (2003). *Applied multiple regression/correlation analysis for the behavioral sciences* (3rd ed.). Hillsdale, NJ: Lawrence Erlbaum.

Collett, D. (1991). *Modeling binary data*. London: Chapman & Hall.

Cowles, M. (2001). *Statistics in psychology: An historical perspective* (2nd ed.). New York: Lawrence Erlbaum.

Fisher, R. A. (1922). On the interpretation of χ^2 from contingency tables and the calculation of P. *Journal of the Royal Statistical Society, 84*, 87–94.

Fleiss, J. L. (1973). *Statistical methods for rates and proportions*. New York: Wiley & Sons.

Fleiss, J. L. (1981). *Statistical methods for rates and proportions* (2nd ed.). New York: Wiley & Sons.

Fleiss, J. L., Cohen, J., & Everitt, B. S. (1969). Large sample standard errors of kappa and weighted kappa. *Psychological Bulletin, 72*, 323–237.

Freedman, D., Pisani, R., Purves, R., & Adhikari, A. (1991). *Statistics* (2nd ed.). New York: W. W. Norton & Company.

Grossman, D. C., Reay, D. T., & Baker, S. A. (1999). Self-inflicted and unintentional firearm injuries among children and adolescents. *Journal of Pediatric and Adolescent Medicine, 153*, 875–878.

Hauck, W. W., & Donner, A. (1977). Wald's test as applied to hypotheses in logit analysis. *Journal of the American Statistical Association, 72*, 851–853.

Hosmer, D. W., & Lemeshow, S. (1989). *Applied logistic regresssion*. New York: Wiley & Sons.

Howell, D. C. (2007). *Statistical methods for psychology* (6th ed.). Belmont, CA: Duxbury Press.

Leemis, L. M., & Trivedi, K. S. (1996). A comparison of approximate interval estimators for the Bernoulli parameter. *The American Statistician, 50*, 63–68.

Liu, X. (2007). *Fitting proportional odds models to educational data in ordinal logistic regression using Stata, SAS and SPSS*. Paper presented at the Annual Meeting of the American Educational Research Association (AERA), Chicago.

O'Connell, A. A. (2006). *Logistic regression models for ordinal response variables*. Thousand Oaks, CA: Sage.

Pearson, K. (1922). On the χ^2 test of goodness of fit. *Biometrika, 14,* 186–191.

Pearson, K., & Heron, D. (1913). On theories of association. *Biometrika, 9,* 159–315.

Pedhazur, E. J. (1997). *Multiple regression in behavioral research: Explanation and prediction* (3rd ed.). Orlando, FL: Harcourt Brace.

Sheskin, D. (2007). *Handbook of parametric and nonparametric statistical procedures* (4th ed.). New York: CRC Press.

Wisconsin Department of Public Instruction. (2006a). Tips for using WINSS to find test results for your school. Retrieved January 9, 2008 from http://www.dpi.wisconsin.gov/sig/usetips_wsas.html

Wisconsin Department of Public Instruction. (2006b). Wisconsin performance level descriptors. Retrieved January 9, 2008 from http://www.dpi.wisconsin.gov/oea/profdesc.html

Yule, G. U. (1912). *An introduction to the theory of statistics.* London: Charles Griffin & Company.

Zwick, R. (1988). Another look at interrater agreement. *Psychological Bulletin, 103,* 374–378.

Appendix

Values of the Chi-Squared Distribution

cprob[a] alpha[b] df	0.500 0.500	0.750 0.250	0.900 0.100	0.950 0.050	0.975 0.025	0.990 0.010	0.995 0.005	0.999 0.001
1	0.455	1.323	2.706	3.841	5.024	6.635	7.879	10.828
2	1.386	2.773	4.605	5.991	7.378	9.210	10.597	13.816
3	2.366	4.108	6.251	7.815	9.348	11.345	12.838	16.266
4	3.357	5.385	7.779	9.488	11.143	13.277	14.860	18.467
5	4.352	6.626	9.236	11.070	12.833	15.086	16.750	20.515
6	5.348	7.841	10.645	12.592	14.449	16.812	18.548	22.458
7	6.346	9.037	12.017	14.067	16.013	18.475	20.278	24.322
8	7.344	10.219	13.362	15.507	17.535	20.090	21.955	26.124
9	8.343	11.389	14.684	16.919	19.023	21.666	23.589	27.877
10	9.342	12.549	15.987	18.307	20.483	23.209	25.188	29.588
11	10.341	13.701	17.275	19.675	21.920	24.725	26.757	31.264
12	11.340	14.845	18.549	21.026	23.337	26.217	28.300	32.909
13	12.340	15.984	19.812	22.362	24.736	27.688	29.819	34.528
14	13.339	17.117	21.064	23.685	26.119	29.141	31.319	36.123
15	14.339	18.245	22.307	24.996	27.488	30.578	32.801	37.697
16	15.339	19.369	23.542	26.296	28.845	32.000	34.267	39.252
17	16.338	20.489	24.769	27.587	30.191	33.409	35.718	40.790
18	17.338	21.605	25.989	28.869	31.526	34.805	37.156	42.312
19	18.338	22.718	27.204	30.144	32.852	36.191	38.582	43.820
20	19.337	23.828	28.412	31.410	34.170	37.566	39.997	45.315
21	20.337	24.935	29.615	32.671	35.479	38.932	41.401	46.797
22	21.337	26.039	30.813	33.924	36.781	40.289	42.796	48.268
23	22.337	27.141	32.007	35.172	38.076	41.638	44.181	49.728
24	23.337	28.241	33.196	36.415	39.364	42.980	45.559	51.179
25	24.337	29.339	34.382	37.652	40.646	44.314	46.928	52.620
26	25.337	30.435	35.563	38.885	41.923	45.642	48.290	54.052
27	26.336	31.528	36.741	40.113	43.195	46.963	49.645	55.476
28	27.336	32.620	37.916	41.337	44.461	48.278	50.993	56.892
29	28.336	33.711	39.087	42.557	45.722	49.588	52.336	58.301
30	29.336	34.800	40.256	43.773	46.979	50.892	53.672	59.703
40	39.335	45.616	51.805	55.758	59.342	63.691	66.766	73.402

Values of the Chi-Squared Distribution

cprob[a]	0.500	0.750	0.900	0.950	0.975	0.990	0.995	0.999
alpha[b]	0.500	0.250	0.100	0.050	0.025	0.010	0.005	0.001
df								
50	49.335	56.334	63.167	67.505	71.420	76.154	79.490	86.661
60	59.335	66.981	74.397	79.082	83.298	88.379	91.952	99.607
70	69.335	77.577	85.527	90.531	95.023	100.425	104.215	112.317
80	79.334	88.130	96.578	101.879	106.629	112.329	116.321	124.839
90	89.334	98.650	107.565	113.145	118.136	124.116	128.299	137.208
100	99.334	109.141	118.498	124.342	129.561	135.807	140.169	149.449
200	199.334	213.100	226.020	233.990	241.060	249.450	255.260	267.540
300	299.334	316.140	331.790	341.400	349.870	359.910	366.840	381.430
500	499.333	520.950	540.930	553.130	563.850	576.490	585.210	603.450
1000	999.333	1029.790	1057.720	1074.680	1089.530	1106.970	1118.950	1143.920

Note: Values were computed by the authors using SAS 9.1.3 (CINV function). [a]cprob refers to the cumulative (left-tail) probability; [b]alpha refers to the right-tail probability.

Index